PERFECTION
PROCLAIMED

PERFECTION PROCLAIMED

Language and Literature
in English Radical Religion
1640–1660

NIGEL SMITH

CLARENDON PRESS · OXFORD
1989

Oxford University Press, Walton Street, Oxford OX2 6DP

Oxford New York Toronto
Delhi Bombay Calcutta Madras Karachi
Petaling Jaya Singapore Hong Kong Tokyo
Nairobi Dar es Salaam Cape Town
Melbourne Auckland

and associated companies in
Berlin Ibadan

Oxford is a trade mark of Oxford University Press

Published in the United States
by Oxford University Press, New York

British Library Cataloguing in Publication Data
Smith, Nigel
Perfection proclaimed.
1. English religious literature, 1625–1702.
Critical studies.
820.9'382
ISBN 0–19–812879–7

Library of Congress Cataloging in Publication Data
Smith, Nigel.
Perfection proclaimed: language and literature in English radical religion, 1640–1660 / Nigel Smith.
p. cm.
Revised version of author's doctoral thesis.
Bibliography: p. Includes index.
1. English literature—Early modern. 1500–1700—History and criticism. 2. English literature—
Puritan authors—History and criticism. 3. Radicalism in literature. 4. Religious literature,
English—History and criticism. 5. English language—Early modern, 1500–1700—Style.
6. Dissenters, Religious—England—History—17th century. 7. Radicalism—England—
History—17th century. 8. England—Church history—17th century. 9. Languages—Religious
aspects—Christianity. I. Title.
820'.9'382—dc 19 PR435.S6 1988 88–4868
ISBN 0–19–812879–7

Typeset by Cambrian Typesetters
Printed in Great Britain by
Biddles Ltd.
Guildford and King's Lynn

To my parents

Fanaticism is the *fever* of *superstition*. Enthusiasm, on the contrary, implies an undue (or when used in a good sense, an unusual) vividness of ideas, as opposed to perceptions, or of the obscure inward feelings.   Coleridge

PREFACE

THIS study is a revised version of a doctoral thesis researched and written mostly in Oxford between 1981 and 1985. That project was originally conceived as a comprehensive attempt to do justice to the extraordinary qualities of expression and conception in the writing of Civil War and Interregnum religious radicalism. It is a literary and language-concerned work, but it will be evident to any reader that the context is deeply historical. The idea of a literary criticism informed by history and historically oriented theories of interpretation (the 'new historicism') is currently fashionable. If what follows has any contribution to make to that debate, then it is to show that there is no division between fields of evidence and critical approaches which we often define as literary and those which we call historical. The two are continuous. Just as language and 'literary' statements cannot be divorced from the conditions of production and circulation in a given historical location, so evidence of a historical nature, especially that which is written or spoken, is not immune from interpretative perspectives concerned with representation, mediation, and signification. These matters, rhetoric, conventions of behaviour, textual interpretation, the communication of cognition and conceptualization, are part of any modern Western society's make-up.

I am grateful to the following institutions for making the research and writing of this study possible: the Department of Education and Science; St Cross, Merton, Keble, and The Queen's Colleges, Oxford. Thanks should also go to the Bodleian Library, Oxford, Cambridge University Library, Worcester College Library, the British Library, Dr Williams's Library, and Friends House Library, where Malcolm Thomas has always been extremely helpful. I should like to thank Dr G. E. Aylmer, Dr M. M. Dzelzainis, Christopher Hill, Dr David Norbrook, Hugh Ormsby-Lennon, and Dr John Pitcher for reading and commenting upon earlier drafts of particular chapters. Conversations with my thesis examiners, Professor William Lamont and Dr Blair Worden, have been particularly useful, as have those with Frank Boyce, Martin Dodsworth, Kate Flint, Dr Michael Hunter, Dr David Katz, and Kate Pahl. Thanks should also go to Dr John Hoyles, who first stimulated my interest in this subject, and Dr Robin Robbins, my supervisor, for his advice and encouragement. Any errors or shortcomings are, of course, my own fault.

For the past few years Professor John Carey has been a constant shepherd and example in countless different ways. I should like to acknowledge with deep gratitude his support, his kindness, and his remarkable intelligence. Anyone approaching the field of radical religion is indebted to the excellent work of Dr G. F. Nuttall, Christopher Hill, and A. L. Morton. I should like to acknowledge my indebtedness to these historians. Geoffrey Nuttall deserves special mention for the time he has spent reading most of this book, for the lengths to which he has gone in search of useful information, and, above all, for his supereminent friendship, in Bournville and Oberhofen, and through the post.

N.S.

Keble College

CONTENTS

FIGURES

Figures 1–11 are reproduced by permission of the Bodleian Library, Oxford.

ABBREVIATIONS

Add.	Additional Manuscripts, British Library
BDBR	R. L. Greaves and R. Zaller (eds.), *A Biographical Dictionary of British Radicals in the Seventeenth Century*, 3 vols. (Brighton, 1982–4).
BIHR	*Bulletin of the Institute of Historical Research*
BL	British Library
Bodl.	Bodleian Library
BQ	*Baptist Quarterly*
CJ	*Journal of the House of Commons*, 34 vols. (1742–92).
CRW	*A Collection of Ranter Writings from the Seventeenth Century*, ed. N. Smith (1983).
CSPD	*Calendar of State Papers, Domestic Series*
CUL	Cambridge University Library
DNB	*Dictionary of National Biography*
EHR	*English Historical Review*
ELH	*Journal of English Literary History*
HLQ	*Huntington Library Quarterly*
JBS	*Journal of British Studies*
JBSQ	*Jacob Boehme Society Quarterly*
JEH	*Journal of Ecclesiastical History*
JFHS	*Journal of the Friends Historical Society*
JHI	*Journal of the History of Ideas*
JMRS	*Journal of Medieval and Renaissance Studies*
JWCI	*Journal of the Warburg and Courtauld Institutes*
N & Q	*Notes and Queries*
OED	*Oxford English Dictionary*
P & P	*Past and Present*
PMLA	*Publications of the Modern Language Association of America*
Rawl.	Rawlinson Manuscripts, Bodleian Library
RES	*Review of English Studies*
RQ	*Renaissance Quarterly*
SCH	*Studies in Church History*
SCJ	*Sixteenth Century Journal*
TBHS	*Transactions of the Baptist Historical Society*

TEXTUAL NOTE

FOR ease of reference, and where necessary, short titles have been used. Roman and italic type in original titles have been rendered as italic here. Upper-case and lower-case usages in the titles have been normalized: no case of interpretation rests upon their original renderings in this study. In all quotations, however, punctuation, spelling, and italicization remain as in the originals. Unless stated otherwise, the place of publication is London.

Where a modern edition of a seventeenth-century text has been used, quotations have been compared with the original and corrected where necessary.

INTRODUCTION

IN 1617, and in a Yorkshire parish so far west that it was almost in Lancashire, someone may have said something like this: 'That Christians affirmed can never committ a grosse sinne. Grace being wrought in the heart, the spirit quite abolisheth all former knowledge.' Someone else may have said, 'The prophesy of old men dreaming dreames, and young men seeing visions, is now fulfilled in Grundleton Chappell', and someone else still could have said something which approximated to 'They have received such abundance of grace that now they can stand without using the meanes and so will doe when Mr Bryerley goeth.'

Mr Bryerley was Roger Brierley (or Brereley), curate of Grindleton in the parish of Mitton in Craven, Yorkshire.[1] What might have been said occurs in a document entitled 'Certaine erroneous opinions gathered from the mouth of Mr Bryerley and some of his hearers'.[2] This was the written evidence produced by an episcopal investigation into the beliefs and practices of the Grindleton chapel. The cautionary 'might' is used because it is almost certain that the interrogators would have cast the utterances of those whom they questioned into a vocabulary which expressed the errors in a form compatible with the language of established church government. We are not listening to the voice of the Grindletonian.

However, there is another quality in the words of the document. Occasionally, official doctrinal language becomes something else. It is either personal, 'that faith and feeling are things inseparable', or to do with biblical interpretation: 'That the Arke of the Covenant is shut up or pinned in within the wals of Grundleton Chappell'.[3] The nouns and the verbs in these two quotations are pointing towards another kind of language, partly outside 'official' terminology, though definitely reacting with it, and a component, as well as a vehicle, of the 'error' itself.

---

[1] See G. F. Nuttall, *The Holy Spirit in Puritan Faith and Experience* (Oxford, 1946), 178–80; Christopher Hill, *The World Turned Upside Down* (1972), 81–5.

[2] Bodl. MS Rawl. D. 1347, fos. 317ʳ–318ʳ. Another copy exists in Bodl. MS Rawl. D. 399, fos. 196ʳ. The two are substantially the same, differing in the order of errors and occasionally in vocabulary.   [3] Ibid., errors 5 and 36.

The speech or writing of a Grindletonian in this period has yet to be found. Brierley was a learned man, and his writings suggest this. They exhibit the structured conceptualization of a devotional treatise, poem, or sermon—except that within these parameters there may be an attempt to introduce a type of discourse, quite alien to anything in the English reformed tradition.

The members of Brierley's congregation might not have sounded so very different from the members of the separatist congregation in Bristol, a Baptist church by 1640, who mingled what has been called a 'bland language of Canaan' with their own deeply emotional attempts to understand the working of the divine upon themselves.[4] In these early days, one of their number was a black servant called Frances. That a 'blackamoor' should have grace surprised the congregation, and they came to revere her, eventually treating her dying words as a prophetic message for the church: to let *'the glory of God to be dear unto them'*.[5]

The Grindletonians were an early example of the religious communities whose languages are the concern of this book. Though Brierley did not see fit openly to separate from the established church, the Grindletonians were practising a form of worship which could never be tolerated inside it. Like those who did separate, the Grindletonians were searching for the true model of church government and worship, as it was laid down in the New Testament. The rejection of idolatrous 'externals', the assertion that the believer is made perfect through the freely given grace of God, and the feeling that the gift of the Holy Spirit, χάραγμα, could fall upon any individual, characterize the nature of the Grindletonian community, so the evidence tells us. To a greater or lesser degree, and in very many different ways, these were the distinguishing marks of English 'radical religion'. This book is a study of how that culture produced such an extraordinary array of discourses, what the active role of these expressions was in the history of radical religion between 1640 and 1660, and what they meant in the wider perspective of mid-seventeenth-century English society. It is an attempt to build upon the findings of the valuable but few literary studies concerned with the sects which have appeared, largely in recent

[4] *Association Records of the Particular Baptists of England, Wales and Ireland to 1660*, ed. B. R. White, 3 parts (1971–4), ii. 53.

[5] *The Records of a Church of Christ Meeting in Broadmead, Bristol, 1640–1687*, ed. E. B. Underhill (1847), 35.

years, against the background of the wider historiographical interest in Puritanism.[6]

The early dissenters and sectarians thought they were engaged in that further purification and reform of the church which Luther had originally begun, beyond the limits which had been defined by Henry VIII and revised by Elizabeth I. Our understanding of early dissent is determined by the fact that 1640 was the first time the phenomenon had broken out on such a scale, set as it was against the wider background of political and civil turmoil in the following years. It is no surprise that the abolition of episcopal government, the collapse of the censorship, and the absence of a national policy of church government throughout the Interregnum contributed to the expansion and fragmentation. On their road to the re-creation of apostolic Christian society, the radicals, as churches, sects, and individuals, often in debate with each other, created their own distinctive linguistic usages, their own habits of expression and communication, their own literature and culture. For them it was a search for truth, grace, and, in some cases, perfection, separate from the impure and the ignorant. From the outside this often seemed like the presumptuous rejection of a divinely ordained social order and the endangering of spiritual well-being in the sight of God.

The term 'radical Puritan' could be seen as very close to the definition of radical religion, except that this would not do justice to the complex situation in which early radical religion grew up, in the century or so before 1640. As Patrick Collinson has recently suggested, it is wrong to think of the Elizabethan and Jacobean church as a distinct, nationally adopted church polity and practice which could be labelled 'Anglican'.[7] Rather, it was a series of differing positions on theology and church discipline held by clergymen, from archbishops to the lower ranks. The

---

[6] See Luella M. Wright, *The Literary Life of the Early Friends, 1650–1725* (New York, 1932): G. F. Nuttall, *Studies in Christian Enthusiasm* (Wallingford, Pa., 1948); id., *The Welsh Saints 1640–1660* (Cardiff, 1957), 24–5, 48; Jackson I. Cope, 'Seventeenth Century Quaker Style', *PMLA* 71 (1956), 725–54: Owen C. Watkins, *The Puritan Experience* (1972), 91–9, 144–207; Hugh Ormsby-Lennon, 'The Dialect of Those Fanatick Times: Language Communities and English Poetry from 1580 to 1660' (Ph.D. diss., University of Pennsylvania, 1977); Richard Bauman, *Let your words be few: Symbolism of Speaking and Silence among Seventeenth-Century Quakers* (Cambridge, 1983).

[7] *The Religion of Protestants: The Church in English Society, 1559–1625* (Oxford, 1982), 92–140.

Puritans of Elizabeth's reign were those who complained against the impurity of 'externals': bowing at the name of Jesus, kneeling at communion, the use of what were seen as 'Popish relics' in the Prayer Book, and ecclesiastical vestments. This was in addition to the drive of the Puritans to make 'godly' behaviour the code to which all households in the kingdom adhered. While most Puritans desired to reform the church from within, others, like the followers of Robert Browne and Henry Barrow, established their own congregations. They asserted that the congregation should be self-governing, especially in the appointment of its own ministers, and stressed their godly fellowships by making covenants which would ensure their correct behaviour and belief.[8]

In small numbers and in a sporadic and precarious manner, the separatist churches, which were to thrive after 1640, established themselves during the first three decades of the seventeenth century, both at home and in exile. There is no need here to recount at length that history, which has been and continues to be thoroughly researched. A few details, however, are relevant. First of all, this separatism was preceded by an even more spectral presence of radicals, going back to the 1550s, including Anabaptists, 'free will men', and the Family of Love. They challenged predestinarian theology and can be said to have had some influence upon later separatists, both in terms of their ideas and in the way that commentators developed hostile stereotypes of religious radicals in reaction to them.[9]

After the Brownists came the first Baptists, who required adult baptism as a sign of conversion and purified separation. Slightly later came what is known as Independency or 'semi-separatism'.[10] Here, a church would be gathered by the free and mutual consent of believers joining and covenanting together, but there was no absolute rejection of communion with the

[8] See B. R. White, *The English Separatist Tradition* (Oxford, 1971), 49; Robert Browne, *A Treatise of reformation without tarying for anie* (Middelburg, 1582); John Canne, *The Necessity of Separation* (1634), ed. Charles Stovel (1849); Stephen Brachlow, 'The Elizabethan Roots of Henry Jacob's Churchmanship: Refocusing the Historiographical Lens', *JEH* 36 (1985), 228–54.

[9] See I. B. Horst, *The Radical Brethren: Anabaptism and the English Reformation to 1558* (Nieuwkoop, 1972); J. W. Martin, 'Elizabethan Protestant Separatism at its Beginnings: Henry Hart and the Free Will Men', *SCJ* 7 (1976), 55–74.

[10] Murray Tolmie, *The Triumph of the Saints: The Separate Churches of London, 1616–1649* (Cambridge, 1977), 7–27.

parish in the hope that reform would spread to the community at large. There were also areas where practices and beliefs were harboured which could never be tolerated inside the established church, as is the case with the Grindletonians. Though some Baptists (the General Baptists) rejected predestination to damnation, most of these radicals stayed within the limits of covenant theology and shared an extreme hostility to ceremony, increasingly regarding sacraments and ordinances as figurative.[11] At the same time, the complex patterns of conversion, of the passage from reprobation to adoption, assurance, justification, and sanctification, developed by Elizabethan Puritans were the doctrinal stuff of much early nonconformity.[12]

The writing of the early nonconformists is built around this doctrinal language, which has been called a 'morphology of conversion'.[13] Across the Puritan spectrum people would relate their experiences to the process of progression from unbelief and sinfulness to grace: this was called 'experimental' theology. While clergymen, including Independents, developed complex psychological and theological theories to explain the experimental, a personal radical religious discourse began to emerge from this context. The Independents required a confession of the experience of conversion, along with a confession of faith, from every individual seeking to join a gathered church. Records of experience were also kept by Baptists.[14] At the same time, in Baptist and other separatist churches, expounding upon the text, often in dispute with the preacher, led to open prophesying and spontaneous outpouring, the beginnings of later extreme sectarian utterances and styles.

[11] There were further significant divisions within the Baptists and between Baptists and Independents. Some Baptist congregations remained 'Open', not requiring the believer to undergo an adult baptism. Henry Jessey's congregation was one such, and it is interesting to note that under such circumstances the flow of expression and prophesying was considerable. The Seventh Day Baptists emerged during these years, observing Jewish sabbatarian practice. For further details see Horton Davies, *Worship and Theology in England 2. From Andrewes to Baxter and Fox* (Princeton, 1975), 498; Tolmie, op. cit. 50–119.

[12] These aspects have recently been discussed with regard to New England in Charles Lloyd Cohen, *God's Caress: The Psychology of Puritan Religious Experience* (New York and Oxford, 1986), 47–72.

[13] Edmund S. Morgan, *Visible Saints: The History of a Puritan Idea* (Ithaca, NY, 1963), 90–1.

[14] See Katherine Sutton, *A Christian Womans Experience of the glorious working of Gods free grace* (Rotterdam, 1663), sigs. *1ᵛ–*2ᵛ.

It is important to realize that these forms of speech or writing were intimately bound up with forms of worship. In Independent and Baptist services there were no set prayers or choirs. In Baptist churches unison singing was discouraged, but individual singing approved. Katherine Sutton was one Baptist whose gift of singing extended outside worship and became the focus of her 'experiences'.[15] Highly emotional services were commonplace, with extempore prayers and prolix sermons, coupled with the taking of the sacrament in Pauline fashion: the 'breaking of bread' (1 Cor. 10: 16). For the se-baptist, John Smyth, all translation from the original languages of the Scripture was corrupt, as was reading from a text in a service. Expounding from the Scripture should be performed in Hebrew or Greek and from memory. In this way, worship in the Spirit created a superior language which needed no text to mediate divine truth between man and God.[16]

There were less extreme versions of Puritanism which were considered nonconformist before 1640. Having been in decline since Elizabeth's reign, English Presbyterianism, aided by its more successful Scottish cousin, came into its own during the 1640s. Its national hierarchical organization, the absence of a requirement of experiential confessions or the manifestation of gifts in believers, and its open opposition to more extreme forms of Nonconformity exclude it from radical religion.[17]

However, the 1640s also witnessed the emergence of more radical forms of sectarian religion. Some upheld mortalism, the notion that the soul dies with the body until the resurrection,

---

[15] Ibid., pp. 13–16.

[16] See John Smyth, *A Paterne of True Prayer* (1605), in *The Works of John Smyth*, ed. W. T. Whitley, 2 vols. (Cambridge, 1915), 27.

[17] The Independent congregations, sometimes seen as quite close to Presbyterian ecclesiology except in the important matters of congregational autonomy and worship itself, are often excluded from the radical ticket. However, Independency contained a broad spectrum of beliefs and practices the radical end of which is certainly included in this study. From the gathered churches, as much as from the Baptist conventicles, developed the more extreme forms of sectarianism. Nevertheless, it is becoming apparent that the private devotional language of the Presbyterians was not so different from that of some of the Independents. The Independents tended to make public and political what was private for the Presbyterians: Paul S. Seaver, *Wallington's World* (1985), 42. For a stimulating interpretation of Presbyterian and Independent differences as a process of debate in which word-usages became blurred, see John K. Graham, ' "Independent" and "Presbyterian": A Study of Religious and Political Language and the Politics of Words During the English Civil War, c. 1640–1646', 2 vols. (Ph.D. diss., Washington University, 1978), 170 ff.

while others denied the divinity of Christ or entirely rejected ordinances.[18] This was a departure from the respectability of many of the Independent, Baptist, and Separatist churches during the Interregnum, a respectability which to some extent ran along lines of wealth. There were further challenges to scriptural authority, such as the denial that God created the world *ex nihilo*, which was sometimes coupled with rejection of the literal truth of the Bible and the habit of reading it as an allegory of the internal state of each individual, a practice which had characterized the Family of Love and which was to mark out the perfectionist groups of the late 1640s and 1650s, the Seekers, Ranters, and early Quakers. The ways in which the radicals came to express these concepts are a central literary concern of this study.

As has recently been argued, the Baptists provided a major forum for the growth of more radical forms of practice and expression.[19] The Baptists were concerned with the strict maintenance of ordinances, which could restrict the capacity for free and inspired expression. The records of the Interregnum Baptist churches show the constant excommunication of individuals for such professions.[20] This dilemma may well have been a function of the clash of dissenting discipline with what Patrick Collinson has described as a residual 'Pelagianism' in the country.[21] In the potential tension between the compulsion of ordinances and the liberty of the spirit lay a huge creative source.

In the 1640s those who professed the most internalized forms of radical religion were known as Seekers. Despite the confusion generated by the heresiographers, Seekers were in fact any who rejected the validity of external ordinances because they felt that all forms of visible church so far were part of the apostasy. Men

[18] See N. T. Burns, *Christian Mortalism from Tyndale to Milton* (Cambridge, Mass., 1972), 42–164.

[19] J. F. McGregor, 'The Baptists: Fount of All Heresy', in J. F. McGregor and B. Reay (edd.), *Radical Religion in the English Revolution* (Oxford, 1984), 23–63.

[20] *Records of the Churches of Christ, Gathered at Fenstanton, Warboys, and Hexham, 1644–1720*, ed. E. B. Underhill (1854), 8, 12, 94–5, 117, 120. For a separatist like Katherine Chidley, the Lord's Supper was not scriptural and so not reliant upon the minister. This put ordinances on the same level as preaching: Nuttall, *The Holy Spirit*, p. 98. Though Henry Jessey was removed from the living of Aughton, East Yorkshire, for dispensing with ceremonies a year after he had been appointed in 1633, he still defended ordinances in this world: Bodl. MS Rawl. C 409, fo. 64; Jessey, *A Storehouse of Provision* (1650), 29.

[21] *Religion of Protestants*, p. 202.

should wait for the Holy Spirit to give forth a new and proper dispensation. For John Webster the only 'Ordinance' was Christ.[22] The Seekers, like the Antinomians, were not an organized movement in any sense. Indeed, some so-called Seekers were Antinomians, like John Saltmarsh, who questioned the use of covenants and 'externals' but who maintained strong and close communications with Independent congregations.[23] Others went to the opposite extreme in search of perfection, believing in man's own capacity to attain salvation, or even in universal salvation.[24] This should not disguise the existence of small groups of Seekers who met together to discuss the awaited dispensation and the workings of the spirit, in some senses like the Grindletonian example. Such was the group which the some-time Quaker John Toldervy came across in the early 1650s.[25] There were also several independent statements, like those of Robert Read and John Jackson (who was not a Seeker but who spoke from a position of rational criticism which was sympathetic to them), which defined Seekerism as a rising above ordinances rather than a rejection of them, and a consequent searching for the perfected body of the saints in Scripture-reading and prayer: in short, an enthusiasm of devotion.[26]

It was from this context that the practical libertinism of the Ranters briefly flourished in the aftermath of the King's execution and the abolition of the House of Lords, manifested in a mystically justified practice of swearing and free love—though many reports of Ranter activity were invented.[27] At the same time, having received his commission to persuade people that the truth lay in acknowledging the validity of the light within each individual, George Fox initiated the growth of early Quakerism, literally fulfilling the prophecies by coming out of the north of the

[22] John Webster, *The Vail of the Covering*, preached at All Hallows, Lombard Street, 1653 (published 1713), 40.

[23] Saltmarsh, *Groanes for Liberty* (1646), 5.

[24] See the anonymous *Divine Light, manifesting the Love of God unto the whole World* (1646), *passim*.

[25] John Toldervy, *The Foot out of the Snare* (1656), 4.

[26] Read, *The Fiery Change* (1656), 4; Jackson, *A Sober Word to a Serious People* (1651), 2.

[27] In *Fear, Myth and History: The Ranters and the Historians* (Cambridge, 1986), J. C. Davis makes a subtle and astute attempt to show that the Ranters were not a movement or even a collection of individuals with broadly similar ideas. Rather, the identity was a creation of a sensation press in the early 1650s. In denying a Ranter identity, Professor Davis is still left with individuals, most of whom he terms 'spiritual enthusiasts' without really exploring what this means. In this study the intention is to

country.[28] Though most Quakers were soberly self-denying, the direct claim for unity with God through the inner light, the consequent release from sin, and the implicit rejection of predestinarian theology led some Quakers, like James Nayler and John Perrot, to claim a spiritual perfection which was reminiscent of those called Ranters. In any case, the fierce enthusiasm and violent language of the early Quakers led many to fear them as a socially subversive phenomenon.[29] Both Ranters and Quakers, along with those intellectual heretics, the Socinians, were fiercely persecuted in the Interregnum, partly because they appeared to deny the historical Christ, whose atonement had given the saints saving grace.[30] This was the central experience of the saints in the Independent churches and sects, and it marks the theological limits of the considerable degree of toleration extended in the Republic and the Protectorate.

Millennialism touched all the radicals, just as it was a fundamental component in all religious outlooks of mid-seventeenth-century English people. While Seekers, Ranters and Quakers generally looked to an inner reappearance of Christ, the Fifth Monarchist movement of the 1650s expected the bodily return of King Jesus. Fifth Monarchism grew up among Independent and Baptist churches who were dissatisfied about the extent of reform achieved in the Republic and the Protectorate. The foundations for this more active millennialism was laid in part by the millennial language of the Independent clergy of the 1640s.[31] In some senses this was an extension of the

show the relationship between the contradictions and differences which could exist within the writing or behaviour of individual sectarians, and the representations or identities, pejorative or otherwise, which make up historical reality: if the Ranters were a fiction, they were one of their own as well as of others' making. It is the connections which can be made between those called Ranters and other radical Puritans which are significant.

[28] See Job 37: 9; Jer. 4: 6; Ezek. 1: 4, 39: 2.

[29] See Barry Reay, *The Quakers and the English Revolution* (1985).

[30] See John Simpson, *The Perfection of Justification* (1648), 41–2; on Socinian Antitrinitarianism see John Biddle, *Twelve Arguments Drawn out of the Scripture* (1647), 6–7; see also Blair Worden, 'Toleration and the Cromwellian Protectorate', *SCH* 21 (1984), 199–233.

[31] See John P. Wilson, *Pulpit in Parliament: Puritanism during the English Civil Wars, 1640–48* (Princeton, 1969), 222–3. For the history and various ideas of Fifth Monarchism, see B. S. Capp, *The Fifth Monarchy Men: A Study in Seventeenth-Century English Millenarianism* (1972).

millennial themes in Independent sermons before Parliament in the previous decade. The Fifth Monarchists proved a considerable opposition to the Interregnum government and their ideas for reform were communicated in a protest literature which made full use of the experiential and prophetic forms developed in the 'gathered churches'. Though the Fifth Monarchists were literalists in their interpretation of the Second Coming, they still found support from some Quakers, while some Fifth Monarchists who feature in the following pages believed in both an inward and an outward return of Christ.

The quality which most centrally characterizes the subject of this book is the attempt to bear witness in expression and behaviour to the immediacy and *charisma* of the Holy Spirit, however it was defined.[32] It was the search for perfection, or the claim that it had arrived, which led to the most interesting discursive experiments of the Interregnum years. The major actors of this study are the most extreme of the radically religious, those who said they were, or were named, Antinomians, Baptists, Seekers, Diggers, Ranters, Quakers, Fifth Monarchists, and a host of individuals who justified the worst fears of the Elizabethan bishops as 'sects of one'. Pejoratively they became known as 'enthusiasts'.[33] Because of the fluid nature of radical religion it was possible for some to appear as enthusiasts in one context and quite respectable and orthodox in another.

Who were the radically religious? From which social orders did they come? During the Civil War and Interregnum, Presbyterians, Independents and Baptists became some of the most influential people in the nation. It is evident that radical religion itself flourished precisely where learned clergy who had moved into separatist or sectarian positions interacted with the 'middling sort' and artisans. The role of lay members in radical worship is clearly important here. It has often been affirmed that radical Puritanism extended down to the lowest and poorest members of society both in the city and the country. While it is true that some servants and rural labourers did become sectarians (this was especially the case with the early Quakers),

---

[32] For the debate between conservative and radical Puritans regarding the nature and witness of the spirit, see Nuttall, *The Holy Spirit*, pp. 48–61.

[33] See Ronald A. Knox, *Enthusiasm: A Chapter in the History of Religion* (Oxford, 1950), 139–75.

recent research suggests that the bulk of sectarian membership remained among the lower professions and merchants, the artisanal groups in the cities, and the yeomanry in the country.[34] This can be substantiated by a consideration of book prices. In the first part of the seventeenth century, the cheapest single-sheet pamphlets cost 2*d*, just within the means of poorer labourers.[35] Though many radical books were made from single sheets or less, many more were a lot larger and beyond the means of the poorer wage-earners. While book-buying is obviously no final indication of radical affiliation, and while those with books could of course influence or lend to those who could not afford them, reading was an essential component in the transmission of radical religion. It is reasonable to assume that, according to extant evidence, those radical religious pamphlets which went through most editions, and which were clearly intended for the widest possible audience, sold at the cheapest prices, perhaps only as much as twice the price of the cheapest available printed matter. We know too that publications, as much as the preached word, were the way in which the radicals spread their ideas, especially in the cities and in the New Model Army.

From the lay 'mechanick preachers', like Samuel How, came some of the most strident attacks upon orthodox education as a means of fitting men to preach the word.[36] The tendency here was towards a replacement of obedience to any form of church governance with a personal claim for direct inspiration from the divine and hence enormous and absolute personal authority in discerning the divine will. The clearest and most crude example of this was Lodowick Muggleton and John Reeve's claim that they were the Two Witnesses from the Book of Revelation. Anyone who did not believe them and who did join their sect would be damned. Many artisan radicals were of course simply members of Independent or Baptist congregations (and others were open Royalists and episcopalians or Presbyterians), but it does seem that the claims for such extreme forms of prophetic authority came from this section of the social hierarchy. Those radical churchmen who had received a university education or those

[34] Barry Reay, *The Quakers and the English Revolution* (1985), 20–31.

[35] Margaret Spufford, *Small Books and Pleasant Histories: Popular Fiction and its Readership in Seventeenth-Century England* (Cambridge 1981), 91–8. I am very grateful to Tessa Watt, for an illuminating conversation on publishing.

[36] See Samuel How, *The Sufficiencie of the Spirits Teaching* (1st edn., 1640).

who were supported by congregations (though not ordained) were not so notable for such claims, though there were examples, such as the case of John Pordage (see below, pp. 205–12).

The obvious remark to be made with regard to such men, be they beneficed, appointed and supported by their congregations, army chaplains during the Civil War and Interregnum, or men who were able to survive by proselytizing on journeys through the country, is that they occupied the positions of pastor, preacher and/or prophet, though of course in terms defined by particular radical religious precepts. The problem of pastorship was reflected in the writings of the radicals, especially in experiential terms, forming a large concern in the pages which follow. Though their function was to make the Word available to believers, to facilitate the regenerate's capacity to interpret divine truths correctly and in a context of true liberty of conscience, radical churchmen did influence the shaping of congregational life, expression and thought, and were often regarded as figures of powerful (even Messianic) authority by congregation members. On the other hand the disputes which could break out within congregations over ordinances, authority, or ethics, are a record of the freedom of debate tolerated in radical religion without 'soul-tyranny', as well as another facet of a developing form of oral and written expression.[37] The fluidity of church membership should be remembered here, together with the experience of isolation and failure of communication between individuals as separatist affiliations cut across domestic ties.[38]

One social group which made a significant impact upon society from within the radical religious field was women. Excluded from all professions including the cloth, women were regarded as the natural and, in orthodox terms, the spiritual inferiors of men. The history of the plight of women in early modern Europe need not be recounted here. What should be noted is the tendency among some Puritans (the more radical the Puritanism, the greater the tendency) to regard women as the spiritual equals of men: '*Christ was one in the Male and in the Female; and as he arises in both*'.[39] Women were singled out for their ability

---

[37] E. S., *The Saints Travell From Babylon Into their owne Countrey* (1643), 3.

[38] See David Brown, *Two Conferences Between Some of those that are Called Separatists & Independents* (1650), 9.

[39] Sarah Blackborrow. *The Just and Equal Ballance* (1660), 13.

to prophesy and in this respect they were allowed to speak in meetings. Gifted sectarian women displayed particular types of expression and language which are not dissimilar to those of medieval female mystics and anchoresses. While women prophets were exerting an influence upon the millenarian politics of the 1650s, and the behavioural politics of individual congregations throughout the entire Civil War and Interregnum period, other women were sustaining the organization of conventicles and keeping alive the memory of sectarian tradition, like Katherine Chidley; or as printers and publishers they helped to maintain the flow of radical religious literature.[40]

The significance of language existed in an area anterior to the experiential and the reflection in writing of modes of worship. All Christian thinking has, of course, to do with the interpretation of the Scripture. It is language-based in that such interpretation involves translation across several languages and a consideration of the nature of signification in biblical language. It is literary in that the Bible itself, or forms of worship derived from the Bible, provided the literary archetypes which determined radical religious expression. The search for the true church was also a quest for true signification. Scriptural language, as the radicals expounded it, provided the residual structures of their expression. The most unusual debates, statements, and consequences arose from their comprehension of scriptural language. Moreover, like their worship, their comprehension and use of Scriptural language endowed their expression with recognizable signs or codes: of fellowship and shared enlightenment for those in the sect, and of incomprehensible, ridiculous, or dangerous otherness for those outside to vilify.[41]

Protestant theology is usually understood to entail a return to the original texts of the Bible (Hebrew and Greek as opposed to the Latin of the Vulgate translation) and a discarding of the complex medieval systems of interpretative allegory for a literal and historical appreciation of the texts. Upon these grounds were based the various interpretations of Scripture from which were derived the different forms of church organization within the

---

[40] See Katherine Chidley, *A New-Yeares Gift* (1645), 7–10.

[41] See Anne Coppins, 'Religious Enthusiasm from Robert Browne to George Fox: A Study of its Meaning and the Reaction against it in the Seventeenth Century' (D.Phil. thesis, University of Oxford, 1983).

reformed spectrum. Inevitably the decoding of Greek words,
such as 'baptism', was accompanied by attempts to make the
language of the Old Testament significant in the light of the
Gospels and the Pauline Epistles.[42] Another feature was, during
the course of the sixteenth century and into the following
century, an extension of the strict definition of typology whereby
events or figures in the Old Testament could be seen to prefigure
events in the life of Christ or Christ Himself. So, in Independent
theology, types were promises fulfilled in Christ and his church,
and valid prefigurations of future kingdoms. Old Testament
types might be abrogated by New Testament antitypes, but
because the New Testament promises a millennium, types could
be applied as examples of eternal verities, both historical and
real. In the New Kingdom, in heaven or on earth, all believers
were renewed in the glorious image of Christ and became like
Him in spiritual love and virtue. This spiritual fulfilment of types
was the great end of the history of redemption.[43]

Most Puritans believed that the Scriptures should be understood literally but with the power of the spirit guiding the
individual's comprehension. The sectarians generally deviated
from this mean in two distinct but related ways. The Brownists
and the Baptists were extreme literalists or 'Biblicists', despite
their witness to the spirit. They rejected any moderating claims
of reason and the weight of traditional interpretation and looked
painstakingly through the Scriptures to find passages which
supported their notions of church government. Hence the
fascination of the Baptists with Scriptural concordances and the
massive lists of references which their works contained.[44]

On the other hand those connected with the Antinomian and
perfectionist sects tended to read the Scriptures allegorically and
analogously. Biblical passages described processes which took
place within every individual. It was possible for literalists to
come to a position where they were allegorical since they resorted

---

[42] 'the Greek Verb βαπτίζω (whence the participle βαπτίζοντες here
used commeth) doth properly signifie to dip in water; So the 70. Interpreters use the
word, 2 Kings 5: 14 And he dipped himself seven times in Jordan.' Hanserd Knollys,
The Shining of a Flaming-Fire in Zion (1646), 3.

[43] On this issue, see especially David Walker, 'Thomas Goodwin and the Debate
on Church Government', *JEH* 34 (1983), 85–99.

[44] See Henry Jessey, *The Exceeding Riches of Grace Advanced* (2nd edn., 1647), sigs.
a4ᵛ–a8ᵛ; id., *An English–Greek Lexicon* (1661), especially sig. (i)3ᵛ.

to figurative readings in order to interpret obscure scripture: 'the spiritual impression affecting . . . hearts, and making them *God like*'.[45] Both literalists and allegorists could speak similar discourses of *scriptura rediviva*, though initial preoccupations and presumptions were different.

Whether encouraging conversion or repelling antichrist the power of this biblical rhetoric, as the Puritans quickly discovered, was its capacity to transform any person, object, or event into an intimation of δόξα (glory) imminent or immanent. As this language became to some extent continuous with the personal experience of the spirit, so the Independents were noted for their vocabulary of 'in-comings, out-lettings, and in-dwellings'. It was a form of mysticism which lay at the very heart of Puritan experience, 'being irradiated with the holy and divine nature'.[46]

Church and believer could be identified as different elements in one perfected body. According to one line of symbolism, again from an Independent, John Rogers, believers were jewels or precious stones who would inhabit the temple.[47] However, matters did not stop here as Pauline theology, so influential in early seventeenth-century Puritan thinking, envisaged all human forms and institutions as 'bodies' within which the power of the Holy Spirit could or would reside.[48] The human body as much as the physical building of a church itself could be the receptacle of the divine πνεῦμα. The process of building the church, of reforming, or, as Puritans chose to call it, 'edifying', by a synecdoche, was a search in the language of the Scripture for the external and internal truth of the way in which the divine resided in the individual human being.[49] In this way, the meaning of body became a matter of inter-sectarian dispute.[50] This was seen as analogous to the way in which the breath of life—*rûach*, in the Old Testament—animated the flesh.[51] The Ancient Israelites, not having a distinction between the mental and the physical, talk in synecdoches and metonymies. Godly language was

---

[45] Henry Lawrence, *Some Considerations Tending to the Asserting and Vindicating of the Use of the Holy Scriptures* (1649), 13.

[46] William Sedgwick, *A Second View of the Army Remonstrance* (1649), 25.

[47] Rogers, *Ohel or Beth-shemesh. A Tabernacle for the Sun* (1653), 510–22 (esp. 510). The reference is to Mal. 3: 17. See also Rev. 21: 18–21.

[48] See John S. Coolidge, *The Pauline Renaissance in England* (Oxford, 1970).

[49] See Smyth, *A Paterne of True Prayer, Works*, i. 130.

[50] Simpson, *The Perfection of Justification*, p. 63.

[51] Henry Walker, *A Sermon Preached in the King's Chapell* (1649), 3.

implicitly tropological: as it strove to encapsulate the spirit so the metaphors were the key to the politics of the person and the community. The way was open, by developing what was orthodox Protestant theology, for an internal description of the regenerate or perfected believer, and the relationship between that 'interiorized' perfect (and inspired) humanity and the external nature of the community or fellowship of believers at large: 'the Christian having some glimmerings of this, that the man of sin is subdued in him, then comes he to have his union and oneness with that mystery of God in him.'[52] This was the 'center' (the fashionable word used across the radical religious spectrum) of individual and community, and, in extreme cases, even God Himself, the 'centred centred Center'.[53] In this way individuals claimed to be in a state of hypostasy, part of the Godhead itself.

What is also evident here is that the nature of Puritan theology, radical or non-radical, was predicated upon an intensely rhetorical understanding of Scripture language, and indeed of the world generally, despite the radical castigation of learned rhetoric.[54] Not only was Scripture to be understood in terms of forms of metaphor, symbol, and metonymy, but also the same relations applied to the book of nature and the book of men. The tropologies developed in order to decode the Bible were also employed to construct a comprehension of reality in this world at large. The influence of the Elizabethan Puritans, especially William Perkins, upon the sermon was immense in this respect. For Perkins all material objects in the Bible or in the world were signs or *figurae* for sacred mysteries, and the materiality of the *figura* should be captured in speech: sermons should expound the shape of the object and its significance.[55] It was this rhetorical consensus which the more extreme radicals, especially the Ranters and Quakers, were throwing over in their own writings. For the opponents of the radicals, such language marked the fatal

[52] Thomas Royle, *A Glimpse of Some Truths* (1648), pt ii, p. 8. For the relationship between Reformation theology and the 'interiorization' of sacramental worship, see Walter J. Ong, *The Presence of the Word* (New York, 1967), 262–8.

[53] Thomas Tany, *Theauraujohn his Theous Ori Apokolipikal* (1651), 39.

[54] Robert Browne, *A Treatise upon the 23. of Matthewe* (1582), in *The Writings of Robert Harrison and Robert Browne* ed. Albert Peel and Leland H. Carlson (1953), 175, 182–5.

[55] See Ann Kibbey, *The Interpretation of Material Shapes in Puritanism: A Study of Rhetoric, Prejudice, and Violence* (Cambridge, 1986), 16–21, 47–9, 67, 73, 157–9.

lack of rationality in the Antinomians: 'Theologia symbolica . . . non est argumentativa.'[56] We may see sardonic mockery in Francis Fullwood's charge of 1651 against the perfectionist, Robert Wilkinson, who was accused of going beyond the heights of Socrates, Plato and the Ranters to Aristotle's sea, the 'ens entium', but the fact that he does compare two types of the most extreme radical with the philosophical giants is an attestation to what radical religious discourse was trying to do.[57] In this sense radical religion facilitated a changed form of consciousness in which figures were found to describe and manifest the return of πνεῦμα in the present.

The desire to expand vocabulary in the interests of further 'leadings' is evident in the role played by continental mystical and spiritual works. In the late 1640s and early 1650s it is possible to identify a group of individuals with various radical religious affiliations who adopted a perfectionist or illuminist stance and who were interested in mystical and spiritualist literature. The connection between radical Puritanism, especially its enthusiastic elements, and mysticism has been denied in an article which shows how the processes of mystical illumination were antipathetic to the immediate revelation demanded by the enthusiast. The enthusiast claimed to be where the mystic wanted to go.[58] Subsequent scholars have accepted this argument, failing to see that it was possible for radical Puritans to read mystical works in a certain way in order to appropriate them, sometimes wholly, for their own visions. Radical religious writers, especially learned ones, were using medieval and sixteenth-century Catholic, reformed and radical, mystical and spiritual writings in order to extend the boundaries of their own spiritual experiences, both psychologically and politically. That Catholic works were used should come as less of a surprise when it is realized that the emphasis upon direct divine inspiration put them in the same position as Catholic spiritual writers.[59] The list of individuals and writings which Robert Rich compiled in 1666 is an anatomy of the radical spiritualist milieu and its reading matter.[60]

---

[56] Thomas Gataker, *God's Eye on his Israel* (1645), sig. d1ʳ.

[57] Fullwood, *Vindiciae mediorum & mediatoris* (1651), 86.

[58] J. L. Davis, 'Mystical versus Enthusiastic Sensibility', *JHI* 4 (1943), 301–19.

[59] See G. F. Nuttall, 'Puritan and Quaker Mysticism', *Theology*, 78 (1975), 518–31.

[60] *Love without Dissimulation* (1666), 6.

Taken as a whole the radicals made an undeniably unusual and extraordinary literary contribution which became one of the hallmarks of 'enthusiasm' for the next century. Versions of self were created which moved increasingly towards the merging of the individual with the Godhead, the ultimate claim for perfection. As experience gave way to prophecy so the distinction between expression and behaviour disappeared: writing, speech, and gesture combined in imitations of Old Testament prophetic behaviour. The complications this created, both inside and outside the text, with regard to the dramatic or theatrical way in which existence was conceived, were considerable. An inner world of archetypes, confident in its glorification, was created across the tumultuous central twenty years of the century. Undoubtedly the language of radical religion was founded upon irrationality in theory and in practice as the difference between the internal and the external, the literal and the figurative, disappeared. Self, church, and Godhead become one.

The experiential was not limited to the self. The broad culture of spiritual enthusiasm was not one simply of indigenous, autochthonous scriptural interpreters. That culture was able to appropriate a range of influences from the continent, not only in the interest of self-illumination but also as an attempt to understand the cosmos and the place of the divine in it. Power, authority, and truth were associated with knowledge of God's operation in the natural world and the way in which the language which described that operation simultaneously defined truths in the individual. For most, this led to a series of highly complex, highly exploratory, and very varied discourses. A field appeared in which an 'inner self' was defined and explored for the sake of the divine working within it. At their most extreme the radical prophets looked beyond human language in an attempt to capture divine language and substance itself. The result was a lapse into solipsism and incomprehensibility, while the extent of sectarian autodidactism was revealed. Yet the radicals needed to communicate, so that, however mysterious their words or gestures were, they still adopted rhetorical and stylistic forms which were recognizable developments from less extreme Puritan traditions. The radicals had to find their own solutions to the problems which faced all forms of religion in early modern England. Order was maintained and these forms

combined with practices of gesture (which symbolically communicated a divine truth), wholly denying the worldly impure.
In the attempt to capture the unattainable and to communicate
it some of the most striking and fascinating uses of language in
the seventeenth century may be found. Yet, if startling, through
the 'liberty of the spirit' this language also displayed a wide
degree of sensitivity and variation in its attempt to capture the
authenticity of God's working within each soul and within the
nation. Without an appreciation of this, no study of this subject
can be complete.

I
The Sense of Self:
From Saints to Quakers

1
Prophecy, Experience, and the
Presentation of the Self

I

RADICAL Puritans thought that they were in contact with God
in a special way all the time. If it were possible to meet every
radical Puritan and sectarian and to assemble all the evidence we
might ever hope to have about any one person, then we would be
able to construct a picture of each radical's sense of this relationship, their sense of self, how they expressed themselves, and how
contemporaries saw them. Though such a huge task is not
feasible, there is sufficient evidence, especially in printed works,
to explore the emergence of a series of radical religious notions of
self, defined within the terms of conversion narratives and
prophecy. Puritan diaries and spiritual autobiographies as
genres which record a sense of self are familiar examples of the
ways in which the godly examined themselves in relation to
Providence. Indeed, for many Puritans, writing on a regular
basis was considered a spiritual duty.[1] However, specific to the
radical churches and sects were types of expression and identity,
inextricably linked to ecclesiology and soteriology. It was here
that the personal emerged as part of the incendiary public world
of radical religious and national politics in the 1640s and 1650s,
as believers and prophets developed discourses to express
inspiration, grace or perfection, giving specific shape along the
way to treatments of gender, sexuality, the body, and time.

Customarily the conversion narrative, or 'confession of experience', is regarded as separate from the prophetic outpourings
which typified the worship and pamphlets of sectarians. This is
partly because confessional narratives have been seen as a
precursor of autobiography proper.[2] But within the contemporary

---

[1] See Owen C. Watkins, *The Puritan Experience* (1972). For the most recent study of
writing as a duty, see Paul S. Seaver, *Wallington's World* (1985), 10, 195 (see also
pp. 174, 183).

[2] See Joan Webber, *The Eloquent 'I': Style and Self in Seventeenth-Century Prose*
(Madison, 1968), 58–79; Watkins, *The Puritan Experience*, pp. 3, 91–9, 144–59; Dean

understanding of prophecy, both categories were defined as examples of divine inspiration. The dream or vision exists also as the climax of both confession and prophecy. True enough the confession of experience had a distinct place in theories of church government but confessions and prophecies contained similarities in the vocabulary of personal experience. The movement from conversion narrative to the most extreme form of prophecy is one in which the central features of internalization, the collapse of the literal and the metaphorical, became more intense, while the tendency to elaborate colourful fictive and symbolic narratives was frequently invaded by the no less vivid claims of hypostatic experience.

Confessions of 'experience' were given by individuals when they joined a gathered church, along with their confession of faith. One congregation took their imperative for giving confessions from Mal. 3: 16 and 1 Pet. 3: 15.[3] Not all 'experiences' however were given in this manner, contrary to the emphases of a recent critic: some were written down beforehand and submitted to the minister while others were of a longer nature and were published separately as complete works by themselves. In this instance some of these works were not so much a recounting of events in one's life as a very detailed expounding of the Scriptures.[4] Clearly 'experience' could mean several modes of spiritual expression. Just as any attempt to depict a linear development in radical ecclesiology is in a sense based upon a false precept (since individuals derived similar principles of church government from the Scriptures but in isolation from each other), so also it is impossible to draw a clear picture of the development of the confession of experience as a condition of church membership.[5]

It should be emphasized that 'prophesying', the oral expounding from the Scriptures, was something quite different and was common to separatist and Independent churches as a whole, whereas the confession of experience was peculiar to the

---

Ebner, *Autobiography in Seventeenth Century England: Theology and the Self* (The Hague, 1970), 22–71, 119–45.

[3] Henry Walker (ed.) *Spirituall Experiences, Of sundry Beleevers* (1653), sig. u4ᵛ.

[4] Patricia Caldwell, *The Puritan Conversion Narrative* (Cambridge, 1983), pp. ix, 1; Jane Turner, *Choice Experiences* (1653).

[5] G. F. Nuttall, *Visible Saints: The Congregational Way, 1640–1660* (Oxford, 1957), 51–5.

Independent or Congregational churches. However, unlike the formal prophesyings of the Elizabethan Puritans, later radical religious prophesyings often included an inspired outpouring or 'groaning' which, though dense with 'Scripture language', was an original utterance, somewhat divorced from a close exegetical relationship with any biblical passage. The two were similar in that they facilitated in different ways the free expression of the spirit within the individual. In meetings of gathered churches, 'prophesyings' were not always accompanied by confessions of experience, but prophesying did play a major role in the continuing experience of believers. In a few celebrated cases of inspired women prophets, prophesying with an inordinately large degree of authority was one of the ends of a traumatic process of coming to grace, the process of which could be detected in the popular published accounts of their lives. These publications constitute expanded versions of the confessions of experience, though the women did not necessarily record their stories by themselves. In each case the constraints placed upon these women in the family and in the church is balanced precisely by the authority which they claimed through a special access to the divine.

The prophetic writings associated with the Ranters and the Quakers are concerned with the place of God in the person of the prophet. For the Ranters the presence of God within the individual threatens to obliterate the self, so that the persona speaks with the identity of God. Accordingly the speaking voice in each pamphlet represents an unstable identity, while still attempting to maintain persuasive authority. The Ranters also consciously adopt symbolic gestures and behaviour, associated with Old Testament prophets in particular, as a sign of their inspiration and a measure of their subversiveness. The mystical element in Ranter writing, the denial of self in the presence of the divine for the sake of union between individual and divine, is taken to a greater extreme in Quaker writing, where the ultimate aim is not prophetic expression but silence, though Quaker behaviour did involve complex forms of symbolic gesture. Quaker writing moves beyond imitation of biblical characters, and the perception of biblical characters as types or examples, to a direct appropriation of biblical voices, which takes place in the absence of a distinctive Quaker *persona*.

Ultimately both Ranters and Quakers transcend the 'fleshy' finite self by means of the elaboration of allegories which describe self in natural imagery. 'Experiences' and more radical prophetic behaviour share certain terms and kinds of self-presentation, especially regarding the description of individual regenerate believers in heightened language. Both categories also behave in some accordance with seventeenth-century notions of prophecy, and these notions are useful in fostering a more accurate understanding of the radical prophetic self. However, though prophecy rather than autobiography is the governing principle, the presentation of self moves towards its own conditions, which lie outside biblical prophetic models and notions of prophetic behaviour.

II

In the seventeenth century 'prophecy' was defined in several distinct but related ways. Generally 'prophecy' referred to divinely inspired utterance, the prophet being God's agent for speaking to the people. That the prophet foretells the future, which is the primary twentieth-century meaning, was subsidiary to the general meaning. In Puritan theology 'prophecy' was understood as the interpretation or expounding of Scriptures. Prophecy as the interpretation of the writings of the Old Testament prophets was practised in the early apostolic churches (see 1 Cor. 12: 14) and Luther revived this sense, casting himself as *homo spiritualis*, reinterpreting the Word in preaching which would have the same authority as the Old Testament prophets, bringing on the new age of the Holy Spirit. Calvin made 'prophecy' a ministerial office in his *Institutes* (4. 3. 5), so authorizing the appearance of new 'prophets' who would rail against iniquity and corruption.[6] In England 'prophesier' came to mean a Puritan preacher in the seventeenth century.

Prophecy was related to the Puritan patriarch William Perkins's notion of 'experimental theology' which described the way in which a regenerate man may discern his possession of the knowledge of saving faith by applying syllogistic reasoning to his

---

[6] See also Zwingli's notion of prophesying, developed in opposition to the personal claims of inspiration made by Anabaptists: *Preface to the Prophets* (1529).

conscience.[7] 'Experimentall knowledge' became extremely wide-spread in English Calvinism. By the 1630s, though the logical strictures of Perkins remained in the sermons of Richard Sibbes, for some preachers and congregations the emphasis was upon an intense *emotional* questioning of 'experience'. Such was the case with John Everard and Roger Brierley. For the Independent Vavasor Powell it was an assurance for both intellect and emotions: '*Experience* is like steel to an edged tool, or like salt to fresh meat, it seasons brain-knowledge, and settles a shaking unsetled soule.'[8] 'Prophesying' was thus accompanied by the communal sharing of 'experiences' in Independent congregations, where each member would recount significant 'experiences' as a sign of his or her election in order to join the congregation.[9] Hobbes slightingly identified one congregational meaning of prophecy as the singing of praises to God, but the communal bond in John Rogers's congregation in Dublin was maintained by shared prophesying, so extending the fellowship affirmed in confessions of experience, and enhancing experiential knowledge itself: '*one by one*, which the Church *kept* so *sweetly*, and I was very much *convinced* of your *walking together* in *love* and *unity* of spirit.'[10]

The greater the belief in inspiration of the individual by the spirit, the more 'experience' looked like 'prophecy'. The point was made implicitly in the use of Rabbinic commentaries by the Cambridge Platonist John Smith in his *Of Prophecy*, the most comprehensive and perceptive seventeenth-century statement concerning prophecy, published in his *Select Discourses*. All inspirational communication, prophecy or otherwise, says Smith, is the 'conversation of souls', a divine whispering or breath, as in the Hebrew *Bath Kol* בת קול.[11] For Smith, this divine breath is a necessary prerequisite for prophecy proper to take place, while the radical Independent John Rogers uses *Bath Kol* to define

---

[7] See R. T. Kendall, *Calvin and English Calvinism to 1649* (Oxford, 1979), 8–9, 80.

[8] Epistle in Walker, *Spirituall Experiences*, sig. A3ʳ⁻ᵛ.

[9] For a thorough discussion of the interpenetration of prophecy and experience in the gathered churches, especially those in New England, see Caldwell, *The Puritan Conversion Narrative*, pp. 45–80.

[10] Thomas Hobbes, *Leviathan* (1651), ed. C. B. Macpherson (1968), 457; John Rogers, '*Experience* of Rebecca Rich', in *Ohel or Beth-shemesh. A Tabernacle for the Sun* (1653), 413.

[11] John Smith, *Of Prophecy*, in *Select Discourses* (1660), ed. Henry G. Williams (4th edn., Cambridge, 1859), 268.

'experience' itself. For Rogers, these *'soule-whisperings'* are not enthusiastic fancy but a *'reall* truth . . . a *pleasant irradiation* or *brightnesse*, beaming upon the *soule'*, which he relates to Paul's idea of man receiving the spirit of God in 1 Cor. 2: 12.[12]

Nevertheless, Smith does elevate the prophet above mere soul whisperings, and it is instructive to follow his definitions of the different types of prophet. A prophecy is a revealed truth 'by which God flows in upon the minds of men, extrinsically to their own proper operations'.[13] Following Maimonides, Smith holds that prophets are influenced from the Deity in the rational faculty primarily and that such inspiration is transmitted in the second instance to the imaginative faculty by the mediation of the active intellect. There are similarities here with a learned radical like Rogers. Both Smith and Rogers feel that divine truth which comes through 'scripture incarnate' is vulgar compared with prophecy. Both stress the importance of the rational faculty. Rogers says that even an 'experience' is taken up and arrested by the *'intellectuall* and *cognoscitive faculties* of their *soules'*, especially if they are dreams and visions.[14]

After the initial postulation however, Smith proceeds to make the traditional distinction between most of the Old Tesament prophets who received messages by dreams and visions, and Moses who received the highest form of vision since he conversed with God 'on familiar terms' while he was awake and without an angelic medium. This, the *gradus Mosaicus*, meant that Moses could prophesy all the time, while his vision was *in speculo lucido*, unlike the obscure riddles, visions, and oracles of the other prophets, who saw *in speculo non lucido*.[15] Rabbinic knowledge provided a further refinement in the form of four different types of prophecy: first, when the prophet is dominated by the imaginative faculty and sees only 'parables, similitudes and allegories'. The second is where the rational and imaginative balance each other while the third is where the rational faculty is predominant. The fourth and highest stage, the *gradus Mosaicus*, is where all imagination ceases and the representation of truth remains in the highest stage of reason and understanding

---

[12] Rogers, *Ohel*, p. 373.   [13] Smith, *Select Discourses*, p. 178.
[14] Ibid. 173, 179; Rogers, *Ohel*, pp. 449–50. Rabbi Joseph Albo held that the rational faculty was mediated by the 'fancy or otherwise': Smith, *Select Discourses*, p. 180.   [15] Ibid. 181–3, 272–5.

in man.[16] With the exception of Moses prophets see only in part while it is also possible for a prophet's actions to be prophetic, though the prophet may not be aware of this, as in the case of Samson.

Most Protestants, of course, accepted that the age of prophecy had ended with the birth of Christ, after which the spirit of prophecy in the Old Testament sense gradually faded away, Justin Martyr being the last to receive such inspiration.[17] Patristic writers had connected prophecy with scriptural exegesis, while medieval Schoolmen viewed prophecy as philosophy charged with divine illumination. With the Reformation Foxe and other Marian exiles were regarded as prophets in their advocacy of a historically justified and reformed state church. More than this radical Puritans increasingly stressed the validity of prophecy as divine inspiration, either in the manner in which it could act through congregations of regenerate Christians or in the rebirth of the prophetic spirit in the mid-seventeenth century. In *Sions Lamentation* (1649), Lady Eleanor Davis (or Douglas) saw a direct continuation of the gift of prophecy from Old Testament times to her own day (pp. 5–6), and it is clear that John Rogers applies a Neoplatonic and Rabbinical theory which was developed to relate historical events in the Old Testament to the psychologies of his contemporaries and himself.[18]

Others were less sympathetic to the radical theory of prophecy. Burton, not surprisingly, regarded prophecy as a symptom of melancholy, a delusion of learning based on astrology, or enthusiastic frenzy bred from fancies, and sometimes induced by drugs as in the case of the Sibylline prophets. False prophets, ancient, pre- and post-Reformation are singled out for abuse, and of the latter especially 'Cretinck, Knipperdoling, and their associates, those madmen of Munster in Germany' as well as 'Brownists, Barrowists, Familists . . . led all by so many private

---

[16] Ibid. Again, following Albo, *Bath Kol* becomes the lowest form of prophecy in this light.

[17] Ibid. 181–2.

[18] Lady Eleanor did predict future events, however, such as the death of her husband, Sir John Davies, as well as the assassination of the Duke of Buckingham in 1628 and the execution of Charles I. Astrologers played an important role in predicting the course of political and military events: see Harry Rusche, '*Merlini Anglici*: Astrology and Propaganda from 1644 to 1651', *EHR* 80 (1965), 322–33; id., 'Prophecies and Propaganda, 1641 to 1651', *EHR* 64 (1969), 752–70; B. S. Capp, *Astrology and the Popular Press: English Almanacs and Religion 1500–1800* (1979), 67–101.

spirits'.[19] Burton recommends the suppression of conventicles and the punishment of individual sectaries. He proceeds to explain that Christ's prophecy of the Second Coming, Millennium and Last Judgement, was final, and no one living after Christ could alter or challenge the authority of this prophecy. Smith takes the same line, admitting that Saul's inspiration may well have been a form of melancholy madness. He supports the Patristic diagnosis of Montanism as ecstasies and abruptions of the mind, '*sybyllae crebro se dicunt ardere, tormente vi magna flammarum*', though he uses a theory of inspiration which is the same as that employed in defence of present inspiration by some of the radicals.[20]

Whether the prophet operated by inspired ravings, dreams, or visions on the one hand, or by inspired interpretation of the Bible on the other, prophecy posed a threat to social and political authority, as Calvin realized, since any individual could claim enormous, unquestionable authority for him or herself.[21] It is therefore not surprising, as Keith Thomas has pointed out, that prophets should come largely, though not exclusively, from those excluded from positions of social, political, and religious authority: notably women and artisan 'tub-preachers'.[22] On the other hand, claims to prophetic inspiration also seem to have come from Puritan preachers, as the millennial atmosphere of the 1640s increased. The movement seems to have been strongest in the Parliamentary Army, amongst preachers who were described by their opponents as 'tub-preachers', though some had had no small degree of orthodox education, such as Henry Pinnell and Abiezer Coppe.[23]

The focus was upon the way in which the prophet behaved. In one sense Calvin had tried to minimize this aspect. He felt that only God could be speaking through the prophet, since when not actually receiving a vision many prophets, such as Hosea and

[19] Robert Burton, *The Anatomy of Melancholy* (1621), ed. H. Jackson, 3 vols. (1932), iii. 371. See also i. 141, 428; iii. 310, 344.

[20] Smith, *Select Discourses*, pp. 260, 201–02.

[21] *Commentaries*, trans. and ed. Joseph Haroutunian, in collab. with Louise P. Smith (1958), 86–8.

[22] *Religion and the Decline of Magic* (1971), 135–79, though on pp. 155–6, the presentation of the early English Reformers as prophets is also discussed; id., 'Women and the Civil War Sects', *Past and Present*. 13 (1958). 42–62.

[23] See the biographical details in Anne Laurence, 'Parliamentary Army Chaplains, 1642–1651', 2 vols. (D.Phil. thesis, University of Oxford, 1981), ii. *passim*.

Ezekiel, behaved in foolish ways. Beyond the actual moment of inspiration what a prophet said or did was not prophetic. However because of his sophisticated psychological models of inspiration, based upon a varying mixture of rational and imaginative components, Smith regards the individual's behaviour as part of the prophetic gift. Thus it may be, in the case of obscure messages, that wise and experienced men are required to interpret a 'dull spirit of divination', as Plato had advised.[24] Here monitions and instructions, heard as voices in the mind of the prophet, do not qualify as true prophetic visions, while, from the example of the Jews, the greater the perturbation and sense of physical exhaustion, the greater the vision.[25] The strange behaviour of some prophets, such as Hosea taking a harlot for his wife or Ezekiel shaving his head, was explained by the adoption of Maimonides' notion that the behaviour of prophets constituted parables designed to be as instructive as the visions of the prophets themselves.

Though one Rabbinic source, Abarbanel, held that all was literal except for the prophet's dream, the Talmudists confirmed that visions could appear as narratives. So the action of the prophet could be taken inside the category of divinely sent symbolic message. The idea of visions as dramas which took place on the stage of the prophet's mind is expanded so that the prophet plays a symbolic role in his waking life, and the divine is felt to be constantly present around him. Smith points to Jer. 13, where Jeremiah hears God's command to put on a linen girdle, and Jer. 14, where Jeremiah speaks about himself in the third person, as examples of symbolic behaviour. Maimonides argued that Ezekiel probably never shaved his head since he was a priest. In this instance it is likely that Ezekiel saw a vision of himself which he recorded in the narrative: 'a history of the visions themselves which appeared to them, except we be led by some farther argument of the reality of the thing, in a way of sensible appearance, to determine it to have been any sensible thing'.[26] The prophet is actor as well as *spectator*, and both Pareus and Mede defended the repetitions and obscure plot development in Revelation as an example of John following dramatic

[24] Smith, *Select Discourses*, pp. 197–8; Plato, *Timaeus*, 72B.
[25] Ibid. 203.   [26] Ibid. 227–37.

decorum.[27] Likewise, in a pamphlet of 1636 the playwright Thomas Heywood described two 'tub-preachers' by means of the dramatic analogy, depicting the tyranny of a distracted mind over a body whose gestures are accordingly not commensurate with the convention of preaching which should govern them:

> At every place of Scripture cited, he turnes over the leaves of his Booke, more pleased with the motion of the leaves, than the matter of the Text: For hee folds downe the leaves, though he finds not the place: his eye being still fixt on his paper, or the Pulpit: Hee lifts up the whites of his eyes towards Heaven, when he meditates on the sordid pleasures of the earth, his body being in Gods Church, when his minde is in the divels Chappell.[28]

There is no notion among the radical Puritans of the prophet as *vates* or inspired poet who can prophesy the future in a mythic vision, a tradition which was so important for Renaissance poets, especially the Spenserians. The idea of *vates* came from classical notions of divine contemplation, and Lady Eleanor Davis, though not a sectarian, does emphasize the distinction between biblical prophecies and both pagan divination and 'gross . . . Romish miracles'.[29] Still, Eleanor Davis follows the popular tradition of using forms of knowledge, astrology, numerology, and the significance of particular letters, as well as scriptural exegesis to interpret contemporary events. So while there is an anagram for 'O:Cromwel' in 'Howl Rome', the birth of the fated Lord Hastings is prophesied in the birth of Josias in 1 Esdras 1 and the assassination of Buckingham in August 1628 is seen as the work of the Beast.[30] This was part of a long Reformation tradition of prediction and the difference between Lady Eleanor Davis and the radicals is that while she is concerned with the interpretation of divinely inscribed knowledge the radicals are concerned with the nature of the inspiration itself, either as 'experience' or prophecy, so turning entirely from knowledge to power, from a concern for comprehending God's intentions for mankind to a concern for God working in the self.

[27] David Pareus, *A Commentary upon the Divine Revelation of the Apostle and Evangelist*, trans. Elias Arnold (Amsterdam, 1644), 20; Joseph Mede, *Clavis Apocalyptica* (1627) trans. Richard More as *The Key of the Revelation* (1643), 61.

[28] Thomas Heywood, *A True Discourse of the Two infamous upstart Prophets* (1636), 3.

[29] *Sions Lamentation* (1649), p. 6.

[30] *The Benidiction* (1651), sig. *2ʳ; *Sions Lamentation* (1649), 8. 1 Esd. 1 contains the death of Josias. His birth is recorded in 1 Kings 13: 2 and Matt. 1: 10; *The Excommunication out of Paradise* (1651), 10.

III

The pattern of the confession of 'experience' consists of a presentation of the self as body and soul acted upon by the divine, either in the form of dreams and visions, as we have already seen, or in the form of a relationship with the process of spiritual regeneration and God's Word in a waking state. Characteristically the metaphor employed to explain this is taken from literary activity. So for the Quaker Anne Audland the mind is the 'Book of Conscience' upon which the Scriptures are written.[31] The significant moments in each 'experience' come when, as it were, the imprint is made and when the individual learns to read the book God has given to him or her. This verbal impulse is common in sectarian prose and Bunyan's *Grace Abounding* is now the most famous example. Bunyan personifies the Scriptures so that they act upon him with human force:

> Now about a week or fortnight after this, I was much followed by this scripture, '*Simon, Simon, behold, Satan hath desired to have you*', (Luke 22. 31). And sometimes it would sound so loud within me, yea, and as it were call so strongly after me, that once above all the rest, I turned my head over my shoulder, thinking verily that some man had behind me called to me.[32]

The radical Puritans, however, present themselves as mechanisms which can be affected by the Scriptures for which they become a repository: 'I was *carried much* after the *Word*'.[33] Bunyan's autobiography is one of continuous confrontation with a concretized Scripture which moulds his behaviour despite his successive revolts against the Scriptures' authority. Bunyan's personification betrays a sense of God acting on and against him. However for the radicals their figurative language betrays a sense of God acting from within the individual or desiring to penetrate the individual.

The purpose of publishing the collections of 'experiences' made by John Rogers, Henry Walker, and Samuel Petto was to declare publicly the regenerate nature of each congregation and the presence of free grace within the heart of each member as a

---

[31] *A True Declaration of the suffering of the innocent* (1655), 2.

[32] *Grace Abounding to the Chief of Sinners* (1666), ed. Roger Sharrock (Oxford, 1962), 30.

[33] Rogers, '*Experience of* Ruth Emerson *as it came out of her own mouth in the Church at Dublin*', in *Ohel*, p. 411.

means of 'assurance'. Stating that the pourings out of the spirit are the greatest gift of the latter days, Samuel Petto affirms that he wants to offer something substantial on assurance in order to give hope to the perplexed against deceptions, he himself having just reached such a state of certainty.[34] In part the purpose was also educative and proselytizing. In his preface to Walker's *Spirituall Experiences, Of sundry Beleevers* (1653) Vavasor Powell indicates that this purpose will be served if the experiences are published rather than being kept in manuscript within the congregation.

It should be remembered that only a fraction of the confessions of experience given were ever published. The common pattern is one of an initial portrayal of a sinner ('in my apprehension I could not fit the part of any good thing with the people of God'[35]), who passes to assurance and salvation, by way of the Scriptural trigger, '*Come unto me all yee that are wearie and heavie laden.*'[36] Most of the experiences do not give details of individuals' entire lives. Instead they focus upon the events, often deeply emotional, which lead to eventual regeneration. On the other hand there are a few examples where the believer imparts a precise and detailed account of the way in which the supernatural has moulded their lives as is the case of John Rogers himself.

At the simplest level the presence of God in the events of an individual's life is not explored but simply recorded.[37] Similarly, the sense of self is merely an 'I' who has no background but simply a place in the congregation, and no more emotional life than a quiet sense of assurance. More sophisticated confessors are concerned with the relationship between body and the state of salvation in the soul or spirit. The inner state always affects the outer: John Rogers recalls that he used to hide from others when smitten with a sense of guilt and despair, which is reminiscent of Bunyan's inability to exorcize his sense of guilt on hearing the sound of bells ringing, by reporting that whenever he stood near the church he feared that the bell or steeple might fall down upon

---

[34] *The Voice of the Spirit* (1654), sig. A6^r.

[35] Walker, *Spirituall Experiences*, sig. A3^v.

[36] Walker, 'Experience of T. A.', in *Spirituall Experiences*, p. 3. The biblical reference here is Matt. 11: 28.

[37] 'through Gods inlightning mee, I knew that despaire brought hell and destruction, but those that trust in him doe never miscarry'. '*Experience* of G. D.', in *Spirituall Experiences*, p. 251.

him and kill him.[38] The believer is always a 'poor soule' prior to actual rebirth while the individuals are consistently visited by feelings of fear, temptation, and suicide. Here the sense of physical brutalization is intense and not figurative:

O the *leaps* that I have made! the *frights* that I have had! the *fears* that I was in! which continued off and on to the *beginning* of these times! Besides great outward *afflictions* which I met with, were of much force to *bring me into this condition*, being often (and doubtlesse I might *deserve* it too too much) beaten, bruised, turn'd out of doors, whirl'd and kickt about, hardly and unkindly used; at which times I should sometimes be *tempted* to *murther my self.*[39]

Nevertheless, the powerful providence of God is felt in the events of individual lives. Most of the London Independent congregations were heavily Calvinist with a leaning towards free grace, and the providentialist emphasis is most prominent in Walker's congregation. Here there is a peculiar sense of horror which can be derived from the graphic detail of the descriptions of the 'trials' which the believers feel God has put in their way. But at the same time there is a sense of the individual's emotional distance from the experience, no doubt largely because the individual has attained regeneration and salvation:

The Enemy took *Liverpoole*, and killed my Husband, and a childe, both before my face, and stript, and wounded me, and a childe of five years old; and it was thought I could not live. And this was a strong tryall; and I was much tempted, my senses me thought were going from me, and my heart I thought would have melted in pieces.[40]

This woman's place in the separatist community and the type of religious devotion which such a place demands function as a therapy which enables her to escape from the numbing depression, shock and distraction which she describes as the consequence of her brutalization.[41]

There are two other points of import in this particular 'experience'. First, the sense of a divine pattern is enforced in that the woman's husband, though enjoying 'abundance of joy and comfort' at one point in his life, was 'troubled in mind' to the

---

[38] Rogers, '*further* Experience of John Rogers', in *Ohel*, p. 426; Bunyan, *Grace Abounding*, pp. 13–14.

[39] Rogers, *Ohel*, p. 427.

[40] Walker, 'Experiences of M.W.', in *Spirituall Experiences*, p. 11.

[41] Ibid. 11, 16–18.

extent that he expected to die in the near future. In effect he predicts, or 'prophesies', his own death. Secondly, the passage finishes with the Bible performing a redemptive act upon the conscience of the woman. The very words affect her, and the scriptural passage itself appears in the text:

Yet I prayed, and the Lord heard me, I thought it was too much for me to beare: but I remembered my Saviours words, *He that will not forsake Father, or Mother, or Sister, or Brother, or Husband, or Childe for Christ, is not worthy of him*, and I desired to give glory to his name.[42]

Also, there is a record of the interaction of human and divine wills, of faith and grace. The woman implores God's help yet she seems to regard herself as responsible for discerning the necessary aid in the Scriptures: she 'remembers' Christ's words. Again, though, the passage ends with the conclusion that 'my heart said, that God was just in all his dealings with me'.[43]

Ultimately self is realized in terms of the Bible. Unlike the Ranter assumption of God's name, 'I am' is adopted by the self to emphasize the total negation of ego in the presence of Scripture: 'I am, in and through Gods free grace, what I am; not for any thing in me, or that I could do; but as in Titus 4.5.'[44] The pattern of realization of grace comes to resemble a complex process, which is rooted in the classic apostolic sense of knowing Christ through contraries: 'my *strength was made perfect in weaknesse*; 2 Cor. 12.9. most gladly *therefore will I glory in my infirmities*; and vers. 10. *when I am weak, then am I strong*.'[45] In John Rogers's own 'experience', the pattern is part of a narrative autobiography which traces Rogers's oscillation between a reliance on the Word and desperate feelings of sin and lack of salvation. The repetitive interruptions of Scripture begin on the auditory level, when, as a boy, Rogers is affected by the zeal of William Fenner's preaching, 'you *knotty! rugged! proud piece of flesh!* you *stony, rocky, flinty, hard heart!*'.[46] The spoken word dominates the written. Like one of his congregation, Ann Megson, Rogers was given to taking down sermons word for word in his youth and before going to bed he

---

[42] Walker, '*Experiences of* M.W.', in *Spirituall Experiences*, pp. 11–12, see also Matt. 19: 29: Mark 10: 29.   [43] Ibid. 12.

[44] Walker, '*Experiences of* D.R.', in *Spirituall Experiences*, p. 125; Titus 4: 5 is a false reference for 1 Cor. 15: 10.

[45] Rogers, *Ohel*, p. 418. Rogers is attracted in a similar way to Donne, referring to pp. 658, 139 in the 1640 edition of Donne's sermons; ibid. 378, 390.

[46] Ibid. 419.

would appease his sense of sin by repeating Hall's *Catechism* over and over to himself.[47] At the intervals when Rogers feels grace the transcendence from 'form' to 'power' is marked by the singing of songs and psalms as a sign of deliverance. The prevalence of the spoken word is apotheosized in the auditory hallucinations of hearing supernatural voices: 'My minde and all was taken up with their *howlings* and *screechings*' says Rogers, as he is persecuted by a hoard of demonic voices.[48]

Rogers's own particular sense of sin is determined by an extreme asceticism, which is marked by periods of fasting and mortification. Indeed, when in a state of severe poverty he feels that he should even eat himself.[49] Rogers in fact undergoes a prolonged process of alienation from himself: the ideals which he feels he should attain (at one point, to exceed the strict asceticism of the scribes and pharisees) are not commensurate with his actual sense of self. This division is rendered in military metaphors so that the divine 'repulses' him from vain practices of magic and astrology. As his body comes to reflect directly his inner state the distinction between internal and external realities does disappear. The same occurs in prophetic discourse proper but there the speaker always uses a rhetoric drawn closely from a biblical prophetic book. Rogers, however, makes even the external environment symbolic of his state of mind as the external, nature, reacts with his physical body: 'the very isicles hung on my hair or cheeks, a conflux of tears that came hot would thaw them, which fell abundantly from me in the open fields'.[50] Rogers's passionate despair melts the ice but both tears and ice exist as an emanation of piteous hopelessness which drains away into the ground. This pathos is juxtaposed with a sense of God as an absolute, omnipotent presence, who can be reasoned with, railed against, and fought against, but who is unmoved by the sinner. Here Rogers flings himself into tantrums and sobbing rages as he feels that his prayers have no effect: 'rise up and appear for thy self thou *great God*!' he demands.[51] After his final conversion Rogers admits that he still meets spiritual troubles but that he is armed to cope with them now. On the other hand some of his Dublin congregation say that even

[47] The text has 'Hall' but it is most likely to have been one of the catechisms of John Ball. There were two published, one in 1615, the other in 1630, the former going through nine editions before 1640, the latter, two editions.   [48] Ibid. 430.
[49] Ibid. 434.   [50] Ibid. 433.   [51] Ibid. 430.

after a saving 'experience' they still walk in 'darkness', and place all their hopes in the regeneration of the congregation as a whole.[52]

Separation from social groups, especially the family, is reported as a common cause of spiritual disruption. In *Ohel or Beth-shemesh*, Humphrey Mills tells how the death of his father, a high sheriff, caused the dispersal of his family. This he takes as a punishment wrought by God and he is surprised when his business flourishes in Dublin. He appears to attribute this success to his membership of Rogers's gathered church, a sign to God of his regenerate nature.[53] Rogers himself suffers estrangement first from his family, especially his father (a Laudian who severely punished his son's Puritanism), and then his friends, as a consequence of his extreme asceticism.

The larger the time scale the greater is the intervention of the power of Providence. In Henry Walker's collection one man comes to regard his rescue from death at his birth as a divine intervention, though significantly it is an understanding he comes to have only later in life. Here a common episode which features Providence is the experience of being saved from near or partial disaster on a sea voyage. Generally the voyage and rescue is a significant point or watershed in the larger, figurative voyage of life.[54]

The features which have been described so far are common to both of the collections of 'experiences' which are being analysed here. However, those in Rogers's *Ohel or Beth-shemesh* are more radically spiritual than those in Walker's *Spirituall Experiences, Of sundry Beleevers*. Though 'experiences' from both collections speak of free grace, the character of Walker's congregation seems to be more traditionally Calvinist, with a greater emphasis on sinfulness. Rogers's congregation is more prepared to express the sense of Christ being within the regenerate individual, a 'free gratian' stance rather than open Antinomianism. This difference is registered in the differing nature of some of the confessions. The

---

[52] Rogers, '*Experience of Ruth Emerson*', in *Ohel*, p. 412.

[53] Rogers, '*Experience given in by* Humphrey Mills', in *Ohel*, pp. 409–10.

[54] Walker, '*Experiences of* E.R.', in *Spirituall Experiences*, pp. 358–9; ibid., '*Experiences on a Voyage* from Lishborne to Brasile in the yeare, 1648', pp. 387–9. The voyage as both physical and spiritual journey is a common device in Renaissance and seventeenth-century literature. For other examples, see Frances Cook, *Mris. Cooke's Meditations* (1650); John Cook, *A True Relation of Mr. John Cook's passage by Sea from Wexford to Kinsale* (1650); John Perrot, *Battering Rams against Rome* (1661).

believers in Walker's congregation, also Independents, seem largely versed from their childhoods in Puritan soteriological classics: Perkins's sermons and works by Erasmus.[55] The imperative for spiritual regeneration stays within these boundaries, as the believers admit that the classics have been some help at least towards their rebirth. However the emphasis in Rogers's collection is often upon rather different sources. Though Luther was not usually cited by Puritans in the soteriological sphere, Rogers displays a profound understanding of *homo spiritualis*, of perceiving and acting a mysterious truth through contradictions:

> God hath a way of himself, as *Nazianzen* says, to make himself the more *admired*, and he doth most of his *workes* as *Luther* said, in *mediis contrariis*, by *contrary meanes* in *contrary wayes*, which makes him the more *glorious*.[56]

Rogers himself places the emphasis much more upon the 'self-annihilation' of the inner self, or ego, in order to become spiritually one with God, to let God into the individual's heart: 'And souls exalted in Christ are the more low, and nothing in their own eyes.'[57] Rogers claims that all the 'experiences' he records display the conditions of self-annihilation which he finds in Giles Randall's *A Bright Starre* (1646), the English translation of the third part of Benet of Canfield's *The Rule of Perfection*.[58] *A Bright Starre* recommends an extreme form of *unio mystica* based upon Bernard and the *via negativa* of Pseudo-Dionysius. Though Rogers's introduction to the 'experiences' is the only place where 'self-annihilation' is specifically mentioned, there is a greater awareness of realizing spiritual immanence than in Walker's collection. The self is annihilated, on one level at least, for the sake of the whole of the congregation. Major Andrew Manwaring, for instance, says that Rogers has convinced him of the 'oneness' and 'unity' of the regenerate in their church, while the experience of letting Christ into the individual's heart or soul is commonplace.[59] It seems that membership of Rogers's

---

[55] Walker, '*Experiences of* M.K.', in *Spirituall Experiences*, p. 161. On the inheritance of three-part sermon structure by writers of experiences, see J. H. Taylor, 'Some Seventeenth-Century Testimonies', *Transactions of the Congregational Historical Society*, 16 (1949), 64–77 (esp. 66), and Rogers, *Ohel*, p. 393.   [56] Rogers, *Ohel*, p. 418.

[57] Ibid. 381.   [58] Ibid. 382; see below, ch. 3, pp. 136–42.

[59] Ibid., '*Experience* of Andr. *Manwaring*, Major', inserted gathering, p. 3. Other indications of the Dublin congregation's more radical and spiritual stance are the lack of inclusion of confessions of faith alongside or within confessions of experience, as

congregation results in his influence upon the shape of each 'experience'. Indeed, the power of preachers is often stressed. For Ann Hewson, wife of Colonel Hewson, though Nathaniel Culverwel tried with great and unceasing effort to preach her into a sense of salvation, only Samuel Bolton with his emphasis upon Christ's immanence in the regenerate individual and the transcendent state of self-denial can finally claim her for God.[60]

The roles of Rogers and Walker in determining the structure of 'experiences' work also on the rhetorical level, though it is a rhetoric designed to facilitate the communication of a soterio-logical matter. The narrative presentation of 'vocation' (the action on the part of God of calling persons to a state of salvation or union with Himself) is, for Rogers, a 'comment' upon election. That is, 'vocation' is a sign of election. 'Experiences' are useful in that they make individuals bold for the future, continually humble, yield further obedience to God, renew pledges and are a release for the individual: since each narrative is a sign of grace, each narrative allows the individual to lessen self-censure. Rogers fits each 'experience' into three parts, each of which is named in the margin. The first is the recounting of the moment of calling, with details of when and where the calling occurred. Second, how the calling was made is set out. Finally the effects of the calling are recorded. At the same time further margin notes are inserted to show the transition from 'legal' to 'Gospel' Christianity, that is, from 'notional' (outward) to 'spiritual' (inward) worship, which corresponds to the radical Puritan insistence upon the transference from type to truth, from form to power. This rhetorical imposition, simple, uniform, and effective, serves almost as an ordinance itself for the congregation, so that spiritual transcendence, union with the divine, is made into an institutionalized pattern of literary representation.

The requirements of constituting a gathered church determine the structure of the confessions of 'experience' on a rhetorical level. These utterances were designed to facilitate the com-munication of a soteriological occurrence. The role of the ministers here is considerable.

with Walker, and the elevation of events into one unified experience, or complete narrative, as opposed to Walker's preference for the plural, where experiences become a distinct series of events.

[60] Walker, '*Experiences of* Ann Hewson', in *Spirituall Experiences*, p. 412.

Among others whom Rogers attacks are the 'formal Independents', the more conservative congregationalists to whom the churches of both Walker and Samuel Petto are somewhat closer than the extreme spiritualism encouraged by Rogers.[61] The difference is the degree to which spiritual experience is liberated from ordinances and 'legal' behaviour and it is illustrated in the different nature of the experiences. While those in the Dublin gathered church have a structure imposed upon them by Rogers, those in both Walker's and Petto's congregations often contain certain points of use inside them together with confessions of faith, both put there by the believers themselves. Rogers does admit that some people need to depend upon the externals of worship and belief and never rise above this, but in Petto's collection in particular, the force of externals alongside the experiential 'intercourse' with Christ is more evident.[62] 'A.M.' depends upon the ordinances first to put her in a solitary state of mind where the Scriptures can work on her. It is only when she is unable to attend church that, in a state of meditation, she sees the difference between Legal and Gospel Christianity.[63] Petto's list of effects of the experiences is concerned with much more basic matters of conversion than is Rogers's, propounding conviction to the unrenewed, direction and encouragement to those in like condition, confirmation and consolation, and provocation:

When they see what progresse others have made in the wayes of God, and what communion with Christ they have injoyed herein; it giveth occasion unto their reflecting upon themselves, and may create shame for former negligence, and become a spur unto future diligence.[64]

Yet the sense of self-annihilation sometimes approaches that of Rogers himself without any actual knowledge of the mystical tradition: 'I understood that, to be one with Christ, was to have our will melted into the will of Christ.'[65]

Rogers proceeds to divide 'experiences' into ordinary and extraordinary ones, the former registering this-worldly encounters with God's will concerning legal and evangelical matters and the latter recording inspiration through dreams and visions. He admits that he has truncated the ordinary 'experiences' so that

[61] Ibid. 51.
[62] Ibid. 450; Petto, 'Roses from Sharon', in *The Voice of the Spirit* (1654), sig. O4ᵛ.
[63] Ibid. 2, 11–12.   [64] Ibid. sig. O5ᵛ.   [65] Ibid. 6–7.

he has effectively rewritten them. Though the confessions appear to be genuine, they are shaped by Rogers's own concern with the supernatural and the whisperings of spirit over and above the scripture:

> I must *contract* much their *experiences* as they were taken, least they be too *voluminous* . . . I shall gather the *stalk longer*, least I hurt the *beauty* and *hide* the *excellency* of those *flowers*; yet without *hurt* to the rest, in those which are *ordinary*, I shall be very short.[66]

Claims are also made to stress the oneiric or visionary 'experiences' because the already-published collection of Walker contains many excellent ordinary experiences. The ordinary experiences contain a higher incidence of formal and technical theological vocabulary: 'I have had my soule stayed upon Christ, by some direct act of faith formerly; and have been in some measure established by a reflex act.'[67] In *Choice Experiences* (1653) Jane Turner proceeds to the experiential workings of the spirit only after setting out moral, legal, and gospel considerations (p. 180). Though Rogers's chapter on experiences is set within a much wider analysis of Church discipline, so that it is easy to forget his concern for externals by concentrating on this chapter, he does emphasize in experiences the excellence of the 'double testimony', of the Spirit working without the individual's spirit bearing witness, and the testimony of Word and Spirit together.[68]

Rogers seems to have spent several years collecting various experiences from every place where he had been a minister. The last 'experience' in *Ohel* has nothing to do with the Dublin congregation. It is in fact the account of the conversion of John Osborne of Purleigh, Essex, who thought himself damned because he had committed adultery. Rogers himself was pastor at Purleigh at the time: he performed the conversion, and wrote up the account for the church register. Thus it is not a believer's self-composed 'experience' but a narrative written in the third person, and in this sense Rogers's control of the presentation of the believer's self is even more absolute.[69] The middle of the 'experiences' section contains what appears to be a cancelled

---

[66] Rogers, *Ohel*, p. 392.
[67] Petto, '*Experiences of* A.M.', in *The Voice of the Spirit*, p. 1.
[68] Rogers, *Ohel*, p. 372.
[69] Ibid. '*An eminent* Experience, *or* relation *of* John Osborne', pp. 440–8.

gathering, which could mean that Rogers re-edited some of the confessions while the book was being printed.[70]

Unlike many spiritual autobiographies in the period, including Bunyan's, there is a tendency among the radicals to transform entirely the appearance of material objects, especially people, so that they become identified with the transcendent world. Rogers describes each member of his congregation in terms of Bernard's metaphor of the soul as a violet.[71] By contrast, without resort to a figure, *Spirituall Experiences, Of sundry Beleevers* achieves a transcendent effect by making each individual the specific focus of Christ's attention, '*Come unto me all yee that are wearie and heavie laden.*'[72] The extreme end of this method is to be found in the Ranter appropriation of the Song of Solomon, so that the object of each Ranter's address becomes 'my *love*, my *dove*'.[73] At the same time, and more so in Rogers's imagination and congregation, imagery of sanctification is based upon a physical analogy for spiritual inspiration. Elizabeth Avery's heart 'melts'. It is a union where the divine physically penetrates the believer. Characteristically the heart of the individual is pierced by the prospect of the crucified Christ or the Word: 'I desire much to hear the Word, and am troubled that sometimes it doth not so pierce into my heart, as I desire.'[74] This imparts a sense of God acting much more intensely upon the individual than the image of God's imprint lying in the heart of the believer: 'The Lord hath given me an heart to discern a beauty.'[75] Walker and Rogers were both preachers, and we know also that Rogers was a clergyman's son, but Walker's 'experience' is no different from the others in his collection, except in so far as it betrays his considerable learning.[76] On the other hand Rogers takes the

---

[70] At p. 412 the pagination is interrupted. This is the end of the gathering, and the next one begins with pagination from p. 1 upwards again for the following two gatherings. The gatherings are however in sequence with the rest of the signatures in the book. The conclusion is that, since pagination begins with p. 413 two gatherings later, either the initial pagination was faulty or that Rogers interfered with an original gathering, possibly having a new one made up which was paginated from p. 1.

[71] Ibid. 380.

[72] Walker, '*Experiences* of T.A.', in *Spirituall Experiences*, p. 3; ibid., '*Experiences* of T.P.', pp. 7–8.

[73] For example, see Abiezer Coppe, *Some Sweet Sips, of some Spirituall Wine* (1649), in *CRW*, p. 51.

[74] Rogers, *Ohel*, p. 404; Walker, '*Experiences* of F.P.', in *Spirituall Experiences*, p. 240.

[75] Ibid., '*Experiences* of I.I.', p. 24.

[76] Ibid., '*Experiences* of H.W.', pp. 286–90.

'pneumatic', enthusing style of the Puritan spiritual sermon inside the autobiographical 'experience', not only in his own account but in those in which he has clearly had a hand in writing. Thus there is the heightened emotional appeal in the frequent vocatives, the rapturous renaming of the addressees, and one cannot avoid the suspicion that Rogers has suggested the mystical readings which some of the individuals, like Ann Megson, record.[77]

There is also a concern to achieve a comparison between biblical characters and individuals. One woman is reminded of Job's and David's sufferings in her own by another woman: 'she opened to me the troubles of *David*, and *Job* and gave me sweet comfort, saying, God is by me, and I did not see him, as *Job* wished, so she wrought upon my hart to wish, *O that I could see him, O that I could behold him*'.[78] Similarly, writing from prison in *Mene, Tekel, Perez* (1654), Rogers complains with Job against his persecution, alluding to Job 19: 19–20, where Job says that others have used God's Word against him in reproach (sig. A1ʳ).[79] An even closer identity can be maintained by simply copying biblical speech, as with Paul's '*O Wretched man that I am*'.[80] There is here the influence of Foxe's *Acts and Monuments* when, for instance, one woman presents herself as the hopeless victim of persecution and imprisonment once she becomes separated from her husband, though the narrative is not so extensively or self-consciously martyrological as Lilburne's pamphlets are.[81]

Though there is some concern for humble and selfless behaviour, there is no notion of *imitatio Christi*. As has been pointed out by J. Sears McGee the Puritan stress was rather upon the saving grace offered by Christ's crucifixion, and the imagery of Christ's redemptive suffering is prominent in radical Puritan writing as well as in that of more orthodox Puritans.[82] In *Ohel* Rogers is convinced that the hearts of believers will be

[77] Rogers, '*Experience* of Ann Megson', in *Ohel*, pp. 416–18.

[78] Walker, '*Experiences* of D.M.', in *Spirituall Experiences*, p. 37.

[79] This relates to a general trend in seventeenth-century devotional literature where typologies are personalized.

[80] Walker, '*Experiences* of M.H.', p. 221. This reference is to Rom. 7: 24.

[81] Rogers, *Ohel*, 'A *Fuller* testimony *as it was taken from* Elizabeth Avery', in pp. 404–5. For Lilburne's self-presentation, see *The Prisoners Mournfull Cry* (1648).

[82] J. Sears McGee, 'Conversion and the Imitation of Christ in Anglican and Puritan Writing', *JBS* 15 (1976), 20–39.

'melted' by the prospect of the crucified Christ.[83] By contrast enemy figures or forces are envisaged as distinct characters who have no internal life, while the regenerate Christian is presented in vital contact with the Word.

In *Newes Coming up out of the North* (1654) George Fox creates a character for Cain, the archetypal sinful man (p. 10). In Rogers, the biblical sinners and drunkards become identified with the past iniquitous lives of several characters in their confessions.[84] Such a close relationship with the Scriptures allows the self to establish vividly dramatic meanings for Biblical riddles and analogies: 'That *Scripture* of Christ, in *Revel.* 3.20 *Standing at the doore and knocking*, did *work* upon me, and then I understood *Christ* must come in, and all *evill* be put out.'[85]

The literary recounting of 'experiences' does, however, tend to be turned into prophetic utterance with regard to the actions of the individual, just as dreams and visions are part of 'experimental' and prophetic discourse. The link was consciously made at the time, and actively manifested: Rogers removes the historical divide between the age of prophecy and the mid-seventeenth century by affirming that Jews often received 'experiences', while Tabatha Kelsall's 'experiences' include frequent shakings.[86]

IV

Prophesying and experience were brought together in the gathered churches most closely through several pamphlets which recounted, in part in their own words, the experiences of several women prophets, the most important of whom were Sarah Wight and Anna Trapnel. Both became bedridden for long periods during which they practically fasted and alternated between periods of silence or dumbness and frenzied, inspired outpourings, which appear to be a development from the oral prophesyings of the Independent and separatist churches. The story of Sarah Wight was put before the public eye by the Independent-Baptist and Hebrew fundamentalist Henry Jessey in *The Exceeding Riches of Grace Advanced* (1st edn., 1647; quotations which follow are

[83] Rogers, *Ohel*, p. 361.
[84] Ibid. '*Experience* of John Chamberlain', inserted gathering, pp. 8–9.
[85] Ibid. '*Experience* of Ann Megson', p. 416.
[86] Ibid. 356, '*Experience* of Tabatha Kelsall', inserted gathering, p. 2.

from the 2nd edn., 1647). The tract became very popular among the Independents, seven editions being published between 1647 and 1658. The traumatic behaviour which Jessey describes was of particular interest to him: a much shorter account which he wrote on the experiences of a child called Mary Warren was published in 1672, while his own deathbed throes echo Sarah Wight's tribulations.[87]

Sarah Wight, the daughter of a Puritan gentry widow, fasted for 75 days, the important points in the narrative being when she became bedridden and when she took food again and was able to walk. She seems to have felt completely unworthy of redemption, damned in fact, but found a sense of salvation so that she became transformed from an 'empty nothing creature' to a 'handmaiden' of the Lord, a phrase which Anna Trapnel frequently used to describe herself. Jessey sees this as an example of light coming out of darkness, after 2 Cor. 4: 6, which, like a confession of experience, contains a *'pattern* of grace'.[88] But more than becoming the member of a gathered church (Jessey's church was an 'open' Baptist congregation), Sarah gains the authority of an inspired and wise woman within the community who may be consulted for spiritual advice.

She seems to have been an anxious child, like her mother before her. She is sixteen when the experiences occur and they appear to stem from an uneasy relationship with her mother, as her impure utterances have left her with a sense of insufferable guilt:

If any one see and feel what I have seen and felt they would take heed of murmuring against God and a Parent. You never murmured so much against God, and against my Mother, as I have done; Ah, ah, ah, sighing and weeping as she spoke (p. 30).[89]

The events take place very much in the centre of the gathered churches, many of whom pray for her during her illness. Their prayers are answered when she finds mercy. In fact Jessey was already writing her story before grace arrived, so that presumably he had to change the direction of his narrative accordingly. Like Trapnel, Sarah has a relator who provides the substance of the

[87] *A Looking-glass for Children* (1672).

[88] *The Exceeding Riches of Grace Advanced* (2nd edn., 1647), sig. A3ʳ. This is echoed by Anna Trapnel in *The Cry of a Stone* (1654), 38.

[89] Jessey emphasizes the familial authority and bond structure in *A Storehouse of Provision* (1650), 152.

narrative and the conversations which occur within. The godly community give support to Sarah when she is in need and take it from her when she has recovered. Jessey makes sure these 'visible saints' are clearly seen by name. Such an appearance becomes a worthy contribution to a helpful tool of salvation: no one need fear public mention since they are all earning spiritual credit, though anonymity is available for those who want it (sig. A8^r).[90] There is a good deal of social exclusiveness in this: Independent ministers and aristocratic women receive the most prominent mentions, together with Anna Trapnel, who visited Sarah, and who was possibly suffering from a similar 'sickness' in July 1646, though her own period of fame did not come until the mid-1650s (pp. 43, 139).

Sarah's inspired speech took the form of scripturally based phrases, which Jessey 'combed' through afterwards, identifying the biblical passages in them and emphasizing Sarah's authenticity by showing how some of her outpourings were closer to the Hebrew or Greek of the original texts. For instance, the repetition of *Love him, Love him* nine or ten times is comparable with the repetition of 'Holy, holy' (Rev. 4: 8) nine times in Plantin's Polyglot Bible (p. 20). The trauma of guilt took the form of intermittent sighings and weepings, together with very quiet speaking in order to let Christ speak. This latter aspect becomes automatic and an extremely literal interpretation of communion with the divine when Sarah becomes dumb for long periods of time. She dreams alternately of grace and terror, but such an alternating state does not stop her giving advice (p. 44). The hope which Sarah advises is given to women whose experiences are not unlike her own. One woman believed that she was in a room full of smoke when her mouth was penetrated by fire which went down to her stomach and remained there, 'flutter, flutter'. She rose out of her bed at this point and heard a voice telling her she was damned, smelt brimstone and saw devils in her house (p. 77). The depths of Sarah's experience come when on 6 April 1647 she threatened suicide. Having seen a vision of Satan as a roaring lion who convinced her that there is only a hell in the conscience (a Familist heresy), she very nearly

---

[90] While the members of Rogers's congregation are identified by their names in full, those of the congregation of Walker and Petto remain veiled by the use of initials though, of course, they would have been more recognizable to contemporaries.

threw herself from a roof. Though a voice saved her from this, she
still managed to concuss herself. Still feeling worthless, she
attempted to kill herself with a knife and was later found by
ministers on Lambeth Marsh contemplating throwing herself to
the dogs kept there (pp. 59, 128–30).

The fasting comes from a literal comprehension in bodily
terms of the imagery of the atonement. She wants the food which
Christ has to offer, and can keep nothing else down because it is
impure. This is the time when the Lord is most at work, since he
sustains her without food for so long. During this time prophetic
speech is generated by an imitation of Christ which explores the
symbolism of water:

Desiring water, shee said, *Give me a little water good people; Christ hath given
you water freely.* Then she drank her *little white cup* full once, and againe,
and said, *I pray you give me some more: Jesus Christ when he turned water into
wine, he turned not cups full, or glasses full; but firkins full. If you give a cup of
cold water as to a Disciple, you shall not loose your reward.* Then shee drank
two cups more: and proceeded in the same tender-hearted manner.
(p. 21)

The water becomes a direct symbol of her spiritual sustenance.
Significantly the symbolism is derived from a Scriptural text,
unlike the concern with food as a sacrament among medieval
pious women. In this way her experience is more directly located
in Puritan soteriology than the inspiration of the more radical
prophets. Thus she sees in an orthodox way, by extension from
her water symbolism, that Christ's blood washes guilt away,
which corresponds to justification, while Christ's tears wash the
filth of sin away, which is sanctification. The narrative becomes a
platform for the Calvinism of the Independents as she firmly
states that justification preceeds sanctification, the latter being
wholly in the hands of God as 'free grace'. She answers questions
on the use of the Covenant, the Ordinances and the Law and a
series of causes and uses are enumerated (sig. Al^r. pp. 23, 65,
91–2, 121). Jessey finishes this at the end of the pamphlet by
suggesting, with further examples, that superiors should not lay
heavy oaths on people since it gives them a sense of responsibility
which leads to an unnecessarily fierce sense of damnation. Such
was the case with a young man who was so distraught that he
ceased from all written expression because he felt he produced
only 'bad writing' (p. 155).

Sarah continues the feature in the confessions of experience of comparing herself with biblical figures, notably Job, Jeremiah, and Judas (pp. 16–17, 129), while repeating the Pauline emphases on feeling the power of the spirit and the interchangeability of name and power (Acts 4: 7, 10) (pp. 90, 137). Unlike more spiritual radicals, she follows Jessey in maintaining that the Word is the Letter of the Spirit so that there is an equivalence between Scripture and inspired speech. When she eats again it is seen as the return of her faith and power. Her recovery is taken as a sign of enhanced unity in the gathered church. She appears before a meeting in a veil after the practice of the Pauline churches (this however was by her own choice since she still felt unworthy in God's sight), after which there is a prophesying and a giving of instructions based upon what has been learnt from Sarah's plight (pp. 86, 137–8, 143–4).

Anna Trapnel could be said to have modelled herself on Sarah Wight. The initial events in her prophesying career are remarkably similar to her predecessor, as if Sarah Wight had established the required behaviour and rhetoric for a gathered church prophetess. Anna Trapnel was the daughter of a shipwright and she lived in Hackney. She was converted by John Simpson in 1642 (when he was accused of Antinomianism), though she had been zealous for prayers since the age of 14, and had looked to the ordinances as a prop: she would fast under the terms of the law.[91] Like Sarah Wight she seems to have been deeply affected by her relationship with her mother, who chided her for excessive formal worship and who died abruptly on the first day of 1642, calling down a double blessing upon her daughter from God as her last words. This seems to have contributed to Anna's growing sense of inspiration. She took Sarah Wight's mode of prophetic behaviour into another, more sensitive political arena. Her experiences vary in subtle ways: the essential sense of divine union within the bounds of the gathered chuch is augmented through fast-induced trances where she hears Scriptural instructions and sees visions, which bear critically upon the Protectorate. There are hints in her pamphlets of the sense of anxious unease which enabled Anna to make prophetic interpretations. During what appears to be the end of the Barebones Parliament, she expresses distress at the curfew imposed, but sees a vision of the

[91] Trapnel, *A Legacy for Saints* (1654), 4.

New Jerusalem and finds further comfort by interpreting the view from her bedroom of the Army and Blackheath hill as hills of salvation and of the reduction of intransigence.[92]

She was frequently ill but she saw this as an 'outward' affliction, while inwardly she kept reviving. Increasingly the inner life was seen as the removal of her soul from her body for communion with the divine. Today her fasting might be explained as anorexia, a rejection of food for the sake of personal control over the body, as if she were trying to make herself pure. In the 1650s the condition was constructed within the terms of the saving of souls, and the religious politics of the Interregnum. So her self-denying modesty was coupled with a special claim to interpret the Bible, as the two days spent by Christ in the tomb became for Anna the two weeks which she spent in bed in Whitehall. Her time as a celebrity began when she came to Whitehall during the questioning of Vavasor Powell by the Council of State in January 1654. She stayed for most of the day in a side room, but later took to her bed in the room of the warden, Mr Roberts, and spent the next twelve days there, eating only a little toast and small beer once every twenty-four hours and often throwing it up, since, like Sarah Wight, it was too impure for her spiritual state. There were prophesyings during this time every three to four hours which consisted of the pouring forth of the visions she had seen and ecstatic songs containing the critique of Cromwell. She then recovered and returned to Hackney, so the report goes, with full strength.

While in bed the closeness of her inner self to God was registered by her outer body ceasing to operate: she did not move and her faculties of sense did not function, especially during her speeches, visions and prayers. She could not be roused, even by the impatient magistrate who pinched her during her later tour of Cornwall. Singing was a form of particular spiritual liberation for her and a sign of the nature of what she was prophesying. Thus she raised her note when she sang of Christ and displayed

[92] *The Cry of a Stone*, pp. 10–11. For accounts of women in Civil War activities, see Keith Thomas, 'Women and the Civil War Sects', *P&P* 13 (1958), 42–62; Phyllis Mack, 'Women as Prophets during the English Civil War', in Margaret Jacob and James Jacob, (edd.), *The Origins of Anglo-American Radicalism* (1984), 214–30. Surprisingly, the latter makes no reference to Anna Trapnel. For a comparison of Trapnel and Lady Eleanor Davis, see Christine Berg and Philippa Berry, 'Spiritual Whoredom: An Essay on Female Prophets in the Seventeenth Century', in Francis Barker (ed.), *1642: Literature and Power in the Seventeenth Century* (Essex, 1981), 37–54.

dependence on a minister when she was younger by refusing to let him go until he had sung with her. After the tour of Cornwall, she was imprisoned by the Council of State in Bridewell and prophesied her release by singing though when she was actually freed, by symbolic contrast, she was struck dumb.[93]

Like Sarah Wight her feeling of not being close to God led to suicide attempts: she threw herself into wells and ditches and took a knife to bed with her. Also like Sarah Wight she identified the temptation to leave the gathered church as a Familist or Ranting error: Wight and Trapnel needed to be part of godly communities in order to have the authority to prophesy. Indeed John Simpson formally examined the grounds of Trapnel's theology during her fast, and this satisfied him and confirmed Anna further in her power. At Whitehall she was visited by many people, members of the government and respectable society as well as Fifth Monarchists.[94] As with Wight, a relator took down her speech, though he had difficulties with the songs and with the quietness of Trapnel's voice as she moved closer to the spirit. Despite the hold of the trance, she was able to communicate with those around her, since she warned the relator during prophesyings to take down a particularly important part which was coming up. Significantly prayer was followed by prophecy as it would have been in a gathered church meeting, so that it is properly seen as a gift which God gives when asked. Moreover, Trapnel seems intent on validating her own role as 'seer' alongside the spiritually gifted who occupy ministerial office.[95] One witness felt that Trapnel was genuine because of her abnormal physical state during a trance which lasted eight days:

[93] *The Cry of a Stone*, 2–3, 5–7, 10, 12–14, 21, 43, 74–6; *Anna Trapnel's Report and Plea* (1654), 21, 48. For further details, see B.S. Capp, *The Fifth Monarchy Men* (1972), 102, 111, 119, 133, 141–2, 144, 151, 174, 183, 186, 189–90, 266.

[94] *The Cry of a Stone*, p. 8; ibid. 2 lists among the visitors the following members of the Barebones Parliament: Robert Bennet, Henry Birkenhead, John Chetwood, Francis Langdon, and William West. Other visitors included Christopher Feake and Ladies Vermuyden and Darcy. There is a similar case with Sarah Wight whose visitors included the Independent ministers Thomas Goodwin, Nicholas Lockyer, Joshua Sprigge, John Simpson, Morgan Llwyd, and Hugh Peters, as well as two consistent witnesses to spirituality, Lady Vermuyden and Lady Fine (Fiennes). See Jessey, *The Exceeding Riches of Grace Advanced* (1647), 8–9. Lady Fiennes appears to be Frances, wife of James Fiennes, Viscount Saye and Sele. After his death in 1647 she married the Independent Joshua Sprigge: G. E. Cokayne, rev. Geoffrey H. White, *The Complete Peerage* (1949) ix. 489.

[95] See, for instance, *Anna Trapnel's Report and Plea*, p. 5.

she became extremely cold, ate very little, and spoke louder and faster as the claims of the spirit increased. At the same time he felt that she was subconciously regurgitating what she already knew, rather than undergoing direct inspiration. She prophesied nothing new but gave forth 'only what she hath beene conversant in before'.[96]

Nevertheless, according to Trapnel and her supporters, she had a power of prediction which stemmed from her close contact with God. Her visions are predictive and occur on significant days.[97] The attack on the Protectorate is not covert. Francis Rous, the Puritan mystic and speaker of the Barebones Parliament, is singled out for a deceptively godly exterior, but the main target is Cromwell, whom Anna identifies as Gideon. The criticisms are made in terms of hopes for eventual reform: she sings a hymn for 'Gideon', and engages in praise and prayer for specific social groups, like the merchants and the poor. There is also a specific pacifist message in her outpourings, so that she speaks in a more traditional pastoral manner.[98]

Anna Trapnel is often accused of being cynically manipulated by the leaders of the Fifth Monarchy movement, instanced in the tour of Cornwall. As much as this might be said to be the case, so also the Fifth Monarchists genuinely believed her prophesyings and her prophetic power, as much as she did. Comparing herself to the Biblical Hannah (1 Sam. 1: 2), she connected her inspired text with the Saints directly: 'Is not the Narrative come from Heaven concerning what thou art doing?'[99] God's plot is the unfolding narrative of Fifth Monarchist activity. Much of what she says is consistent with Independent ecclesiology, which would bolster her authenticity for radicals. She attacked university language, and desired a voice for the 'New Covenant'. She describes the workings of free grace in herself, and sees this as a resolution of Law and Gospel, rather than the transcendence of the latter over the former. Her language here is an enriched version of experiential discourse:

But this conceit, free grace laid in the dust, and Divine Light shewed me the spawn and seed of all sin within my corrupt nature, which made me to lie in the dust, and to cry out, Lord let free grace own me, else I am

[96] *The Cry of a Stone*, p. 40; Bodl. MS Rawl. A. 21, fo. 325ʳ–ᵛ.
[97] Anna Trapnel's visions are discussed below Chapter 2, Sections III and IV.
[98] *The Cry of a Stone*, pp. 30, 33, 52.   [99] Ibid. 44.

undone; when the Law of the Spirit came, then sin revived, and I died; it shewed me every secret sin that I saw not before, so that all my sins were set in order before me.[100]

Interestingly, though she was accused in Cornwall of witchcraft, she was also accused on her own terms of being possessed with an 'extraordinary impulse of spirit'.[101] There were those who viewed her cynically but the potential for doing so in her time was less than it would be in ours today. This is compounded with the illuminist vocabulary which is found in Independent and sectarian writings elsewhere. She speaks of seeing into the 'center' of the universe and beholding Alpha and Omega, and this 'Holy Center' is Christ. Prison for her is a purifying fire which actually encourages her spiritual liberty: her body can be confined but never her spirit.[102]

V

Eventually the sectarian sense of direct inspiration by God leads to a variety of obviously prophetic stances, usually with an emphasis upon recording the experience of union. The sectarians had a sense of the prophets as authors: the profession of belief at the end of *Spirituall Experiences, Of sundry Beleevers* contains an affirmation that the Bible is the product of the prophets, who were inspired by God for enhancing the faith of the people.[103] This sense of prophetic authorship was adopted by some sectarians, so that the pamphlets were written in the form of prophetic epistles after Paul, with the difference that the sectarian letters, especially in the case of the Quakers, are dated and the place where they were written is also noted.[104] Furthermore, the notion which has already been seen in John Smith, that prophecy is a dramatic experience with the activities of the prophet being possibly a different type of vision in the mind of the prophet, is reflected in the 'experience' of at least one

---

[100] Trapnel, *A Legacy for Saints*, p. 5. See Rom. 7: 9.
[101] *Anna Trapnel's Report and Plea*, p. 26.
[102] Ibid. 27; see also Trapnel, *A Legacy for Saints*, pp. 60–4.
[103] Walker, *Spirituall Experiences*, sig. u8ʳ.
[104] See e.g. Thomas Tany, *Theauraujohn High Priest to the Jewes* (1651) and Isaac Penington, *Severall Fresh Inward Openings* (1650). Essential communication between Lodowick Muggleton and his followers was made by means of letters.

individual who refers to her own life as a 'tragi-comedy'.[105]
Effectively the woman has constructed her life as a drama which
she can comprehend as a vision of her soul's progress. Here there
are again continuities between the understanding of 'experience'
and prophecy. There are differences between the two, however, in
that the sectarians regard prophecy as something which must be
set down with great urgency, unlike the 'experience'. Similarly,
for the Quakers 'experience' is renamed 'declaration' or 'testimony', though it is important to remember that Quaker
testimonies were understood to speak to truths in all people. In
addition the time span covered by most prophecies is generally
much shorter than the autobiographical stress of 'experiences'.

The radical religious prophets conceived of a historical link
between biblical figures and themselves. It lies at the forefront of
their writing: George Fox states that the Quaker refusal to pay
tithes is a fulfilment of Peter's prophecy in 2 Pet. 1.[106] This is in
fact an extension of the tendency in Reformation typology to
regard contemporary events as fulfilments of biblical prophecies,
biblical types as examples for contemporary behaviour. For the
Ranter Abiezer Coppe, biblical characters become types for
particular qualities which can be transposed allegorically onto all
mankind in the present:

And that this house of *Jacob* may like fire fall upon the house of Esau (I
say) *Esau* (which is as stubble and now as stubble fully dry) upon this
house of which is rough, hairy, red, fiery, fierce, rugged flesh, hatred,
strife, envy, malice, evil surmizing &c. and utterly consume them, that
there be not any remaining of the house of *Esau*.[107]

Radical prophets asserted the inspiration of God in themselves
even when not experiencing a vision. The notion of the prophet
as inspired social leader against iniquity, oppression, and
corruption which Luther stressed is an important component
here. If the radicals did not have a conscious knowledge of this
tradition, which is unlikely given the prophetic rhetoric of
striving for the New Jerusalem in mainstream Puritan preaching,
the role that the Old Testament prophets played as leaders of
their people is clear in the Bible.[108] John Saltmarsh adopted such

---

[105] Walker, '*Experiences* of M.K.', in *Spirituall Experiences*, p. 160.
[106] *A Warning from the Lord* (1654), 16.
[107] 'An Additional and Preambular Hint' in *CRW*, p. 78.
[108] See Paul Christianson, *Reformers and Babylon: English Apocalyptic Visions from the*

a prophetic stance when criticizing Cromwell, as did William Sedgwick when seeking the imprisoned Charles I's ear in 1648. Coppe, following James 5: 1–7, implores rich people to give their possessions to the poor, and in doing so he adopts a gesture based upon Sedgwick's own non-violent altruism: '*Wil. Sedgewick* (in me) bowed to that poor deformed ragged wretch, that he might inrich him, in impoverishing himself.'[109] A true prophet must have courage. The prophet's self-presentation is crucial for the communication of inspired authority, and the term developed by modern biblical commentators, 'pseudepigraphy', is appropriate for this analysis.[110] By definition 'pseudepigrapha' were spurious writings, generally of early Christian origin, falsely attributed to biblical or Patristic sources. However, the specific qualities of pseudepigraphic writing include details of the prophet's life, his background, birth, and habits which make him special, apart from other people, and so enhance his authority. In this sense radical prophecies are 'pseudepigraphic' in so far as they are displaying, explicitly and implicitly, the way in which the character of an Old Testament prophet comes into the life of the radical prophet. In the two *Fiery Flying Rolls*, Coppe appropriates Ezekiel's identity, rhetoric, and gestures.[111] Coppe comments upon this in chapter 4 of *A Second Fiery Flying Roule* where he notes how the '*divine majesty*' within him has made him adopt Ezekiel's 'postures'. All prophets are established as 'signs and wonders', says Coppe, after Isa. 8: 18, but Ezekiel stands above the rest: being a son of *Buzi*, Ezekiel is also a son of contempt, so stressing his transgressive role. Again the prophet is cast as rebel, which compares with the Independent John Goodwin's portrayal of Elisha as an insurrectionist in *Anti-Cavalierisme* (1642, 13–14). Coppe uses a familial analogy: he is Ezekiel's brother, since both share visions and strange postures, and Coppe's point is that it is this shared behaviour, caused by the indwelling 'divine majesty', that is subversive. Coppe then refers to Ezek. 24: 3, 19 and Hos. 2 to show that strange behaviour is inexplicable in human terms: though other people in the sects might threaten to punish

Reformation to the Eve of the Civil War (Toronto, 1978), 132–43; K. R. Firth, *The Apocalyptic Tradition in Reformation Britain, 1530–1645* (Oxford, 1979), 204–41.

[109] *A Second Fiery Flying Roule* in *CRW*, p. 109. For Sedgwick's career, see *BDBR*.
[110] For the latest discussion of this subject, see Christopher Rowland, *The Open Heaven* (1981), 69–70.
[111] For another example, see Lady Eleanor Davis, *Ezekiel*, n.p., n.d., p. 22.

him they are nevertheless amazed by his prophetic power.[112]

Coppe was also acutely aware of the general prophetic climate and that Ezekiel is not the only model of prophetic posture that is adopted by the indwelling God. Throughout *Heights in Depths* Joseph Salmon puns on his near namesake, Solomon, using the model of Ecclesiastes for his meditation. There is also a general assumption of a Jewish identity here.[113] Thomas Tany claimed himself to be the risen King of the Jews, while Coppe and George Foster undergo name changes by divine injunction. Coppe spells his name in Hebrew characters, and in the Hebrew it means approximately 'the Lord is my strength', while Foster is called Jacob Israel so that he is reborn as Hebrew prophet and patriarch.[114]

The pose is of a divinely instituted madness. In Foster's *The Pouring Forth of the Seventh and Last Viall* (1650), Paul's madness is seen as a worthy previous example: 'you may reade that Paul was counted mad, but he said whither he was mad, or whither he were besides himself, it was for their sakes, and so say I', and so Paul is praised for turning the world upside down, which Foster also compares with Jesus's attack on the Pharisees (sig. a1ʳ). Christopher Hill has suggested that madness was a useful guise to adopt to avoid persecution, especially when the 1650 Blasphemy Act was instituted to repress the Ranters.[115] However, it also seems that the radicals were able to maintain a conscious and even astute awareness of themselves while experiencing what they reported as the intensely violent nature of the indwelling God. So Coppe and Foster can make comparisons between themselves and Old Testament prophets. An even more rational usage of such madness occurs in the anonymous *Divinity And Philosophy Dissected, and Set Forth, by a Mad Man* (1644).[116] The speaker mocks those who attack prophets, but in a coy fashion

---

[112] Coppe, *Some Sweet Sips*, in *CRW*, pp. 103–4.

[113] Millenarians showed a general interest in Jewry, who would have to be converted prior to the Second Coming. Moves to have them admitted to England were seen as a way of bringing the Millennium on. See D. S. Katz, *Philo-Semitism and the Readmission of the Jews to England 1603–55* (Oxford, 1982).

[114] George Foster, *The Pouring Forth of the Seventh and Last Viall* (1650), sig. A4ᵛ.

[115] *The World Turned Upside Down* (1972), 220.

[116] R. M. Jones, *Spritual Reformers in the Sixteenth and Seventeenth Centuries* (New York, 1914), 254, 261–3, claims that this pamphlet was written by Giles Randall. However, as Jones admits, the style is not characteristic of Randall's prefaces to his translations, and there is no definite evidence to determine his authorship in this instance. The

asks the reader to decide whether he is really mad. He claims not to be ignorant and asserts that he is only as 'mad' as any other pamphleteer. Like Salmon's recantation in *Heights in Depths* the speaker here befriends the reader in a persuasive way—'Deare Friend and Reader'—but disclaims any interest in talking to the world at large. Here 'madness' has become a purely literary posture, private to the prophet's mind ('my intention is to declare the matter according to my own mad minde') where the reader is admitted as a privileged audience—'I have thrust my selfe upon the Theatre in this mad posture and act.'[117]

The 'transgressive pranks' of *A Second Fiery Flying Roule* are preceded in Coppe's earlier pamphlet, *Some Sweet Sips, of some Spirituall Wine* (1649), by a presentation of the self not as explicitly 'mad' but as an emanating centre of extreme exhortative phrases. The frenzy and breathless repetition seem to belie an unstable personality:

Deare hearts! Where are you, can you tell? Ho! where be you, ho? are you *within*? what, no body at *home*? Where are you? What are you? Are you asleepe? for shame rise, its break aday, the *day* breaks, the *Shaddowes* flie away, the *dawning* of the *day* woes you to arise and let him *into* your *hearts*.[118]

The unity of the speaker's voice is only maintained by the almost comic and dramatic employment of the register and vocabulary of the bridegroom in the Song of Solomon: 'The day *star* is up, rise up my *love*, my *dove*, my fair one, and *come away*.'[119] It is a rhetoric of unity in which Coppe, and Joseph Salmon in *A Rout, A Rout* (1649), pose as invigorated lovers and Christ figures wooing the reader to let the spirit enter into them. In Clarkson's *The Lost Sheep Found* (1660) is also found the implication that the Song of Solomon was used as a ritual invocation in Ranter orgies, though it is made clear later that Clarkson derived his libertinism from Solomon's identification of man with beast in Eccles. 3: 19.[120]

In *A Second Fiery Flying Roule* Coppe's behaviour becomes wholly subversive through its association with the keyword 'base'

tract is also attributed by Richard Baxter to the perfectionist Robert Wilkinson with a sense of certainty in *Plain Scripture Proof* (1651), 147.

[117] *Divinity And Philosophy Dissected*, sig. A2ʳ. Coppe presents the prophet as a mechanism fuelled by divine power '(. . . the great God within that chest, or corps) was burning hot toward him: and made the lock-hole of the chest, to wit, the mouth of the corps, again to open', *A Second Fiery Flying Roule*, in *CRW*, p. 102.

[118] In *CRW*, p. 51. [119] Ibid. 52. [120] Ibid. 182.

(1 Cor. 1: 28; 2 Cor. 10:1). Coppe envisages a levelling apocalypse in which material possessions will be destroyed and man will live in a community of spirit with God, a return to a 'base' level. As a prototype spiritual man, and a prophecy of what is to come, Coppe engages in 'base' behaviour, a series of 'transgressive' animal gestures which presents his self as contrary to the state of union with God which he originally posits. Chapters 5 and 6 of *A Fiery Flying Roll* are partly repeated in chapter 5 of *A Second Fiery Flying Roule*, where Coppe extends love, friendship, and respect to the poor and the deformed: 'As also in falling down flat upon the ground before rogues, beggars, cripples, halt, maimed; blind, &c. kissing the feet of many, rising up againe, and giving them money, &c.' (in *CRW*, 105).[121] The gestures are a parody of courtly, even Cavalier, behaviour, and Coppe aptly makes the point that he has postured in London and Southwark while Cavaliers and gentry have passed him. The graphic description of physical deformity, 'a poore deformed wretch . . . who had no more nose on his face, then I have on the back of my hand, (but only two little holes in the place where the nose uses to stand)', is matched by the abnormal stance adopted by Coppe: 'my hand stretched out, my hat cock't up, staring on them as if I would look thorough them, gnashing with my teeth at some of them' (ibid.). Here Coppe transcends social divisions with his behaviour. He coyly mentions 'that notorious business' with 'Gypseys and Gaolbirds', which seems to refer to some form of free love: 'I have gone along the streets impregnant with that child (lust) which a particular beauty had begot' (ibid. 105, 108).

In fact Coppe's lust is centred on the act of kissing and this is 'base' because it is a gesture of spiritual levelling, though there are lewder sexual connotations in the analogy of being pregnant with lust. Coppe realizes that his actions are seen as licentious so he deliberately mocks public morality by adopting its own language for his rather different enterprise. He sees himself as an imitator of David in 2 Sam. 6: 13–26 'confounding, plaguing, tormenting nice, demure, barren *Mical* . . . by skipping, leaping,

---

[121] In *Copp's Return to the Wayes of Truth* (1651) the author tells how when young, and stricken with guilt, he would tie a label to each wrist, one with 'yes' written on it, the other with 'nay' written on it (*CRW*, p. 134). Clearly, gesture was very important for him from an early age. As a younger man, he was under Presbyterian patronage in Warwickshire: see *DNB*.

dancing, like one of the fools; vile, base fellowes' (ibid. 106), and observes, that if he had been courting ladies rather than 'gypseys' in this way, Michal would not have been so ashamed. Michal thus becomes a symbol of hypocritical public religious morality, while Coppe exceeds David's play: 'I sate downe, and eat and drank around on the ground with Gypseys, and clip't, hug'd and kiss'd them, putting my hand in their bosomes, loving the she-Gipsies dearly' (ibid.). Coppe, of course, feels that he is not only imitating Old Testament prophets. The spirit of the prophets makes him act in the strange way that he does. Thus the speech of the religious radical becomes the speech of the spirit of God. Swearing, then, cannot be a sin if a divine voice is the utterer: 'And [I] had rather heare a mighty Angell (in man) swearing a full-mouthd Oath; and see the spirit of *Nehemiah* (in any form of man, or woman) running upon an uncleane Jew . . . and tearing the haire of his head like a mad man, cursing, and making others fall a swearing'.[122] However, Coppe's ability to register precisely the presence of God within is compromised. He does make the distinction between his own body or self and the divine: 'My most Excellent Majesty (in me) hath strangely and variously transformed this forme'.[123] But at other times Coppe moves without making the distinction from his prophetic voice to what is surely the authority and identity of the 'divine Majesty': 'It is my good will and pleasure.'[124] In this tract, Coppe refers to himself as the 'Author', though in his preface to 'I.F.' 's *John the Divines Divinity* (1649) he puns on 'Author' so that it could mean the human author or God, the motivating force. Finally there are places where Coppe clearly collapses identities. God and prophet are now one, as Coppe makes the indwelling God the maker of gestures: 'my most Excellent Majesty, the King of glory, the Eternall God, who dwelleth in the forme of the Writer of this Roll . . . hath i'th open streets, with his hand fiercely stretcht out.'[125]

However, aside from prophetic behaviour, most of the radical prophets register the actual presence of God within in a manner which is continuous with the language of 'experience'. Gerrard

---

[122] *A Fiery Flying Roll*, in *CRW*, pp. 91–2. For a similar inversion of morality, with sexual innuendo, see A *Justification of the Mad Crew* (1650), 22–5.

[123] Ibid. 81.

[124] *A Second Fiery Flying Roule*, in *CRW*, p. 105.

[125] *A Fiery Flying Roll*, in *CRW*, p. 97.

Winstanley, for instance, notes the entrance of the spirit which results in the 'inward power of feeling experience'.[126] The Ranter Joseph Salmon is also aware of the way in which he is pierced to the centre, but this time the imagery of purgation is extremely violent:

Angry flesh being struck at heart with the piercing dart of vengeance, begins to swell, and contracting all the evil humors of the body of death into one lump, to grapple with this throne of wrath, at last violently breaks out, and lets forth the very heart and coar of its pride and enmity.[127]

The bodily experience continues and develops into recurrent figurative vomiting, 'disgorges its foul stomack upon the very face, and appearance of Truth', 'tumbling in my own Vomit', as Salmon feels that he has had the serpent living inside his body.[128] Salmon is here regretting his former Ranter ways and the inner trial which he records is accompanied by self-portrayal as a false prophet who is distinguished by nakedness, filthiness, and bestiality.

When 'experiences' talk of an inner divine presence it is usually that of the 'Spirit' or the 'spirit of Christ'. For the Ranters, however, it is a much stronger presence of God himself as trinity and unity at once, as Coppe makes clear.[129] The root of the resultant hypostatic experience moreover lies in a return to the womb, apparently an image for the centre or essence of the universe, as Salmon points out: 'I have run round the world of variety, and am now centred in eternity; that is the womb out of which I was taken, and to which my desires are now reduced.'[130] Again, the most vivid account of this return is in Coppe, where the sense of re-birth is multi-sensual and not just imagistic. Salmon's experience is clearly figurative but Coppe gives the impression that he is actually experiencing the return:

I was utterly plagued, consumed, damned, rammed, and sunke into nothing, into the bowels of the still Eternity (my mothers wombe) out of which I came naked, and whetherto I returned again naked. And lying a while there, rapt up in silence, at length (the body or outward

[126] *The New Law of Righteousness* (1649), 22, 106.
[127] *Heights in Depths* (1651), in *CRW*, pp. 212–13.
[128] Ibid. 213.
[129] 'An Additional and Preambular Hint', in *CRW*, pp. 73–5.
[130] Salmon, *Heights in Depths*, in *CRW*, p. 216.

forme being awake all this while) I heard with my outward eare (to my apprehension) a most terrible thunder-clap.[131]

The excessive use of parenthesis reveals the interpenetration of inner and outer, subjective experience and objective perception, as Coppe is able to intimate the apocalyptic feelings of spiritual hypostasy while looking down upon himself in the womb, as it were. Later on Coppe similarly describes himself as the ark carrying the covenant of God.[132]

In this context the use of the prophet's 'I' becomes increasingly important as the speaker becomes obsessed with his own identity. For the Ranters in particular the fact that there is no guarantee of the morality of the outward act focuses all importance upon the intention within the individual. This is reflected in the naming process. Apart from the significance of Hebraic identities, discussed earlier, the Ranters assume the identity of God, though they use the words of Paul and John of Patmos: 'I might have a new name, with me, upon me, which, I am', and 'I am that I am.'[133] It is a process of self-deification, self-exultation, which passes through a yearning for enunciation, through intense desire, to the climax of knowledge and naming, 'heart-knowledged by divine inspiration'.[134] The speaker becomes deprived of the surface identity (at least his 'old name' on the printed page) and inscribed throughout the process of illumination. However there is still an ambiguity. In Salmon's *Heights in Depths* there appears to be a habit of using a roman 'J' when the inner self is referred to, and an italic '*I*' when the outer, 'fleshy' man is depicted, and when Salmon is referring to himself as a distinct historical figure undergoing trials, unlike his present spiritually regenerate self. This convention is not entirely consistent because of the rarity of typesetting standards and the possibility of inconsistency in Salmon's copy, but it does seem

---

[131] *A Fiery Flying Roll*, in *CRW*, p. 82.

[132] *A Second Fiery Flying Roule*, in *CRW*, p. 103.

[133] *CRW*, pp. 83, 79. The biblical references are Isa. 62: 2; Rev. 2: 17, 3: 12; 1 Cor. 15: 10. See also ibid. 50, and Thomas Speed's record of an interrogation in *The Guilty-Covered Clergy-man Unvail'd* (1657), 'For the said person being again, and again asked by the Mayor, *What she was, (not what was her name*, at that time she gave the following answer) answered, *I am that I am*' (p. 72). When signing themselves by initials, Quakers would often reverse the order of the letters in order to signify a new name 'known to few'.

[134] Thomas Tany, *Theauraujohn His Aurora in Tranlagorum in Salem Gloria* (1655), sig. A2ʳ.

that the sense of inspiration is ordered here, in the same way that
Coppe uses parentheses:

To declare to all men what J now am, onely in what *I* am not: if thou
(Reader) art so wise as to discover my spirit by what *I* shall here
declaim, thou wilt spare me the labour of making an after profession of
my Faith, which *I* confesse *I* shall hardly be drawn to declare to any
man.[135]

For other sectarians God may manifest himself by an inner
dialogue with the prophet, so that while God the speaking
subject is in the prophet, he has a separate identity, giving the
impression that he is outside and around the prophet. This
clearly stems from the tradition of biblical prophecy where the
prophet hears divine voices instead of, or as well as, seeing a
vision. In *The Pouring Forth of the Seventh and Last Viall* George
Foster has a dialogue with God with the purpose of interpreting
Foster's vision, and to predict Foster's 'shakings'. God's voice is
distinguished by repetitive phrasing and italics. Each of Foster's
visions is followed by God's interpretation which is usually about
ten times as long as the vision, and includes God's terrible
warnings that there will be a harsh levelling if people do not give
their money to the poor. Such is the potency of God's speech that
by a third of the way through the pamphlet, God has totally
assumed the dominant identity: God and Foster are one
(pp. 7–10). The same is true of Coppe, so that the injunctions to
share in *A Fiery Flying Roll* are made by the voice of God, as are
the voices which explain Coppe's prophetic experiences.[136]

It is clear then that the radical religious prophets were
involved in complex modes of address connected with the
conviction that they spoke the words of God, or that God spoke
directly through them. Unlike the writings of other radicals, such
as the Levellers, and the pamphlets of Royalists and Parlia-
mentarians, there is no narrator figure of apparent common sense
and good will, an impartial observer of events. Neither is there
a satirical or jesting 'persona' which is not implicitly part of a
larger prophetic stance.[137] There is no sequence of events, or

[135] Salmon, *Heights in Depths*, in *CRW*, p. 206.
[136] In *CRW*, pp. 82–3, 86.
[137] For a wider definition of satire in Ranter pamphlets, see Byron C. Nelson,
'Play, Ritual Inversion and Folly among the Ranters of The English Revolution',
(Ph.D. diss., University of Wisconsin-Madison, 1985).

history, which is recounted by a narrator for a persuasive end. The prophetic 'I' nevertheless functions in a persuasive way, be it with the emotional depth and force of Coppe or the self-assured enthusiasm of Salmon or Jacob Bauthumley. The way in which Salmon tries to wheedle his way into the reader's affections seems to be an admission of the heretical nature of his views. It is not so much a question of flying a colour of political or religious identity, as might a polemicist, but a strategy of driving home the locus and consequence of the Antinomian experience: 'But I tell you . . . whilst you are embracing his body of self-safety and outward Liberty, he is dying and departing from it, though you see it not.'[138] The repeated 'you's force the reader to confront the presence of God in and around him or her, so that there is an impression of a shared experience between speaker and reader. The reader is then denied fully entering it and so is enticed onwards by the sheer fervour of the statement.

For the Ranters this form of affective strategy bridges public and private, since the same 'I' occurs in both the pamphlets and in the letters of Coppe and Salmon: 'I live in yor peace and freedome because I dwell in my selfe att Coventrie.'[139] Here the pamphlet becomes an appendage of the self, a direct reflection of the prophet's self. For Lady Eleanor Davis her pamphlets go forth to the public as 'babes', as if they were her offspring, while for Salmon *Heights in Depths* is couched in 'homely language' which is 'like my self'. Like Salmon himself, the pamphlet will steal 'like a Thiefe upon the benighted world', but it will only take from the reader that which the reader is willing to give up: selfishness and 'fleshy' pride. Accordingly the language of the pamphlet withdraws from the outer world into Salmon's own symbolic discourse, though allegiance to the Commonwealth is affirmed, since the pamphlet is Salmon's recantation.[140]

The persuasive authority with which Coppe's 'I' is invested involves a crude assumption of superiority. Coppe hurls his utterances out and expects their power to communicate itself to the reader. It is not wary and clandestine propaganda but a blatant confrontation with the reader: 'wherein the worst and foulest of villanies, are discovered, under the best and fairest

---

[138] *A Rout, A Rout* (1649), in *CRW*, p. 195.

[139] Coppe, Letter to Joseph Salmon and Andrew Wyke in *CRW*, p. 117.

[140] Davis, *The Restitution of Prophecy* (1651), sig. A3^r; Salmon, *Heights in Depths* in *CRW*, p. 204.

outsides'.[141] This is coupled with a pathos which comes from *imitatio Christi* and prophetic behaviour but which Coppe exaggerates. So Coppe's voice 'pities' those who mistake him and attack him, and commands the 'great ones' not to laugh at him since he is sanctioned by divine authority. When Coppe encounters the beggar, it is almost as if massive authority and self-deflation are compounded to avoid persecution, as well as displaying the sublimity of prophecy: 'yet I rode back once more to the poor wretch, saying, because I am a King, I have done this, but you need not tell any one.'[142]

Though it does seem that the act of 'thundering' is a means of maintaining a connection with the One—indeed, Coppe styles himself a 'Boanerges', a roaring pulpit-thumping priest whose forerunners are Ezekiel, Joshua, and Christ—the speaker still operates by means of an awareness of the possibiilty of persecution. Coppe notices that the Blasphemy Act is passed while he is in prison, so making him guilty before trial.[143] This insight is compounded by his own self-abnegation: he acts 'not for my own sake', thus reasserting himself, in a manner characteristic of Lilburne. Then Coppe offers a pun on 'enlarge' as his supposed selflessness goes hand in hand with his continued imprisonment. Having created such an omnipotent utterance sustained by the accusatory, large signifiers, 'Weakness', 'Malice', 'Ignorance', 'Mistake', the speaker can, in this case, clear his own slate against the attacks of enemy pamphleteers. So *A Remonstrance of The sincere and Zealous Protestation* (1651) ends with the speaker denying his own involvement in both utterance and action, while drawing a distinction between his opponents and the 'authority' of the Parliamentary imprint.[144] Such is Coppe's own sense of persuasive authority by now that he can accuse his enemies of making ridiculous identifications: his supposed she-disciples are none other than the soldiers who are guarding Coppe.

By contrast the speaker in Jacob Bauthumley's *The Light and Dark Sides of God* attempts to obliterate the distinction between himself and the reader: the reader is not mentioned but is

[141] *A Fiery Flying Roll* in *CRW*, p. 80.
[142] *A Second Fiery Flying Roule*, in *CRW*, p. 103.
[143] *A Remonstrance of The sincere and Zealous Protestation* (1651), in *CRW*, p. 119. 'Boanerges' (Mark 3: 17) is glossed in the Geneva and Authorized Versions as 'sons of thunder'.   [144] Ibid. 122–3.

assumed to be engrossed in following the discourse. Simultaneously the speaker makes his presence omnipotent by admitting that he has no objection to any opinion but then couches this inside the governing explanation (in *CRW*, 288). Indeed the negation of self entirely, beyond the claims of ecstatic inspiration, becomes the major means of signifying inspiration after the state of prophetic vision has been passed through. It is, of course, a consequence of the indwelling God, but also it involves a degree of renunciation of prophetic imitation. In fact it is already present in Coppe: he feels that his name will 'wilt away' as the divine comes inside him, while his entire identity will be obliterated by God's literal ownership of his body. When the 'great ones' 'professe me', it is not Coppe that is referred to but the 'Divine Majesty' within.[145] Similarly, by an inversion of the normal expression of the spirit within, Winstanley talks of the unregenerate man as one who 'falls out of his maker'.[146] Salmon seems to have engaged in prophetic 'strange' behaviour in Coventry, under the influence of Coppe: 'wicked Swearing and uncleanness, which he justified and others of his way, That *it was God which did swear in them, and that it was their Liberty to keep company with Women, for their Lust.*'[147] However, in his recantation, the indwelling spirit leads the prophet to silence: 'My great desire (and that wherein I most delight) is to see and say nothing.' The circle becomes a symbol of worldly nothingness. 'Wisdom it self is but a womb of wind', though the eternal womb is still to be returned to: 'I have run round the world of variety, and am now centred in eternity; that is the womb out of which I was taken, and to which my desires are now reduced.'[148] Here, the negation of self is made so that all attention focuses upon the mysterious symbol, as Henry Pinnell pointed out: 'In Ezekiel's vision you have a wheele, an internal mystery in an externall appearance, forme or dispensation; the spirit of life within keeps this wheele in motion.'[149] To complete the process Salmon describes how he disappears from the 'stage' of 'outward appearances' where as Ranter prophet he has 'acted a most sad and Tragicall part', though he does not leave the biblical imitation behind. Indeed,

---

[145] *A Fiery Flying Roll* in *CRW*, p. 94.
[146] *The New Law of Righteousness* (1649), p. 2.
[147] Bulstrode Whitelocke, *Memorials* (1682), 446, col. 1.
[148] Salmon, *Heights in Depths*, in *CRW*, p. 216.
[149] *A Word of Prophesy* (1648), sig. A6ʳ, where the reference is Ezek. 1: 15–21.

Heights in Depths adopts the voice of Solomon in Ecclesiastes: 'Vanitie of Vanities, All is Vanitie saith the Preacher', and he leaves the prophetic stage for the 'close Galleries' of the Song of Solomon.[150]

VI

The most extreme form of self-denial comes with the Quakers, who generally subordinate the sense of self entirely to the light within. This has been seen as a mystical negation quite peculiar to the Quakers.[151] As I hope has just been shown, there are strong traces of such self-denial in Ranter, Seeker, and Independent writing, and it should not be forgotten that some of the sectarians in these groups eventually became Quakers, such as Salmon himself and Isaac Penington. It is possible to see in what follows where Quaker versions of self differ from the types of prophetic awareness in previous radical religious groups, and what qualities these groups shared.

There is not so much a desire in early Quaker discourse to imitate a particular prophet as a comparison of Quaker works with those of the prophets, without claiming the need to perform prophetic gestures or to receive visionary inspiration. George Fox himself felt that customary gestures were vain, though he was not unchallenged during the 1650s from within the movement.[152] The tendency is rather to refer to a prophet locally within the Quaker's own peculiar prophetic discourse. Isaac Penington names Paul in this way as a prototype for his own self-representation as a voice of freedom.[153] Likewise Margaret Fell sees the prophet Moses as a self entirely outside of her, and with a distinct historical existence.[154] Similarly the Muggletonian prophets John Reeve and Lodowick Muggleton betray the quiet assurance of the Quakers, though they do see themselves as the

[150] Salmon, *Heights in Depths*, pp. 207, 216.
[151] Jackson I. Cope, 'Seventeenth-Century Quaker Style', *PMLA* 71 (1956), 725–54 (esp. 725–6).
[152] *Concerning Good-Morrow, and Good-Even* (1657), 14. The episodes of Nayler riding into Bristol on a donkey in imitation of Christ, and of Perrot refusing to take his hat off at all are famous in Quaker history. Quaker gesture seems to take place beyond writing, though Quaker plain style was seen as symbolically pure in itself, and thus still connected with gesture.
[153] *A Voyce Out of the thick Darkness* (1650), 14.
[154] *An evident Demonstration to God's Elect* (1660), 2–3.

two witnesses referred to in Revelation (11: 34). On the contrary, false prophets are identified with evil biblical characters, which was a tactic employed by opponents of the sectarians: Ranters in particular were often labelled as Simon Maguses. In this way Gerrard Winstanley uses the name Thomas Didymus from John 11: 16; 20: 24; 21: 2 to attack those with 'lying imaginations'.[155] Thus, opponents are diminished. But both Quakers and Ranters use biblical character types: the thief and robber, as symbols of release from and loss of the carnal, are employed by both Coppe and Christopher Taylor.[156]

The Quaker presentation of the self is not so much to do with *elevating* the self *into* the divine through prophetic behaviour. Rather, as with the Independents' 'experience', it is an impulse concerned with *merging* the self with the One Light. Rogers asks his flock to perceive with 'the light of the eye', to become one with the 'Ocean of Love'.[157] Similarly George Fox asks his followers to look at Matt. 6: 22, where 'the light of the body is the eye'.[158] The eye here is the spiritual eye, the 'single eye' of Luke 11: 34, so that visual perception becomes a metaphor for spiritual insight, though it should also be noted that Fox specifically refers to the body as the object which should be illuminated. Indeed, for some Quakers the body—the physical self—is something which should be harnessed by the light: for Humphry Bache the light is a 'bridle' on the tongue.[159] In an important essay Jackson Cope detected the standard pattern in which Fox addressed his reader, from warning to instruction to exhortation, and finally to the glorification of the reader, an end common with Independent 'experience' and Ranter prophecy, so that the 'Day star arise in their hearts'.[160] Fox, however, goes as far as to make illumination a condition of being:

All Magistrates, and Ministers, and People whose mindes are turned from this light, and makes a profession of the Gospel of Christ, of God, of the Prophets and Apostles, and have gotten the form of their words

---

[155] Winstanley, *The New Law of Righteousness*, p. 42.

[156] Coppe, *A Fiery Flying Roll*, p. 88; Christopher Taylor, *The Whirl-wind of the Lord gone forth As A Fiery flying Roule* (1655), 55.

[157] Rogers, *Ohel*, p. 357.

[158] *Newes Coming up out of the North* (1654), 45.

[159] *A Few Words in True Love* (1659), 9.

[160] Cope, 'Seventeenth-Century Quaker Style', p. 734; Fox, *Concerning Good-Morrow*, p. 12.

that did proceed from their life, and having not the life, and loving not the light, with the light all such are condemned.[161]

There is a concern with light in Ranter writing, but the emphasis is upon establishing its relationship with darkness, particularly in the moral sphere, and by means of intense scriptural analysis, rather than the appropriation of the self by light.[162] The relationship between light and self, however, depended upon individual definitions of the two words. John Toldervy was one who passed in and out of Quakerism, and afterwards he came to regard the Quaker inner light as a high point of egotism: '*Self for the justifying of Self*' where all was 'Resolved into Self'.[163] His own position was confused, however, in that he reports an experience akin to ranting hypostasy while he was a Quaker, so that his rejection of Quakerism comes from a reaction against a language of self-negation attempting to accommodate what Toldervy later felt was prophetic egotism.[164] Still, for Joseph Salmon the self willingly becomes a centre which is dominated not explicitly by the light, but the collapsing together of finite and infinite, time and eternity, into nothing, the silence of the self.[165]

Nevertheless, early Quaker writing exhibits all of the exhortative force of a Coppe, as is evident in the words of Milton's future amanuensis, Thomas Ellwood:

Houl, Houl you Merchants of Babilon, for the time is coming wherein none shall buy your merchandise. Houl and roar you children of Babylon, for your mother the false woman, the great harlot, the scarlet Whore shall shortly be stripped out of her false coverings.[166]

The Quakers are not apparently worried by the search for the relationship between self and indwelling divine, once it has been established that the light is indeed there. Speech follows biblical prototypes as if the speaker in the text were disembodied. So William Dewsbury lets the voice of Hosea speak (for Hos. 14: 1):

O England, who lies in the *faln* and *lost* estate, separated from the true and living God, by thine iniquities, notwithstanding all thy profession of

[161] Fox, *Concerning Good-Morrow*, p. 26.
[162] See Laurence Clarkson, *A Single Eye All Light, no Darkness* (1650), in *CRW*, pp. 161–75.
[163] *The Foot out of the Snare* (1656), sig. A2ʳ, p. 7.
[164] Ibid., *passim*.
[165] Salmon, *Heights in Depths*, in *CRW*, p. 216.
[166] *An Alarm to the Priests* (1660), 2.

his Name, in outward forms and observations; Repent, repent, and turn unto the Lord God Almighty, who waits on thee to be gracious, unto thee, and to make thee the glory of all the Nations of the world.[167]

Here, the sense of self with light is characterized by simple words and phrases interspersed with biblical phrases. Cope maintains that scriptural references are rare in Quaker tracts.[168] However, it is more accurate to say that there are generally fewer scriptural references in Quaker pamphlets than in those of the other radical religious groups. For the Quaker there is no end in Scripture or prophetic imitation in writing, though biblical rhetoric cannot be escaped. The point is well exemplified in *The Resurrection of John Lilburne* (1656) where Lilburne records, in confessions and letters, his conversion to Quakerism. He registers his rebirth into the light within, but the last four pages of the fourteen-page pamphlet are taken up with a last-ditch effort to match his experience of the light to the Scriptures, and the margins are dense with references.[169]

Quaker rhetoric now involves another kind of auditory hallucination than that experienced by the Independent congregations and the Ranters. Where the latter two groups hear the voice of the Lord, the Quakers simply allow this dread voice to speak with no necessary and final identification: it is either God or Quaker prophet or both. Given the Quaker emphasis upon correct knowledge of the Word through the Light, the emphasis in the speaking voice becomes distinctly Johannine. Margaret Fell repeats the maxim, '*I am the Resurrection and the Life*' (John 11: 25) while Thomas Stubbs warns against ignoring the light:

But in hating the light of Jesus Christ, and giving liberty to your vain minds, you run on the broad way to death, Hell, and destruction, and the light in the conscience is your condemnation, *John* 3, 19, 20, 21 and Jo. 8, 12, so all people take heed to the light, by it you are left without excuse, *Rom.* 2. 16.[170]

Here, however, the speaker's register of social complaint follows that of the Ranters so that Stubbs, like Coppe and Foster, demands repentance from the rich who must 'howl and weep'.

---

[167] *A True Prophecy of the Mighty Day of the Lord* (1654), 1.

[168] Cope, 'Seventeenth-Century Quaker Style', p. 731.

[169] *The Resurrection of John Lilburne* (1656), 10–13.

[170] Fell, *An evident Demonstration*, p. 4; Thomas Stubbs, *Certain Papers Given forth from the Spirit of truth* (1659), 8. The section quoted was written in 1653.

Quaker *personae* become angry or glorifying according to the demands of the occasion. The reader sees only the surface rhetoric with very little revelation of why the prophet is saying what he is, and how he came to be as he is. The experience of the light is beyond language and it can be registered only in the simple admission of the power of the light (the closest the Quakers come to actual silence in their writings) or in the evocative power of scriptural phrases. Discursive reason is not necessary, so that the self transcends language by means of progressively shorter clauses which accelerate into a Pauline epiphany:

For it is receiving Christ and his Righteousness by which Man is justified, and not by taking of it, even by the free gift of righteousness, which is but one, and wrought by one, yet it must be received in all who receiveth Christ, who is Gods righteousness, without which none can be justified, as is plain, *Rom.* 5.15, 16, 17, and Christ in the Saints is the hope of glory, *Colos.* 1. 27.[171]

The result is no different, when looked at from outside the mind of each believer, than the 'experience' of the Ranter's hypostasy, though the route taken to arrive there is slightly different.

From this it follows that Quaker style, a form of *scriptura rediviva*, is imposed upon the record of the lives of individual Quakers in the real world. Metaphorical abstractions break down the barrier between conceptions and things, or objective events: 'I saw a purity strike through Magistrates.'[172] Nevertheless, and contrary once again to Cope's argument, there are detailed descriptions of persecutions in Quaker writing:

The 16. day of the 11. month, this Priest *Townsend* came to this Prison of *Norwich*, and said that sprinkling of Infants was the seal of the Covenant, and that it was an ordinance of Christ, and that it was to the seed of believers and he sprinckled a womans Child in this prison aforesaid, who was imprisoned for whoredom, and for sprinkling of it, he took twelve pence.[173]

---

[171] James Nayler, *Antichrist in Man, Christ's Enemy* (1656), 12.

[172] Fox, *A Warning from the Lord* (1654), 26.

[173] Christopher Atkinson *et al.*, *Ishmael, And his Mother, Cast out into the Wilderness* (1655), 13. It should be noted that records of Quaker sufferings may be regarded as a separate genre from testimonies, though the two overlap for the purposes of this chapter.

Here, facts are divorced from the light. In general though, Ranters and Quakers make no distinction between inner, spiritual, subjective, and outer, objective worlds, since all is taken into the individual's mind. Ultimately this results in the self being reconstituted in allegorical terms. Jacob Bauthumley disseminates his speaker across the entire network of creation, so that the 'I' appears to become identified with and reborn through the anatomy of the universe.[174] Coppe constructs an inner dialectic. He focuses upon the connection between gesture, action, and morality, achieving a stunning identity between wealth, possession, and corruption. The image of the 'WEL-FAVOURED HARLOT' inside Coppe, who 'flattereth with her lips', suggests a connection between money and illicit seduction, and she exists for the reader as a force of privilege and selfish appropriation (for Coppe, the false standards of behaviour which exist within the gathered churches and the Baptist conventicles, the homes of the 'spiritual notionists'). She has the potential to possess the speaker, but fortunately 'divine Majesty' roars out the imperative, again from within Coppe, to give all to the poor.[175] The allegory here is part of Coppe's prophetic behaviour still. Like Bauthumley, however, the Quaker John Perrot achieves a genuine splitting up of himself into creation. Perrot's self becomes first worm, then regenerate seed which swims in a sea, or lies buried in an earth of spiritual persecution:

> I am a Worm *poor* and *low*, which in the Earth doth creep,
> Hid as the *tender Plant* with *Snow*, in time of winter deep
> So saith the Seed, grievous *Oppressions* long have bin
> My weighty *burthens*: ages spreading clouds of sin
> Have *wrapt* me up, and *roul'd* me under trouble;
> I stand *the same*, they *perish'd* as a *bubble*[176]

Perrot stands at an extreme in Quaker discourse where the self becomes an allegorical quality as well as admitting that allegorical qualities like light, seed, and serpent operate inside the self. This is to go further than any Ranter had done in relating the Word to the self and the body. But the more extreme

---

[174] 'I see that all the Beings in the World are but that our Being, and so he may well be said, to be everywhere as he is, and so I cannot exclude him from Man or Beast, or any other Creature', *The Light and Dark Sides of God* (1650) in *CRW*, p. 232.

[175] *A Second Fiery Flying Roule*, in *CRW*, p. 102.

[176] *A Sea of the Seed's Sufferings* (1661), 3.

prophets, Ranters and Quakers included, had elaborated a series of accounts of the self in which the divine entirely defined the body, so that all utterance and every movement constituted a symbolic language which was supposed to exert powerful control over beholders. This was to go beyond the confines of the conversion narrative, even though such narratives clearly contained the roots of some forms of prophetic speech, and though some prophetic narratives were clearly conditioned by ministers or church politics in a manner similar to the confessions of experience. All the subject-matter of this chapter has nevertheless been concerned with the ways in which radical religious people conceived of themselves. Here, for all radical Puritans and sectarians, the apex of experience was communication with God, usually by means of dream or vision, and it is this aspect of experience which is the concern of the next chapter.

2
Dreams and Visions

I

IT has become widely accepted that Renaissance people explained behaviour which did not conform with a rational, sane
norm in terms of the intervention of supernatural forces. Such
behaviour included delusions, mania, delirium, dreams, and
visions. This is an extremely complex picture in which divine or
demonic inspiration co-existed with secular categories which
explained mental behaviour. As a consequence, while dreams
could signify a supernatural visitation, mental abnormality, for
instance, was defined as melancholy. This was until the
ascendancy of rationalism in the later seventeenth century, by
which time an educated élite had ceased to believe in divine
inspiration and Swift could see religious enthusiasm and
madness as the same thing defined in two different words.[1] However, as Michael MacDonald has shown, in the earlier part
of the century, although ravings may have suggested mental
disorder, as long as they signified supernatural visitation few
classified them as signs of wild irrationality.[2] Extra-rational
behaviour was tolerated and regarded as a means of sublime
communication by inspirational forces. The deluded spoke in an
incoherent language which conveyed understandable ideas, a
language made up largely of elementary and demonic lore, of
allegorical struggles between good and evil.[3] Such expression
could be subversive yet still tolerated since it was seen as
originating from a source outside the utterer's control. Similarly,
radical Puritans and sectarians regarded dreams and visions as
manifestations of supernatural inspiration, valid prophecies
which told a truth and which bolstered the authority of a
particular sect or individual. Certain religious radicals also
believed in healing powers and miracles as direct divine

---

[1] As in *The Mechanical Operation of the Spirit* (1704).
[2] *Mystical Bedlam: Madness, Anxiety and Healing in Seventeenth-Century England*
(Cambridge, 1982), 169.   [3] Ibid. 142–7.

manifestations.[4] In every case of inspiration among the radicals, a supernatural manifestation acquired a subversive meaning because of the millennial content which went against the established political and religious order.

These attitudes fostered the characteristic feature of mid-seventeenth-century radical religious prose, the expression of extremes of emotion as a supernatural encounter. As the previous chapter demonstrated, this was defined as an 'experience' and was applied to any sublime meaning. 'Experience' was the 'inward sense and feeling', and 'a Copy written by the Spirit of God upon the hearts of beleevers'.[5] Not all the sectarians subscribed to this convention. Isaac Penington dismissed the claims of relevatory inspiration, preferring a more sober, rational sublime:

And for such of you who break forth through Visions and Revelations into new apprehension, I profess I know you not, this is not the way of breaking forth of my life, which must not be steered by these, but be able to judg these, which when once I feel with clearness, Majesty and power, I may then be drawn to beleeve that I begin to taste life.[6]

This, though, is part of another tradition among the sects. Of the '*Treatises of experience* newly put out' by the Independent pastors, at least one third involved the recounting of dreams or visions. In order to comprehend their occurrence in these publications it is instructive to consider seventeenth-century definitions of dreams and visions.

For most Puritans a vision was something seen vividly and sometimes heard by supernatural revelation. For most Puritans, too, a dream constituted a vision: without a vision it almost failed to qualify as a dream, or 'visions of the night'.[7] This was an idea elevated by a long line of theologians, Aquinas being the prime

---

[4] The most famous case is of the early Quaker, James Nayler, raising Dorcas Erbery.

[5] Vavasor Powell, Epistle in Henry Walker (ed.) *Spirituall Experiences, Of sundry Beleevers* (1653), sigs. A2ᵛ–A3ʳ. For the theological definitions of 'experience' see above, pp. 26–8 and R. T. Kendall, *Calvin and English Calvinism to 1649* (Oxford, 1979), esp. 8–9, 80.   [6] *An Eccho From the Great Deep* (1650), sig. A3ʳ.

[7] Abiezer Coppe, *Some Sweet Sips, of some Spiritual Wine* (1649) in *CRW*, p. 64. See Job 4: 13; 20: 8; Isa. 29: 7; Dan. 2: 19; 7: 2. Keith Thomas discusses dream as prophecy in the sixteenth and seventeenth centuries in *Religion and the Decline of Magic* (1971), 151–4. He concludes 'Most of the "visions" and "revelations" which were so common during the Interregnum were probably what we should call dreams' (p. 153). See also Peter Burke, 'L'Histoire sociale des rêves', *Annales*, 28. 2 (1973), 329–42.

example, and it served to enhance the continuity between waking consciousness, sleep, dream, and vision which so irritated Hobbes:

The most difficult discerning of a mans Dream, from his waking thoughts, is then, when by some accident we observe not that we have slept: which is easie to happen to a man full of fearfull thoughts; and whose conscience is much troubled; and that sleepeth, without the circumstances, of going to bed ... For he that taketh pains, and industriously layes himself to sleep, in case any uncouth and exorbitant fancy come unto him, cannot easily think it other than a dream.[8]

Likewise, the radicals' revelations were often defined as uneasy juxtapositions of visions and dreams. Anna Trapnel, for instance, had a vision of an angel in white, before she slept.[9]

Identifying dreams as visions, the Presbyterian minister, Philip Goodwin, posited a sliding scale of dream, good to bad, according to the nature of the supernatural visitant.[10] It should be emphasized that the supernatural cause is fundamental, though Goodwin exercises a wealth of knowledge, classical, patristic, and otherwise, to argue with considerable flexibility. In this way the reader sees the intensely personal nature of dreams. Waking life, says Goodwin, is essentially social, while sleep and dreams take individuals into private, discrete worlds, a notion which Goodwin derives both from Heraclitus and Bernard on Cant. 7: 11, 12.[11]

The supernatural theory was not the only account of dreams in the period. A physiological account, with its roots in Artemidorus, was also given credence. Artemidorus posited *somnium* as proleptic experiences, and *insomnium* as nightmares which reflected matters of mind and body in the dreamer's present life.[12] To this can be added Aristotle's statement in *De Anima* that dreams are examples of the imagination working in the absence of the waking senses, and are therefore false, or, in Hobbes's words: 'no

---

[8] *Leviathan* (1651), ed. C. B. Macpherson (1968), 91. For Aquinas's view, see *Summa Theologica*, 'Secunda Secundae', Q. 95, Art. 6c.

[9] *A Legacy for Saints* (1654), 14.

[10] Goodwin, *The Mystery of Dreames, Historically Discoursed* (1658).

[11] Ibid. 292.

[12] Manfred Weidhorn, *Dreams in Seventeenth-Century English Literature* (The Hague, 1970), 38–42 contains an account of Artemidorus, whose *The Judgement of Dreams* was first published in English in 1518. There were fourth and fifth editions in 1644 and 1656 respectively.

Imagination . . . but what proceeds from the agitation of the inward parts of mans body'.[13] Sir Thomas Browne set both viewpoints together, supernatural and natural, in his 'On Dreams'. He chides Aristotle for not admitting divine visitation in sleep, but also professes that Cato's fondness for cabbage resulted in his uneasy sleep. The secular and supernatural theories were interdependent to a large extent. Browne uses several examples from the Bible to show how virtuous behaviour when awake leads to good dreams, as with Plutarch and Aquinas, according to Goodwin.[14] Working in the opposite direction, Browne suggests that men can use their dreams for the better understanding of themselves: 'wee may more sensibly understand ourselves. Men act in sleepe with some conformity unto their awaked senses, & consolations or discoureagments may bee drawne from dreames, which intimately tell us ourselves.'[15] Still Browne stresses the widely held contemporary belief that dreams are 'fictions and falsehoods'. We may be deceived, he says, by the vision, and by mistaking the 'Naturall and animall dreams' (those generated by the self) for a divine or demonic dream.

These were the opinions of the learned minority. Learned or unlearned, radical religious writers did not distrust dream visions in this way. Their degree of commitment to the super-natural verity of dreams is paralleled by the elaboration of Neo-platonic theories of dream. It should be noted here that many of the radicals were familiar with versions of mystical and occult ideas, of which Neoplatonic dream theory was a part. Neo-platonists emphasized the blur between consciousness and sleep, arguing that the soul escaped in sleep. In Plato's *Timaeus*, dreams reflect in an irrational way the rational functioning of the higher part of the human soul by means of sense impressions. In effect the soul employs the imagination to communicate with the mind. The closest state to pure intellect therefore occurs in dreams. According to Manfred Weidhorn, in the early fifth century Synesius of Cyrene linked this theory with the notion of *sympatheia* between cosmos and organism.[16] So dreams register the stirring of the human microcosm by events in the macrocosm.

[13] Aristotle, *De Anima*, 3. iii; Hobbes, *Leviathan*, p. 90.

[14] 'On Dreams' in Sir Thomas Browne, *The Major Works*, ed. C. A. Patrides (1974), 475–9; Goodwin, *The Mystery of Dreames*, p. 339.

[15] Browne, 'On Dreams', p. 477.   [16] Weidhorn, *Dreams*, pp. 20–1.

The seventeenth-century version of this had come to England through the alchemical, hermetical, and Paracelsan tradition. Here the imagination is conceived as a mirror of images from the microcosm. Though Thomas Tryon's *A Treatise of Dreams and Visions* (1689, 2nd edn., 1695) was written at the end of the century, it explores dreams in a manner consistent with the explanatory system of Jacob Boehme.[17] The 'general cause of dreams' for Tryon is a 'Radix [or divinely instituted root] *whence they derived from Nature*' (p. 26). In natural terms man is the image of God and so partakes of the ethereal. Since God never sleeps, neither does the soul. Only the body sleeps. So, in sleep, the soul and spirit 'goeth on forming, figureing, and Representing of things as real, and substantial' (p. 39), while a residue of bad natural functions impedes the human facility to remember dreams. Here dream is inextricably linked to an idea of divine communication and vision, a form of representation which demands self-denial, enlightenment, and perfection to be fully appreciated as a 'sublime truth'. Though couched in Behmenist terms here, the notion of dream as a representation, where God imprints divine impressions, was not foreign to orthodox Calvinists. Consequently for Goodwin as well as for Boehme, 'A good soul is a fit soyle for such seed.'[18]

Goodwin's Calvinist viewpoint merits further consideration because it reflects upon the emotional engagement of all Puritans with dreams. Goodwin associates dreams with visits from the devil, which can be bad or, worse still, defiling. Such were the dreams which Epiphanius saw as leading the Sodomites into delusion.[19] Goodwin divides dream theories into two categories, firstly the passive school of Vatablus, Aretius, and Erasmus; and secondly the active school of Pareus, Piscator, and Calvin.[20] In the former, men are seen largely to be tempted in their dreams, while in the latter, men are actually 'filthy' in their dreams, despite the threat of eternal punishment. This corresponds partly to Goodwin's threefold distinction between *Delusi in somniis*, where men are bewitched in dreams; *Demersi in somniis*, where men drown in filthy dreams; and *Devicti in somniis*, where men are vanquished in dreams. Again, image is important, as Satan

[17] According to John Everard, *The Gospel-Treasury Opened* (2nd edn., 1659), ii. 307–14, dreams allow the individual to return to God as essence.

[18] Goodwin, *The Mystery of Dreames*, p. 275.

[19] Ibid. 98. See also p. 88.   [20] Ibid. 93–4.

'embraces the representations he tenders'. Goodwin, in fact, places equal emphasis upon demonic and divine visitation in dreams, though again the image can be deceptive. Hence, Luther is cited with regard to his statement that the Anabaptists' inspiration was really a series of deluding dreams. Similarly Burton follows Polydore Vergil on the dreams of monks and nuns, which are seen to 'proceed wholly *ab instinctu daemonum*'.[21] What separates the more orthodox Protestant from the radical sects is his Scripturalism, however. Goodwin admits that God gives man sleep and dreams as a token of his love, but he questions the need for illumination in dreams beside the light of the Scriptures.

II

If the dreams which feature in radical religious pamphlets are examined, they are seen to consist of images, actions, and emotions. Most striking are the visual images. Thomas Browne was intrigued that 'phantasticall objects' should appear large in dreams. This was their 'mysterie of similitude'.[22] It was the dramatic element which was most noted. Indeed the radical Royalist prophet, Arise Evans, labels encounters with Satan in dreams and visions as 'conflicts'.[23]

On what might be called the lowest level of dream interest in radical writing, the dream itself, as a collection of images and actions, does not in fact occur. In *Wonderfull Predictions* (1648) John Saltmarsh says that he experienced a dream in a trance-like state. He does not record a dream narrative as such but simply uses the fact of its occurrence as an admonitory prophecy against the New Model Army. Though Saltmarsh may have had a dream, he places whatever happened in it immediately in the language of the Millennium. Only the authority of the dream as divine inspiration remains to enforce Saltmarsh's veiled critique:

That the great and dreadfull day of the Lord is neare, when all men shall be judged by Jesus Christ, And then shall the wayes, and actions of all men appeare, Beleevers stand on a glorious Gospell, spiritual Bottome, supported by their Saviour: And

---

[21] *The Anatomy of Melancholy* (1621), ed. H. Jackson, 3 vols. (1932), iii. 344.

[22] Browne, *On Dreams*, pp. 476, 478. 'Oneiric' will be used to describe that which is typical of dreams.

[23] *Mr. Evans and Mr. Pennington's Prophesie* (1655), 2.

Infidels, clasping about the stones and Pillers of the World, and fleshy phancy, be thrown downe to hell forever. (p. 3)

With the Independent dream of 'experience', images and actions function as a locus of inspiration and salvation inside the dream structure, while the dream itself justifies the narrative of experience since it marks the transition from repentance to grace. For instance, on 4 January 1651 John Cooper dreamed that he was riding down a wide green sward with his minister, John Rogers, his commander, Colonel Hewson, and his Lord, the Lord of Clogher. The narrative is no less than a compressed romance. The four riders pass down the path towards a gate which opened by a prayer. Inside is a garden, some stairs, and scattered bones and bodies, up and through which the party passes. Rogers's superior state is revealed when only he sees these skeletons as '*full* and *perfect*'. Cooper and his fellow Saints are passing through the place of judgement, the climax of which is a deep pit with a pike over it. Cooper's anxiety regarding salvation is dramatized in that while the others pass easily over the pike, he is unable to cross until Rogers calls down aid from heaven for him. On the other side, all sit together in a room (the shelter and fellowship of the gathered church) and music is heard. Rogers, however, announces that he will have to leave his flock soon. This is reminiscent of Christ talking to the Disciples, so that Cooper's impression of Rogers's saving power is so great that he subliminally conflates the roles of minister and messiah in his dream.[24]

Two points of import are worth noting here. First there seems to be little distance between the subject of the dream, and the speaker who describes the dream. The 'I' connects John Cooper the recounter with the saved John Cooper in the dream, so that the dream becomes an intimation of bestowed grace in the present. Secondly Cooper the dream subject faces judgement alongside the leaders of his society. His place in this society,

---

[24] Rogers, *Ohel or Beth-shemesh. A Tabernacle for the Sun* (1653), 400. These gates refer to the 'strait gate' of Matt. 7: 13. The same motif occurs in the allegory of Bunyan's *The Pilgrim's Progress* (1678), ed. Roger Sharrock (1965), 41. Alice Browne, 'Dreams and Picture Writing: Some Examples of this Comparison from the Sixteenth to the Eighteenth Centuries', *JWCI* 44 (1981), 90–100, makes the significant point (p. 91) that dreams were thought of differently before the invention of the cinema: cinema provides a descriptive metaphor for dream preferable to that of second life. However, the dream as second life is still a dramatic narrative.

which is also about to receive grace, is validated and assured as Cooper is encouraged and helped across the pit by the words of his pastor, Rogers. In both cases the dream functions as a divinely sent message of salvation to the individual and his society. Given that most of the dreams in *Ohel or Beth-shemesh* belong to the members of Rogers's congregation in Dublin, who are all seeking salvation and the knowledge that the spirit of Christ is within them, the dream seems to be determined by the context of salvation in the gathered fellowship of saints.

The intensification of violence in the dream is coupled with the connection between dream or vision sequence and the body of the subject, breaking down the barrier between the internal sleeping and external waking worlds. John Rogers claims that he underwent a waking vision when young, after he took God's name in vain. He was confronted with a narrow gateway and once through it he was in the field of judgement. Then a fiercely sharp blade cut Rogers, which he later interprets as 'coming close to death'. Just as John Rogers was cut by a sword in his vision, so John Osborne bit through his tongue during his sleep. Osborne claims that in his dream he knows that his friends and neighbours are praying for him, so that inner and outer worlds meet in the consciousness of the dream-subject and in the interpretation which is offered later. Since Osborne's interpretation is based closely on the memory of his dream, interpretation and dream become part of the same spiritual experience.[25] In Henry Walker's *Spirituall Experiences, Of sundry Beleevers* (1653) the continuity between dream and consciousness need not necessarily involve the dreamer in his or her own dream. Satan as a jester figure appears to one woman in her dream, which encourages her to think that she 'has played the hypocrite with God'. In the 'experience' her actual bodily movements become significant: she rises up in bed as a sign of grace.[26]

The same pamphlet contains examples of dream narratives which are of considerable length, and their symbolic and imagistic significance expands accordingly. As with the previous dream the demonic element remains but the context is far more complex. Like John Cooper's dream T.M.'s dream is framed by the bounds of sacred and secular society. T.M. is an apprentice

---

[25] Rogers, '*further* Experience *of* John Rogers', in *Ohel*, p. 423.
[26] Walker, 'Experiences of E.C.', in *Spirituall Experiences*, p. 82.

and therefore probably male, which is interesting because of the degree of female role-playing which takes place in the dream narrative. On the other hand there were female apprentices so that a female T.M. may have used the role of motherhood in her dream to explore her relationship with salvation and divine authority. At first the description is markedly patriarchal: after seeing his or her minister T.M. 'returned backe from my Master to my father's house, lying downe once upon a bench I fell asleep'.[27] The apprentice is somewhat anxious because the master is ungodly. The dream follows with the subject in a green meadow with good and evil, frightening beasts and monsters which change their shape often. T.M. does not say whether good creatures turn into evil ones or vice versa but the general impression is one of eerie and fantastic instability.

The vision is capped with the appearance of a 'great red Dragon', which proceeds to move menacingly towards T.M. Clearly this is a version of the serpent, the dragon in Rev. 12, the forces of Satanic evil, perhaps T.M.'s master. As the dragon approaches a child is put in T.M.'s arms—surely the Christ child, another symbol of salvation. T.M.'s attention is entirely occupied with the child and the overtones are maternal: the child is so 'beautifull and comely' that he forgets the dragon. Neverthless the dragon chases man with child up a hill. It seems that T.M. has at least been given the impetus to try to save them both, though nothing is explicitly stated. At the top of the hill divine salvation is present as emanation: 'there appeared a brightnesse from heaven, which gushed forth like a flash of Lightening, and split the dragon in peeces, at which I rejoiced exceedingly'.[28] Now a dialogue takes place between the apprentice and the child which is essentially ontological. He asks the child its name; it replies 'Emmanual', while its father is called '*I am*' and its mother '*Eternity . . . which was lost*'. The child further decodes the dream by saying that he has been sent to save the apprentice. Modern interpreters of dream from Freud to Lacan have stressed the particular feature in the dream of the naming of the subject's father.[29] If we allow ourselves the liberty of

---

[27] Ibid., '*Experiences* of T.M.', p. 370. For another reading, see Caldwell, *The Puritan Conversion Narrative* (Cambridge, 1983), 17–20.   [28] Ibid. 370–2.

[29] See Sigmund Freud, *The Interpretation of Dreams* (1952 edn.), trans. J. Strachey (New York, 1971), 288–9, 461–7, 89–96, 516. See also M. Foucault, 'The Father's

comparing the modern theory with the seventeenth-century example, it seems, in one sense, that the dream allows T.M. to discover his or her true father, God, rejecting the reprobate master, while the earthly father remains in the waking world as a controlling authority: he enters his son's or daughter's room to wake him or her from the dream. The homecoming has been accompanied by an assurance of the saving grace of Christ. What is also important is that, whether male or female, T.M.'s discovery has been made through a traditional receptacle of mercy, the role of woman as mother.

The presence of animals is another recurring feature in the radical dream. A fearful terror is intimated in this most traditional envisaging of Satan:

My *first call* was upon a *dream*, which *I had of a great black terrible dog*, which seized upon me, and *took hold* on *my ear fast*, which *I thought* was the *Devil*; at which, *I waked* with *shreeks* and *cries*, and such *frights*, as for *three weeks I thought I should* have gone *distracted*.[30]

On the other hand, the importance of the perfectionist connotations of communion with animals and inanimate nature is also evident in Abïezer Coppe's *Some Sweet Sips, of some Spirituall Wine* (1649), one Mrs T.P. reports in a letter a dream where she found herself standing among many animals, wild and tame, beside a clear running river. These animals are seen to be 'recreating' themselves, in the sense of a physical and spiritual re-invigoration, while T.P. communicates with them: 'yea, we had so free a correspondence together, as I oft-times would take the wildest of them, and put them in my bosome, especially such (which afore) I had exceedingly feared, such that I would not have toucht, or

---

"No" ', in *Language, Counter-Memory, Practice*, ed. and trans. D. F. Bouchard (Ithaca, NY, 1977), 68–86. The interpretation of dreams here lies within the confines of *psychoanalytical* method, that is, investigation which brings out the unconscious meaning of the words, actions, and products of the imagination (dreams, phantasies, delusions) of a particular subject. (See J. Laplanche and J.-B. Pontalis, *The Language of Psycho-Analysis* (1980), 367.) This chapter is not concerned with the application of this body of theory as such to radical religious dreams. Rather, it seeks to see similarities between seventeenth-century notions of dream and modern ideas, in order to facilitate greater comprehension of the experiencing of dreams by people in the past. By 'naming' is meant the recognition of paternal authority, implicitly or explicitly.

[30] Rogers, '*Experience* of Edward Wayman', in *Ohel*, p. 409. See also Alan MacFarlane, *The Family Life of Ralph Josselin* (Cambridge, 1970), 187.

come nigh: as the Snake, and Toade, &c.'.[31] It seems, as T.P. later admits, to be a vision of perfect harmony: 'a very glorious libertie, and yet a perfect Law'.[32] However, T.P. then describes how she takes the wildest animal, the tiger, and puts a collar on it to make it hers, whereupon the tiger struggles to free itself, and though T.P. tries to keep the tiger, it finally runs away. This she later sees as an example of human weakness, which is selfishness, of 'appropriating of things to our selves, and for our selves'.[33]

Sarah Wight's dreams automatically allegorize animals. She sees a vision of a roaring lion which she interprets as Satan, who tells her that there is only a hell in the conscience—the Familist error. It is as if the dream's violence challenges Sarah's cosmology so that it threatens to become her total reality, which she resists: this is not a dream of wish-fulfilment. Later on she dreams she is on the top of a hill by the sea, which has red, white and black horses swimming in it. She is carried violently down the hill to the sea but is then carried away by a man who interprets the horses as her 'spiritual enemies'—significantly the image of horses as waves in a stormy sea was also seen as a symbol of illness in the individual. The spiritual enemies are within her, which refers to her unsettled familial relationships (see above, p. 46). The man takes her to the top of the hill so that she can look down and appreciate her mercy better. He speaks biblical language to her and she describes him as glorious: he is an angel at least. When she wakes up she has characteristically wet cheeks from crying with joy, and she is able to fix her mind on the relevant biblical passages which he has spoken and which she hears: Matt. 3: 17 and Ephes. 1:6 give a sense of great regenerative release.[34]

If a small digression is permissible, there is an interesting comparison to be made with Milton. In *Paradise Lost* Eve is in Eden when she has her dream at the beginning of Book V, *ll.* 35–93, and already has a communion with the animals, a harmonious and perfect life. This is the reverse of T.P.'s situation in Coppe's pamphlet. She sees what she has to gain in her dreams, and also what she has to lose. Eve has all there is to gain on earth, and all there is to lose is to come. It must, of course, be said that Eden in *Paradise Lost* is an actual world, whereas T.P.'s

[31] Coppe, *Some Sweet Sips*, p. 65.   [32] Ibid.   [33] Ibid.
[34] Henry Jessey, *The Exceeding Riches of Grace Advanced* (1647), 148–50.

utopia is a vision which she regards as symbolic and representative of a certain spiritual state. Nevertheless Eve's dream itself is symbolic, and the crux of it is Satan's urging of Eve to eat the fruit of the Tree of Knowledge of Good and Evil.[35] Once she tastes the apple, Eve the dream subject flies up above Paradise, so breaking her place in the order of creation and becoming more like a God. T.P. wants nothing more than the spiritual perfection which Eve has, but Coppe was later to claim a higher degree of spiritual perfection as a Ranter, or so his enemies claimed. The point of importance is that the knowledge and liberty with which Satan tempts Eve in her dream are a version of the enlightenment which the radicals desired or even claimed to have, though for Milton it is a distorted picture. So the devices which Milton uses to portray the dream are the reverse of those with which T.P. and Coppe treat the radical dream. Eve's dream is a parody of a love song and Eve is clearly frightened by her dream, while Coppe greets T.P.'s dream by drinking the wine of illumination, employing figurative references to and echoes from the Song of Solomon, among other biblical passages, to celebrate the coming enlightenment in an exhilarated fashion.[36]

III

Clearly, there is a similarity between seventeenth-century radical religious dreams and visions and others of the Bible, which would seem to suggest a relationship of influence of the latter upon the former. The sectarians imitate the Bible. Dr B. S. Capp, however, has stated that he sees only a slight resemblance between radical, particularly Fifth Monarchist, dreams and biblical ones.[37] Capp's opinion derives from the fact that he does not distinguish between dreams and visions which are of complex psychological and literary interest, and more simple prophetic visions containing one symbol, and relating to one event in the real world. Such is the case with Owen Lloyd's vision of a black panther which overcame the world until destroyed by God. When the vision was reported to John Rogers in the mid-1650s,

---

[35] See the gloss provided in John Milton, *Paradise Lost*, ed. Alastair Fowler (1968), 258–61.   [36] Coppe, *Some Sweet Sips*, in *CRW*, pp. 66–71.

[37] *The Fifth Monarchy Men: A Study in Seventeenth-Century English Millenarianism* (1972), 186.

the panther clearly referred to Cromwell, though when it was published as a pamphlet in 1662 the animal was seen to refer to Charles II.[38] In one sense Capp is correct, and these types of prophecy are mixed up with a welter of popular prophecies and those of Paracelsus, Nostradamus, and Joachim of Fiore.[39] Here Capp seems to follow Hobbes's equation between dreams, visions, and superstition: apparitions, from which 'did arise the greatest part of the Religion of the Gentiles in time past, that worshipped Satyres, Fawnes, Nymphs, and the like: and now-adayes the opinion that rude people have of Fayries, Ghosts, and Goblins'.[40] But even here there are cases to prove the exception. In *Mr. Evans and Mr. Pennington's Prophecie* (1655) Arise Evans refers unpretentiously to William Pennington's dream that England will be visited by seven years of plenty, to be followed by seven years of famine. It is a popular prophecy, applied to the 1650s, but it is also a direct plagiarism, as it were, from the story of Joseph (Gen. 41: 18–36).

The word 'prophecy' is important here again. A venerable tradition of scholars had, since the Reformation, been interpreting biblical prophecies which involved dreams or visions, particularly the Books of Daniel and Revelation, in terms of the events in recent history, so that, in effect, they were able to give precise dates for the Second Coming of Christ.[41] But it was as important, if not more important, for the sectarians to feel the Second Coming as a *spiritual immanence* within themselves. Consequently, just as some of the sectarians expressed their sense of inspiration by adopting Biblical prophetic styles, so the radical prophets relive the archetypes of biblical dreams and visions.

Biblical dreams have been described as 'characteristically violent, highly symbolic, fantastical'.[42] This is particularly the case with the Old Testament Prophets and John of Patmos. In fact, in the same way that a distinction can be made between

---

[38] Ibid.

[39] Rogers, סגריר *Sagrir. Or Doomes-day Drawing Nigh, With Thunder and Lightening to Lawyers* (1653), 131–2. See also pp. 28–9 for Rogers's attitude to Hildegard of Bingen as a prophetess.

[40] Hobbes, *Leviathan*, p. 92.

[41] See Wittreich, *Visionary Poetics* (San Marino, 1979), 3–47, 273–7; K. R. Firth, *The Apocalyptic Tradition in Reformation Britain, 1530–1645* (Oxford, 1979), 21, 63, 120, 144, 162, 194, 222, 229.

[42] Adolphe Lods, *The Prophets and the Rise of Judaism*, trans. S. H. Hooke (1937), 51. See also pp. 52–7.

radical dreams and visions and simpler modes of popular political prophecy, so the first Old Testament prophets, Joel, Jeremiah, and Ezekiel, condemned the original Hebrew 'prophets' who were essentially conjurors and occultists, devoid of any direct visionary inspiration. Among biblical prophecies, Luther distinguished three types: that of Moses, which featured words only; that of Daniel, which included words and pictures; and the pictures-only version of John, a 'concealed and dumb prophecy'.[43]

Following Luther's second category, Daniel's dream, in chapter 7, which prefigures the visions of Revelation, is genuinely sublime, and was certainly one model for the radicals. Animal imagery is characteristic, compounded with violent imagery:

Behold a fourth beast, dreadful and terrible, and strong exceedingly; and it had great iron teeth: it devoured and brake in pieces, and stamped the residue with the feet of it: and it *was* diverse from all the beasts that *were* before it; and it had ten horns. (Dan. 7: 7)

Typically Daniel has a divine messenger to tell him the meaning of his dream in a directly symbolic way: the four beasts stand for four kings who 'shall arise out of the earth'. In a similar manner, Daniel was able to interpret Nebuchadnezzar's dream in chapter 4. In chapter 7 Daniel simply has a presence he can converse with, 'one of them that stood by', as well as the Ancient of Days to make plain the vision, a function he could play himself in chapter 4. Another characteristic effect is for the body of the prophet to be affected by the vision, so that in chapter 8 Daniel faints and is sick after his vision (v. 27). Similarly, Ezekiel and John register physical ecstasy and pain respectively after swallowing their heaven-sent rolls.[44]

In Anna Trapnel such dream sequences are mirrored and they are closer to the original than the general biblical landscape which typifies the dreams collected by Rogers, Walker, and Coppe. Trapnel locates the horns of Daniel and Revelation in *The Cry of a Stone* (1654), and her interpreter in the vision refers her back to the Bible for the meaning:

[43] See Jer. 27: 9; Joel 2: 28, which is echoed in Acts 2: 17; Luther, 'Preface to the Revelation of St. John' in *The Works of Martin Luther*, ed. A. J. Holman, 6 vols. (Philadelphia, 1932), vi. 480.

[44] Dan. 8: 27; Ezek. 3: 3; Rev. 10: 9–10. In medieval dream vision theory a dream with an interpreting figure in it is called an *oraculum*.

He gave them many pushes, scratching them with his horn, and driving them into several houses, he ran still along, till at length there was a great silence, and suddenly there broke forth in the Earth great Fury coming forth from the Clouds, and they presently were scattered, and their horns broken, and they tumbled into Graves; with that I broke forth, and sang praise, and the Lord said, mark that Scripture, *Three horns shall arise, a fourth shall come different from the former.* (p. 13)[45]

The difference from Daniel's dream is that the bulls here are involved in actions much closer to the speaker, so that the speaker actually comes to take part in the action, as with T.P. Also as in the Bible, Anna Trapnel has a divine voice to interpret the vision for her: this time it is God referring directly to Revelation. God speaks in 'similitudes', reinscribing scriptural dreams inside the dreamer's mind and as the vision proceeds, Trapnel refers each vision back to its scriptural root to enhance the vision's authority.[46] Here there is also the sense of being physically touched by the divine, another prophetic experience. As John Jecock says, 'the *Law* laid *hold* upon me', while for Anna Trapnel, 'an arm and an hand clasped me round, a Voyce said, I will be thy safety'.[47]

Trapnel uses natural imagery to hint at the Second Coming. It is thus not a prophecy made from scriptural analysis, and there are similarities with the reported dream, though both do use biblical vocabulary. The central vision is framed in the typical way, though it is not specifically identified as a dream: she is 'kept indoors', probably by a physical seizure connected with the visionary state which kept her in bed, and she proceeds in her mind to the 'Vally of Visions'.[48] Her vision of creation withers away before the reborn tree, Christ:

Another Vision I had at the same time, of many Oaks, with spreading branches full of leaves, very great limmed; I looking to the root, which lay but very little in the ground, & look't dry, as if it were crumbling to dust, and above the ground was only a little dry bark, on which limmed and spreading Oaks were set; a few shrubs which being by, were lovely and green, these great Oaks fell suddenly down, and cover'd the other;

[45] The reference is to Dan. 7: 8. Gerrard Winstanley also uses Daniel's vision openly in *Fire in the Bush* (1650), 24–6.

[46] *A Legacy for Saints* (1654), pp 33–4.

[47] Rogers, '*Experience in* Mihil *made out by* John Jecock *Captain*', in *Ohel or Beth-shemesh*, p. 399; Trapnel, *The Cry of a Stone*, p. 13.

[48] Ibid. sig. a2ʳ.

presently I saw a lovely tree for stature & compleatness every way not to be paralleld by any thing that ever I saw.[49]

Here, there is no communion with nature, as an allegorical or literal representation of perfection. A closer attachment to the biblical vision is apparent in the nature of the dreaming subject's perceptions. Her role as speaker here though is more distanced, while the vision focuses upon the mantic qualities of the trees rather than any action in which the speaker might become involved. The surreal quality of the vision is also clear. Where T.P. communicated with animals, Anna Trapnel's perceptions seem to defy physical laws as she looks through the ground at the 'little' roots of the trees.

The prophets were in fact great stylists, and the radicals imitated the conventions of the biblical originals. Seventeenth-century people paid close attention to what they saw as generic and stylistic features in the Bible.[50] Particularly striking was the fact that the prophets spoke in rhythmic poetry, and Philip Goodwin wrote that the raptures and visions which visited the Apostles were an early example of prosopopeia. All the prophets seem to have turned physical gesture into a literary convention, while Ezekiel's rhetoric has been subdivided by a modern critic into histories, allegories, parables, answers to points of law, prophetic invective, lyrical outpourings, descriptions of visions, and symbolic gestures, all of which are delivered in a mode of fantasy.[51] Against Dr Capp's assertion again, it can be demonstrated that the radicals appropriated these more specific elements, sometimes beyond the boundaries of dream and vision.

The relationship here between Bible and radical religious vision is thus one of considerable complexity, which deserves to be spelt out. In terms as simple as possible, whereas the great tradition of dream visions treats dream as a literary convention, quite separate from the actual act of dreaming, the radicals were recording genuine dreams and visions which closely resemble

[49] Ibid. 12. The reference is to Isa. 1: 29. Having received a letter of encouragement from Anna Trapnel, John Rogers dreamed that he lay underneath a mulberry tree in which Christ trod the berries, the juice of which flowed into Rogers's mouth and stomach, and refreshed him: *Jegar-Sahadutha: An Oyled Pillar: Set up for Posterity* (1657), 28–9.

[50] See B. K. Lewalski, *Protestant Poetics and the Seventeenth-Century Religious Lyric* (Princeton, 1979), 72–110.

[51] Goodwin, *The Mystery of Dreames*, p. 329; Lods, *The Prophets*, pp. 222, 228, 244.

biblical dreams and visions, even though the latter were expressed in a highly conventional manner. The radical religious vision seems to follow the conventional biblical one. This is the case for Anna Trapnel's vision rather than for those collected by Rogers, Walker, and Coope. In the latter the dream is functioning merely as an intimation of salvation and grace but in the former the dream is part of a distinct prophetic stance and style on the part of the writer.

Here it is important to recognize several biblical motifs which are significant for radical dreams. Usually they take the form of a transposed parallel. As in Isa. 29: 8 Dorothy Emmet heard Christ describe himself as a fountain in her sleep, and she wakes up refreshed but still 'thirsty' after Christ.[52] This is the reversal of the Artemidoran thesis so that sleep influences waking sensations rather than vice-versa, and, like T.P.'s dream, it is another example of wish-fulfilment. Indeed the radicals were attracted by the biblical analogy made between dream and liberation, as in Ps. 126: 1–2: 'When the Lord turned again the captivity of Zion, we were like them that dream. / Then was our mouth filled with laughter, and our tongue with singing.' Beyond dream and vision, at the extreme of the radical religious experience lies ecstatic union with the divine, and here the radicals were attracted by the 'archetypal' image of the womb as a place of silent withdrawal, prior to spiritual rebirth. After the story of Ishmael and Sarah (Gen. 16, 17), the womb could become a place of divine visitation. This is bolstered by Job's emphasis upon the womb as a place of origin, prior to life, 'I should have been as though I had not been; I should have been carried from the womb to the grave', and in Ps. 22: 6, 9, 10, 23, 30, the connection is made between womb, worm, and seed. In despair the Psalmist identifies himself as worm or sinner, but then states that he is given hope, made one of the 'seed of Jacob' by being taken from the womb of God: 'But thou *art* he that took me out of the womb: thou didst make me hope *when I was* upon my mother's breast' (Ps. 22: 9).

Just as there is confusion between what is dream and what

---

[52] Rogers, 'Experience of Dorothy Emmet', in *Ohel or Beth-shemesh*, inserted gathering, p. 1. The dream and interpretation could work equally well from demonic visitation: John Rogers saw a dragon and then a tree full of dragons, but he is told in his dream that he would not be harmed. He then sees the dragons dead and wakes up refreshed: *Jegar-Sahadutha*, pp. 41–2.

is vision for the radicals, so there is confusion between dream vision and the sense of a direct presence of God within the individual, or of a direct encounter with a supernatural being. The immediacy and intensity of this experience seems to grow out of the degree to which the dream subject is involved in the dream. In the final instance death for the dream subject is connected with Christ's Second Coming, as a prelude to the 'new rest'. The concern is with the body. Serpents eat John Osborne in his dream as a form of punishment. Though he does not seem to register any pain in his dream, there is a ghoulish portrayal of an everlasting devouring.[53] A similar threat is made towards Anna Trapnel in *The Cry of a Stone*. She is confronted by a field of horned bulls, one of whom eventually charges at her. Here the threat just touches on the sexual, though one is not entirely convinced: 'they prompting him and fawning upon, he run at me, and as he was neer with his horn to my breast, an arm and an hand clasped me round', and Christ saves her.[54] Another type of vision is where the subject's senses are dulled and anaesthetized in anticipation of a divine command. So William Pennington had a vision in which he fell into a snowy ditch where his head was covered with salt and he heard voices telling him to denounce Babylon.[55]

Here the vision seems to take the aspects of disproportion and fantasy to an extreme. Coppe's vision in *A Fiery Flying Roll* is rendered in terms which try to excel each other with respect to the quality they are defining: 'the very blacknesse of darknesse'.[56] Similarly the 'whiting' sweeps the image of a picture from a wall so that Coppe's capacity to juxtapose images, to dream and envision, is removed. It is an annihilation of sensory perception which Coppe sees as a spiritual, inward re-invigoration, apparent to the 'outward eye' as streams of light. Again the sense of physical contact is aroused as Coppe feels the hand of God upon him. At this point, devoid of all senses, divine figuration occurs. Coppe sees three hearts in front of him with emblematic distinctness. The inability to define clearly is important: 'I saw

---

[53] Rogers '*An eminent* Experience, *or* relation *of* John Osborne', in *Ohel or Beth-shemesh*, p. 446.

[54] *The Cry of a Stone*, p. 13.

[55] Evans, *Mr. Evans*, 1. Dr John Pitcher, of St John's College, Oxford, has suggested to me that snow and salt perhaps represent the salvation of the individual or eternity generally since they are agents of preservation.   [56] *CRW*, p. 82.

three hearts (or three appearances) in the form of hearts, of exceeding brightnesse.'[57] This might symbolize the presence of the Trinity, though Coppe does not say so. The hearts then expand to form an 'innumerable company', so that Coppe receives his sense of the unity of creation, a description which again leaves words and images behind:

And methoughts there was variety and distinction, as if there had been severall hearts, and yet most strangely and unexpressibly complicated or folded up in unity. I clearly saw distinction, diversity, variety, and as clearly saw all swallowed up into unity.[58]

The vision then develops in successive layers, each one of which presents new vision, just as in biblical prophecy. What is more, as the vision proceeds so Coppe's perceptions alter, until he reaches an ultimate state of consciousness. In the presence of the divine, he is seeing *through* its eye, rather than *with* his own. Before this vision Coppe had returned to the womb, 'the bowels of the still Eternity', where he had heard a voice promising salvation after visions of both hell and eternity, and after the latter, Coppe hears the voice again interpreting his vision of diversity in oneness: '*The spirits of just men made perfect*' (*CRW*, p. 83).

In George Foster's two pamphlets the divine presence in his body is rendered in just as somatically painful terms, though, unlike Coppe, the propensity for the vision itself to range beyond the image is not so pronounced. Where Coppe is 'utterly plagued, damned, rammed and sunke into nothing' (*CRW*, p. 82), Foster achieves a self-posturing in his vision, an active dialogue with God which seems analogous to dialogues in biblical dreams between subject and the dream interpreter who appears in the dream. In *The Sounding of the Last Trumpet* (1650) vision and possession are closely and causally connected, so that each validates the authority of the other: having seen the recurring vision of the army being routed, Foster hears a voice which tells him he shall be afflicted with a shaking fit which is as violent as the vision of the rout: 'in a very little while *I* was taken so; and *I* desired my brother that lay with me, to lie upon me, and so he did, to try whether I should then shake, and I did tater him up and down and shake so much' (p. 22). The figure of symbolic gesture is again apparent, connected with the Hebrew notion

[57] Ibid.   [58] Ibid.

that the prophet can be so touched by the future that his actions are affected by this knowledge.[59] Just so, Anna Trapnel passed into trances where she shook, trembled, and spoke with a 'lownesse of her voice', as the spirit, she said, descended into her 'center' to produce the 'rapture'.[60]

The purpose of Foster's fit is a kind of purgation, the 'tearing of proud flesh', a cauterizing of the outer man. Moreover, the sequence vision-fit can occur in the opposite order, so after more fits, Foster sees further symbolic representations:

Four black horses all in harnesse, drawing and tugging as if they had bin in a cart that was set, and strived harder then ordinary to get out: And *I* said Lord, what is the meaning of this (sighing and groaning until *I* had an answer) and I was answered, that these do represent the powers of the world that do oppose God in his people, & all powers that they are now ready to be drawn in pieces.[61]

Like Daniel, Ezekiel, and Coppe, Foster has a voice within his vision to interpret it, though this time the subject's presence is even more active since he actually asks the meaning of the vision. As becomes apparent, the dialogue with God is continuous throughout the pamphlet, and the sense of personal disruption, of living through the fit, is placed within the visionary sequence by the constant interruption of 'I's. Like Ezekiel, John, and Coppe, Foster eats when the angel gives to him, while singing greets the appearance of the Lord. The similarity of the vision with Coppe's is indeed striking, especially the simple vision of eternity. Foster hears an unceasing roaring torrent, and sees:

A company of men and women standing upon *Sion*, having harpes, and made musick; and then came some others and they danced; and there was one more glorious then the rest in the midst of them. And I beheld till he that was in the midst of them did go into them all and they became as one.[62]

---

[59] Lods, *The Prophets*, p. 216.   [60] Trapnel, *The Cry of a Stone*, p. 58.
[61] *The Sounding of the Last Trumpet* (1650), 5.
[62] Ibid. 6. Similar to Foster's visions and meetings with angels are those in Joshua Garment's *The Hebrews Deliverance at Hand* (1651). Garment was a follower of John Robins and the only one of this group of Ranters to leave an authentic personal record.

IV

These dreams and visions have contexts which are evidently more than just personal. The dreams in confessions of 'experience' which we looked at first were collected and published so as to enhance the spiritual confidence of particular congregations. The heavily stylized prophetic visions were designed to bolster the authority of the writer as much as to speak a particular truth. The next stage was to have visions referring directly to events in the world of public events. Foster, for instance, communicates political comment direct through his visions. The recurrent vision in *The Sounding of the Last Trumpet* is one of the New Model Army being defeated and routed for its selfish and 'fleshly' behaviour: 'as soon as I saw the Army routed, and the General slaine, I cryed out, they are now cut downe' (p. 11). Where Coppe shouts with a prophetic voice to 'have all things in common',[63] Foster, in *The Pouring Forth of the Seventh and Last Viall* (1650), presents visions in which he has seen such behaviour prefigured:

I saw in a vision a man giving away his money to another, and also giving away food to feed him, and cloth to cloath him. And I heard a voice say, this man lends unto the Lord, that man that feeds the hungry and cloaths the naked, lends unto the Lord. (p. 1)

Dr Capp describes this type of revelation as 'transparent' as if to imply that the political or moral statement in the dream or vision did not really happen.[64] It is merely placed inside the vision in order to give it divine sanction. We do not have sufficient evidence to tell whether these dreams and visions really happened or not, except that they were reported in considerable quantity, and have certain common characteristics which cannot be attributed simply to literary convention or proselytizing cynicism. It seems reasonable to argue that, in the millennial milieu of the late 1640s and 1650s, it was possible for prophetic writers to take their public concerns into their dreams and visions, experience revelations connected with the public context, and then to use that experience as a manifestation of their role in the millennial movement.

---

[63] *A Second Fiery Flying Roule* (1649) in *CRW*, pp. 112–13.
[64] Capp, *The Fifth Monarchy Men*, p. 186.

The most important case here is that of Anna Trapnel. Stranded in the field of bulls in *The Cry of a Stone*, Trapnel is under threat from the New Model Army, and her immediate danger comes from a familiar figure:

I saw great darkness in the Earth, and marvellous dust, like a thick smoke descending upward from the Earth; and I beheld at a little distance a great company of Cattel, some like Buls, and others like Oxen, and so lesser, their faces and heads like men, having each of them a horn on either side their heads; for the foremost, his countenance was perfectly like unto *Oliver Cromwels*; and on a suddain there was a great shout of those that followed him, he being singled out alone. (p. 13)[65]

The bulls give a suitably rousing chorus of cheering support for the bovine Oliver who then charges at Anna. This vision became an important witness to the verity of the Fifth Monarchist cause. It is repeated in part in another Trapnel pamphlet, *Strange and Wonderful Newes from White-hall* (1654), and in *A Legacy for Saints* (1654) she refers to it as a reflection of the struggle between Fifth Monarchists and Parliament: 'I have now Related, that you may take notice of the horns running at my breast' (p. 57). Notice that she uses exactly the same phrase as she had done some time earlier, consistently presenting herself as the inspired prophetess impaled upon the weapons of a brutal and vindictive enemy. So subversive and contentious was this vision that it was read aloud at her trial as a major piece of evidence against her.[66]

How much of this hypostatized repetition is *scriptura rediviva* is made clear in Trapnel's treatment of the symbolic qualities of horns. The first section of *Strange and Wonderful Newes from White-hall* is a vision which is modelled on the horns in Daniel, more precisely than that in *The Cry of a Stone*. The concern was widespread among the radicals. Mary Cary, for instance, in *The Little Horn's Doom and Downfall* (1651) related the prophecy of the little horn in Dan. 7: 8 to the event of the 1640s and 1650s. Anna Trapnel's vision is distinguished by the symbolic qualities of the four horns which appear to her. The first horn, identified as the

---

[65] The biblical origin here is Ps. 22: 12. In the same pamphlet Trapnel envisages Cromwell as Gideon (p. 6). The apocalyptic hieroglyphs at the end of the astrologer William Lilly's *Monarchy or no Monarchy* (1651), 2nd series, 1–23, feature one woodcut of a rampant bull in a field. It is entirely possible that Trapnel saw this work. For further dreams which feature the Protector, see Alan Macfarlane, *The Family Life of Ralph Josselin* (Cambridge, 1970), 91, 186.

[66] *A Legacy for Saints*, p. 56. See also *Anna Trapnel's Report and Plea* (1654), 25.

Bishops, is broken, and the second would appear to be the King, for the horn had joined to it 'an head, and although it seemed to bee more white than the first, yet it endeavoring to get aloft it was suddenly pulled down and broken to pieces'. The third horn had 'many splinters joyned to it, like the skales of a fish, and this was presented to be a Parl, consisting of many men, having fair and plausible pretences of love', though it 'scatters' with its diversity. Finally the fourth horn appears, pointing at Cromwell as the prelude to the Apocalypse, as it 'was very short, but very sharp, and full of variety of colours sparkling, red and white, and it said to her, that this last *horn* was different from the other three, because of great proud and swelling words, and great promises of kindness'.[67]

The balance between divine authority and political commentary is always finely kept. Trapnel claims that her visions are 'Scripture' which 'came in with a very great strength in the middest of Divine contemplation', and 'these Scripture languages were spoken to me in the spirit'.[68] In yet another vision she sees troops trying to ignite a 'white Tower', in which the Saints dwell, and the interpreting presence of the 'Scripture' relates this to Babel, and to Psalms and Proverbs', '*The Name of the Lord is a Strong Tower*, wherein those factious ones, as they called them, sat in safety, and shall be preserved all their days.'[69] In fact, Trapnel is conflating two contradictory stories, since Babel is to be destroyed, its languages 'confounded', though God protects those in the Tower of Strength. Similarly, George Foster's vision of union between God and man is rooted in the old allegorical reading of the Song of Solomon, which he envisages dramatically as a woman dressed in white, whom he sees carried around a room and then placed in the centre of it, and elevated, by a man.[70]

All of this raises the question of how these dreams and visions were interpreted in the seventeenth century. There is little doubt that those who wanted to believe in them, for what they prophesied and for the basic assurance of the divine presence, did so. John Rogers was in no doubt what happened when a

[67] *Strange and Wonderful Newes from White-hall* (1654), 4–5.
[68] *A Legacy for Saints*, pp. 27–8.
[69] *The Cry of a Stone*, p. 12. See Gen. 11: 4–10; Ps. 61: 3; Prov. 18: 10.
[70] Foster, *The Sounding of the Last Trumpet* (1650), 40–1.

person was visited with a '*dream* and *vision*', for it is taken up and arrested by 'the *intellectuall* and *cognoscitive faculties* of their *soules*', an assertion which mirrors that of Goodwin on Paul: 'His visions were not to the ocular part of his body, but to the intellectual part of his mind.'[71] As has been shown, following the example of the Bible, the radical dreams tend to contain their own interpretation. For dream theorists this feature is accepted without question, so that Thomas Tryon sees dreams as 'Forms and Figures represented, with the *Interpretations* thereof'.[72] Browne feels that there need not be an interpreter, so that representation and interpretation become the same symbolic function:

Many dreames are made out by sagacious exposition & from the signature of their subjects: carrying their interpretation in their fundamentall sence and mysteries of similitude, whereby hee that understands what naturall fundamentall every notionall dependeth, may by sumbolicall adaptation hold a readie way to read the characters of Morpheus.[73]

The same opinion is voiced by the millenarian Arise Evans, though in a simpler way: '*These Visions I had the last Somer . . . are so plaine . . . that they need no interpretation.*'[74]

Evans's dreams themselves, as a consequence of this attitude, combine a recounting of the dream images with direct political observation. In one version they are a continuation of Evans's political life as he would like to see it. Without an apparent oneiric distortion Evans dreams that he finds himself in a room with Cromwell, and admonishes the Lord Protector for executing Charles I. Cromwell retires to cry in guilt for his sinful act. In *The great and Bloody Visions* (1653) Evans combines a series of dreamlike symbols, which resemble the elements of popular political prophecies, in a bizarre narrative which was reported to him by one John Farly. Initially there is a sexual innuendo connotative of temptation: a woman appears in a coach and the subject is asked by a man on horseback, 'How do you like her?' Then six youths appear in blue caps and beside them an image of the moon hanging on a sign, with a spot of blood on it. Following this, two men appear with candles, one of whom says, 'I thank

---

[71] Rogers, *Ohel*, pp. 449–50; Goodwin, *The Mystery of Dreames*, p. 266.
[72] *A Treatise of Dreams and Visions*, p. 43.
[73] 'On Dreams', in *The Major Works*, ed. C. A. Patrides (1974), 475–9 (esp. 476).
[74] *The Euroclydon Winde Commanded to Cease* (1653), 10.

you all for beholding the same.' Then a chariot appears, pulled by white horses, and surrounded by fire and sparks. At this, the subject runs in fear of the chariot's heat. He sees another chariot and flies down a street, thinking he is free, but then he meets a man with a torch in his hand. The subject thinks it is doomsday and falls to the ground.

The man is an angelic visitor, it would seem, for he blows into the subject's ear and says that the subject must be bathed in Christ's blood in order to be saved. He then appears naked and washed in blood, and runs into a temple-like building whose columns are smeared with blood. He tries to escape, but is surrounded by many bladders, all of which disappear, except for three, one great one and two 'pots', at which point the voice the subject has heard before says, 'there will not be left the worth of a half-peny remaining of all this sight'. The subject wakes up, then falls into another 'trance' where he sees himself in a field of newly sown wheat, where there is a circle of doves with an exceedingly bright dove in the middle of them.[75]

Evans's admonishment of Cromwell is a dream which is similar to the soteriological dreams analysed earlier in this chapter. The obscure symbols in *The great and Bloody Visions* operate in rather different ways. They 'need no interpretation' because on one level they are clearly connotative of an apocalyptic experience. The moon with the spot of blood is transposed from the Biblical passages where the moon turns to blood as part of the apocalyptic process (Joel 2: 13; Acts 2: 20; Rev. 6: 12). The two men with candles are the two witnesses from Rev. 11: 3–4, the chariot is a version of the vision in Rev. 6: 2. The angelic figure refers to the appearance of the son of man in Rev. 1: 13, while the torch appears to be based upon the

---

[75] *The great and Bloody Visions* (1653), 3–5. In 'The Case of Arise Evans', *Psychological Medicine*, 6 (1976), 351–8, Christopher Hill and Michael Shepherd argue that the accounts which Evans gives of his visions prior to 1640 and the way in which he was treated by others then indicate that he was suffering from an 'atypical mental psychosis of a revelatory' nature, characterized by the expression of autochthonous ideas. After 1640, however, Evans's visions become more closely related to millennial ideas and images, while the millennial atmosphere in society meant that he was not taken for an insane person. Indeed, as has been seen, Evans took to collecting and publishing other prophetic visions. However, given that Evans did continue to experience visions into the 1660s, the article does not sufficiently explain the precise state of Evans's psychology. Even if he was not regarded as an insane person, the nature of his post-1640 visions remain largely uncharacterized, except in so far as they are seen to be relevant to the political situation.

chariots of Nahum 2: 3, which refers back to the previous vision. The bladders in the temple refer to the ceremony of the purification of the Jews (John 2: 6), analogous to the subject's own sanctification, though they are conflated with the image of sacrifice and apocalypse (the latter from Joel 2: 30, so that the columns in the temple are as pillars of smoke). The doves are the sign of grace, and the astrologer William Lilly's symbols at the end of *Monarchy or no Monarchy* (1651) similarly feature several flying doves just before the symbol denoting eternal salvation.

This, however, is not the interpretation given by Evans. Rather, Evans employs his own art of oneiromancy (divination through dreams), Browne's 'sumbolicall adaptation', to decipher the dream.[76] So, the woman in the coach symbolizes, according to Evans, an enemy passing by, and the moon, a star, which is a sign that the enemy will vanish. The interpretation of the chariot and the pots is where Evans's own particular apocalypticism takes full control. In his own words, the chariot is 'a violent interest to be set up, so that all will in that day be forced to shut up their shop windows and doors for fear'.[77] Similarly the two pots represent three men who will shortly come to power, before the final arrival of the Millennium, symbolized by the doves in the field. The potential is certainly present then, for a dream or vision sequence to be interpreted as an admonition of final days and Second Coming, though the actual reporting of the sequence is largely obscure, which itself is part of the biblical prophetic tradition of leaving a prophecy veiled in half-light. Evans treats the vision sequence as a second Scripture to be interpreted allegorically.

It is possible, however, to show that the dreams and visions were controlled by the people who experienced and reported, not just for the sake of a millennial or political end, but for the sake of ordering or explaining a continuous spiritual experience. Here, the two major terms used by modern dream theorists to explain this type of manipulation, wish-fulfilment and censorship, both of which are interconnected, are useful. The exercise is not anachronistic. Wish-fulfilment was familiar to seventeenth-century people in the analogy from Isa. 29: 8, where the hungry

[76] Browne, 'On Dreams', p. 476.
[77] Evans, *The great and Bloody Visions*, p. 5.

man dreams that he eats, but wakes up still hungry. Second, the notion that people suppress information when they dream is present, as Tony Tanner has suggested, in Milton.[78] In *Areopagitica* Milton claims that Jerome must have been 'whipt' by the devil or deluded by a 'fantasm bred by the feaver which had then seis'd him' for reading Cicero.[79] If it was an angel, says Milton, then Jerome would have been chided merely for the vanity of florid writing, rather than Cicero's subject-matter. As 'phantasm' or devil, it is Jerome registering his own guilt for reading Cicero. Milton's explanation is still linked inextricably to the supernatural, but he does admit that an individual could deceive himself by subconscious self-censorship.

During the long process of his conversion John Rogers experienced the recurrent dream of seeing his father's coach-house on fire. He is unable to interpret it, though a friend offers an interpretation:

Dr. *Draiton* D.D. he declared to me, for *severall reasons*, that this must be more then a *meer dream*, as *working of fancy*, and that something was to *come* which I should finde this to *predemonstrate*, instancing in some of the *like kinde* which himselfe, his wife, and others had met with as *warnings* and *predictions*; and therefore he *wished* me in no case to *slight* or *contemn* it; for that he was confident it did show some *fiery* and *angry* dispensation upon all our *family* and my *father*, and the *rest* should lye under some *trouble* by the *times* or otherwise; and my self should be set *free*, and at this liberty to *pray* for them, and that by *degrees* they should be *recovered* and *brought* out, and the fire *abate*: which interpretation . . . is for the most part *verified* at this day.[80]

Some years after this interpretation Rogers dreams that on the way to his father's house he passes a beautiful house on a path which he feels to be correct for his salvation. The house is in a beam, which Rogers avoids because he knows the beam represents false opinions, while the house (which is on his left side) represents the glory of the great ones of the world. Once past the house, he is approached by men who accuse him of setting fire to the house and who arrest him. This dream repeats itself word for word. The repetition suggests Rogers's continuing

---

[78] 'License and Licensing: To the Presse or to the Spunge', *JHI* 38 (1977), 3–18.

[79] In *Selected Prose*, ed. C. A. Patrides (1974), 210.

[80] Rogers, '*further* Experience *of* John Rogers', in *Ohel*, p. 425. Thomas Drayton, together with Robert Gell and William Parker, were known as perfectionists: see *Conway Letters*, ed. M. H. Nicolson (New York, 1930), 109, 275, 280 n., 350 n.

fear of his father's hold over him, and guilt that his family is endangered, though the beautiful house catching fire suggests his own desire and the fear that he may lose salvation or endanger his family.[81] Once Rogers has a rational intepretation of his original dream, he is seen to refashion the dream according to his own continuing anxieties, and so he is seen to become responsible, in a sense, for his dream and his subconscious.

With the prophetic visions, repetition becomes a question of re-organizing biblical models. In *A Fiery Flying Roll* (1649) Coppe inhabits Ezekiel's waking vision and swallows the Fiery Flying Roll under the imperative to write down and print as much of his inspiration as he possibly can, though the imperative to write is taken from John's inspiration in Rev. 1 (in *CRW*, p. 83). Coppe is using the voice heard in a divine vision to escape from a censorious authority imposed from outside. Coppe has actualized his wish by having God within him, and his intention in *A Fiery Flying Roll* is to exhort people to relinquish their selfishness and guilt, their 'plaguey holiness', effectively to stop censoring themselves, since every action is justified under the auspices of the divine presence within. A similar process of inspiration takes place with William Pennington. Here the model is John. In sleep Pennington dreams of a 'glorious sight' and hears a voice saying 'Pen my son pen.' Then he sees an angel at the top of some stairs who blows a vision of London undergoing the apocalypse into his ear.[82] The actualization of fulfilled wish, as prophecy, is self-reflexive and self-authorizing: the pamphlet itself is the record of the command to write the pamphlet in the first place.

Still, for the religious radicals, dreams were not so much to be interpreted for their imagistic and narrative content as for their capacity to resemble, in a verbal way, scriptural passages. In *Some Sweet Sips, of some Spirituall Wine* Coppe's interpretation of Mrs T.P.'s dream is made in terms which are entirely different from the dream itself. Coppe relates the simple fact that there has been a divinely inspired dream to his own spiritual typology, so addressing T.P.: 'I know you are a *Vessel* of the *Lords House*.'[83] Coppe then takes T.P.'s descriptive language and matches it with the relevant biblical passage. The picture in the dream of

---

[81] *Conway Letters*, pp. 435–6.
[82] Arise Evans, *Mr. Evans and Mr. Pennington's Prophesie* (1655), 1. In the same vision, London is vanquished by smallpox.   [83] *CRW*, p. 66.

the animals 'recreating' themselves is related to Rom. 9: 19–24, reflecting Coppe's concern with spiritual regeneration. 'Recreation' is equivalent to regeneration and to salvation. The myth of the serpent in the Bible is next stressed, so that the reptiles in the dream are equated with the idea of the serpent or worm within man, which is to be slain and replaced by the inner presence of God. The communion with the animals, far from being a pantheistic union, is seen by Coppe as an allegorical representation of the neutralization of evil:

Serpents stings shall be pulled out, are they not? We shall *beare* them in our *Bosomes*; Doe we not? And they shall not sting us; Doe they? . . . *Lions in us*, . . . but they are as *tame*, as if they were dead; Dead they are, and a honey-combe in their carkasse.[84]

The river takes on much stronger associations (in Coppe's mind) of a universal stream of perfected life, as the '*chiefest good*' and the '*Fountaine of Life*', and indeed, it is identified with God, 'in *Him* (*the river*) *all things consist*'.[85] The river is a symbol of that pure spiritual life which is to be obtained when 'forms' are abandoned.

At the same time Coppe authorizes his ability to speak about T.P.'s dream in this way by referring to his divine inspiration. Like Evans he does not seem to be conscious of interpreting the dream. Rather, he amplifies T.P., calling on the images of classical pastoral, 'I am your eccho, in that which followeth in your Letter', yet Coppe mixes this with his own continuing inspiration: 'I heare a voyce from heaven, saying to me, *write*; *Blessed* are the dead, which thus *die in the Lord*'.[86] Though T.P.'s dream narrative has been considerably broken up so that in Coppe's analysis it little resembles the original sequence, Coppe has succeeded in imposing his own highly spiritualist exegesis. The force with which he does it suggests that his followers would not necessarily have disagreed with him.

The resemblance which Coppe sees between dream and Scripture is nevertheless imagistic. For Coppe, T.P.'s vision of union with nature recalls Deut. 11: 10, 11: 'a *land* of hills and valleys, and drinketh water of the *raine* of *heaven*'.[87] In Coppe's view it is an allegory of spiritual liberty, which is what T.P. said

---

[84] Ibid. 70.   [85] Ibid. 70–2.   [86] Ibid. 66.   [87] Ibid. 68.

it was; though she did not go to these lengths to elaborate it. Like Anna Trapnel, Coppe sees dream images and narrative as a form of Scripture, correspondences for which can be found in the Bible itself. However, Trapnel and Coppe both regard dream language as connotative, unlike the mantic and mysterious symbols in the Book of Daniel. The correspondence between dream and Scripture seems to enhance Coppe's sense of enlightenment so that he begins to participate in the dream-Scripture interpretation he has created. This results in affective devices which appeal to the outward senses as figures for the inner spiritual: the song motif returns and the speaker participates in consuming the produce of the valleys: 'Drink, oh friends; yea, drinke abundantly oh beloved! it is lively wine, liquor of life, it will make the lame man leap like a Hart, causing the lips of those that are asleep to speak; for it is the *New Wine* in the *Kingdom* . . . good wine, the best wine, of the *best Vine*.'[88] We are witnessing a form of prophesying upon this second Scripture of dream. The same type of rapture is typical also of Anna Trapnel, though she places vision language automatically inside her exhortation:

Oh how glittering, how glorious are they: what Sparklings are there!— Thou hast a great Gust to come upon the Earth, a great wind that shal shake the trees that now appear upon the Earth, that are full of the leaves of Profession; but they have nothing but outward beauty, or outward flourish; but thy Trees O Lord, they are full of Sap.[89]

To summarize, the dreams and visions which have been examined here were, for the radicals, genuine intimations of the proximity of the divine. The dreams mirror social contexts and make the constant presence of God, in the millennial sense, more apparent, especially with the soteriological episodes. The dreams and visions are important in affirming the purpose of congregation or sect. If we accept these phenomena as experiences which are faithfully reported by the individuals, then we are defining cases of subconsciously generated sectarian propaganda. The visions which fall within the wider sphere of prophetic behaviour constitute stylistic imitations of biblical prophetic visions. Such imitations seem genuine rather than contrived not only in the detail of the recounting, but also in the capacity of prophetic possession to disrupt the sectarians' own sense of conceptualiza-

---

[88] *CRW*, p. 69.   [89] *The Cry of a Stone*, p. 17.

tion. Likewise the radical interpretation of the dream tends to reduce oneiric images and actions to phrases and verbal echoes which correspond to a scriptural original, so that the final emphasis is upon the divine voice or style, a presence active in the individual, and one which is sometimes most perceivable during sleep.

II
The Culture of Illumination

3

The Translations of John Everard and Giles Randall: *Theologia Germanica* Sebastian Franck, Nicholas of Cusa, and Benet of Canfield

I

FOR many years a body of writings mostly with continental origins, pre-, post-, and Counter-Reformation, and concerned with personal illumination, has been acknowledged as a significant component in English seventeenth-century devotion, though never as an interconnected whole.[1] These writings may be described as mystical, Neoplatonic, and occult: they taught illumination either through the attainment of personal union with the Godhead, or through a superior insight into the created world. The following three chapters are concerned with the nature of three major groups of these writings and their influence upon or significance for English radical religious writers.

Since the Reformation, mystical and occult texts had worried more orthodox Protestants and Puritans for two main reasons. First, they encouraged claims of personal perfection upon earth to the extent that individuals could claim to be deified or to be in a state very close to this. However quietistic any individual mystic might be, the theological and social subversion inherent in such notions was evident to some, especially if these ideas reached the unlearned. Second, these illuminist ideas had their origins in a form of scriptural interpretation which elevated the power of the spirit in the individual over the letter of the scriptural text as a witness to divine truth. The result was manifold, including the elaboration of personal allegories which mythologized biblical episodes, forms of ecstatic inspiration, mystical sublimity, and a sceptical criticism of Biblical texts themselves, all of which are features of the European radical

---

[1] See R. M. Jones, *Spiritual Reformers in the Sixteenth and Seventeenth Centuries* (New York, 1914), 208–339.

Reformation, as much as they are the characteristics of English radical religion in the 1640s and 1650s.

The heresiographers of the 1640s and 1650s were fond of seeing similarities between the heretics of Luther and Calvin's time and the sectarians they sought to vilify, to such an extent that some heresiographers, especially Samuel Rutherford, attempted to show how the roots of English religious radicalism lay in earlier German heresy.[2] Such a stance is an over-statement, since the capacity for extreme opinions regarding perfection and scriptural interpretation to develop autonomously through Scripture reading and separately from any particular tradition was as sure as was the case with ideas of church government. However, it would be equally wrong to deny the importance of such a tradition or to dismiss it as a dim, numerically insignificant corner of a much more important native field. Even when due significance is attached, the continental writings are often grouped together as a whole without any investigation into the different components and the specific make-up and appeal of any one text or author.[3]

It is the case that a body of mystical and occult writings were translated into English (usually, though not always, by Englishmen) and made available by a number of publishers many of whom were radicals or were connected with radical religious groups, like Benjamin Allen, Giles Calvert, John Sweeting, and George Whittington. Few would deny the significance of the book in the dissemination of ideas since the Reformation across the complete spectrum of the social scale. What is not sufficiently acknowledged at present is the way in which the mystical and the occult could appeal in different ways to groups and individuals involved in different kinds of activity. The writings of Cornelius Agrippa could appeal as a source for speculation to a contemplative alchemist, or as a revelation of internal apocalypse and regeneration to an enthusiast. Several radical Puritans fall into both categories. At the same time the authorities were well aware

---

[2] Rutherford, *A Survey of the Spirituall Antichrist*, 2 parts (1648), ii. 1–4, 161–74.

[3] See e.g. William Haller (ed.), *Tracts on Liberty in the Puritan Revolution, 1638–47*, 3 vols. (New York, 1934), i. p. 43; id., *The Rise of Puritanism* (New York, 1938), 207–12; Murray Tolmie, *The Triumph of the Saints: The Separate Churches of London, 1616–1649* (Cambridge, 1977), 34. For the European perspective, see Leszek Kolakowski, *Chrétiens sans Église. La conscience religieuse et le lien confessionnel au XVIIe siècle* (Paris, 1969), esp. 31–55, 615–24.

of the association of some texts with radical religious movements themselves. Many radicals (not just the Quakers) who used mystical writings and who were persecuted or examined by episcopal or Commonwealth authorities became apparent quietists during the rather different context of the Restoration, though they continued to disseminate this writing at home and abroad. In this way, radical religion played its role in a much more general and rich European intellectual tradition, though its roots lay firmly in the activities of the 1640s and 1650s.

In the middle twenty years of the century in particular a ripe context existed, especially in London, for the dissemination of the continental mystical and occult tradition. The widespread interest drawn by the self-proclaimed prophet Matthew Coker is a testimony to the popularity of perfectionism and spirituality in the Interregnum.[4] This was made possible by the intimate connections between learned perfectionists, who may not have had any radical religious bent, and unlearned or self-taught sectarians and separatists. John Perrot's eventual despair of Boehme is a characteristic representation of the interaction of mystical literature, separatist treatises and authentic spiritual inspiration in the individual: 'God appeared *brighter* by *Behman* and *Brown*; but they which built their *Travels* as *Towers*, the LORD *confounded* with many *Languages*, and even running up to the height, *Baptists*, *Seekers*, and *Ranters*, some made *bounds* for the *pure*, and others in their *lusts* revolted.'[5] This milieu did not only constitute itself in private meetings, or through connections between publishers, printers, and authors: traces of the mystical and the occult may be found in gathered churches even of the less extreme variety. It would not be true to say that the English radicals were reproducing in their own work the precise sentiments of the continental mystics and spiritualists, but they were not averse to the idea of a spiritual and devotional process employed as a means of attaining illumination. Where necessary, the radicals forgot the dogmatic parts of Catholic spiritual writings, and the sections concerned with the outward life.

The result was, in the writings themselves and the manner of their translation into English, a modification of the affective and

[4] See *Conway Letters*, ed. M. H. Nicolson (New York, 1930), 98–101, 103–4.

[5] Perrot, *Battering Rams against Rome* (1661), 11–12; see also William Bayly, *A Collection of the Several Wrightings of . . .* (1676), sig. D1ʳ. This quotation also reveals that Perrot was familiar with the works of Sir Thomas Browne.

expressive capacity of the English language itself. Also, in some cases, native writings can be shown to have incorporated continental vocabularies and concepts into their own forms of rhetoric and argument. In some cases, such as the writings of the Familist leader, Hendrik Niclaes, it was the texts themselves which guaranteed the survival of an earlier sectarian tradition, one which was to be modified in the context of the Interregnum.

II

A considerable amount of energy has been expended on the study of the elusive figure of John Everard (?1582–1640).[6] Though he played no part in the establishment of the separatist churches in London during the second, third, and fourth decades of the seventeenth century—indeed, he did not condone separation— he was a prolific preacher of radical and popular Puritan sermons, and was seldom free from persecution by the Jacobean and Laudian authorities. He spent the 1620s sheltering with the aristocratic circle surrounding the Earls of Holland and Mul- grave at Holland Park, near Kensington, and combined a formidable scholarly talent with the desire to invigorate and inspire with Godly language *'Tinkers, Coblers, Weavers, Poor sleight Fellows'*.[7] An earlier commentator over-enthusiastically described him as the combination of a Rosicrucian, an Anabaptist, and a Jesuit![8]

Everard left behind him scattered official references to his persecution, a string of translations which reveal the way in which he constructed his own individual theology and epistem- ology, and a collection of his sermons, published posthumously in 1653 as *Some Gospel-Treasures Opened* and in 1657 as *The Gospel- Treasury Opened*.[9] Because of his interests in natural philosophy and Hermetic texts, Everard was known personally to several men of learning, including Elias Ashmole and Oliver Hill, fellow of St John's College, Oxford. In the light of these connections, his

---

[6] The best biography to date is Paul R. Hunt's 'John Everard: A Study in his Life, Thought and Preaching' (Ph.D. diss., University of California, 1977).

[7] Everard, *The Gospel-Treasury Opened*, 2 parts (1657, 2nd edn., 1659), i. 86. For Everard's incumbencies in Dorset and Essex during these years, see *DNB* and *BDBR*.

[8] Theodor Sippell, *Werdendes Quäkertum* (Stuttgart, 1937), 5.

[9] The change of title was possibly to avoid a clash with Bunyan's first work, his attack on the Quakers, *Some Gospel-Truths Opened* (1656).

noble patronage, and the fact that some of his congregation seem to have been essentially well-to-do London merchants, Paul R. Hunt has argued that Everard's alleged connection with radical sectaries is wrong and based upon faulty hearsay, and the distorted memory of Everard's biographer, Rapha Harford, who was writing thirteen years after Everard's death.[10] Hunt, however, is referring to Everard's congregation when he was lecturer at St Martin-in-the-Fields, and not to the later period, after Everard had been deprived of this post. Everard was then appointed to the lectureship at St Mary Abbot's, Kensington, under Holland's patronage, some time between 1624 and 1628. What is significant here is that a confession made by one Giles Creech before Laud's Ecclesiastical Commission Court in 1635 has several interjections by Sir John Lambe, who was in charge of the commission, five of which link Everard with the sectarian underworld which the confession describes.[11] No doubt much of Creech's statement and Lambe's comments are exaggeration, as is much heresiography of the period. Still, the picture which Lambe gives is made credible by the fact that many of the characters mentioned turn up as later associates of spiritual and Antinomian religion and by the fact that Harford's account partly agree with Lambe's.

Everard, then, was known to many sections of London society, noble, middle-class, artisan, Puritan, and sectarian. His best friends seem to have been those who shared his interests in theology and natural philosophy, and who were also radicals, like John Webster, and the Independent minister Thomas Brooks, both of whom contributed dedications to Everard's collected sermons.

Everard was a member of Clare College, Cambridge, for many years, and it is here that he took his doctorate. His first published work did not appear until 1618. Entitled *The Arriereban*, it is the printed version of a sermon, preached at St Martin-in-the-Fields before the Military Company of the City of London, which arrogantly and provocatively attacks James I's foreign policy, in the name of the unity of Protestant Europe. Its immense learning (Harford was later to call Everard '*Super-Excellent, Super-Eminent*'

[10] Hunt, 'John Everard', pp. 20–7.
[11] Paul S. Seaver, *The Puritan Lectureships: The Politics of Religious Dissent, 1560–1662* (Stanford, 1970), 232; *CSPD* dxx (1648–49), 425–7.

in this respect) is coupled with a figurative reading of scriptural passages, in agreement with the aims of radical Protestant foreign policy at this time.[12] Calling upon Seneca's *Epistle* 89: 2 to facilitate a clear understanding of the Bible, *dividi in partes, non in frusta concidi utile arbitror* (p. 5), Everard proceeds to interpret biblical 'similitudes' and 'symbols'. Thus the horses in Jer. 4: 13 are seen as a synecdoche for an army of men, with the literal implication that these are the armies of Protestant Europe sweeping away Anti-Christ, driven by the power of the Lord, 'his chariots shall be as a whirlwind: his horses are swifter than eagles. Woe unto us! for we are spoiled' (Authorized Version). Everard says that such phrases are the 'forest of proverbs' which he has turned to in a time of need, away from the sweet 'tones and raptures' of the Song of Solomon, which *The Arriereban* initially contemplates (p. 2), an ironic statement given his later recourse to mysticism in the face of persecution. Everard's demand for clear, concise divisions is also an open attack upon the metaphysical complexities of Andrewes's and Donne's sermons, upon a sensibility which allowed the Scriptures to be interpreted not so much by the spirit within the individual as by individual ingenuity.

In reply to *The Arriereban* and other sermons which were not published, James I had Everard imprisoned periodically during the first half of the 1620s. By repute he threatened to make Everard Dr 'Never-out'.[13] Throughout the 1620s Everard lived and preached as a partial fugitive in London.[14] Until 1628 his sermons largely bore the traits of orthodox Puritan soteriology as well as the constant attacks upon pro-Spanish foreign policy.[15] In that year, however, Everard translated the *Theologia Germanica*, which increased the mystical component in his own outlook.[16] In no sense, however, did Everard withdraw from the public forum. Indeed, the manuscript circulation of the *Theologia* merely increased the ire of the Ecclesiastical Commissioners in the

[12] Harford, 'TO THE READER of Dr. *Everards* SERMONS' in Everard, *The Gospel-Treasury Opened*, sig. A4ᵛ. See S. L. Adams, 'The Protestant Cause: Religious Alliance with West European Calvinist Communities a Political Issue in England, 1585–1630. (D.Phil. thesis, University of Oxford, 1972), esp. App. III, 'Thomas Scot Bohemian Propaganda', 448–62.   [13] Harford, 'To the Reader', sig. c6ᵛ.
[14] Ibid., sigs. c6ᵛ–c7ʳ.   [15] See Hunt, 'John Everard', pp 116, 183–4.
[16] The Cambridge MS translation is dated 1628, though the manuscript in which it occurs is dated 1638.

1630s. On 10 October Everard was brought before the Commissioners' court at Lambeth. He was accused of several heretical opinions and of being a Familist. Everard was not a Familist, though his opinions led his prosecutors to make the connection, such were the confessions obtained by Laud's men during the 1630s.[17] Everard did not believe in the earthly perfectibility of man, which was held to be one Familist tenet, though he may have known religious radicals who did profess this.[18] He was accused of pantheism, based upon the notion that God was inside everything: 'The same in a bedpost, stickes, Stones, & Trees, adding that the Creature is nothing but God cloathed with accidents.'[19] It would be more accurate to say that Everard held that the *spirit* of God was inside everything, which, incidentally, is what most perfectionists in the 1630s and after would have believed. Nevertheless, there are other accusations which are confirmed in the translations and in the sermons. He is held to affirm that there is no resurrection and that, after the Day of Judgement (according to Pseudo-Dionysius), all things shall be turned into God as they were before the Creation.[20] This is compounded with genuine Familist elements. God is the author of sin and thus of the Fall of Adam; hell is not eternal, but a state experienced within the individual on earth, while all 'Creatures are but the second person in Trinity, & that their sufferings are as satisfactory as Christ on ye Crosse.'[21]

Above all, it is Everard's translations which are felt to be the worst threat:

[17] Christopher Hill discusses the Laudian perspective in *The World Turned Upside Down* (1972), 184–5.

[18] *CSPD* dxx, pp. 425–6 includes a reference to one Morgan, a tidesman and mortalist, for whom Everard obtained employment by supplication to Sir Abraham Dawes. The manuscript also refers to Everard's connection with Harford and Wolston, a scrivener, who wrote for Everard, and who apparently sold mystical translations to these 'poor people'. The same went for one Fisher, a barber in the Old Bailey. Other translations mentioned in the confession are books by the Familist Hendrik Niclaes (see Ch. 4 below) and the '*Rule of Perfection*' by the Capuchin monk, Benet of Canfield (see below pp. 136–43).

[19] Bodl. MS Tanner 67, fo. 143ᵛ. Another copy of this exists in the same manuscript, fos. 187–8. In the sermons (*The Gospel-Treasury Opened*, i, 374) Everard states that creatures are only accidents which hide God, the Abyss, from us. This is properly defined as 'panentheism' where God is immanent in creation and removed above it.

[20] This doctrine, Annihilationism, is discussed in relation to the Family of Love by N. T. Burns, *Christian Mortalism from Tyndale to Milton* (Cambridge, Mass., 1972), 53–5, 82–9.   [21] Bodl. MS Tanner 67, fo. 114ʳ.

That I have both publiquely & privately extolled certaine Pamphlets that goe under the name of Hermes Trismegistus entitled the one Pymander and the other Asclepias, sayeing that the Trismegist was a more Cleere author for the doctrine of the blessed Trinitye then Moses, & have com[m]ended his booke to be reade by such wth whom I have conferred, & Moreover I have extremely magnified a booke entitled *Theologia Germanica*, telling some, that it was the only booke for salvac[i]on which Author I translated into English and p[r]esented it to a great Parsonage of this Kingdome.[22]

Everard did not challenge these charges: he was ordered to publish a recantation, and was fined £1,000. He satisfied neither of these conditions, but managed to remain in hiding. He continued to translate alchemical works and died in 1640, just as the movement, in which he had played no small part when it was under threat, came to fruition.

III

If Hermes and the *Theologia Germanica* are put aside, the list of Everard's surviving translations is still long, including parts of Tauler, Sebastian Franck, Hans Denck, Nicholas of Cusa, and Pseudo-Dionysius. Everard also translated several alchemical works and provided the marginal notes to a translation of a Rosicrucian tract, *The Way to Bliss*, which Elias Ashmole published in 1658.[23] It is necessary to record the way in which these translations appeared, in order to understand the intentions of the translator and eventual publishers with respect to the functions which the works were supposed to perform.

1642 saw the publication of *The Forbidden Fruit*, a translation of Sebastian Franck's *Von dem Baum des Wissens gůts unnd böses*, first published in 1538 by Philipp Urhart at Augsburg. Unlike later publications of spiritual translations, Everard's translation itself appears to have no connection with *The Forbidden Fruit*. Part of Everard's translation lies in manuscript in Cambridge University

---

[22] Bodl. MS Tanner 67, fos. 144ʳ⁻ᵛ. Hunt, 'John Everard', p. 145, argues that Everard only really made translations for his wealthy patrons, who were beyond the reach of direct persecution by the Ecclesiastical Commission. Even if this were the case, it does not take into account the apparent flurry of MSS circulation among the artisans which is largely why Lambe was so interested in Everard.

[23] In *Medicina Magica Tamen Physica: Magical, but Natural Physick* (1656), sig. A4ᵛ, Samuel Boulton suggests that papers heavily influenced by Crollius which he had originally obtained from one M.B. of Kent came from Everard.

Library, MS Dd. 12. 68. It is entitled 'The Tree of Knowledge of Good and Evill And The Tree of Life' and is dated 1638.[24] This translation appears in both editions of Everard's collected sermons, so that it is likely that Everard's publisher, Rapha Harford, used this manuscript or one like it as the copy text for part of the editions. The Cambridge MS also contains three other principal works, one of which is a version of Everard's translation of the *Theologia Germanica*. The others are fragments of Everard's translation of Cusa's *De Visione Dei* and fragments of *The Mystical Divinity* of Pseudo-Dionysius. We cannot be certain whether this manuscript was made for one of his patrons, as other translations were, or whether Everard intended it to circulate among heretical circles, especially Antinomian clergy.[25] However, whatever its origins, the freer conditions which allowed the publication of *The Forbidden Fruit* imply that it should have sold as a popular spiritual manual, not only for convinced Puritan 'spiritualists' but also to spread the word to the public at large.

There are other translations which occur at the end of the collected sermons. Some of these have also survived in manuscript, and they do contain small prefaces by Everard dealing with their origins and their purpose.

Concerning the residence of the spirit within the letter, Everard recommends two passages from Tauler's *Opera* (Cologne, 1548) and one from Denck's last work, a recantation of sorts, entitled *Widderuf*, written just before his death in 1527.[26] All three passages intimate the central point in Everard's theory of interpretation: that the letter of the Scriptures cannot be understood properly until the reader allows the 'mystery' of the spirit to determine the truly divine meaning behind the letters. There is also a striking parallel between the lives of Everard and his German predecessors, especially Denck, and it may be that Everard saw Denck as an exemplary *homo spiritualis*. Like Everard's, Denck's persecution led to a spiritual withdrawal, and a renunciation of any particular sectarian stance. It is thus understandable, though still remarkable, that Everard was able to contain a copy of the *Widderuf*: it was produced in Basel in 1528 in one edition of no more than 500 copies. The tract was

---

[24] The title on fo. 1ᵛ appears as the title page for the Franck extract in both versions of the printed sermons.

[25] Bodl. MS Tanner 67, fos. 144, 188ʳ.

[26] G. H. Williams, *The Radical Reformation* (1962), 179–80.

and is extremely rare, and no copy has survived in a major British library.[27]

More serious and more influential was the *Theologia Germanica* project. Two manuscript copies of Everard's translation have survived. One lies in the Cambridge manuscript already mentioned, and the other in the Folger Library at Washington, MS V. a. 222. The latter would appear to be the copy made for the Earl of Holland.[28] A printed edition first appeared in 1646, and another in 1648, both published by John Sweeting, who is more famous for his editions of poems and plays, including editions of Donne.[29] This edition of the *Theologia*, subtitled a 'Little Golden *Manuall*', seems to have been intended, like *The Forbidden Fruit*, as a popular pious, devotional work, in the vernacular, especially for those who were 'illiterate and unexpert' in German and Latin. The edition was prepared for publication by Giles Randall, apparently a graduate of Lincoln College, Oxford, who had become a radical preacher in London: both Samuel Rutherford and Thomas Edwards refer to him as a leading 'Familist'.[30]

Randall's relationship with Everard has been a subject of some controversy. R. M. Jones assumed that Everard and Randall were friends and collaborators. However, Randall claims that the translator of the *Theologia* is 'to me altogether unknown', and he does not acknowledge Everard in the published translations of Cusa. On the other hand, the 1646 and 1648 editions are connected with the Cambridge MS at least because it contains some of the fragments which occur after the *Theologia* in the Cambridge MS. It is incorrect to say that the manuscripts and the printed edition have no connection, even though it has been established that the printed edition is an entirely different translation from the Cambridge MS (the Folger MS also differs from the Cambridge version).[31] One clue to the mystery seems to lie in Giles Creech's confession with Lambe's interjections:

[27] Denck, *Schriften*, ed. Georg Baring, 3 vols. (Stuttgart, 1955–60), i. 38–40, ii. 87–110.

[28] Hunt, 'John Everard', p. 145; *CSPD*, dxx. p. 425.

[29] H. R. Plomer, *A Dictionary of Booksellers and Printers . . . 1641–67* (Oxford, 1907, repr. 1968), 145. Sweeting also published several works by the Antinomian and Baptist Henry Denne, as well as memorial verse for the Antinomian Tobias Crisp.

[30] *Theologia Germanica* (1646), sig. A4ᵛ; R. M. Jones, *Spiritual Reformers*, pp. 253–4; Rutherford, *A Survey of the Spirituall Antichrist*, i. 167; Edwards, *Gangraena* (1646), iii. 25.   [31] Hunt, 'John Everard', p. 264.

H.N. his books and the 'Rule of Perfection', but especially that cursed book called 'Theologia Germanica'; ther are [several copies] of them in Latin and manuscripts. There is one Fisher, a barber in the Old Bailey, who writes and sells them. [*Added in* Dr. Lambe's hand] he sells old books, and got 'Theologia Germanica' translated into English by a minister at Grindleton, in Yorkshire, called Brierley, or Tenent, this was the man who brought it of Wolston, in Ch [urch] Lane, and lent it to Dr. Everard, who was translating it, and did two [copies] of them, one for the Earl of Holland, and another for [Edmund] Earl Musgrave [*sic*].[32]

As we shall see, Everard's own translation is stylistically different from the 1646 and 1648 texts, since he seems to be attempting a closer imitation of Latin syntax (see below, Section IV). If Lambe is correct, then Everard may well have taken some of his fragments from Brierley's or Tennant's translation, although this view does no justice to Everard's immense learning. At any rate, Randall need not have seen Everard's translation at all, if the fragments did have origins in a Brierley or Tennant translation, though Randall's edition of Cusa bears a very close relationship to the Cusa fragment in the Cambridge Everard MS. There seems to be a large hint that Randall could have used Brierley's work: Brierley was attracted by the metaphor of civil war for spiritual state. Attached to his sermons was Josuah Sylvester's translation of George Goodwin's Latin poem 'Auto-Machia: Or Selfe-Civil-War', which expresses sentiments akin to those of the *Theologia Germanica*:

> Unto my self I do my self betray . . .
> My self agrees not with my self a jot . . .
> I trust my self, and I my self distrust . . .
> I cannot live, with nor without my self.[33]

Tellingly the fragments suffixed to the 1648 edition of the *Theologia* contain the following unidentified four-line epigram, very similar to Sylvester.

> In war, that I am undertaking
> Against my self, my force doth spend me:
> Sith with my self war I am making,
> O from my self then God defend me.   (p. 146)

[32] *CSPD*, dxx. pp. 425–6. For Brierley, see above, pp. 1–2; Richard Tennant was rector of Burnsall from 1619: A. G. Matthews, *Walker Revised* (Oxford, 1948), 399–400.

[33] *Poems*, p. 94, appended to *A Bundle of Soul-Convincing, Directing and Comforting Truths* (2nd edn., 1677).

If these lines were written or simply appended by Brierley, then Randall was using more than Everard's translation with which to produce his own version. Randall may have been able to translate from Latin and French (see below, Section IV). His purpose in using other translations, then, was to produce the most accurate, cogent, elegant, but simple English edition.

The *Theologia Germanica* itself had become a symbol of spiritual, if not Anabaptist, separatism in Europe during the sixteenth century.[34] Luther had discovered it in a manuscript and it was dated as late fourteenth or early fifteenth century. The author was presumed to be a Teutonic lord though in the eighteenth century it was assumed that the author was Tauler himself. In the mid-nineteenth century a manuscript of the *Theologia* was found and dated 1497. However the original work was produced in the fourteenth century, not later than approximately 1350, since the manuscript refers to Tauler as an already well-known figure. The author has been taken to be a member of the 'Gottesfreunde', monks and nobles who withdrew from a chaotic society to practise pious devotion, and who concealed their individual identities as much as possible. It is now generally accepted that Luther's text, especially the second edition of 1518, was derived from a manuscript which was closer to the original than the text of the 1497 manuscript. Luther's text was replicating a simplicity which was more like the original state of the work than the somewhat expanded 1497 manuscript.

From the first printed edition in 1516 the *Theologia* enjoyed immense popularity as a vernacular devotional guide, a truly *German* theology, separate from Rome, during the early stages of the Lutheran Reformation. It advocated an extremely personal form of religion, not all of which was commensurate with Luther's developing ideas. Nevertheless one result was the appearance of a different translation, issued by Berthold von Chiemsee in Latin, which emphasized the authority of the Roman church.[35] As Luther became more concerned with church organization and dogma, so the *Theologia* lost its popularity with the Lutheran mainstream. It became increasingly associated with the spiritualist and Anabaptist opposition to

---

[34] Stephen E. Ozment, *Mysticism and Dissent: Religious Ideology and Social Protest in the Sixteenth Century* (New Haven, 1973), 14–60.   [35] Publ. 1561, Salzburg.

Luther and was adopted as a breviary by some Anabaptist and Waldensian communities.

Everard himself (and also apparently Brierley or Tennant) translated the *Theologia* from a Latin edition of 1558, translated by Sebastian Castellio, a spiritualist writer and former protégé, turned bitter enemy, of Calvin. On the execution in Geneva of Michael Servetus, Castellio penned *De Haereticis*, the foremost defence of intellectual liberty in the Reformation. The use of Castellio's text partly explains the occurrence of appendages to the English *Theologias*. Castellio had based his Latin translation upon the German edition of Louis Haetzer (1528), which, apart from many amendments to Luther's edition (effectively emphasizing the personal role of the Holy Spirit),[36] also suffixed a series of meditative sayings by Denck, the *Hauptreden*.[37] In the English editions, and in Everard's sermons, the *Hauptreden* occur as 'Certain grave sayings by which the diligent Schollar of Christ may search into himself'.

Another appendage to the 1648 but not the 1646 edition was '*The Communication of Doctor* Thaulerus with a poor beggar' attributed to Tauler.[38] This first occurs in English in John Yakesley's 1613 translation of Francis of Sales's *An Introduction to the Holy and Devout Life*, printed at Douai. This work, as Helen White and Louis Martz have shown, was immensely popular in England and went through several editions, including one printed in London in 1616.[39] Yakesley's translation itself was taken from the third edition of the French original. Francis of Sales's book was an attempt to broaden the appeal of the Counter-Reformation, replacing Jesuit rigour with a mode which was 'gentle, easy, moderate'. It was very popular with the Anglican community at Little Gidding, though a Puritan outcry forced the suppression of the 1637 Paris edition.[40] The important point here is that the dialogue was seen by the radicals as a valid spiritual text, despite its origin.

[36] Ozment, *Mysticism and Dissent*, pp. 25–8 gives an account of Haetzer's version of the *Theologia Germanica*.

[37] Printed at Augsburg, 1531 by Alexander Weissenhorn.

[38] The other pieces appended to the 1646 edition were two summarizing pieces: 'The Author's Institution contained in three points' and 'Perfection in the first, second, third, and fourth degrees'.

[39] Helen C. White, *English Devotional Literature [Prose], 1600–40* (Madison, 1931), 111–13; Louis Martz, *The Poetry of Meditation* (New Haven, 1954, rev. edn., 1962), 6.

[40] White, *English Devotional Literature*, p. 113.

In addition, the printed *Theologia* of 1648 also contains 'Definitions Theological', 'Definitions theological and Philosophical' and a schematic illustration of different philosophical conceptions of the soul, entitled *De Anima*. The first two appear to be distillations of the *Theologia* and of Franck's *Von dem Baum des Wissens*. Since they are signed with the epigram which may have been Roger Brierley's work, these short pieces may also be his, though again there is nothing else to suggest this. They may have been added by Randall but original work by Randall is uncharacteristic, apart from his prefaces to his translations. Though none of the three occurs in any known Everard manuscript, *De Anima* at least displays the breadth of learning which few radical spiritualists have shown elsewhere, apart from Everard.

The text of the 1648 edition is a somewhat 'up-market' version of its 1646 predecessor. The production is superior and in places the phrasing has been made more elegant, sometimes with the insertion of Latin commonplace words. The 1646 edition seems to be closer to a manuscript. Randall's involvement in this second edition might be doubted too. He does not explain the additions, and he disappears from sight after 1646.

Everard's identity as translator of editions of works by Cusa in 1646 and 1651 has been affirmed in the first instance, the case of *De Visione Dei*, by the fragment of the translation in the Cambridge MS. This identifies closely, though not entirely, with Randall's edition of 1646, 'Οφθαλμὸς 'Απλοῦς *Or the Single Eye, Entituled the Vision of God*. Randall had recourse to an Everard translation, though he seems to have altered punctuation and word order slightly. The 1650 Cusa translation of the *Idiota* as *The Idiot* has been attributed to Everard by T. W. Hayes because Everard's name appears on an advertisement for the book prepared by the publisher.[41] Though not a devotional guide, Cusa's works are certainly highly meditational. They were important for Everard himself because they enabled him to forge a link between the mystical bent of the German writers and the concern for the divine knowledge of nature which is such a feature of Hermetic theory. Like the *Theologia* and the Franck translation, they were published in the popular octavo form,

---

[41] See T. W. Hayes, 'John Everard and Nicholas of Cusa's *Idiota*', *N & Q*, NS, 28 (1981), 47–9.

whereas Cusa's works had remained hitherto in large folio volumes, essentially the possession of universities, rich clergy and nobles. In addition Everard translated at least one further work by Cusa, the *De dato Patris luminum*, a manuscript of which was found recently, appended to the Folger manuscript version of the *Theologia Germanica*.[42]

Last but not least, Everard's translation of *Hermes Trismegistus* was published in 1650 by Thomas Brewster, with a preface by the alchemical writer John French. In 1657 a second edition of the *Pymander* was published with the *Asclepias* appended. Hunt argues that since no manuscripts of these Hermetic translations of Everard have survived, and since the translation of the *Asclepias* is unsigned, there is no reason to connect Everard with the translation of it.[43] This seems to me to be a false assumption. In the first instance, Hunt ignores the MS Tanner evidence which accuses Everard of producing the *Pymander* and the *Asclepias* together, while both customarily appeared with each other, notably in Ficino's 1576 edition of Hermes, from which Everard presumably translated. Stylistically the 1657 *Asclepias* is similar to the *Pymander*, so that at least it seems very likely that Everard translated it.[44]

IV

The actual process of translation involved in Everard's work is significant because it shows how Everard was able to determine the lexical, affective, and argumentative potential of his own language, and how the original versions affected Everard's intentions. It was a matter of no small concern for Everard. In *The Gospel-Treasury Opened* he speaks of the necessity for the 'right translation' in order to comprehend the 'obscure' meaning specifically in the epistemological sense.[45] This process is more

---

[42] T. W. Hayes, 'A Seventeenth-Century Translation of Nicholas of Cusa's *De dato Patris luminum*', JMRS 11 (1981), 113–36.   [43] Hunt, 'John Everard', p. 268.

[44] Three translated Hermetic fragments survive, two at Bodl. MS Ashmole 1440 (a part of the *Smaragdine Table* with gloss, and an extract from Basilius Valentinus, *Theatrum Chemicum* (1613)), and one in British Library, MS Sloane 2175. R. M. Schuler, 'Some Spiritual Alchemies of Seventeenth Century England', *JHI* 41 (1980), 293–318 (esp. 307), identifies this fragment as Valentinus's '*Practica, una cum XII clavibus et Appendice*' from Michael Maier, *Themis aurea* (Frankfurt, 1618). For Everard's alleged possession of manuscripts from Sir Thomas Hariot's circle, see Christopher Hill, *Milton and the English Revolution* (1977), 328.

[45] Everard, *The Gospel Treasury Opened*, ii. 506.

than one of merely finding English words to match those in German, Latin, or Greek. Everard often translated not from an original, but from a translation in another language so that the English version is the second translation, at two removes from the original. The result is highly significant in the development of prose style in radical Puritanism at large, and it is implicitly bound up with, if not Everard's, then certainly Randall's aim, inherited from the Anabaptists, to make serious 'divinity and philosophy' available to Puritan readers at large, even Luther's 'simple folk'.[46]

Everard translated most of his texts from Latin versions of German originals, where they were not in Latin in the first place. We cannot be sure that he did not know German. No Latin text of Denck's *Widderuf* exists, for instance. However, Latin texts of the other works were probably more available in England, and Everard would have felt far more at home with Latin. Indeed, his translations from the Latin are remarkably precise and faithful to the original. The disparity comes with the realization that the Latin version of *Von dem Baum des Wissens guts unnd böses* and the *Theologia Germanica* are distinctly stylized versions of the simplified and rarified language of German spiritualism.

Everard translated Franck's work from a 1561 Latin version, *De Arbore Scientiae Boni et Mali*, printed at Mulhouse by Peter Schmidt. The translator from the German is unknown. The Castellio version of the *Theologia Germanica* from which Everard also worked was printed in 1558 by Christopher Plantin at Antwerp.[47] The original *Theologia*, displaying the influence of both Tauler and Eckhart, is written in a Strasbourg dialect with a vocabulary which did not have corresponding words in Latin. According to Luther it was 'bad German, crabbed and uncouth words'. Castellio's preface apologizes for the creation of new words in Latin, 'Egoitas, Ipsitas, Meritas, Velitur, Deificatus, Displicentia, Personalitas'. His excuse was that Cicero had already done so before him, 'quam Cicero, qui Appiitate & Lentulitatem non dubitavit dicere'.[48] Haetzer, though, had

---

[46] See R. W. Scribner, *For the Sake of Simple Folk: Popular Propaganda for the German Reformation* (Cambridge, 1981).

[47] CUL, MS Dd. 12. 68, 50ᵛ contains a transcription of Plantin's colophon and his licence to print the *Theologia Germanica*.

[48] *Theologia Germanica* (Antwerp, 1558), 4; Cicero, *Epistolae ad Familiares*, 3: 7.5.

already done much to radicalize the *Theologia*, making stylistic changes which were commensurate with Anabaptist postures. In chapter 6, for instance, 'Meister' was dropped from Boethius, and 'Sanctus' from Paul.[49] Also, the 'seed' or image of God within man was stressed, along with the notion of freedom through a unity with the will of God by means of resignation, *gelassenheit*, of the ego. In the English, Castellio's inventions become unfamiliar English words, 'Inesse, selfnesse, Minenesse, It is willed, Godded, Displeasingnesse, & Personality' ('Egoity, Selfness, Meity, Deified, Disposence, Personallity' in the 1648 edition).[50] Throughout Everard's and Randall's texts there are certain recurrences of this vocabulary, 'egoity' for instance. However, Randall in particular finds simple English words without resorting to Castellio's Latin creations. Though Everard and Randall may never have looked at a German version, the English finds some form of correspondence with the German, effectively eliminating the Latin bridge in a number of cases. So 'Velitur' becomes 'willfulness' (Randall) or 'willed' (Everard) and 'ipsitas' becomes 'selfhood' ('selbheit' in the original).

If the versions are compared, it can be seen how the English loses the nominative concentration in the German, the concentration upon the subject's state of being, through the economy of the Latin:

Auch ist geschriben: So meyn ich, das ist icheit vnd selbheit, mer ab nympt, ßo gotis ich, das ist got selber, mer zu nympt yn mir.

Hoc item scriptum est: Quò magis decrescit meum ego, hoc est, egoitas, & ipsitas, eò magis in me crescit Dei ego, hoc est Deus ipse.

This is also written, by how much more my I, yt is my Iinesse, & selfnesse decreaseth, by soe much more, gods I, that is g. hims: increaseth in me. (Everard)

This also is written, the more that my self doth decrease (that is, egoity or selfness) the more doth in me increase the I of God, *id est*, God himself. (1648 edn.)[51]

---

[49] Other changes which Haetzer made were to emphasize the Truth over the Scripture in ch. 2, to make the prayer at the end theocentric, even Antitrinitarian, and to replace Luther's preface with Peter Schoeffer's. Denck's *Hauptreden*, a commentary upon the *Theologia Germanica*, is couched in a rhetoric which put it beyond censure: anyone who does not understand it does not have the spirit within them. See Ozment, *Mysticism and Dissent*, pp. 25–8.   [50] CUL, MS Dd.12. 68, fo. 51ʹ.

[51] The page references here are, in German ('*Der Frankforter*' ['*Theologia Deutsch*'] *Kritische Textausgabe*, ed. Wolfgang von Hinten, Munich, Artemis Verlag, 1982), 92;

Here Randall, noticing an unfamiliar concept for his readers, aids understanding by referring back in parenthesis to the original principle of individual self-awareness. Elsewhere, the presence of God in that self is rendered thus:

Sich, diß sal seyn vnd ist yn der warheit yn eyme gotlichen ader yn eyme waren, vergotten menschen, dan er wer anders nicht gotlich adder vergottet.

atq. hoc & esse debet, & reipsa est, in diuino, siue in verè deificato homine, alioquin non esset diuinus, aut deificatus.

And this both ought to be, & is indeed in a divine, or in a truly deified or godded man: otherwise he were not divine or deified. (Everard)

and this both ought to be, and in truth is, in a divine and truly deified man, otherwise that man were neither divine nor deified. (1648 edn.)[52]

Here Randall clearly stays closer to Everard, although he still polishes the prose by inverting verb order and reducing pronouns. The full result in English in both versions is a breathless sequence of short clauses, with the specific spiritualist vocabulary half sedimentary, half visible as an import from the German:

Auch sal man mercken, wan man spricht von eynem menschen, das do ist alt, vnde von eynem nuwen menschen. Sich, der alt ist Adam vnd vngehorsam vnd selbheit vnd icheit vnd des gleich. Aber der nuwe mensch ist Cristus vnd gehorsam.

Hoc quoque animaduertendum est: Cùm sit veteris & noui hominis mentio, sic res intelligentia est: Vetus est Adamus & inobedientia, ipsitas, egoitas, & similia: at nouus homo est Christus & obedientia.

This is also to be noted, when yr is mention made of the ould & new man; the matter is thus to be understood: the ould man is Addam, disobe: himself-nesse I-nesse, & the like, but ye new man is ch: & obedience.

This is also to be observed when mention is made of the old and new man, the matter is thus to be understood; the old man is *Adam*, disobedience, selfness, egoity, &c. But the new man is Christ and obedience.[53]

---

in Latin, ed. Castellio (1558), 32; CUL MS Dd. 12. 68, fo. 63ʳ; assembled by Randall (1648), 30.

[52] von Hinten, p. 117; Castellio, p. 63; CUL MS fo. 74⁴; Randall, pp. 66–7.
[53] von Hinten, p. 90; Castellio, pp. 29–30; CUL MS fo. 62ᵛ; Randall, p. 27.

The translation of Franck presents a slightly different problem because the German original, *Von dem Baum des Wissens*, is partly a paraphrase of Cornelius Agrippa's *De incertitudine & vanitate omnium artium et scientiarum*. The language is thus a mixture of the simplified biblical and spiritual terminology, as in the *Theologia Germanica*, and the expression of sceptical humanism. Cornelius Agrippa's Latin is already simplified by Franck for the German reader: 'eine erbaulich gehaltere Volksausgabe der Stilubung des Meisters', a 'worthy and edifying popular translation of the practice of the masters', which is the 'Thorechte wort', the 'word of the Law'.[54] The translation enhances this. A fluid balance and lucidity is added by splitting the prose into paragraphs and by merging sentences:

Etenim universus mundus exterior, & quicquid externum est atq; sit, est duntaxat accidens quaedam & significans figura uerae rei & naturae interioris. Idéoq; nihil uerum est in ijs omnibus quae conspiciuntur ob oculos. Nam huius mundi species intereat oportet, quippe qui sit aliud nihil, quam imaginarius quidá mundus, figura recti, ueri, aeterni, & per sese constantis mundi.

for the exterior world, and whatsoever outwardly is to be seene or is done, is onely an accident and a certaine signifying figure of the true and interior nature: and there is nothing true in all those things which are seene with the eye, that is substantiall; for it behoveth that the frame of this world perish, because it is nothing else but an imaginary world, and a figure of the right true eternall, and by it selfe the constant world.[55]

There is another concern displayed by Everard and Randall (and Franck and Castellio) with 'Author, Nature, Matter, Method, and Style'.[56] It is a desire to make the language in the texts incite in the reader the state of mind and being which is the subject of the texts themselves. This is connected closely to the notion of an essential truth lying within the outer 'shell' of language, and the visible, material world itself. In *The Gospel-Treasury Opened* Everard juxtaposes a series of meditational statements in both English and Latin, so that 'where the one Language shall be obscure, it may be helped by the other'.[57]

---

[54] C. Dejung, *Wahrheit und Häresie. Eine Untersuchung zur Geschichtsphilosophie bei Sebastian Franck* (Zürich, 1979), 39. The 'Thora' or 'Torah' is the Mosaic Law.

[55] *De Arbore Scientiae Boni et Mali*, p. 2; *The Forbidden Fruit*, p. 4.

[56] Randall, 'To the Reader', in *Theologia Germanica* (1648), sig. A3ʳ.

[57] Everard, *The Gospel-Treasury Opened*, ii. p. 506.

Similarly the translations are simple not only because of any intended readership but also to encourage a state of intense meditation: the text is 'often to be read over, and that with diligence'.[58] Thus there is justification for the fact that 'the shortness it is somewhat obscure', even though Randall bemoans the fact that the English lacks the 'elegance' of the Latin.

V

Everard's translations fall into two groups. The first is concerned with exploring the correct godly behaviour of the individual, the state of the individual in his or her higher relationship with the divine. The *Theologia Germanica* and the translation of Franck form the main texts here. Secondly, through Cusa, the Neo-platonic tradition including Pseudo-Dionysius, and the Hermetic tradition, the relationship of man and God to the rest of the universe, is explored. The two groups are not separate, and they share certain elements, not least of which is the notion of God as action, and phenomena as manifestations of the divine, active will. The mystical annihilation of selfish will to become one with God also corresponds to the Hermetic *gnoses*, where the *magus* achieves a state of spiritual and physical mastery over creation through the contemplation of Hermetic knowledge. The mystical writings include metaphors of perception and intuition based upon space and geometry common in Christian Platonic writing, while the Hermetic works are couched in terms of a meditational exercise, which is not unrelated to the mystical instructions given in the former.[59]

The *Theologia Germanica* instils hope in the reader for the arrival of the spirit within, the birth of the new man, the death of the old. This is seen as analogous to the death of Adam and the birth of Christ within. Adopting the biblical prophetic figure, 'I speak as a fool' (2 Cor. 11.23), the speaker in the *Theologia* expounds a dialectic where the individual is exhorted to negate the selfish covetous will so that man becomes 'deified' (*vergottet*) or 'divine'. With such a man lives God, though the divine does not have a separate identity: 'But where God, as God, is man, or where God

[58] Castellio's preface in *Theologia Germanica* (1648), sig. A5ʳ.

[59] Everard also translated the *Pymander* of *Hermes Trismegistus* in such a way that it would have biblical rhythms.

liveth in some Divine or Deified man, there is something belonging unto God, which is only appertaining to him, and not to the creatures.'[60] The manuscript translation contains an expansion which reveals Everard's own precision here: 'But where G. is as god in man, or wher god liveth in some divine or deified man; thersomth: pertaines unto g: wch is proper to him; & apertaineth to him alone, not to ye creatures, by originall & essence, not by forme or action.'[61] It is an open imitation of Christ in so far as this must involve the realization of the location of the will, which is a submission to God's will:

> Now, of all freedoms, nothing is so free as the wil, and whosoever maketh it his own, and doth not leave it to its own noble liberty, free nobleness & free nature, he doth ill; this doth the Devil and *Adam*, and all their Imitators.[62]

On the other hand it is not an enforcement of *imitatio Christi* in terms of works, and so it is commensurate with the Puritan tendency to concentrate all attention upon the saving grace of Christ's atonement.[63] Accordingly a woodcut of the crucifixion accompanied many of the early German editions of the *Theologia*.

By connecting the imperfect with the perfect the *Theologia* could be seen to imply that it is possible to become perfect in this life.[64] This is couched within the distinction between the outward fleshly man and the inward spiritual man, 'a true inward and sincere humility'. So Christ's soul had an outward 'left eye' which comprehended worldly distinctions and suffered pain and calamity, and an inward 'right eye' which beheld the 'perfect use of divine nature'. Something like a hypostatic state is reached where Truth is perceived in the abandoning of the senses. This is the *via negativa* of Pseudo-Dionysius where the experience of the divine is rendered by the denial of any sensory or cerebral mode's ability to know that experience. The reader must lose him or herself in God by learning to rely upon nothing: 'Such a one ought both to extinguish, and also to have

---

[60] *Theologia Germanica* (1648), 62.

[61] CUL, MS Dd. 12. 68, fo. 73ʳ.   [62] *Theologia Germanica* (1648), 123.

[63] See J. Sears McGee, *The Godly Man in Stuart England* (New Haven, 1976), 51 n., 107–13, 152, 164, 230, 251.

[64] *Theologia Germanica* (1648), 2. This was the type of statement which the Antinomians could distort. In another seventeenth-century translation of the *Theologia Germanica* taken from Castellio's version in BL, MS Sloane 2538, fo. 54ʳ, the attack on libertines in ch. 38 is marginally glossed 'Antinomian'.

extinguished in him all delights and pleasures, bred by such mortal creatures as are without God, of what sort soever they are.'[65] Man's sin, disobedience, appetitiveness, lustfulness, is a blindness which is voluntary, for 'Boethus saith, yt we doe not love the best, it is long of sinne', or as Randall explicates, 'it is our fault that we do not love that which is best'.[66]

The truth requires that an individual reaches the essence of being. Knowledge, reason, and will ought not to be 'profitable to it self, or to the use of it self, but to be of his of whom they had their Being, and to obey and flow back again into him, and in themselves, that same is to be turned into nothing in their own selfness'.[67] Knowledge thus belongs to eternal wisdom, just as imperfection stems from perfection. In Cusa scholarly learning is rejected in favour of 'knowing ignorance' which relies on intuition to apprehend the spiritual principles which exercise causality.

Intrinsic to this problem of perception is the familiar paradox of describing in language a mystical experience: that is, one in which some kind of union with or closeness to a divine or other-worldly presence is felt, which is beyond the scope of language to express. The state of perfection is, not surprisingly, described in terms of illumination imagery: lights are equated with grace, the spirit is the candle shining in the chamber of the mind, heart or body, as with Prov. 20: 27: 'the spirit of man is the candle of the Lord', while the owl uses the 'light of the night', showing the ubiquitous presence of the divine as this light is 'darker then the most darksom part of the day'.[68] Here the *Theologia* reveals the influence of the Pseudo-Dionysius's *via negativa* while the mental struggle required to comprehend this paradox suggests the transcendent complexity of Truth.

One answer to the problem of describing mystical experience is to employ a sensory analogue. For instance, the mind has to 'taste' perfection as well as see the light. The organization of perceptions in Pseudo-Dionysius and in Cusa becomes a conflict between the potency intimated in abstract terms and the principles of emanation, of continuity between finite and infinite

[65] *Theologia Germanica* (1648), 12, 144.
[66] CUL, MS Dd. 12. 68, fo. 56ᵛ; *Theologia Germanica* (1648), 10.
[67] Ibid. 119.
[68] Ibid. 143. This is a reversal of the more usual use of the owl as a symbol of spiritual blindness.

in concrete images. As will become evident, this is possible for a description of God's presence in the universe, but with the description of essence itself imagery falls away. The problem becomes one of making definitions stand separately in a situation where the objects of description are nevertheless parts of the same whole, indeed, interdependent parts of the same definition. In the *De dato Patris luminum* Being is a question of reverting to essence, to the origin of life. Essence simply is essence, so that the Word becomes irreducible and the effect contains its cause:

> But humanity is a most simple essence which receiveth specifically the generall essence in which are, as in a simple power, all those things which in the variety of men are individually partaked . . .
>   Therefore the essences of sensible things are insensibly in the species. The specificall essences are in their genders without specification, & the genericall essences themselves without generality are in the absolute essence, which is God blessed for ever.[69]

Another descriptive correlative lies in the use of number, the prime metaphor in the mind of the creator. It is another Pseudo-Dionysian concept, elaborated upon by Cusa's Idiot:

> When thou considerest that number is made of the multitude of unities, and that alterity doth contingently follow multiplication; and markest the composition of number to be of unity and alterity, the same and divers, even and odd, divisible and indivisible . . . then thou mayest after some fashion reach unto it, how the essences of things are incorruptible, as unity, whereof is number, which unity is entity.[70]

To make distinctions is finally pointless, because all finite objects are ultimately connected with the infinite: 'All things are all that they are, because God is.'[71] In this sense the divine is everywhere, as Hermes Trismegistus was held to say, 'God may be called by the name of all things, & all things by the name of God.'[72] Wisdom, God's understanding, is that mist of unknowing '*Wholely* UNKNOWN, by the *Cessation* of all *Knowledge*: and in that he knoweth *Nothing*, Knowing *Above* any *Mind* or *Understanding*'.[73]

  In Franck knowing the divine presence or spirit depends upon

---

[69] *De dato Patris luminum*, in Hayes, *JMRS* (1981), 134.

[70] *The Idiot* (1650), 99.

[71] 'Definitions Theological', in *Theologia Germanica* (1648), 169.

[72] *De dato Patris luminum*, in Hayes, *JMRS* (1981), 12.

[73] *The Mystical Divinity of Dionysius the Areopagite*, in Everard, *The Gospel-Treasury Opened*, ii. p. 498.

a comprehension of the 'inner word' inside the surface language of the Scriptures. Paying attention only to the 'outward' word is subjection to the 'idoll' of the Letter, and a 'certain snare to wicked men'. The inner word however is a part of the divine essence:

The interior word containeth both of these which sometimes is called the Kingdome of God, sometimes the Spirit, sometimes Christ dwelling in us. For it is not only a Light, way, and guide, but also Spirit, truth, and Life; that is, which not onely teacheth man that he may understand, but also moves him that he works.[74]

In the *Theologia Germanica* the relationship between essence and creation is rendered in unmistakably spatial terms. God is a fountain of perpetual emanation: 'God is one, and unity existeth, and floweth from him alone, and yet not out of him, otherwise it should decrease and become less.'[75] Cusa takes this concept to a further stage of sophistication. There is a sense in which divine and human identity merge:

God & the Creature are the same thing; according to the manner of the Giver, God; according to the manner of the gift, the Creature. Therefore it shalbe but one thing though, according to the diversity of the manner, it have here divers names.[76]

God extends to the creation by 'descentions', by which every creature is 'filliated' to the divine. God is neither 'abstracted' nor 'too infinite'. Nature becomes a metaphorical expression of God's mind. The human mind becomes a metaphor for the universe itself. The consequence is the image of absolute sight in *De Visione Dei* where the perception of the divine, the universe, and human cognition are brought together in the simultaneous association of eye, circle, and globe:

wherfore the appearance of sight in the Picture cannot so well as the conceipt approach or come neare the height of the excellency of absolute vision or sight, and consequently it is no whit to be doubted, but that whatsoever appeares in that Image is excellently and perfectly in the absolute sight.[77]

---

[74] *The Forbidden Fruit* (1642), 176.

[75] 'Certaine grave sayings' in *Theologia Germanica* (1648), 138.

[76] *De dato Patris luminum*, p. 126; see also Sir Thomas Browne, *Pseudodoxia Epidemica*, ed. Robin Robbins, 2 vols. (Oxford, 1981), ii. 2 (pp. 10 ff.).

[77] Ὀφθαλμὸς Ἁπλοῦς *Or the Single Eye, Entituled the Vision of God* (1646), 4.

God can become a series of similitudes, and operations, instanced in the visual paradox of the mirror or 'glasse':

the eye is of the nature of Glasse, and a glasse though never so little will figuratively represent a great Mountain, and all things that are in the surface thereof, and so the species of all things are in a glasly eye.[78]

Cusa makes God distinct from the world, but there is no separation of sensible and super-sensible: through the notion of similitude things are images of ideas, or rather, the idea, which is God, essence, infinity. This notion is enhanced visually in the 1646 translation of *De Visione Dei* by a woodcut in the shape of a circle, with a microcosmic landscape within, and the eye of God looking down upon it from the edge of the circle.

Everard's translations of Cusa reflect the prevalence of scholasticism in fifteenth-century thought and method despite Cusa's own rejection of it. The parataxis which is indicative of this is more prevalent in the Cusa translations than it is in the *Theologia Germanica* and *The Forbidden Fruit*:

yet alterity in simplicity is without alteration, because it is simplicity, for all things that are said are affirmed of absolute simplicitie, coincide, or are the same with it, because there to have, is to be, the opposition of opposites, is their opposition without opposition, as the end or bo[u]nd of things infinit is no end or bound without end or bound.[79]

In Cusa's methodology this is termed *visio intellectualis*, an exercise involving the comprehension of the coincidence of opposites. The concept fits into Cusa's understanding of the role of metaphor in the universe, for while abstract terms are not strictly representative, they are forced into a metaphorical pattern, as an aspect of the shape of God. So 'singularity' and 'plurality' are exceeded in the 'infinite Sphericity' of the 'Eye' of God.

Under these conditions the positive uses of human reason are questioned. If disciplined and subdued before divine reason, then, as Tauler's beggar says, human reason is an assurance of grace. For Cusa man has in his mind the 'discerning light of Reason' but this is 'darkened with many shadows in this sensible body'. Like Cusa's attacks on the schoolmen, Franck's paraphrase of Cornelius Agrippa includes a genealogy of knowledge imparted

---

[78] Ibid. 42.   [79] Ibid. 77–8.

to man by the light of God, which acts upon 'Adam, Abel, Noah, Lot, Abraham, Job, Mercuries [Hermes Trismegistus], Plotinus, Cornelius, and all other upright-hearted Gentiles'.[80] Here, as in Terence, all things have been said before, in some language or other, and it is only for man to turn back to a deep spiritual knowledge of God again. Nevertheless, the author of the *Theologia Germanica* cites Tauler's belief that the imagination can aid the achievement of truth, through the process of 'Purgation', 'Illumination', 'Union'.[81]

VI

Everard's sermons themselves display the influence of the works which he was translating. From the sermon headings and glosses, it would appear that they were set from copies made as Everard delivered them and were then corrected by him afterwards.

Everard's mode of explication is fiercely Pauline, emphasizing the need for the godly to let the Spirit enter them. It is an evocative style which matches the clarity of Sibbes but which outstrips Sibbes in terms of energy and vivaciousness:

> what manner of People are these, that so champ the Letter between their Teeth, and troul it on their Tongues (For God's sake) what are they in their lives? have they got any Virtue from Christ, by being so conversant with him?[82]

But alongside this the delights of the withdrawn, divine life, with the spirit of Christ living within, are evident:

> Are they transformed and made *New Creatures*? Do they live *The Inward and Spiritual Life* of the Word? Are they dead to the world, and the world to them? Doth Christ's life shine in them and by them, so that they live not any longer in themselves?[83]

This is the self-denial recommended in the *Theologia Germanica*, the pursuit of a 'Spiritual, Practical, and Experimental Life'. The imperative to experience the workings of God in the spirit is enforced in the stress upon prophetic behaviour: the individual should not neglect foolish things. This is compounded with

---

[80] *The Forbidden Fruit*, p. 166.   [81] *Theologia Germanica* (1648), 24.
[82] 'Shadows Vanishing, Some Rays of Glory appearing', in *The Gospel-Treasury Opened*, i. p. 417. Christ is realized as an experimental teacher over ordinances: ibid. 431–2.   [83] Ibid.

praise of the evangelism, both active and passive, of the early Christians. The constant urges to self-denial, self-annihilation, and resignation are compounded with sensory imperatives: the reader must 'see, know and feel' the truth. The theme of the imitation of Christ also recurs, but this time it is balanced by satirical character portrayals, similar to the writings of the Puritan satirists, Thomas Scot and Richard Overton. Doctor *Honour* pursues 'a fine, smooth, moderate way, and so shalt thou please all the world'; Dr Profit 'gets riches' for himself; Dr Pleasure 'fills and satisfies' himself with 'Recreations' (a pun on the theological terms for spiritual regeneration), while:

And then comes up *Doctor Reason*: Oh! He is a great man, He is a *Learned Doctor indeed*, He is *Doctor of the Chair* at least: when all the rest are silenced, yet he must be heard; and he will believe nothing that you cannot bring within his Bounds.[84]

Everard's critique of self-approbation in *Some Gospel-Treasures Opened* is matched by the almost hagiographical praise which Harford, Webster and others give to Everard: he becomes the best example of the way of life he is proposing. The 1653 edition includes a woodcut of Everard, dressed as a Puritan and holding a Bible, with a small poem below it which sees Everard's integrity as an example of his preference for 'Truth' over 'Type'. It is this integrity which leads Harford to the judgement that Everard stands as a mid-point on the scale of 'experimental' religion, between 'Rationalist' and 'Formalist' on the one hand, and 'Familist' and 'Ranter' on the other.

In the sermons Everard's system of belief consistently refers to the life of the spirit within. This mystery, a 'shining jewel', is tied to a notion of the Trinity as One. Experience of this One is an experience of Trinity as a process. The influence of Cusa is clear:

Now you see here is Three things named, *The Loving, the Loved, and the Love*. Yet All is but *One and the Same thing*. So much at present concerning this *Occult, Hidden and Secret MYSTERY* of the Blessed *Trinity*: This hath been to me an *Experimental Vision*, others may be otherwise *Satisfied*.[85]

---

[84] 'The Starre in the East, Leading unto the true Messiah', in *The Gospel-Treasury Opened*, i. pp. 88, 90.

[85] Ibid. 109. Augustine defines *caritas* in a similar way: *De Trinitate*, 8. 10. 14. The marginal gloss here is 'As the vision of God lively sets forth'. It is significant that Everard describes his 'vision' as part of 'experimental theology'.

Pseudo-Dionysius is also present: God, the abstracted unknow-able essence is described as the 'Unknowable, Infinite *Abysse* of BEING', an 'ocean' of divine truth.[86] At the same time, the figure of Christ is prominent on several levels. Biblical Christ is typical and representative of divine behaviour, while the redemption of man in the crucifixion is rendered in intensely figurative terms:

> If Great Sins opened the *River* of Blood in Christ's Side, and *Current* of Blood in his Hands and Feet, the Smallest sins then are the Thorns, and make more wounds on his head, or at least they opened a Pore in his *Sacred* Body.[87]

But above all this is the profound presence of the spirit: 'The Truth is, Christ was conceived in us as soon as ever we were born.'[88] This is accompanied by a critique of 'types'. Their presence in Jewish ceremonies, says Everard, raises false, literal expectations. The Rabbis are seen to require a 'sensuall sign' rather than the spiritual knowledge released in the apprehension of Christ crucified. This is a bondage to form, a concept which occurs later in the writings of Abiezer Coppe, Jacob Bauthumley, and John Warr. Everard's desire is to confound this 'language of Babel' and he sets against it the image of treasure for the perfect life, a consideration of the 'eye of love', the heart, and an imperative to heed what is '*Radiant* and *Convincing*'.[89]

The attack upon 'types' and 'forms' is extended to scriptural interpretation. However, Everard is careful to maintain a literal understanding of the Bible and bluntly rejects 'mere Allegorical interpretations', though he has been accused of considering biblical verses out of context.[90] He argues for interpretation afforded by the light of God working inside the individual and hidden inside scriptural discourse. Commentaries must not force a meaning upon the text: there is a high degree of literal use of biblical words, a close textual reading which encourages the hearer or reader, as Coppe was later to do, to throw away 'silver

---

[86] 'The Rending of the Vail, Or Some Rayes of Glory from the Holy of Holies', in *The Gospel-Treasury Opened*, i. p. 23. In 'All Power given to *Jesus Christ*, in Heaven And In Earth', in *The Gospel-Treasury Opened*, ii. p. 464, Everard encourages a 'drowning' in words in order to understand a mystical union with Christ.

[87] 'The Starre in the East', in *The Gospel-Treasury Opened*, i. p. 111. For the typical Christ, see below, p. 144, n. 1.   [88] Ibid. 112.

[89] Everard, *The Gospel-Treasury Opened*, sigs. a3ᵛ–a4ʳ.

[90] Hunt, 'John Everard', p. 133.

and gold' in order to reach a state of purity. At the same time Everard thoroughly extricates every level of meaning with biblical words which do have symbolic status. In the sermon headed 'Christ the true Salt of the Earth', salt is seen to possess a long list of analogical meanings, including 'wisdom and discretion in Speech', 'Holiness and Sincerity in Life and Conversation' (as in Matt. 5: 33), and the final vision of Christ as an alembic of incandescent fire and salt.[91] The result is an interdependence of word and spirit which effectively evangelizes Franck and Denck's notion of biblical interpretation. With the spirit thus operating upon the word, enthusiasm is generated by a swift, almost manic syntax which carries a startling integration of biblical narratives:

> He tramples all under foot, and is content to expose himself to whatever their Malice could bring about: He reposes no Confidence in whatever Parts he had equal with them; and sayes, that he expected; and was content to be accounted a Fool and to hide himself, and be as one that had nothing in him . . . He knew that would do no good: For he had Experience, *that of Disputations there was no End*: for every one stuck so fast and unmoveable to his own Opinion.[92]

On the surface Everard's sermons do appear to bear all the traits of the Puritan sermon. The plain style is there, and the insistent tone, as well as the penchant for individual interpretation of parts of the Bible.[93] However, another look reveals the Neoplatonic and spiritualist reading of Everard, and the features of his style are determined by this. So, what is knowledge in the translation becomes a potentiality in the sermons:

> Yet all this being but external, all was nothing, they for all this had seen nothing; though they lived in the Light; they never saw the Light, their Eyes were but half open, they could not see perfectly.[94]

Obviously Everard's works cannot be said to have had an overwhelming influence on later sectarian writing, though his interests are certainly reflected in the sermons of John Webster,

---

[91] 'The Rending of the Vail', in *The Gospel-Treasury Opened*, i. pp. 19–22.

[92] 'The Starre in the East', in *The Gospel-Treasury Opened*, i. p. 50.

[93] Accordingly Hunt, 'John Everard', p. 267, notes how Everard increases *divisio* by launching straight into moral allegory, while ignoring the structure of formal objection. Therefore Everard appears to be spontaneous, though this does involve careful and practised calculation.

[94] Everard, *The Gospel-Treasury Opened*, i. p. 56.

Matthew Barker, and Thomas Brooks.[95] Nevertheless, he was the centre, in the fifteen years prior to his death, of an enterprise devoted to Anglicizing the central mystical anthropology of Medieval German spiritualism as it had been interpreted by the sixteenth-century German spiritualist and Anabaptist movement. It was a concern also to find a means of expressing the interpenetration of spiritual and natural worlds, and to that end, Everard's incorporation of his learning into his own sermons results in a form of expression which heralds the sublime style of later sectarian writers. Though the precise relationship between Everard and the other translators, Randall and Brierley, cannot be reconstructed, it is clear that, when the translations reached the stage of printed publication, an English version of the German spiritual tradition had been produced which accommodated the demands of a specific terminology while still adhering to the Anabaptist (and indeed Lutheran) demand for a simple and elegant popular expression.

VII

The little information we have concerning Giles Randall is gleaned from his translations and from a handful of hostile references scattered among the documents of the heresy hunts of the 1630s and the heresiography of the 1640s.[96] It would seem that he was connected with the mystical and perfectionist Puritans of the 1630s and was identified with the Antinomians in the early 1640s, when he had a following of his own. It is clear that he was frequently preaching in public a version of the Neoplatonic and mystical theology which was the subject of his translations, and his preaching methods, as they were reported, furnish an example of the way in which complex concepts were distilled into simpler forms to be digested by the popular audience.[97] Our concern here is with Randall's translation of the

---

[95] See, e.g. Matthew Barker, *Jesus Christ The Great Wonder* (1651), 16, 19.

[96] Thomas Edwards, *Gangraena*, 3 parts (1646), iii. 25, reports that Randall frequently preached at the Spittle to large gatherings of people, one of his texts being the story of the sower going forth to sow (Matt. 13: 3) which was used to demonstrate all creatures being held forth by Christ, and the notion that all creatures and actions are sacraments.

[97] Thomas Gataker also accuses Randall of saying that Christ could sin and of having a following of '*Silly Women*': *God's Eye on his Israel* (1645), sigs. a2ᵛ, c2ᵛ, d4ᵛ. For further details, see N. Smith, ' "The Interior Word": Aspects of the Use of Language

third part of Benet of Canfield's *The Rule of Perfection*, a key work in Counter-Reformation spirituality and mysticism, which circulated among several radical and Independent groups and congregations before and after 1640.[98] That Randall was prepared to translate a Catholic work helps to explain the pejorative naming of him as a Familist, though whether this evidence is taken by itself, or whether it is set beside other evidence concerning Randall's activities, no definite identification of Randall as a Familist can be made.

The Rule of Perfection was composed in about 1593 and circulated in manuscripts until it was printed in French, Latin, and English in 1609–10. Benet wrote the work originally in French and translated the first two books into English. The third part was considered too dangerous for the popular reader, dealing as it did with the supereminent life. It was felt by Benet, and even more so by his superiors, that approaching such a mode of being without proper consideration of the first two parts and especially without the tutelage of a master would lead to claims of perfection by a lay readership.[99] Nevertheless pirated editions in French, Latin, and Italian of the third part did appear, and these forced Benet to produce the definitive French edition of 1610 in Paris, which was to be the text for many subsequent reprintings. It is quite probable that Randall translated from this text, though there is insufficient evidence to construct any relationship between Randall's published translation and the manuscript translation referred to in the confession of Giles Creech.[100]

Randall is characteristically unclear as to whether he had actually translated the work or was merely publishing somebody else's work. From the evidence of his other publications, it is possible that he may have revised an original English version. What is also clear is that any egalitarian proselytizing in Randall (such as has already been seen in John Everard) must be somewhat qualified:

and Rhetoric in Radical Puritan and Sectarian Literature, c. 1640–c.1660' (D.Phil. thesis, University of Oxford, 1985), 84.

[98] See above, Chapter 1, p. 39.

[99] Jean Orcibal, *La Rencontre du Carmel Thérésien avec les Mystiques du Nord* (Paris, 1959), 9–12, 40–1.

[100] Randall's translation omits the last chapter of the 1610 edition (ch. 21, 'Summa totius praxis').

That therefore the brightened Sun might not be clouded, and the cleerest glory vailed from the eyes of poore suiters; I have been induced to attempt the publishing of this most excellent and spiritual piece of incomparable price to the use and view of the more common and vulgar people in their owne Mother tongue, not doubting but the light breaking forth, it shall finde entertainment, and leade and cause to grow up as calves in the stall.[101]

The translation was published under the title *A Bright Starre Leading to, & Centering in Christ our Perfection* in 1646, printed by Matthew Simmons for Henry Overton. Curiously it was registered in the Stationers' Register and 'licensed by the most learned and judicious' (sig. A5[r]).[102] However, no name of a censor appears and the phrase may have been intended to slip the book past the gaze of the Presbyterians and more orthodox Independents. This was a failure in any case as the heresiographers were soon denouncing Randall's translation. Nevertheless one of the licensers in 1646, John Bachelor, was sympathetic towards some of the Antinomians, such as Robert Bacon. Possibly Bachelor looked favourably upon Randall, though there is no evidence for this in *A Bright Starre*. 1646 was an active year for Randall for it was also in this year that he published his edition of the *Theologia Germanica* and John Everard's translation of Cusa's *De Visione Dei* which drew slightly less fire from the Presbyterians.[103]

The third part of *The Rule of Perfection* deals with what is called the supereminent life, the highest stage of mystical illumination. The first and second parts of the work are concerned with the active and contemplative lives respectively. The third part is at pains to emphasize the progression from active or exterior through the contemplative or interior to the supereminent or essential, though, as has been pointed out recently, the radical aspect of Benet's work lies in the degree to which the supereminent is seen ideally to permeate the active and contemplative spheres.[104]

As with the *Theologia Germanica*, and especially Cusa's works by which Benet was greatly influenced, the point of *The Rule of*

---

[101] *A Bright Starre Leading to, & Centering in Christ our Perfection* (1646), sig. A3ᵛ.

[102] William Wethered entered the edition on 13 March 1646: *A Transcript of the Register of the Worshipful Company of Stationers, From 1640–1708 A.D.*, 3 vols. (1913–14), i. 220.

[103] See Samuel Rutherford, *A Survey of the Spirituall Antichrist* (1648), ii. 118.

[104] Kent Emory Jr, 'Mysticism and the Coincidence of Opposites in Sixteenth and Seventeenth-Century France', *JHI* 45 (1984), 3–23 (pp. 9–10).

Perfection is to inculcate in the reader a denial or *annihilation* of self in order to achieve a union with the Godhead, with no apparent barriers in between. This is achieved by a process of successive stages of increasing illumination, each stage being marked by nine points of (remaining) imperfection. In this way a catalogue of good and false rests is built up. Following the negative dialectic of Pseudo-Dionysius, which was reiterated by Bona-venture and Cusa, Benet stresses the need for speculation in mystical writing, specifically the three-fold division of theology into the sensible (the realm of the imagination), the rational, and the intellectual (the mystical). Though Benet is spiritually radical, what is more important for the English context of publication is the rigid adherence to a broadly Bonaventuran framework. This results in a language which is in many ways very different from and indeed hostile to orthodox Puritan spiritual writing. It does however contain certain affective features whose roots would have been familiar to English Puritans, so facilitating a development of their own awareness towards an intense sense of illuminated union.

In the first instance Benet presents man as a temple (similar to the procedure of Hendrik Niclaes, using the Pauline analogy of man as a temple: 2 Cor. 3: 13–16; Eph. 2: 14), in which the divine operates in different ways, according to the three different spheres of outward, inner, and inmost. The exterior or active concerns external behaviour and should conform to the law, while the interior consists of 'contemplations and sweetest meditation of the inner man'. The soul having passed through the 'partition wall' of the temple (sig. A5^r)[105] and the veils having passed away, the soul is left 'denuded and unclothed of all forms' (p. 2). This is the state of annihilation, where the self is 'annihil'd and spiritualiz'd', in which all selfhood is lost and replaced by the inner presence of God. As with the German mystics Benet envisages a stage of Purgation prior to Illumination and Annihilation (p. 52).[106] Like Cusa, Benet describes and demands of his reader an appreciation of the divine as the absolute All over creation, including man. Creation is nothing. The result of this thinking of the unthinkable is meant to be the annihilation or supersession of the will and ratiocination. After Bonaventure the

---

[105] See Niclaes, *Revelatio Dei* (1649), pp. 76–87.
[106] As with the *Theologia Germanica*: see above, p. 132.

intellect is seen as blots and hindrances (p. 105) while one who is 'disannihilated' is compared to a Beast. Annihilation itself rests upon the necessity of prayer in order to come to the intimate, and remembrance.

It might plausibly be argued that it is impossible to know or even write about annihilation since it is the absolute opposite of rational cognition, far more extreme than the self-denial with which most Puritans were familiar. Benet provides a partial answer in that he assigns a certain knowledge, experience or reflection of annihilation to the contemplative sphere. Thus, while genuine union, passive annihilation, is not possible all the time, active annihilation, the means to union partly through the remembrance of past unions, is:

'Tis therefore expedient that this Active Annihilation mediate to annihilate the Acts of this Practick Love, which otherwise might hinder that enjoying, and raise so many middle walls between God and the soule. As therefore the Passive Annihilation nothings all things by deading all our feeling of them, and transchanging them into enjoying Love. (pp. 11–12)

Indeed, active annihilation, preserving the essence if not the experience of ecstatic union, is where the image of the Passion may be internalized: ''tis most excellent, saith the same Saint, to behold him in his Passion within ourselves' (p. 203). Thus, while annihilation in the passive sense is the end of images, active annihilation brings the soul and the crucifixion together, refashioning for the Puritan the strong emotional appeal of the atonement, as opposed to the notion of *imitatio Christi* in actions, which was never a primary Puritan interest. In fact, the third part of *The Rule of Perfection* goes so far as to extend the super-eminent into the active and contemplative lives, to take the realm of *unio mystica*, the purest operation of the divine in the human sphere, into everyday acts of devotion. Hence the appeal to Antinomians: though the Law should operate in external behaviour, the sphere of the external is dominated by the interior and the inmost where illumination and annihilation persist.

The key point, exemplified in Pauline references and quotations, is that we should bear the Passion in ourselves. However, this is not false 'in-turning' because the logical and necessary operation of 'in-turning' still involves the self. To think of the interior in this way is merely to evoke its opposite, the exterior: 'Inturning therefore I say is to be rejected because Out-turning is never to be admitted, but to live constantly in the Infinite of this Divine Being, & the Nothingnesse of all things' (p. 127). This effectively transcends much spiritual thinking in English radical religion based as it is upon notions of internal and external. The same goes for the 'Diapason [entire harmony or concord] of the Will' (p. 197) which helps to make Christ present, but which does not contribute to the supereminent sense.

Benet's heavy reliance upon Pseudo-Dionysius and Cusa, as well as Bonaventure, not only explains his attractions for Randall, but also closely identifies *A Bright Starre* with Everard's own writing, his sermons. It would seem that Randall renders Benet in an English which both relies heavily upon newly invented words to express actions in the mystical process and borrows vocabulary from the English soteriological tradition. Thus Randall has a reference to 'experienced Christians', akin to Everard's emphasis upon 'experience' as mystical illumination, though it should be added that in the work itself there is the Catholic definition of Light as Faith which 'Reason helps, experience ratifies and confirms' (p. 115). What is happening is that the Catholic position is appropriated for the radical and mystical Puritan position.

Benet distinguishes this metaphor of sexual union with an operation of exchange, so that as the burning desires flow into God, so the 'practicke Love' is exchanged with the 'fructive' (p. 35), and this is the way the Soul proceeds on her journey. The desire imagery pervades the first part of *A Bright Starre*, so that the Beloved comes to lodge between the breasts of the soul (p. 48), while later on, the image becomes one of unmistakable copulation: 'Here she opens her selfe, and entertaines this Being, not as a vessell receives what it holds, but as the Moon does the shine of the Sun. Here she throwes abroad her white and Lilly armes, to fold and close' (p. 61). The bride does not merely contain the bridegroom, she reflects his love, as if it were a trace or seed left in her. A curious sense of detachment is manifested by the combination of the erotic (for example 'the perfect *uncloathing of the Spirit*' (p. 49) with the pastoral: the Soul follows the *Lamb* wherever he goes (p. 60). Union and parenthood are combined in the image of the vine:

He that cleaves to God in one spirit; whence it comes that our sufferings are common. For, in what degree our Spirit hath Communion with the Spirit of God, God again by fervour of Love, & by Compassion, answerably beares our sorrowes. Wherefore he saith to *Saul*: *Why persecutest thou me?* He said not my friends or servants, but mee; whose members they are. For, *I am the Vine, and yee the branches.* And as the same radicall moysture is common to Boale and Branches; so is the feeling of sorrowes and sufferings to Christ and Christians. (pp. 190–1)

At the root of *A Bright Starre* lies the Neoplatonic doctrine of the coincidence of opposites. Each spiritual and corporeal act reduces to one point, immediate union with God. Nature becomes a mirror in which to contemplate the *vestigia* of divine majesty, but it is always seen in relationship to its merging with the transcendent One. Also, the coincidence of opposites explains the limiting of the crucifixion to the sphere of Active Annihilation, because Christ's humanity and divinity must not be mixed or contemplated together. The paradox of the Cross is the paradox of All (Active Annihilation) and Nothing (Passive Annihilation).[107] The paradox annihilates the very act of reason in trying to contemplate it, Benet expresses this through the metaphor of God as endless ocean, so that his readers are exhorted to be 'drown'd in the Bottomlesse Ocean of this Infinite Being' (p. 86). This represents the triumph of Active over Passive: 'though an Idea of Jesus Christ crucified present it self to us, yet the Ocean of Faith drownes and annihilates the same' (p. 189). In 1645, one of Randall's supposed followers, Cullumbeame, a grocer in Thames Street, was held to express what he had heard Randall say either in a private meeting or at a public preaching, that 'a man baptized with the holy Ghost, knew all things, even as God knew all things, which himselfe greatly admired as a deep mystery, and likened it to a great Ocean, when there is no casting anchor, nor sounding bottom'.[108] Clearly Randall was distilling Neoplatonic mysticism for popular consumption, in the year before his translations appeared.

The translations which Everard and Randall, in their similar ways, made available, were of sufficient concern to Laudians and to Presbyterians, to merit investigation, censure, and vilification.

---

[107] See Emory, 'Mysticism', pp. 13–14.
[108] John Etherington, *A Brief Discovery of the Blasphemous Doctrine of Familisme* (1645), 2.

Their role as disseminated radical religious material is not negligible, even if not pervasive. To regard these writings as a very minor manifestation of an enthusiastic quietism misses the importance of their role in making available a version of subjectivity based upon mystical doctrines of annihilation which denied the efficacy of any form of reformed religion. The problem for the modern historian is that these writings were the reading matter also of respectable quietists. Most of all, Everard and Randall were expanding the language of English Puritanism and radical religion, making German medieval mysticism and radical spiritualism, and also a version of Counter-Reformation mysticism, part of a native inheritance. This process is confirmed not only in their translations but also in their own writings, and in those of a few others. Not every continental tradition shared quite this fate, as can be seen in a search for the supposed presence of the Family of Love, the subject of the next chapter.

4

The Writings of Hendrik Niclaes and the Family of Love in the Interregnum

I

THE place of the writings associated with the Family of Love, primarily those of the Familist leader and prophet, Hendrik Niclaes, in mid-seventeenth-century England is difficult to locate with precision. Evidence concerning English Familists in the sixteenth and seventeenth centuries is patchy and obscure, though what is known grows steadily. In the seventeenth century the term 'Familist' was applied willy-nilly to any professor of perfectionism or Antinomianism. 'Familists' were seen also as those who met privately for Scripture readings outside of church services so that genuine Familists, who were always good at covering their tracks, are often obscured by the mass of hostile and inaccurate accusations made against others. Generally speaking, current knowledge of the production and circulation of Familist pamphlets is still extremely vague.

Nevertheless Familist tracts were re-published and read during the late 1640s and 1650s. In a ground-breaking pamphlet of 1954, which went far to contextualize and comprehend accurately the activities and writings of the Quaker James Nayler after three centuries of distortion, G. F. Nuttall spoke of a 'Familist milieu' in the 1650s in which Nayler moved, though the phrase was used loosely in order to avoid raising hopes or suspicions.[1] Nuttall was referring to the context in which, in the absence of an established church, spiritual and mystical writings, of which Niclaes's works constituted no small part, were read and discussed. Nevertheless, there is very little evidence to suggest that the Family of Love existed as an organized sect as it had done in the sixteenth century.

By analysing the conditions of production, translation, and re-publication of Familist works, this chapter elaborates upon

---

[1] A 'Familist' for Nuttall is anyone who believed the historical Christ to be a type: *James Nayler: A Fresh Approach* (1954), 2.

previous investigations into the popularity of Familist writings in the Interregnum. As with the works of Jacob Boehme, those of Hendrik Niclaes appealed both to intellectual spiritualists and to sectarians, helping to form that 'Familist milieu' in which individuals could be said to have a foot in both camps. By examining aspects of expression and style, including vision, allegory and emblem, the extent of Niclaes's affinity with and possible influence upon native sectarian and spiritualist writing can be demonstrated. The hitherto unnoticed sophistication of Niclaes's use of genres and the complexity of his allegorical and affective strategies are not reflected in English writers, though there are similar uses of particular vocabulary and qualities of vision, together with a certain affinity of biblical reference.

The Family of Love was established by Niclaes in the 1540s.[2] A merchant of Emden, Niclaes had as a child openly challenged the tenet that Christ's atonement provided sufficient grace for mankind, asserting that mankind was too sinful. A vision followed soon afterwards, which he later interpreted as a representation of the ideal union of man with the Godhead and of the history of the Family of Love. The vision forms the turning point in what later became the hagiographic account of Niclaes's life. Niclaes developed his own version of the Christian myth, which has been seen as influenced by several late medieval and sixteenth-century spiritualists and mystics, specifically Tauler and Franck, à Kempis, *Theologia Germanica* and David Joris.[3] Man, through Adam, had fallen from his original state of oneness with God. Christ's crucifixion had lifted the veil between man and God, but few realized this. It was Niclaes's own responsibility to bring men to a state of spiritual re-birth and near perfection on earth, to become 'godded with God'. Grace was to be found simply by joining the Family of Love and abiding by its rules, and anyone who did not would be damned. Niclaes established a hierarchy of elders, a system of devotional practices, and groups of Familists sprang up in the 1550s and 1560s in several cities

[2] See W. N. Kerr, 'Henry Nicholas and the Family of Love' (Ph.D. thesis, University of Edinburgh, 1955); N. H. Penrhys-Evans, 'The Family of Love in England, 1550–1650' (MA thesis, University of Kent, 1971); Alastair Hamilton, *The Family of Love* (Cambridge, 1981); J. D. Moss, ' "Godded with God": Hendrik Niclaes and His Family of Love', *Transactions of the American Philosophical Society* 71. 8 (Philadelphia, 1981).   [3] Hamilton, *The Family of Love*, pp. 6–23.

and regions of Northern Europe, France, and England. The Family was outward conforming, intended as a secondary, more intense engagement with the divine, across and within all churches. Niclaes himself professed to be a Catholic: he based the organization of the Family upon the Roman Church order, and criticized Protestants for their biblical literalism, which he regarded as a false understanding of the Scriptures. On the continent the Family of Love appealed to learned humanists, men like Christopher Plantin who were indifferent to outward religion, as well as to disaffected Anabaptist artisans. In England the sixteenth-century membership was largely among the lower (but by no means the poorest) orders, though there is evidence of Familist clergy.[4] Indeed, while on the continent literacy was a condition of membership, in England illiterate people were admitted as novices, while Bishops and Elders were chosen from those who could read.[5] There was never a large membership, but because of his own wealth, genius and connections, Niclaes was able to publicize his cause out of all proportion to the size of his following.

While European Familism died out with the death of Niclaes, the English Familists continued to exist into the early seventeenth century. This was in part due to the somewhat different organizational circumstances of the English branch, which remained unaffected by the changes in organization after Niclaes had moved to Cologne in about 1567. It has been suggested that the English Familists came to resemble the earlier Lollards especially in terms of their meetings to read the Scriptures together.[6] Moreover, if interrogated by the clergy, English Familists tended to confess their heresy only if the evidence against them was overwhelming. They would then recant but

[4] I. B. Horst, *The Radical Brethren: Anabaptism and the English Reformation to 1558* (Nieuwkoop, 1972), 152–4; Felicity Heal, 'The Family of Love and the Diocese of Ely', *SCH* 9 (1972), 213–22; J. W. Martin, 'Elizabethan Protestant Separatism at Its Beginnings; Henry Hart and the Free-Will Men', *SCJ* 7. 2 (1976), 55–74; id., 'Elizabethan Familists and Other Separatists in the Guildford Area', *BIHR* 51 (1978), 90–3; id., 'Christopher Vitel: an Elizabethan Mechanic Preacher', *SCJ* 10. 2 (1979), 15–22; id., 'Elizabethan Familists and English Separatism', *JBS* 20 (1980), 53–73; id., 'The Elizabethan Familists: A Separatist Group as Perceived by their Contemporaries', *BQ* 29 (1982), 276–81; J. D. Moss, 'Variations on a Theme: The Family of Love in Renaissance England', *RQ* 31 (1978), 186–95.

[5] Moss, ' "Godded with God" ' (1981), 23–4.

[6] T. W. Hayes, 'John Everard and the Familist Tradition', in Margaret Jacob and James Jacob (edd.), *The Origins of Anglo-American Radicalism* (1984), 60–9 (esp. 61–3).

might easily have reverted to membership of the sect afterwards.[7] The Familists, notably the groups in Surrey, Ely, and Warwick, provoked a wave of suppression, while the circulation of Niclaes's tracts in translation prompted outraged replies from several divines.[8] Recent evidence suggests that Familist affiliation could be totally assimilated into the parish structure, given the toleration of the local community and the failure of episcopal authorities to detect the heresy.[9] Despite petitions from Familists for toleration, Elizabeth and James I outlawed the sect in 1580 and 1606 respectively, and most of the communities disappeared by the second decade of the seventeenth century.

Even so, the idea of the Family of Love exercised a considerable hold over the popular and literary imagination for most of the century. The most famous examples are Jonson's and Middleton's inaccurate portrayals of Familism as sexually licentious but the obsession has been shown to be far more extensive.[10] Though the charge cannot be sustained, the popular image is significant in that it emphasizes the use of coded language and gestures in the sect as a means of signalling that heightened status which begoddedness brings.[11] On the theological level, several rejections of and attacks upon Familism were made in pamphlet form during the 1620s, and Laud's Ecclesiastical Commission did charge men with Familism in the 1630s. As has been seen, Niclaes's works appear to have circulated in London in the 1630s in English and Latin, and the evidence suggests that John Everard may have been familiar

---

[7] Heal, 'The Family of Love and the Diocese of Ely'; Martin, 'Elizabethan Familists' (1978); L. F. Martin, 'The Family of Love in England: Conforming Millenarians', *SCJ* 3 (1972), 99–108.

[8] See Stephen Batman, *The Golden Booke of the Leaden Goddes* (1577); John Rogers, *The Displaying of an horrible Secte of grosse and wicked Heretiques* (1578); id., *An answere unto a wicked & Infamous libel made by Christopher Vitel* (1579); John Knewstub, *A Confutation of monstrous and horrible heresies, taught by H.N.* (1579); William Wilkinson, *A Confutation of Certaine Articles delivered unto the Family of Love* (1579).

[9] Christopher Marsh, ' "A Gracelesse and Audacious Companie?" The Family of Love in the Parish of Balsham, 1580–1630', *SCH* 23 (1986), 191–208.

[10] Ben Jonson, *The Alchemist* (1610), V. v. 117; Thomas Middleton, *The Family of Love* (1607). See also J. D. Moss, 'The Family of Love and its English Critics', *SCJ* 6 (1975), 35–52; W. G. Johnson, 'The Family of Love in Stuart England: A Chronology of Name-Crossed Lovers', *JMRS* 7 (1977), 95–112.

[11] See Moss, ' "Godded with God" ' (1981), 24. For the relationship between Familist and 'official' language in the sixteenth century see Janet E. Halley, 'Heresy, Orthodoxy, and the Politics of Discourse: The Case of the English Family of Love', *Representations*, 15 (1986), 98–120.

with Niclaes's writings.[12] It would be wrong, as Laud's Commission did and as a recent commentator has done, to identify Familism with Everard.[13] Though both Niclaes and Everard were indebted to the *Theologia Germanica*, Everard's borrowing is by far the greater in profundity and length. Everard's mysticism derived also from Pseudo-Dionysius, Cusa, and Hermes Trismegistus, none of whom features prominently in Niclaes. While it is true to say that Everard held that all matter was 'accident', this does not make him a pantheist. The corresponding charge that Familists believed that all was ruled by nature rather than God is equally false, though one unspecified group, the 'Familists of the Mount', were suspected of this latter heresy.[14] Familism was also attached to a few more Antinomians, such as John Eaton, whose sermons were circulated in manuscript before they were published in 1643, and in the 1640s, Giles Randall, though neither show an interest in Niclaes's doctrines or works, as far as we know at present.[15]

I I

It is difficult to say exactly where the impulse to re-publish Niclaes's works came from. Certainly those like Randall, Henry

[12] See Chapter 3 above, p. 133, n. 18.

[13] Hayes, 'John Everard and the Familist Tradition' (1984), 65. There is no specific evidence for any substantial debt to Hermes Trismegistus in Niclaes.

[14] *CSPD*, dxx (1648–49), 425. The 'Familists of the Mount' were also held to have all things in common, to live in contemplation together, to deny prayers and the resurrection of the body, to localize heaven and hell and to internalize the Scriptures by allegorical readings of them. They included Edward Hill, a taylor and his wife, Stephen Proudlove, a pedlar, Rapha Harford, a bookbinder (who became a publisher and published Everard's sermons in the 1650s) and Callo, a perfumer and his wife. The confession also refers to the 'Family of the Valley' who held that all was according to the will of God, denied the resurrection of the Body, prayers and giving thanks to God, and denied the existence of devils. The 'Sensualists' or 'Essensualists' denied sin, placing all moral authority in the will of God. There was also a 'Family of the Antinomians'. Stephen Denison used the same categories in *The White Wolfe, or A Sermon preached at Pauls Crosse* (1627), 37–40, adding the 'Castalian Familists', who were presumably interested in the works of Sebastian Castellio, the translator of the *Theologia Germanica*. Denison's information was used by the popular heresiographer, Ephraim Pagitt, in *Heresiography* (1645), 84. Denison was attacking John Etherington who denied being a Familist, though he stressed the baptism of the spirit, and claimed that Esdras, Niclaes's favourite Apocryphal book, was genuine prophecy if not part of the Scriptures because of the similarity between 1 Esd. 8 and Ezra 7: *The Defence of John Etherington* (1641), 37; id., *The Deeds of Dr. Denison* (1642), sig. B2ʳ.

[15] Gertrude Huehns, *Antinomianism in English History* (1951), 64. However the Huntington Library copy of Samuel Pordage's *Mundorum Explicatio* (1661) does

Pinnell, and John Pordage, who could be counted both learned and religious radical, were crucial in the constitution of a readership for both types of work. For instance, a sales list suffixed to Giles Calvert's 1659 edition of the English translation of Paracelsus's *Aurora* lists Niclaes (and Boehme) alongside Cornelius Agrippa, Renodaeus, Gassendi, Samuel Hartlib, Thomas Vaughan, and Robert Gell. The pursuit of the goals of occult philosophy was paralleled by the pursuit of spiritual perfection, which Niclaes's works offered if read by themselves, and not necessarily attached to any form of Familist organization. It is impossible to judge the interest of the sectarians at large here. Calvert was advertising primarily for the learned, whereas the dissemination of Quaker literature did not necessitate advertisement, at least in this type of book, and it may well have been politically indiscreet to do so in any case. However, both John Saltmarsh and William Sedgwick, fathers of radical Puritan spirituality, do appear, though by 1659 the former was dead and quite widely esteemed while the latter had reverted to a submissive Antinomian scepticism.[16] Furthermore, George Fox did possess Niclaes's *Speculum Justitiae* while James Nayler's associate, Robert Rich, refers to Niclaes, among many other radical writers, as someone whom he had read and regarded as part of a distinct and revered tradition of spiritual writers.[17] Clearly Niclaes was popular across a wide spectrum of interests.

Niclaes's writings themselves, intensely prophetic and illuminist, are characterized by the construction of obscure allegories, based closely upon biblical language with some features of biblical myth structure. No one has yet attempted a comprehensive and detailed penetration of Niclaes's language, especially its affective aspects. A close reading reveals how the peculiar lack of clear reference between the literal and the allegorical levels (in some cases to the extent that the literal is omitted) results in a fundamental ambiguity in Niclaes's thought, which he does not explicitly resolve for the reader. The highly complex nature of

contain a frontispiece woodcut which integrates the figures in Familist pamphlets with those of Behmenist symbolism (see below, chapter 5, pp. 191–205).

[16] Thomas Fuller, *The History of the Worthies of England* (1662), ed. P. A. Nuttall, 3 vols. (1840), iii, 434–5 for Saltmarsh; Christopher Hill, *The Experience of Defeat* (1984), 97–109 for Sedgwick.

[17] J. L. Nickalls, 'George Fox's Library', *JFHS* 28 (1931), 3–21, (esp. 9); Robert Rich, *Love without Dissimulation* (1666), 6.

Niclaes's visions, both in generic and rhetorical terms, makes them fundamentally different from those of English sectarians. This is particularly so given that the visions are capable of yielding several layers of interconnected meaning, and are often consciously made to do so by the prophet Niclaes. It might be argued, through a consideration of syntactic, logical, and rhythmic elements in Niclaes's prose style, that there is a broad similarity between Niclaes and English sectarians, but on every level a discerning judgement points to the consciously more intense use made of rhythm and linguistic ritual, to parallel the very distinct nature of Familist doctrine, and the difference is enhanced when the nature of the English translations from the Low German is considered. Though Niclaes's visual representations and some elements in his vocabulary find no parallel or recurrence among English sectarians, it is possible to find similar descriptions of the dispensation of divine jurisdiction, visible through similar vocabulary but anterior to any surface allegory.

The importance of literature as a means of spreading religious ideas and of controlling the Family of Love was always evident to Niclaes. The pamphlets issued during his lifetime were sophisticated and well produced, and this is reflected in the English versions.[18] The number of sub-genres within this whole is very large, including prophetic exhortations, visions, meditations, ballads, psalms, and dialogues, epistles and proverbs. There is also a drama, *Comoedia* (1574, English trans. *c.*1575) which includes stage directions and resembles a morality play.[19] Most of Niclaes's works were published in two periods, 1555–60 and 1570–5, so that the composition of pieces was spread over several decades. Despite this and the variety of forms, the doctrine and language remain essentially the same, though there are some instances of an increasing sophistication.

It has been argued that the simple songs were most effective in England in the late sixteenth century when Familist groups in England supposedly consisted mostly of unlearned artisans and

[18] See H. de la Fontaine Verwey, 'The Family of Love', *Quaerendo* 6 (1976), 219–71. For an interpretation connecting Familist writing with literacy and the rise of the printing press, see T. W. Hayes, 'The Peaceful Apocalypse: Familism and Literacy in Sixteenth-Century England', *SCJ* 17 (1986), 131–43.

[19] C. A. Zaalberg, following the suggestion of J. Wille, alleges that the poet Jan van der Noot was influenced by Niclaes: *Das Buch Extasis van Jan van der Noot* (Assen, 1954), 72–4, 85, 88 n.

rural labourers. Two song sheets, *A New Balade* and *Another of the Same Kynde*, were published in 1574 and a Familist hymnal in manuscript was confiscated from the Surrey community.[20] However, it was the prophetic tracts which were re-published in the seventeenth century, where Niclaes's inner millennium is presented as the union of God and man, through the realization of the spirit within.[21]

Niclaes's appeal lies in his sense of a close relationship with God. *Mirabilia Opera Dei* describes the vision which Niclaes saw when he was young, a *unio mystica* which is repeated in extended and extrapolated form in his own works:

He was compassed about with a mighty great being of the glory of God, and the same was a[s] a very great Mountain of glorious beauty. And when he was surrounded . . . with the glory thereof, then this greate Mountaine wholly united itselfe with him in his whole spirit and mind, so that his spirit and mind, with the same great and glorious Mountaine, become so great and broad, that he became also of an equal greatness and like being, with the same, in altitude, latitude and profundity.[22]

This prophetic stance is at once both distinctly personal and also appropriates the being of God much more than is the case with later English sectarians. Niclaes does not worry about the problem of the distinction between his own identity and God's. His 'I' is simply his prophetic self, unified with God within. Indeed, Niclaes signifies this identity very specifically in his monogram 'H.N.', 'Helie Nazarenus' or 'homo novus', as well as Hendrik Niclaes. What H.N. says is an original prophetic utterance though it seems to rely for its authority at least in part upon the similarity with or repetition of utterances by biblical prophets, especially John, and Christ. So 'I will open my mouth in similitudes' is glossed marginally by references to Psalm 49: 7, 8 and Matt. 13: 13.[23] Simple sense impressions or single

---

[20] Lambeth Palace Library, MS 869.

[21] For a discussion of Familist tracts circulated in the Interregnum, in print and in manuscript, see N. Smith, ' "The Interior Word": Aspects of the Use of Language and Rhetoric in Radical Puritan and Sectarian Literature, 1640–1660' (D.Phil. thesis, University of Oxford, 1985), 101–7. These include some of the works of Niclaes's disciple and eventual opponent, Hendrik Jansen van Barrefelt ('Hiel').

[22] Tobias, *Mirabilia Opera Dei* (?1650), 16–17.

[23] *Terra Pacis* (1649), 7. The biblical reference not in Niclaes's margin is Hos. 12: 10.

faculties are the central indexes of Niclaes's prophetic descriptions, for it is through these that the visionary power gains its focus. Sound, 'I will open my mouth', elevates H.N. as a voice rather than a prophetic persona and it is coupled with instant visual and perceptual reward, '*I looked and behold*'.[24] Sound or silence accompany H.N.'s visions. They are part of the sense of God pouring himself forth: 'The Lord, the God of Heaven, moved me, in his minde, or Spirit; his power encompassed me with a rushing noise: and the glory of the same *God* of Heaven became great in my Spirit of his Love', which heralds the eventual Sounding of the Last Trumpet and the rising of Daniel alongside God to judge.[25] The communication of spirit is what is important, though it is unclear whether 'in' God's mind means the moving of H.N. *into* the Godhead or whether it is simply God consciously operating in a certain medium. After the sound comes silence, the interval in the apocalypse in which all the earth and everything on it are entirely still, prior to the judgement.[26] In fact, the judgement is but the last part of a long process in which H.N. 'cries' out for love, for a requital of his desire for the divine, and he is given in return a series of aural and visual gratifications.

Niclaes is using prophetic and apocalyptic language from the Bible to express his inner revelation and divine union which will extend to all men, should they wish to receive it. In this way the Bible becomes an allegory of the inner change both in terms of the imagery and the narrative structure employed, but H.N. writes as if the experiences were happening to him in the sense that he is undergoing a prophetic vision. It is this personal sense of experience which communicates most effectively to the reader. But then, Niclaes's allegorical method becomes part of the prophecy in another sense, in that it constitutes a clarification of the obscure symbols which H.N. sees. For instance, in *Revelatio Dei* H.N. has his vision in the land called 'Pietas', and he is visited by figures such as '*Testimony of Truth*', 'which distinctly informed me of the diversity of things, and resolved me also (with clear understanding) of the things which I understood not, and

---

[24] Ibid. The centrality of the Apocalyptic element is evident here, the root text being Rev. 4: 1.

[25] Niclaes, *The Prophecy of the Spirit of Love* (1649), 8, see also p. 87; Niclaes, *An Introduction to the holy Understanding of the Glass of Righteousnesse* (1649), 103 features an entire chapter characterized as a trumpet sounding.   [26] *Revelatio Dei*, p. 46.

were shewed unto me' (pp. 4–6, 34). On this level, Niclaes is employing his own allegorical figures which represent his state of mind during revelation, and which dramatize his inspiration, so that the visions look like biblical visions (Daniel has one who stood next to him as an interpreter) while simultaneously setting forth elements in the illuminist doctrines of the Family of Love, which appear as original prophetic revelations.

In *Revelatio Dei* the vision sequence begins in two stages. At the very beginning of the work, H.N. sees a glorious angel and the Lord in Heaven. The descriptive language is limited to little more than this (pp. 4–5), while *Testimony of Truth* appears and proceeds to explain the nature of the body of love, the role of Abraham in leading the holy people, the inward righteousness of Christ and the spirit, and the meaning of circumcision (pp. 12–31). In response, H.N. rejoices so much that he has to be reminded of man's sin. This then broadens out into a vision which derives its energy from the conjunction of male and female principles. Out of the mountain in *Revelatio Dei* comes a woman 'whose body was even as a Gods body, or as a spirituall heavenly mans' (p. 38). She is based on the woman in Rev. 12, though here Niclaes explicitly outdoes the Scriptures since his woman is brighter than the sun, as opposed to the biblical woman who is merely clothed with the sun. In Rev. 12: 5 the woman gives birth to the man child, but Niclaes's woman gives birth to a wind, continuing H.N.'s favourite prophetic *motif* from 2 Esd. The woman is an archetypal principle of revelation, her force stemming from her union with the divine:

This same gave forth her self so great and glorious, that she stretched out her self over all heavens, and also in all heavens, and she was, and remained consubstantiated with the Deitie, and with all heavens; and with the clearness of her body, she gave light in all heavens and over the universal earth, for her body was in clearness, brighter then the Sun. (pp. 38–9)

She then becomes a source of grace for mankind (p. 40). Grace is seen to flow out of her mouth, while the saved are depicted as those who suck from her breasts (p. 45). The image here is echoing Isa. 40: 49 and 2 Esd. 8: 8–10 where Esdras uses procreation as an analogy for God's nurturing of each individual. The prophet's explanation becomes a genuine vision for Niclaes, though the womb imagery is suggested to Esdras by the Lord previously (2 Esd. 4: 40–2; 5: 46). The conjunction of principles is reflected in H.N.'s conception of Adam and Eve. Originally Edenic mankind lived in union with God as the 'Life', and from the 'Life' God created the female 'Memorie' in order to have the original unfallen 'Fellowshipp unto the Life':

And that was the holy Understanding, the Fellow-Life of the Life. And the Life inclyned to the Memorie his Fellowshipp and she was the Woman of the man. But the Life, was a Life of God, and was an everlasting substantiall Being, of one substance with the Godhead. And the Memorie, was a memory of the Life of God, and was the Fellow-Being of God with the life, and with God.[27]

It is the memorial function, womanhood, which breaks the fruit from the Tree of Knowledge of Good and Evil and takes man, the Life, out of the holy Understanding, bearing with herself the memory of culpability.

The second stage of the vision sequence is rendered in a more complex symbolic mode. Seven lights are seen to come out of the side of the Godhead. The description of each at this first appearance is simply that man does not understand the lights, though there is an allusion to the description of the creation in 2 Esd. 6: 38–54. The seventh light is identified as the perfection of the Godhead and what follows is a revelation of world and mankind in terms which relate directly to the woodcuts accompanying Niclaes's works (*Revelatio Dei*, pp. 46–50, and Fig. 1). The seventh light becomes the globe in which the world is 'glassed' or viewed. Despite Christ's atonement (Niclaes took Christ as the seventh prophet and himself as the eighth): 'the world, together with all men on the earth were in all these seven Lights turned wholly into silence, and so insensible that they could not distinguish the lights from the darknesses' (p. 48). While the 'glasse' becomes a medium for prophetic revelation, just as one would see through Cusa's divine 'eye', Niclaes's vision returns to its biblical archetype: the Godhead acts as a womb from which the lights are born.

The climax of the vision in *Revelatio Dei* comes when, after expressing extreme anxiety regarding the fate of man, H.N. is able to see into the Godhead where lies 'great Grace, Love and

---

[27] *The Glasse of Righteousnesse*, Bodl., MS Rawl. C. 554, fo. 3ʳ.

Now is the Iudgement of this World, now shall the Prince of this World be cast out. *Iohn. 12*

Now is come falvation, and ftrength and the Kingdome of our God, and the power of his Chrift. *Apoca: 12.*

Fig. 1. Hendrik Niclaes, *Revelatio Dei* (1649), Sig. A1ᵛ

Mercy' which appear to give him the knowledge of all the secrets of God. At this point, we are not told any more. H.N. cannot tell more until *Testimony of Truth* provides the answers. In its voice, the hills which H.N. saw when he looked down upon the earth are said to be the continuing variance and diversity, just as the images in the dream of Nebuchadnezzar which Daniel interpreted (Dan. 2). Once again, similarity of H.N.'s vision with a biblical one provides a measure of authenticity, though this time it is more specific as *Testimony of Truth* explains that the wind which came from the woman in H.N.'s vision was like the stone in Nebuchadnezzar's dream, a symbol of judgement, while the Word of God is Christ himself (p. 53). The next chapter allows *Testimony of Truth* to interpret the seven lights which are seen to come out of the Godhead as seven days or historical periods, so taking the allegorical framework to a further level of significance. This interpretation is both a reading of human history and a history which is contained within each individual. The first day is identified as paradise, the second as the law, the third as righteousness (signified itself by the consubstantiation of the divine with true Spirits and holy Angels), the fourth as the dominion of God and the capacity to become 'begodded', the fifth as the stool of majesty in man, the sixth as the vision of peace in perfection, and the seventh day as the anointed. To this is added the eighth day, H.N. being the eighth and last prophet, the New day when all the saved walk together in righteousness.

The vision of individual figures culminates with the appearance of the dispenser of justice:

one cloathed with an Habergion and Harness, and girded with an iron chain. And both his hands, and from his girdle-forth, even unto the very end of his feet, he was very red and wet of bloud, and he had in each hand a sword; the sword in his left hand was also very red and wet of bloud, but the sword in his right hand was altogether a glowing fire, [which] glinsened [*sic*] and crakt very terribly, with many fire flames, and there stood written on his forehead, *The vengeance of God.* (pp. 114–15)

The imagery, drawn from various parts of the Bible, is sensory and blatantly violent.[28] It illustrates the literary aspect of Niclaes's discourse in so far as this image is a fairly typical construction in sixteenth-century religious writing. The same figure, for instance, occurs in the *Enchiridion Militis Christiani*

[28] 2 Esd. 13: 3–5; Sap. 18: 15–16; Job 41: 26; Nch. 4: 18; Rcv. 6: 4–8.

(1515) of Erasmus.[29] The usage of the figure also raises another question regarding the reading of Niclaes's allegory. Given that an internal apocalypse is being described, is it taking place inside the individual or inside several people simultaneously? If the former is assumed, then the allegory remains closed and supports the notion that heaven and hell were states of mind, a belief attributed to many English Familists. If the latter is assumed, an external and objective element is introduced, enhanced by the very visual, concrete figure. It is as if the allegory is breaking down to admit a literal reading of the Day of Judgement at this point. Niclaes most probably did mean to support the internal apocalypse here, but the specific nature of his allegorical figures sometimes puts that in doubt.

Nevertheless the figurative emphasis is given further support by the sophistication of the exploration made possible by the use of allegorical figures. *Testimony of Truth* and *Vengeance of God* are not the only externalizations and personifications of Niclaes's prophetic consciousness. *Searching Providence* and the *Accuser* are also called forth by H.N.'s plea for knowledge (p. 62), the former being a Promethean figure. Between them they explore the relationship between human transgression and obedience, partaking as they do both of internal human and transcendent qualities. They have taken man's earthly, and in their terms, 'experimental' knowledge and judgement, as far as is possible, and seem now to look forward to something more: to challenge God's will and therefore to take control of destiny. With the now familiar sign of judgement and revelation, the wind or 'vehement rushing', *Searching Providence* and the *Accuser* are whisked to God's presence where the challenge is made:

There is great injury ministred unto me *Searching-providence*, on the earth, for against mine Office and my Righteousness there is another entred into mine Office; by whom both I and the man (in his understanding) have been constrained (oftentimes) to suffer disturbance. (pp. 68–9)

The *Accuser* echoes this, and the consequence is a trial where *Searching Providence* chooses *Testimony of Truth* as a judge, while God chooses the *Memory or Understanding of the man* (p. 70). Niclaes's intention is to show the union of God and man's

---

[29] English translation (1533), ed. Anne M. O'Donnell (Oxford, 1981), 53.

destiny, and to do this, *Testimony of Truth* is dispatched to earth to be with *man's understanding*. Thus, God has been relegated from his usual all-powerful position, while the arena of earth seems to emphasize the fact that judgement takes place inside man. As the allegory eventually makes clear, the identities of the original actors are not properly constituted so that the allegorical narrative is a process of revealing true identities and purging the positive elements or qualities from corruption. To do this Niclaes has telescoped biblical narrative patterns and history both ways, so that the entire Bible is compressed into the allegory, while the prospect of revelation seems to focus attention rather more on the last book, and this is supported by the heavy use of the language of apocalypse, though for Niclaes, all biblical elements are simply 'figures' or 'similitudes' which may be used to illuminate his own vision or 'similitude' of divine truth in any appropriate way.

The appearance of *Testimony of Truth* by *Man's Understanding* takes the form of a union between the former (male) and the latter (female) in archetypal terms which Niclaes has employed previously in the same work.[30] *Man's Understanding* (earthly knowledge) has reached her teleological end. The other further consequence must be to receive *Testimony of Truth* or divine knowledge, the 'joyful Message'. In one sense, the divine purpose is already revealed according to God's will: both His judge and *Searching Providence*'s have been brought together as one inevitably, though God had originally chosen what to the reader would not make the most reliable judge, *Man's Understanding*.

Man's Understanding is at first reluctant to merge with *Testimony of Truth* since *Searching Providence*, the source of all previous knowledge, has departed, leaving only a disquieting silence. Man is unfamiliar with the new, a clear comment upon human behaviour. *Testimony of Truth*, by revelation of mysteries and repetition, eventually convinces *Man's Understanding* who seems to be impressed by her joint role as judge in accordance with the principles of Right and Equity, Niclaes's moral and juridical absolutes (p. 74). The union of 'one beeing with each other' (p. 77) finally mirrors the nature of each individual's relationship with Niclaes and the Family of Love, and it is put forth in terms which suggest the allegory of the Song of Solomon: 'then opened the whole minde of the *Understanding* it self, and received

---

[30] However, Niclaes is not positing unfallen man as androgynous here.

Testimony of Truth very lovely with joy, and believed him with whole heart, And submitting her self obediently under his Requiring' (p. 76). The image of union is repeated three pages later, and the affectivity enhanced by the image of the con-joined principles gazing at each other in wonder. Then follows another vision of the Godhead pouring out of his heart and mind the new light or eighth day. This is the removal of the 'middle wall' (Eph. 2: 14) from *Man's Understanding*, who then becomes *Holy Understanding*, and the hosts may be gathered for judgement.

Against the desire of *Searching Providence* to be superior to God, God actually presents himself for judgement to show that he is all-powerful (p. 87). God is presented as an entirely self-sustaining emanating essence, or light, as in the vignette which often occurs on the title page of Familist pamphlets (see Fig. 2). At *Searching Providence*'s request, God declares his omnipotence as creator and divorces Providence from Searching by explaining that Providence is superior and part of God's body, its eye or sight, through which God sees all. Effectively man and Providence had fallen away from the true Light: all three should be one.

This constitutes the first sentence of judgement. The second demands that all give themselves over to God's understanding, so repeating the original allegorical vision of merging. Niclaes thus makes his allegories repeat the central tenet of becoming 'godded' in different ways and on different levels. The third sentence follows the vision of the great one, the Peace of God, sounding the trumpet to call up the dead so that Righteous Judgement can take place. In fact, the third sentence repeats the exhortation of the second one to come into the being. In the meantime, Niclaes's internal eschatology is set forth. *Searching Providence* is split in two. *Providence* returns to the same Being of Love, while *Righteousness* arises from death and becomes inconsumable (p. 112). The *Accuser* (the devil) and the newly revealed *Curious-Searching* depart from Eternity into the bottomless pit or everlasting spiritual death (p. 113). The notion of inner judgement becomes unmistakable here, as earthly being and the natural loving equity set themselves in upright form and being on the earth. This is connected to the actual worship of the Family of Love as the upright form is accompanied by the upright ordinance. The vision of vengeance follows and this in turn is succeeded by a vision and sound of joyous angels who announce

REVELATIO DEI.

THE
REVELATION
OF
GOD, and his *Great Prophesie,*
Which God now (in the laſt day)
Hath ſhewed unto His *ELECT.*

Set forth by *HN.* and by him peruſed a-
new, and more diſtinctly declared.

Tranſlated out of Baſe-Almaine.

O all ye people that dwel on earth, look now to it, that the
ſame come not over you, which is ſpoken of in the Prophets; behold ye diſpiſers, and wonder, and periſh : for I
do a work in your times, which ye ſhal not believe, when
any one ſhal tel it unto you. *Habac* 1. *Act.* 13.

London, Printed for *Giles Calvert,* at the ſign of the
Black Spred-Eagle, at the Weſt-end of *Pauls.* 1649.

FIG. 2. Hendrik Niclaes, *Revelatio Dei* (1649), Sig. A2ʳ

the new day, gather up the iniquity into a heap and cast it into hell. The remainder of *Revelatio Dei* compounds Niclaes's rhetoric of repetition. H.N. repeats that the allegory just expounded is the meaning of the seven lights, so giving his vision a sense of perfect closure. He also stresses its authority in that it fulfils the Scriptures of both the Prophets and the Evangelists (p. 119), while stressing his own unique prophetic powers which are repeated (albeit in slightly different forms) in his other works, specifically *Evangelium Regni* (pp. 120–6).

To English readers, the allegory of *Terra Pacis* might seem more familiar.[31] Here, the individual is seen to take progressive steps to become 'godded with God' by reaching the city in the Kingdom of God, and the journey structure facilitates the most tightly written Niclaes work. The Family of Love is identified with the divine kingdom of Christ. It is a framing device, so that the Family is ever present in the narrative both as society and spiritual experience. The figure of the holy city, popular of course throughout the Christian tradition, was an important figure for reformed churches, and especially for sectarians, with their desire to convert Babylon to Jerusalem, and this no doubt contributed to the popularity of *Terra Pacis* in Interregnum England.[32] However, the figurative treatment of the city here is entirely Niclaesian. A comparison with both traditional and radical Puritan versions is instructive. According to Augustine's interpretative system there are four interpretative levels: the literal, the allegorical, the tropological, and the anagogical. Allegorically, biblical Israel foreshadows the Church on earth, tropologically represents the soul of man, and anagogically presages the heavenly nation of Christ's reign. At the other extreme is the simple typology of the Münster Anabaptists and the Fifth Monarchy Men, where Jerusalem is a type, pure and simple, for the literal kingdom of Christ on earth. Niclaes does not deny that the city of the Family of Love has an outward existence in the actual members of the sect. However, the description of the city becomes indicative of the spiritual inner man: 'this good City, named *God's Understanding*', a '*land that is*

---

[31] Because of its linear structure, *Terra Pacis* resembles Bunyan's *The Pilgrim's Progress*, but Niclaes's work is unlikely to be the source for Bunyan.

[32] Augustine, *De Civitate Dei*, xiv. 11. The city in sectarian political theory is discussed in Michael Mullett, *Radical Religious Movements in Early Modern Europe* (1980), 20, 30 and more generally, 1–32 (ch. 1).

void of all molestation, and a City that is very peaceable which also is inhabited with no maner of vexation or unprofitable labour, but with joy, in all peace'.[33] Niclaes wants to communicate all of Augustine's senses, without making distinctions between specific levels of meaning.

Some confusion is inevitable for readers. On the one hand, the internalized nature of the allegory is enhanced in the simplified geography. The 'Land of Ignorance' has 'this forementioned City (named *Ignorance*) [which] hath two Gates; the one standeth in the North, or Midnight, through the which, men do go into the City of Darkness, or of Ignorance'.[34] There is the familiar departing of the veil or flesh of Christ in the heart of the believer, the falling away of the middle wall. On the other hand personal progress is judged by the juxtaposition of a catalogue of opposites: 'bitterness' and 'falsehood' are set against 'unity of heart' and 'nakedness', and it was such terminology, especially the later term, which led some to see Niclaes as an apostle of depravity if they read the text literally. Alastair Hamilton is right to point out the *lacuna* in *Terra Pacis*, that death is not mentioned before the city of God's understanding is reached, so that the individual becomes perfect in this life, unlike the authors of the *devotio moderna*, who warned against this despite their notion of the *vergottet* man. But this is precisely what Niclaes did believe, though he also maintained that the souls of the regenerate went to heaven after death. This, finally, shifts the emphasis to the inner nature of Niclaes's allegory so that the river before the city is named 'A desire in the pleasure of the flesh', with fishes standing for related qualities like *'Meate of the temporal delights, instead of the everlasting good'.*[35]

The appeal of Niclaes's allegories also relies upon a close integration of verbal and visual symbols. Detailed and sophisticated woodcuts accompany the text, functioning as an extension of Niclaes's emblematic imagination. Two vignettes are frequently used. The first shows two hands meeting across a heart with the words 'Love' and 'Truth' beneath them, symbolizing the Familist ideals of piety and community (see Fig. 3). The second,

---

[33] *Terra Pacis* (1649), 14. The marginal references are to Isa. 60: 65; 35: 4 and Jer. 33.   [34] Ibid. 27.
[35] Hamilton, *The Family of Love*, 36–7; *Terra Pacis* (1649), 63. The gloss here is Rom. 6, Eph. 5: 4; Jer. 5, Phil. 3; 2 Pet. 2.

Our Heart is the Minde of God most high.
Our Beeing amiable, as the sweete Lillie.
Our faithfullnes Love and Trueth vpright,
Is Gods Light, life, and Cleernes bright.

FIG. 3. Hendrik Niclaes, *Revelatio Dei* (1649), Sig. 14[r]

often to be found on title pages of Niclaes pamphlets, shows a
circle, possibly a rope for bonding, with an emanating tetragrammaton in the centre (see Fig. 2), which is in fact similar to
the vignette on the title page of the French editions of Benet of
Canfield's *The Rule of Perfection*, the Catholic mystical work
popular with English sectarians (see above pp. 137–42). This is
the true centre of the Word and God and the rays emanate to a
quotation from 2 Esd. 5: 42 (in the vignette, it is identified as '4
Esd.', from the Vulgate location), 'Coronae assimilabo iudicium
meum'. In their context God's words here mean that his dealings
with man are the same at all times, an index of God's difference
from man, though Niclaes perhaps wants his reader to see the
similarity between the ring, the seven lights or circles in his
vision, and the 'unity of Love' which binds the Family of Love
together as one.

The 'figurations', however, begin in the text, in an eclectic use
of biblical symbols. The opening of the book of the Lamb
signifies the entrance of the spirit, while a similar use is made of
the rending of the veil. Niclaes expands to personify love, so that
it becomes a female image of truth and love, in a way which prefigures Boehme's personification of divine wisdom as 'Sophia':
'The love is her self a nurse unto her children and a sure band
unto all those that are incorporated to the everlasting life, and a
mighty strength, which is able to suffer and to endure all
things.'[36]

In *A Figure of the True & Spiritual Tabernacle* the woodcuts make
the spiritual metaphor immediately more concrete (see Fig. 4).
The first representation 'figures forth' the medieval motif of the
Seven Deadly Sins emitted from the mouth of the serpent. Above
this is a naked man, a microcosm representing the inner man,
who also stands on the globe or world. To his right are
instructions on how to reach the true light and at the top the
tetragrammaton, which passes both blessing, seen in the tree
branch, and cursing, seen in the flaming sword. All are contained
within a circle, representing the inner self, heart, or soul. So this
depicts the operation of grace in the individual. The other
woodcuts show progressively greater stages of spiritual growth.
Each is marked by a picture of corresponding progress in the
temple. Niclaes is using a model similar to Maimonides's image of

---

[36] *The First Epistle* (1648), 12. The gloss is 1 Cor. 13.

FIG. 4. (i) p. 85

FIG. 4. (i–v) Hendrik Niclaes, *A Figure of the True & Spiritual Tabernacle* (1655)

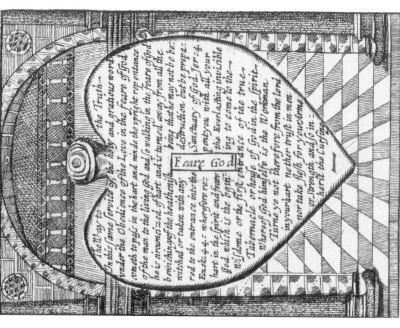

FIG. 4. (iii) p. 95

FIG. 4. (ii) p. 90

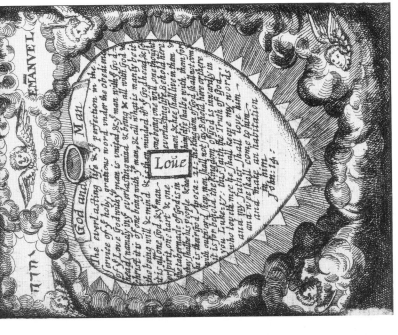

FIG. 4. (v) p. 109

FIG. 4. (iv) p. 104

the Temple of Solomon where different parts of the temple refer to increasing states of divine knowledge according to their proximity to the tabernacle at the centre. The veil covers the centre from sight, and before it are two hearts, which advise fear of God and belief respectively, with explanations written on them. Beyond the veil is the heart with love as its inscription, the aim of the service of love, the union of God and man. Though the hearts are in the traditional iconographic shape, differences of detail seem to match the differing states of growth. The first heart, advising fear of God, shows a sectioned artery at the top of the heart, as if the act of respect demands an inner knowledge. This is called the 'circumcision of the heart', compounding the sense of a cutting away. The second heart, requiring belief, is placed nearer the tabernacle, and represents a higher state of patient faith. The final heart representing the Love is taken out of the temple, and the presence of God in man represented by rays of light which come from the heart. Clouds of angels surround the heart, while the words on the heart, the heart of man that is, are taken from Rev. 21: 3 and John 14: 23, Niclaes's two favourite references for the coming of God inside man, which appear on the title pages of tracts and preliminary woodcuts.[37] As a whole, the woodcuts correspond to the process elaborated in *The First Exhortation*, where grace is the reward for accepting the Family of Love. This is belief, and it is followed by an awareness of sin and sorrow for it (fear of God), an appreciation of Christ's suffering (the veil), and the final baptism of the spirit (see Fig. 4).

Though some of the woodcuts make man the central part of the allegory, the tree is also central to Niclaes as a representation of that which brings the regenerate together. The woodcut attached to the *Speculum Justitiae* is the pictorial representation of this. Fools and unwise people become unfruitful trees (from Jude 1: 12), while trees and fruit become a measure of the rectitude of action. In the *Speculum Justitiae* memory breaks fruit from the Tree of Knowledge, which is a dismembering of love, the pleasant garden of the Lord. Similarly in *Terra Pacis* the traveller is confronted with a set of trees with various significant names, all of whom offer only *Vain Comfort* to him. Quite traditionally,

---

[37] See J. H. Hessels, 'Hendrik Niclaes: the Family of Love', in *The Bookworm* (1869), 81–91, 106–11, 116–19.

however, all believers are elsewhere grafted to the olive branch (Rom. 11: 17–24), an apt image for the notion of belonging which Niclaes seeks to evoke. Many of H.N.'s visions are set in this symbolically populated pastoral landscape: the poor silly sheep are exalted to return to the fold to escape the wolves, bears, dragons, and serpents. Most people, it would seem, are prepared to tolerate this vulnerability. Like hedgehogs they prefer to stay in unclean places.[38]

Though the allegorical figures represent substantial qualities in the inevitable process of spiritual regeneration, there are other moral qualities which lie anterior to the allegory and which Niclaes pushes forward with no small emphasis. The Love has subsumed within it the 'Vertues', so that living in the 'community' of the Love makes the individual take on these virtues.[39] It seems that here Niclaes is moving from the realms of the metaphorical 'body of love' into the active sphere where the application of virtues is made. However, in most of the pamphlets precisely what the virtues are remains unclear, apart from being a general active or behavioural quality associated with the Love, which endows the individual with 'Beautifulnesse'.[40] Like wisdom it proceeds from an understanding of judgement and becomes an object to which devotion must be pointed: 'Love ye the Vertue fervently.'[41]

However, suffixed to *A Figure of the True & Spiritual Tabernacle* is a section entitled 'Of the Eight Vertues or Godlynesses, whereout all Vertues Godlynesses do proceed or spring' (sig. O4[r]). At the start of this section 'Elders or dayed ones in the same' are referred to, who presumably have achieved just such a comprehension and embodiment of virtues. In fact, the description of virtues itself is highly significant for the way in which the very description of each virtue implies its opposite vice by incorporating the same or associated descriptive qualities of that vice. For instance, the first virtue is the 'Lust, Pleasure or Will of the Lord' (sig. O5[r]), which necessitates renouncing one's own lusts. The other seven virtues together with the first one, correspond exactly to the eight lights originally seen by H.N.

---

[38] *Terra Pacis* (1649), 92.

[39] *The Prophecy of the Spirit of Love* (1649), 20. In *Comoedia* (Cologne, ?1574), a debate takes place between the virtues on p. 11[v].

[40] For Niclaes, such love fulfilled the law (Rom. 13: 10), rather than releasing the individual from sin.   [41] *An Introduction*, 2nd pagination series, p. 284.

They are not so much modes of behaviour as states of being, which correspond again to the stages of begoddedness. Thus, the third virtue is 'Lordlyness or Dominion of God, or essentially to Lord with God . . . for that the same might obtain a being-like shape in you, and ye to Lord with God and his righteousness essentially or being-like' (sig. O6ᵛ).

Clearly Niclaes fashions traditions in the Catholic church here to his own ends and the virtues are complemented in the *First Exhortation* by a description of the Eight Beatitudes, from Matt. 5 and countered by an elaboration upon the seven deadly sins, the opposition of the two being represented in a woodcut earlier in the pamphlet (see Fig. 4.4(i)). Here Niclaes does move into a literal interpretation of biblical language in order to expound his behavioural requirements. These are driven by a need to mirror the purity of begoddedness in one's life, so that those 'of the truth know in the Spirit, where-through they have a regard unto a pure procreating with undefiled love' (p. 206).This results in instructions which are not found elsewhere in English sectarian literature in this way. So the upright man and wife are not to use their bed for 'lust', and they are forbidden to lie together during menstruation or 'bloody abominations' for the sake of purity (pp. 205–6). Though one of Niclaes's glosses here, Lev. 15, refers directly to such cleanliness, the other provides an example of a continuing allegorical interpretation within the overall literal framework. Ezek. 22:2 has the word of the Lord asking Ezekiel to judge the bloody abominations of the city, which is referred to in the feminine, so providing the point of identification with woman.

Equity exists as a force of balance, providing mercy for the begodded. The absence of equity is judgement, darkness, and the roaring of bears.[42] As we have seen Judgement comes by Right and Equity, and it should be a complement to love.[43] When Niclaes refers to Equity he does not mean any specific legal process but the biblical usage put to his own ends. The result is an enhancing of the prophetic emphasis rather than the definition of the social extension of Christian charity, which would have been familiar to most English people.[44] In *Revelatio*

---

[42] *An Introduction*, 2nd pagination series, p. 45.

[43] *The Prophecy of the Spirit of Love*, p. 77.

[44] See William Perkins, Ἐπιείκεια: *Or, A Treatise of Christian Equitie and Moderation* (1604), 2. Biblical references to equity include Ps. 98: 8, 99: 4; Prov. 1: 3; 2: 9; Ecc. 2: 21. Niclaes was fond of the references in Isa. 59: 14 and Mal. 2.

Dei vengeance and the casting down of iniquity are preceded by all who are in the upright life in nature achieving a natural equity, which is presumably counterpart to a spiritual equity. It is a state of mind, a quality worth 'praying in', which can have external manifestations, like wisdom (p. 114). This, and the potential in Niclaes for Equity to exist as a force which has grown historically in mankind, make the notion of Equity in Familist literature bear an affinity with the work of the legal reformer John Warr, who posited Equity as a dialectical force of right in human history.[45] A measure of Niclaes's consideration of this-worldly behaviour is that Equity, a 'humane Ordinance', is disastrously forgotten if man attempts to ascend to the Spirit by his wit alone.

The Familist use of different genres to 'figure' divine truths, so that genre becomes a figure itself, is reflected in the works reproduced during the Interregnum. The morality play structure used by H.N. in *Comoedia*, which is reflected to a certain extent in the allegory of *Revelatio Dei*, was appropriated and transformed by the anonymous author of *An Apology for the Service of Love*.[46] The author was supposedly attached to the Elizabethan court and the structure represents something more than a dialogue between three speakers (the Countryman, the Citizen and the Exile) but something less than a masque, which has been one claim made for it.[47] The Exile is a particularly apt name for the representative of the Familists, since his status exactly mirrors the current state of the Family of Love in society: a complete 'communalty' which has been rejected by most of English society despite the success of Familists in their simulation of established religion. The Exile also bears connotations of Christ in the wilderness, and, by his unorthodox clothing, an Old Testament prophet. He also reflects the journey which H.N. is supposed to have made into the forest in *Mirabilia Opera Dei*. In fact the Exile wears the skins of wild beasts, which turn out to be a means of disguise and defence against the beasts: 'Lest otherwise I might be devoured of them'—perhaps a reference to the Familist

---

[45] *Administrations Civil and Spiritual* (1649), 2, 11.

[46] The author puns on 'courtier' in order to identify pious good manners (in the court) with the prerequisites for becoming a Familist: 'You lowly courtiers, courteous by kind, / Lowly, wise, and pleasant in mind, / This little Device from the ground of his heart / The *Exile* hath sent you, take it in good part.' (sig. A3^r)

[47] Moss, ' "Godded with God" ' (1981), 23.

practice of outward conformity (pp. 8–9). The *Apology*, though it is replying to criticisms made of Familist attitudes to ordinances, sacraments, and political authority, is also deriving much of its impetus from the popular theme of withdrawal and exile in the drama. Indeed, the exile of the virtuous man or society is a theme which may have appealed to many European humanists (especially those drawn to Stoicism) who were associated with the Family of Love. At any rate it was a popular means of propagandizing, given the allegedly pervasive popularity from the 1590s onwards of *Mucedorus* (1590) and the attraction it held for Shakespeare in *As You Like It* (1599).

The *Apology* supports Niclaes's insistence that the enlightened should be brought into the unpolluted 'body of Love' by employing a detailed metaphor of social kinship, centred on the relationship between the three characters in order to highlight the persecution against the Family of Love. The Exile has a 'simple mind', a humble, meek spirit of childlike purity as a sign of spiritual ascendancy against the various degrees of hostility manifested by the other two speakers. Significantly it is the countryman who says that the Exile must be a heretic and demands further questions of him. Though the Exile criticizes corrupt patronage at the Elizabethan court, there are some statements which are relevant to the way in which the pamphlet must have been intended for publication and read in the 1650s. For instance, the Exile places an unfailing belief in the early Father, Prophets, Apostles, and the Apostolic, Athanasian, and Nicene Creeds (p. 38), upholding as it were the essentials of the Church of England, together with the desire to sing a song at Paul's Cross, the centrepiece of Elizabethan public preaching. Given the uncertain ecclesiastical policy which prevailed in the Interregnum, at the very least this could have been taken to mean an acceptance of the bare essentials of Christian religion, but with a plea for the necessity of higher spiritual illumination which H.N. offered. The discussion ends with the Countryman lamenting the persecution of Familism and asserting that Familists are honest, not superstitious, and very like English people, notably in their pursuit of brotherhood.

When pressed on the point of sacraments, the Exile says that all images are sacraments (p. 51), so that the externals of worship and the means of exploring the divine in Scripture (the figures) are collapsed together. The latter is an extension of the former and the difference between them lies in the way in which the individual is able to interpret them. Essentially they are part of the same hermeneutic system. Sacraments come to represent true begodding and this, H.N. appears to be saying, is how the early Church understood sacraments and ceremonies. At the other extreme but by the same token the description of begodding becomes a higher form of sacrament itself (p. 47). Since the major collective activity of the Family of Love seems to have been reading the Scriptures, that reading serves as the gateway to the superior sacrament and the begodded state for the individual.

The extent of this connection between inner and outer is demonstrated in *Evangelium Regni*, the explanation of the Family of Love's hierarchy of authority. Moreover, in this connection, the fusion of the literal and figurative types of interpretation are explained. 'Figures' are identified with rituals of worship or 'services':

the true Being of the services of the Images and figures (in the Spirit, and in all truth) erected, in the obedience of the Belief . . . And this aforementioned service of the Image, Figures and Shadows . . . brought forth a serviceable seed of Righteousness (after the manner as is said of *Agar* [Gal. 4: 24]) the which is the Elders Testament. (p. 64)

Niclaes identifies image with word, and image with ritual, all three of which have become a 'type' or 'shadow' for the transcendent spiritual truth. Verbal symbols enact the purification of the believer. Extending the notion of 'Homo Novus' and the 'deified man' of the *Theologia Germanica*, the members of the Family of Love are 'godded with God' under the 'Annointing' and all are 'grounded on Christ'.[48] From the divine side, God 'mans' himself. The special vocabulary seemingly contains within it an impression, in the figurative sense, of the spiritual action which it describes. For Niclaes this was in order to enforce on every level the sense of belonging to the 'body of love', the metaphor he uses to describe the Family itself. It was this rhetoric which so aggravated the early separatist Henry Ainsworth. He saw that Niclaes created his own gospel, 'farr differing from the language of Canaan', which was more 'grosse or wicked'

---

[48] *Evangelium Regni*, 76; Bodl. MS Rawl. C. 554, fo. 2'.

than Mahomet, and which enabled Niclaes to be the 'gaoler' of people's spirits.[49]

The keywords and key phrases employed are at once powerfully effective and plainly representative of the experiential heart of the Family of Love. Such examples, which will be returned to later, are 'God-service' (*Godes dienst*), 'Holy Understanding' (*Heilige Verstândnis*), and 'washing in love'. It was not unusual for radical Puritan sects to develop what has been called a jargon or specific vocabulary to describe specific experiences. What distinguishes Familist vocabulary is the way in which it is so very different from that of any other sect in England, even when compared with later Ranter and Quaker terminology (with which Familist vocabulary was often compared by hostile commentators). Indeed, John Etherington spoke exactly of the 'keys' necessary to understand Familists, as did John Tickell, identifying the 'chambers of imagery' which characterized Familist and Ranter language alike.[50] The cumulative effect is to create an impression of an enveloping bond of love, so that the begodded one is protected. The repentance of the saved takes the form of repetition (which itself enhances the sense of protection and identity with the divine), 'all good willing ones to the good, shall assemble them unto the good', and they are incorporated under the umbrella of Christ:

Therefore have we (which are now in this day of love, adjoyned and incorporated into the body of *Christ*) here in our Consolation among each other, and set our Comfort much more, on the righteous which are dead, then on the living ungodly.[51]

Eventually English fails, as the ultimate realization of freedom is seen as a renunciation: 'Gelatenheyt or free giving over of the upright Circumcision of the forefront of the true Tabernacle of God'.[52]

In one sense Familist vocabulary re-orders the significance of names in Christian myth: Christ becomes a type while H.N. and Hiel (Barrefelt: see above p. 151 n. 21) after him are both self-characterized as the life of God. But for the most part, the

---

[49] *An Epistle Sent Vuto Two Daughters of Warwick from H.N. . . . . With a Refutation of the errors that are Therein by H.A.* (Amsterdam, 1608), 42, 12.

[50] Etherington, *The Deeds of Dr. Denison* (1642), sig. A3[r]; Tickell, *The Bottomles Pit Smoaking in Familisme* (2nd edn., 1652), 46.

[51] *Evangelium Regni* (1652), 21.   [52] Ibid. 40.

'jargon' is concerned with intimating the sense of belonging to the 'body of love' or not. The spatial concern manifest in the allegorical visions operates here too. So to be unregenerate is to be part of 'the defecting or off-falling being' as opposed to 'God's lovely being'.[53] The unregenerate are all under sin while those in the 'upright being' and 'center' are part of the body of perfection: 'That verily is the life which is true, and that life is the light of men, and the head of the holy Commonalty. Who so goeth out of it, cometh to the death, blindnes and darknes.'[54] Diversity and variance, previously characterized as sin, are surmounted by the Unity:

Wherefore for the Unities sake in the Love, O ye children of men, lay downe your contentions under the Love, and have regard unto Gods promises, and to your Calling: and incline likewise your hearts to the obeying of the love, and of the requiring of her service.[55]

Recently the charge has been made against Niclaes that he reduces all to a redundancy, *ad absurdum*, by inventing so many terms to describe a central and rather straightforward spiritual experience.[56] However the vocabulary, like the allegories, is part of a generally consistent and well-planned whole where associated meanings of a central tenet (begoddedness) are developed successively and concentrically outwards from the central truth. This is Niclaes's comprehension of the shape of human understanding in the original state of the 'upright life' which H.N. has recently rediscovered. In this way traditional teaching is refashioned. Christ is not simply reduced to a part of the illumination vocabulary. Instead, the Atonement and the teaching of the Gospels become an entity in the inner self and in the 'body of love': 'confesse him [Christ] out of the shape that he hath in you, through such a cleernesse as his Apostles confessed him by'.[57]

As with the other radical religious sects on this occasion the notion of the seed, spiritually substantial, is seen as the factor which transmits the inward righteousness down from Abraham to Christ to H.N., as in *Revelatio Dei* (p. 20). This is part of the doctrine of filiation, so that those who became 'co-deified', or

---

[53] *The Prophecy of the Spirit of Love* (1649), 18; *A Figure of the True & Spiritual Tabernacle* (1655), 48.   [54] *An Introduction*, 2nd pagination series, 238.

[55] Ibid. 2nd pagination series, 268–9.

[56] Moss, ' "Godded with God" ' (1981), 40–1.   [57] *An Introduction*, p. 271.

'consubstantiated' with or in God are also part of his sonship. Elsewhere the children motif is used to intimate the becoming of part of the mind of Christ.[58] The 'body of Love' metaphor is given substance by the utilization of the image of the Tabernacle of God coming to reside spiritually inside the individual. Other figures support this, such as the Throne of Grace:

(which is appeared and come unto us, now in the last Time, in the most holy of the true Tabernacle of God, to an everlasting Stool of Grace, upon the Earth) the Glory of the Lord becometh manifest.[59]

This is coupled with an exploration in psychological terms of the meaning of illumination. Unlike the 'best-worthy', 'divers others' (and significantly they are *divers* and so associated with sin):

perceive no difference between the illuminated and the vnilluminated Men; and so whiles they are not yet illuminated themselves, they give regard both to their own Imagination of the Knowledge, & also to the Precepts of unilluminated men, because they trust upon such things: & suppose, that in such sort all is well with them.[60]

All of this is couched in very human and individual terms. The necessity of love is described as a 'bond', which calls one to the house of love, and encourages the individual only to present love and wisdom to the unilluminated. By contrast, human wisdom operates as a 'tye' which bewitches the senses and thoughts and prevents one from coming to true illumination. In this way 'serviceability', the obedience to the services and ordinances of the Family of Love, is couched in the most obvious and moving terms as a complete commodity:

Learne of the Love in her Service lowlinesse, long-sufferance, meek-nesse, sobernesse, chastnesse, and righteousnesse, in faithfulnesse and truth; that same shall be wholsome to your [v]eigns, do good to your navell, refresh your bones, and rejoyce your heart, and shall be unto you a living fountain.[61]

However, very definitely at the heart of this usage of specific terminology lies the description of two central experiences, that of Niclaes as prophet himself and that of the Godhead. The

[58] *An Apology for the Service of Love*, p. 21.
[59] *The Prophecy of the Spirit of Love*, p. 37.
[60] *An Introduction.* 2nd pagination series, p. 217.
[61] Ibid. 127.

prophetic gestures which characterize H.N.'s utterances facilitate the expression of simultaneous pride and humility of spirit. In *An Introduction to the holy Understanding of the Glass of Righteousnesse* Niclaes demands that his readers warn the desolate, with a cry, of their spiritual poverty and that the 'Seers', like H.N. himself, weep for the desolation and unrighteousness. This is part of the prophesying which coming to the understanding of God will fulfil (p. 17), while the ungodly, following the apocalyptic warning, continue to fear, tremble and quake as in Isa. 13. At the opposite extreme is the central emanating Godhead: 'God is a Spirit, a Light, or a life.'[62] Though the light is still a symbol for God, it seems to occupy a position superior to the other 'figures' enforced by the assonance of 'light', 'life', and 'like': 'Behold according to all like resemblance, even as God is a very true light and everlasting life, so is also his like-being a true light and everlasting life in the manly creatures.'[63] God is removed from man but also in begodded man. The link between the two is the action of perception, which is rooted in the prophetic experience. Thus, though humble behaviour is always a pre-requisite, the final but by no means least important prophetic component is the notion of the cleansing of the sight in order to see again into God. Coming into the service of the love results in a reform so that 'every mans eyes might be made bright, and become clearer and clearer, to behold with a clear sight of their eyes, Gods Kingdom of heaven'.[64] Characteristically enlightenment also comes with a physical sensation: 'my heart became lighted with cleaness, and my whole inward minde was pierced thorow with winds or life and delectable sweetness.'[65] This comes round to Niclaes's central image of the glass, so that looking into the Holy Glass of Righteousness or 'glassing' oneself daily is that act of renewal of perception and awakening through allegory and figure to perceive the essential Godhead or light.

Just as H.N.'s allegories are extensively detailed to match every aspect of the Family of Love, the rhetorical organization of each work is elaborate so that it is easy to read and very clear. *The First Exhortation* (1656) consists of a series of instructions from a 'Household-Father in the Communalty of the Love of Jesu

---

[62] *A Figure of the True & Spiritual Tabernacle* (1655), 58.
[63] *The First Epistle* (1648), 28.
[64] *An Introduction*, p. 148.
[65] *Revelatio Dei* (1649), 4.

Christ', a dialogue between a Father, the 'Oldest Elder of the Family of Love' and his 'obedient sone', and a series of prayers which combine mystical perception with the moral absolutes of Familism: 'to pray even so unto God when one in-seeth and knoweth that he hath sinned, or overreached himself in any thing: and beareth grief and sorrow therefore, in his Heart, or is full of heavinesse' (sig. A3^r; pp. 84, 161). The longest pamphlets contain summaries at the beginning of each chapter and there is the suggestion that they were intended as daily readings, just as the prayers in *The First Exhortation* are also meant for different parts of the day so that the individual's life should become punctuated with the Service of Love (pp. 134, 148). The more prophetic pieces do depend more upon being read and compre- hended in one piece. This includes not only *Revelatio Dei* but also *Evangelium Regni* which is a 'figurlie' reading of biblical history. Here the seed is transmitted successively through particular characters until H. N. is reached after Christ: the discourse only makes full sense when the last section, explaining the interpretative methods of the Family of Love, has been reached.

The extent of this rhetorical organization is far greater than in most English sectarians, though both share the predilection for invocation and apostrophe: 'Verily, in the same day . . . ', 'For that cause, O all ye people . . . ', 'For after the day of love . . . ', and 'there shall no day of grace appeare any more . . . ' all occur on one small octavo page.[66] What distinguishes Niclaes is his syntax. Displaying the heavier punctuation of German, the first sentence of *Evangelium Regni* lasts the length of two pages. Where English millenarians tend to write in long clausal units, fashioning unwieldy sentences with complicated conceptual turns inside single clauses, Niclaes, through his translators, generally breaks down clausal units, making the sense ductile. The sentence in question contains thirty-nine clauses, twenty-six commas, five semi-colons and seven colons. In the original Low German the effect is of a seemingly endless liturgy:

So zynder vele Volckeren mede betrocken gewesen / die deselue, vor de naerastige under vollentomene Godes-densten / unde Wercken der Gerechticheit did Godt forderde anfagen under gelouede; under van

---

[66] *The First Epistle* (1648), 8.

Velen oict also gedreven unde geleret worden, nomplick / na da wyze /
also idt oict in vohr-tnden, by de Juden.[67]

The expressive function in fact becomes limited by the short
clauses, so that the structure in each sentence becomes that of a
list, the components of which contain one action within a larger
framework. This is obviously more the case with the pieces which
consist of a string of commands or exhortations. The effect is to
evoke a rhythmic counterpart to that Niclaesian vocabulary
which seeks to contain its own action, something which is
reflected also in the early placing of the present participle:

Seeing now (dearly beloved) that we see, heare, and marke evidently, that
the blind wicked world is wholly minded to errour, hunteth for corruption, and destruction, and hasteth to fall into the plagues of the ungodly,
to her own perdition, which all malicious ones, together with such as are
strayed and departed from the upright life, doe take pleasure with, and
are blinded in, and doe daily increase in blasphemie, wicked imaginations, false judgements, malice, and owne-conceitednesse of self-chosen
wisdome: therefore let every one now with earnest love to the good, take
heed to his time, that is to say, that he hate, die from, and forsake all
that which the erring world increaseth in, and followeth after.[68]

The English Familists imitate Niclaes, especially with regard
to the incantatory nature of the prose. *The Apology* is marked
repeatedly by 'It is very true' (p. 35) reflecting both H.N.'s 'Take
it to heart' and more broadly 'O man! who art thou then, or why
takest thou so upon thee . . . and justifieth thy self'.[69] The purpose
of this is to maintain simple clarity, unlike the prophetic passages,
and to this end, Niclaes's pamphlets are littered with short
poems, prayers, and songs, most of which are exceedingly simple
in form. Here was the material popular among sixteenth-century
English Familists, though the author of *An Apology* puts the same
message and imagery into a somewhat more sophisticated form:

> Lest Gods wrath once kindled, unawares hap to fall,
> Where godly Love as a marriage weed,
> In Lowly hearts works all things new. (sig. A3ʳ)

---

[67] *Evangelium Regni* (?1573), 76.
[68] *An Introduction*, p. 28. This is a regular feature of Homilies and legal phraseology.
[69] Ibid. 23.

III

Any consideration of Niclaes's influence in the 1640s and 1650s must take into account how he was read by English people in this period. As has been seen Niclaes himself did not deny the validity of outward ordinances. He simply reserved for his own 'service' that allegorization of biblical language which described inner enlightenment. This symbolism was unique and because of this rejection of literalism he appeared as a sacramentalist to Protestants. For him the Bible was symbolic, a testimony to the Word, which men could only know within themselves. Thus, the woodcut at the front of *Revelatio Dei* extends the allegory to the context of Revelation where the Lamb is seen as Love triumphant over the serpent, and on top of the world (see above Fig. 1).

For the Presbyterian Samuel Rutherford, the Familist 'type' and 'shadow' for transcendent truth posed a radical threat to Reformed and even to Roman religion:

Familists deny the *Pope* to be *Antichrist*, and think the *Masse* and *Romish* Priesthood indifferent, as all Religions are to them, and there is no *Antichrist*, but the Legall Protestant voyd of the Spirit, because he speaks *Greek* and *Hebrew*, and hath some skill in logick, and would have the Scriptures in use.[70]

At the same time the notion of Christ being within the individual appeared to the separatist Henry Ainsworth not only as outrageous but also an example of transubstantiation while the notion of a 'Service of Love' was 'Papist'.[71] Like Ainsworth, Rutherford saw the identification of the spiritual with the symbolic and allegorical in H.N. and found that this offended his sense of biblical history and the real Christ:

Then is Christ not true man . . . nor dyed he really, but only Spiritually in us, when we suffer with the like meeknesse and patience, as he dyed and suffered, and yet he is but an Allegorick or phancied Man to the *Familist*. The like *Familists* say of his Resurrection, Ascension, and judging the world.[72]

Though Familist ideas, such as the localization of hell and inner apocalypse, do recur in English sects, it is hard to show any

---

[70] *A Survey of the Spirituall Antichrist*, 2 parts (1648), i. 202.
[71] Ainsworth, *An Epistle*, p. 47.   [72] *A Survey*, i. 167.

recurrence of Niclaes's way of writing. In his *Divine Dialogues* Henry More felt that the Family of Love directly influenced the early Quakers, who had first to reject Niclaes's sadducism.[73] In my opinion this rejection was paralleled on the stylistic and symbolic level by a refusal of Niclaes's detailed allegory and allegorical systems. Besides this there are recurrences of language which is found in Niclaes in Seeker, Ranter, and Quaker tracts, especially descriptions of the baptism of the spirit, the operation of the seed and the tree. Niclaes's use of biblical characters to represent eternal human qualities is reflected in Abiezer Coppe's early writings.[74] All these recurrences could equally have their roots in other sources. The difference between Niclaes and the English sectarians lies in the different comprehension of prophetic utterance. Where Niclaes spoke in 'shadows' despite being 'godded' himself, George Fox proclaimed the end of signifiying 'shadows', so that his messianic language is identical with the inner light, in the heart of the believer:

Here thou wouldst bring the Children from her mother above, which is *Jerusalem*, to Jerusalem below, and *Sinai*, and so to *Hagar* into the shadow; and the Christians witnessed the end of the shadows and Sabbaths, and witnessed the body Christ Jesus and *Jerusalem* that's above and come to Christ the end of the Law, and into God by him from whence the Law came, and so Christians cannot put signes in their bosome that have Christ within them, and cannot touch the doctrine, Commandments, Ordinances of men.[75]

Allegorical language still remains, interspersed with Quaker attacks on the established clergy, but the sense of experience becomes more personal, not so schematic. The tree of the *Speculum Justitiae*, the work which Fox owned, is expanded by James Nayler in *Two Epistles*, the allegory becoming less specific as a result:

Was there not a Plant planted amongst you once, a tender Plant, which had a little rooting in a tender Ground, which began to appear out of the Earth, more in beauty than all the Wild Trees of the Forest; it also did begin to Blossom, and some tender Grapes did appear; and the Roots and Branches began to spread, and to bend towards him that planted it,

---

[73] *Divine Dialogues* (1668, 2nd edn., 1713), 456.
[74] See 'An Additional and Preambular Hint' in *CRW*, p. 78.
[75] *An Answer To Thomas Tillams Book* (1659), 24. See also the structure of Robert Wilkinson's *The Saints Travel to the Spiritual Land of Canaan* (1650).

and made its appearance towards Heaven; and there were great hopes
of a Blessing in it. (in *A Collection of Sundry Books* (1716), 573–4)

More gives one further clue. He claims that Quaker tracts
were read alongside those of Niclaes because both were admired
for their respective prophetic voices. More feels that both are
'mock' prophets.[76] However, the point of prophetic voices is that
each one is distinct even though similar elements might be used
to authenticate any individual prophetic voice. What seems to
bring Nayler closer to Niclaes, however, is his appreciation of the
power of abstract moral values, 'as once I had been by the living
Virtue thereof'.[77] Elsewhere he praises 'Reason, Equity and
Conscience'. This does invite the prospect of direct influence,
especially with the similar example of John Warr (see above,
p. 171). However, Nayler often uses equity in the context of the
law when talking about the persecution of the Quakers, and he
could be using this sense here. Still, 'Virtue' does seem
reasonably close to Niclaes's meaning, though the distinct
allegorical position of Virtue, as expressed by Niclaes, is missing.
Exactly the same can be said for the comparison between
Niclaes's visions and those of some English sectarians. The
figures which are analysed above are not dissimilar from those
which occur in some Ranter and Quaker visions. George Foster
is one such (see above, chapter 2, p. 95), but then his figures do
not have the explicit allegorical explanations attached to them,
though his presentation as an authentic Old Testament prophet
is very similar to Niclaes's. The comparison emphasizes even
more the conscious and literary deliberation of Niclaes, so that,
even though his original visions might have been the result of
genuine inspiration, he has rewritten them successively as their
significance has changed and as his sect has developed.

It is also clear from a consideration of Niclaes's use of biblical
sources how he is largely different from English sectarians.
Niclaes places the authority of his visions over those in the
Scriptures, though as we have seen, he uses the broad similarity
with biblical visions to bolster his own authority. He stops
history by making his own self, not Christ, the 'original'. There is
however no parity as the marginal glosses from the Bible are

---

[76] *Conway Letters*, ed. M. H. Nicolson, p. 304.
[77] *To the Life of God in All* (1659), in *A Collection of Sundry Books*, i, p. xxxix.

'superscriptions' to his 'testimony of truth'.[78] For his Elizabethan disputant, John Knewstub, this was an allegorization of the Bible akin to Aesop's Fables and Robin Hood. Knewstub was concerned to identify Familist tracts with popular profane literature, as opposed to the small godly devotional treatises. Niclaes, using the Vulgate translation, belongs in fact to a long tradition of medieval symbolism and allegorization, though the end result is quite unique. Being begodded and reading the Scriptures this way are, as it were, something which is 'added' to the Letter.[79] This is the superior sacrament again, and with this Niclaes can attack heathen, Catholic, and Protestant literalists: 'yea, much worse then with the worldly ignorant, which have not heard any better then the manner or Rite of the world, or of the seditious and sectarish Scripture-learnedness'.[80] Niclaes is also capable of a highly concentrated reference to scriptural passages, more so than David Joris, so that there is some claim to the free running together of references in Familist tracts. What is specific about this is that Niclaes will refer in one gloss to several chapters or whole books of the Bible to support his allegory. One reference in *An Introduction to the holy Understanding of the Glass of Righteousnesse* lists Isa., Jer., Deut., Ecc., Thess., and Heb. It is not literal then, as with the Anabaptists, but instead evokes an extremely diffuse set of connotations. There is one English sectarian who glosses like this, Abiezer Coppe, and that is in the pamphlet where he refers to the Family of Love, though the allegory which he builds here is significantly different from Niclaes's.[81] Like Ranters and Quakers, Niclaes often speaks directly in biblical phrases, but the combination of this with his allegorical framework gives the reader the impression that he is telling the Bible what to do. So, Rev. 14: 14–19 is conflated to 'O God, smite now in with thy Sickle'.[82] There is no such distinctive treatment by English sectarians.

The most that can be said in conclusion is that Niclaes's writings contributed several elements in a much wider field of prophetic and illuminist discourse, but that among English sectarians he leaves only traces, as opposed to the more distinct

[78] *Revelatio Dei*, p. 3.
[79] Knewstub, *A Confutation of monstrous and horrible heresies, taught by H.N.*, pp. 81–2; Bodl. MS Rawl. C. 554. fo. 27ᵛ. [80] *The Prophecy of the Spirit of Love*, p. 21.
[81] *Some Sweet Sips, of some Spirituall Wine*, in *CRW*, pp. 50, 55, 70.
[82] *The Prophecy of the Spirit of Love*, p. 86.

influence of the German mystics and spiritualists. Popular Familism, that little amount which can be detected between 1620 and 1640, reduced all to the minimalist notion of begoddedness and, thereby, membership of the body of love. The complexity of Niclaes's allegories seems to have been missed here, though such cannot have been the case with those intellectuals who read H.N. in the 1650s. One is tempted to speculate on the nature of the body of love as an illuminist version of Hobbes's sovereign body in the 1650s, but the evidence to make such a comparison is simply not there. We are left with the pamphlets and the manuscripts, and the unique version of prophecy and allegory which they contain.

5

Jacob Boehme and the Sects

I

OF all the continental spiritualists to influence the radical sectarians during the middle years of the seventeenth century, Jacob Boehme has been the most talked about, but the nature of his influence the most consistently misunderstood. The reception of Boehme's work in England has been the subject of five full-length studies.[1] Each study has noted the wide readership of Boehme's books, across the spectrum of practices of worship, appealing to mystics, spiritualists, and occultists alike. The interest is reflected in vigorous publication. If Boehme was not read in the original German, his works could be obtained in a series of remarkably faithful translations which appeared between 1644 and 1662.[2] Until the late seventeenth century, however, there existed no consistent body of Behmenist (to use the adjective then preferred) works or thinkers. In the pre-1660 period, commentators have tended to note the affinity between Boehme's ideas and those of English writers, from Milton and the Cambridge Platonists to Ranters and Muggletonians, claiming a pervasive influence where none in fact exists.[3] It would be equally erroneous, especially where the radicals are concerned, to argue from the other extreme that, though Boehme was widely read, the profundity of his thought was never reflected and therefore not appreciated.[4] The truer picture is that Boehme had a significant influence upon a handful of important sectarians who each gave their own forms of expression and shapes to

[1] R. M. Jones, *Spiritual Reformers in the Sixteenth and Seventeenth Centuries* (New York, 1914), 190–234; M. L. Bailey, *Milton and Jakob Boehme: A Study of German Mysticism in Seventeenth-Century England* (New York, 1914); Wilhelm Struck, *Der Einfluss Jakob Boehmes auf die Englische Literatur des 17. Jahrhunderts* (Berlin, 1936); Nils Thune, *The Behmenists and the Philadelphians: A Contribution to the Study of English Mysticism in the 17th and 18th Centuries* (Uppsala, 1948); Serge Hutin, *Les Disciples anglais de Jacob Boehme* (Paris, 1960). See also G. F. Nuttall, *The Holy Spirit in Puritan Faith and Experience* (Oxford, 1946), 16–19; Désirée Hirst, *Hidden Riches* (1964), 76–109; D. P. Walker, *The Decline of Hell* (1964), 120, 218–24, 229, 240, 252, 257.

[2] Hutin, *Les Disciples anglais de Jacob Boehme*, 37–45 contains an accurate list of the order of the translations, and identifies the work done by each individual translator. It may have been easier to obtain Boehme in England than on the continent, up to the 1680s: see Frans A. Janssen, 'Böhme's *Wercken* (1682): Its Editor, Its Publisher, Its Printer', *Quaerendo*, 16 (1986), 137–41.

[3] Struck, *Der Einfluss Jakob Boehmes auf die Englische Literatur*, pp. 95–8, 166–74.

[4] Thune, *The Behmenists and the Philadelphians*, pp. 45–7.

Boehme's ideas, making Boehme's unique statements part of a wider knowledge. Boehme's writings themselves belong to the more extensive tradition of European Christian Kabbalah, and the appropriation of his ideas in England is best seen in this context. By concentrating upon several individuals who used Boehme extensively—Thomas Tany, Morgan Llwyd, John Pordage, and his disciples Thomas Bromley and Mary Pocock—it is possible to see how such an interest shaped the epistemological concepts and expressive language of several versions of English separatist and spiritualist thought.

The story of Jacob Boehme, the Bohemian farmer's son and shoemaker who was born in Görlitz in 1575, is well known.[5] Stated briefly, during the first decade of the seventeenth century Boehme experienced a series of visions in which he saw, in his own terms, to the heart of nature, and saw how the divine essence operated in all creation. This insight was first set down in *Morgenröthe* (1612), the publication of which resulted in his persecution by the local Lutheran clergy. Boehme was forced into silence until 1619, when, under noble patronage, he produced a plethora of writings which successively refined and elaborated upon his original vision until his death in 1625. None of these writings was published until the 1630s. His own debts were to Neoplatonic spiritualists and alchemists, Paracelsus, Weigel, and Schwenkfeldians, and his work is often described as achieving a synthesis of the former two thinkers.[6] Boehme appealed to spiritualists and alchemists, and to those who fell into both camps, throughout Europe, as his correspondence reveals.[7] It should not be forgotten that people thought of Boehme in this connection as a prophet, instanced in an anonymous satire of the Synod of Dort and the Thirty Years War:

> Quid quae Behmanni vaticinatur opus?
> Arndum Aquilam vestrum mitto, vatesque minores;
> Teuto, prophetarum messis opima tibi.
> En tibi vaticinans fallace nec ore cometa,
> Schismata, bella, dolos, cum nece, peste famen.[8]

[5] See Durant Hotham, *The Life of one Jacob Boehmen* (1654).

[6] Alexander Koyré, *La Philosophie de Jacob Boehme* (Paris, 1929), 232–3, 258, 307, 429, 463, 495.

[7] See *The Epistles of Jacob Behmen* (1649) and the letter attached to *The Way to Christ Discovered* (1648), sigs. K2ᵛ–K4ᵛ.

[8] Quoted in William Parker, *The Late Assembly of Divines Confession of Faith Examined* (1651), sig. a2ᵛ.

In England interest in Boehme lay first with the men who translated him, the Cambridge teacher Charles Hotham, the lawyer John Sparrow, his brother-in-law John Ellistone, and the publisher Humphrey Blunden. Boehme's works spread rapidly in England in the 1630s, as they did in the rest of Europe, in manuscript and print. Manuscript letters, most probably copied from the tracts, exist to show an interest in Boehme among Elias Ashmole's circle.[9] The Platonists certainly made use of the English translations of Boehme after 1644. Henry More read them, while Peter Sterry has been shown to have taken some of Boehme's terminology, such as the symbol of grace and perfection, the 'Lilly-Seed'.[10] A list of Sterry's library, and another list inside a copy of *A Bright Starre* (1646; Giles Randall's translation of the third part of Benet of Canfield's *The Rule of Perfection*) which belonged to John Salusbury, places Boehme alongside Neoplatonic spiritualist classics: Tauler, Cusa, and Sales.[11] Here, *XL Questions concerning the Soule* (1647) is one identifiable Boehme work which was read. In the 1650s Quakers and Muggletonians also read Boehme (with varying degrees of hostility).[12]

Boehme, the 'Teutonick philosopher', is, however, a good test of the occult interests of the Antinomian radicals. Henry Pinnell, the Antinomian Army Chaplain, and translator of Paracelsus and Crollius, speaks highly of Boehme's insights into nature.[13] William Erbery echoes his sentiments, though this is his only reference to Boehme throughout his writings:

If Christians, with us, turn to be Turks, why may not Turks turn to be Christians? Jacob Behme *compares Christians to that Son who said,* He would go to the Vineyard, but went not. *And the Turks, to the second Son, who told his Father,* He would not go, but afterwards repented, and went.[14]

---

[9] Bodl. MS Ashmole 1499, fo. 279^{r-v}.

[10] *Conway Letters*, ed. M. H. Nicolson (New York, 1930), 297, 306.

[11] V. de Sola Pinto, *Peter Sterry, Platonist and Puritan* (Cambridge, 1934), 57–8.

[12] See Lodowick Muggleton in *A Volume of Spiritual Epistles* (1820), 45. Muggleton refers to the Behmenist Quaker of Nottingham, Rice Jones, ibid., 141. For the Quaker readership of Boehme, see above, p. 109 n. 5. The Library of Woodbrooke College, Selly Oak, has a copy of the 1650 edition of Boehme's *Epistles* (Shelfmark F. 07. 13636) which belonged to the Wiltshire JP, Edward Stokes, who is better known for his attack on the Ranter, Thomas Webbe in *The Wiltshire Rant* (1652). The copy is signed by the owner in the year of publication.

[13] *Philosophy Reformed & Improved in Four Profound Tractates* (1657), sig. A3^v.

[14] *The Testimony of William Erbery* (1658), 333.

The radicals saw their desire for a spiritual reconciliation of all parties into one body, the mystically reformed nation, reflected in the abridged collection of Boehme's prophecies, *Mercurius Teutonicus* (1649). Boehme's appeal here was in his association of material and spiritual worlds. For instance, he maintained that the search for material transmutation of metals was fruitless unless it was accompanied by a genuine inner search for spiritual perfection.[15] It was an extension from inner to outer, achieved by the naming of inner qualities with physical objects, which bolstered the radical Puritans' idealism. So, for John Webster, spiritual and material are one:

And moreover though it be grown to a mighty height of exactness, in vulgar *Anatomy* and dissection of the dead bodies of men, or the living ones of beasts, birds, and fishes; yet it is defective as to that vive and *Mystical Anatomy* that discovers the true *Schematism* or signature of that invisible *Archeus* or *spiritus mechanicus*, that is the true opifex, and depositor of all the salutary, and morbifick linements, both in the seminal *guttula*, the tender *Embrio*, and the formed Creature, of which *Paracelsus, Helmont*, and our learned Countryman Dr. *Fludd*, have written most excellently.[16]

The occult interests of a sectarian like Webster partly explain the incursion of Boehme into radical religious writings. Also there is the familiar connection encouraged by publishers like Giles Calvert and Lodowick Lloyd, who published Boehme alongside radical religious pamphlets. Of the thirty-two separate translations of Boehme published between 1644 and 1662, Calvert was responsible for twelve. Serge Hutin has noted the millennial inspiration and pantheistic spirit shared between Boehme, Ranters and Quakers, but the observation is too general to be of significance here.[17] There are, however, basic shared elements of vocabulary which suggest similar perceptions in Boehme and the radicals. Laurence Clarkson is but one of many to speak of a 'center' for the spirit within him, his ground of being, in a manner similar to Boehme.[18] Similarly Christopher Hill has recently noted that the Muggletonian prophet John

[15] Bodl. MS Ashmole 1499, fo. 279ʳ⁻ʳ.

[16] *Academiarum Examen* (1654), 74.'Opifex': 'worker', 'framer', 'fabricator'; 'Morbifick': 'that produces disease'; 'linements': 'portions of the body or face seen in contour'; 'guttula': 'a small drop-shaped spot' (earliest usage recorded in *OED*, 1887).   [17] Hutin, *Les Disciples anglais de Jacob Boehme*, pp. 47–79.

[18] *A Single Eye All Light, no Darkness* (1650), in *CRW*, 172.

Reeve may have taken some of Boehme's language regarding the notion of the two seeds.[19] In his doctoral thesis of 1975, P. A. Trout argued that the occultists, of which the Behmenists constituted one group, shared hopes for a spiritual millennium with some of the more extreme Puritans.[20] In one sense, this position cannot be sustained since many Behmenists accepted orthodox and relatively conservative forms of church organization which the most extreme radicals, though not all of those examined here, rejected. This argument holds with those radicals like Llwyd who believed in the continuing necessity of external ordinances in order to help people reach the inner truth. Nevertheless, what can be said is that there is to a certain extent a shared vocabulary and structure of thought which makes possible the appropriation of Boehme's ideas by certain radicals.

The most famous English Behmenist was John Pordage, rector of Bradfield, Berkshire, friend of Elias Ashmole and founder, according to Baxter, of the Behmenist sect which later became the Philadelphian society.[21] Pordage is mentioned along with some other Antinomian spiritualists as a 'Familist' in 1645 when he was probably still a curate in Reading, though the source implies that Pordage was known in London.[22] It is not clear when Pordage came across Boehme, but he had developed his version of Behmenism by 1651 and his followers were expressing similar notions as early as 1649.[23] It is possible to demonstrate Boehme's influence upon Pordage in the 1650s. This is confirmed in the Behmenist epic, *Mundorum Explicatio*, which Pordage's son Samuel published in 1661, but which Pordage is generally held to have influenced. Pordage takes Boehme's notions a long way from their original form, and for this reason scholars have been

---

[19] Christopher Hill, B. Reay and W. M. Lamont, *The World of the Muggletonians* (1983), 88.

[20] 'Magic and the Millennium: A Study of the Millenary Motif in the Occult Milieu of Puritan England, 1640–1660'. (Ph.D. diss., University of British Columbia, 1975).

[21] *Reliquiae Baxterianae*, ed. Matthew Sylvester (1696), i. 77, 78. See also Bodl. MS Rawl. D. 833, fos. 64ʳ⁻ᵛ, 82ʳ⁻ᵛ; Hutin, *Les Disciples anglais de Jacob Boehme*, pp. 84–92; Christopher Hill, *The World Turned Upside Down* (1972), 224–6; id., *The Experience of Defeat* (1984), 220–42.

[22] John Etherington, *A Brief Discovery of the Blasphemous Doctrine of Familisme* (1645), 10.

[23] Désirée Hirst, 'The Riddle of John Pordage', *JBSQ* 1 (1954), 5–15, and Hutin, *Les Disciples anglais de Jacob Boehme*, p. 83, after her, cite the anonymous *A Most Faithful Relation* (1650) to date Elizabeth Pordage's visions from 1648 and Everard's arrival in August 1649. Pordage had also studied in Leiden, where Boehme was popular.

reluctant to see such a presence in Pordage's writings in the 1650s.[24] Pordage does not help us in that he published little in these years not only to avoid persecution (though he lost his living in 1655), but also to be in accordance with the aims of his withdrawn spiritualist community at Bradfield.[25]

The Oxford and Oxfordshire–Berkshire milieu is of considerable importance here for the dissemination of Boehme and Pordage's influence. Oliver Hill, fellow of St John's College, was a friend of both John Everard and Pordage, as well as being a founder of the Philadelphian Society later on.[26] Edmund Brice and Thomas Bromley both left Oxford to join Pordage's community, the latter just as he was about to be elected to a Fellowship at All Souls.[27] It is quite possible that Pordage came to Boehme through these connections. Bromley himself was also a founding Philadelphian, though he is important in the 1650s for his authorship of a paraphrase of Boehme's ideas, *The Way to the Sabbath of Rest* (1655). One of Pordage's followers from the late 1640s onwards was Mary Pocock. She defended Pordage when he was before the Reading Assizes in 1654, while her pamphlet, *The Mystery of the Deity in the Humanity* (1649), shows the transformation of Pordage's Behmenism into a popular radical religious epistemology.[28]

Thomas Tany is probably the most individual and most eccentric of the radical religious fanatics. A London goldsmith, he proclaimed himself King of the Jews and claimant to the thrones of England and France in the early and mid-1650s, having already attacked Parliament for not observing the stipulations of Magna Carta.[29] His transcendent prose style has led him to be identified as a Ranter, though he has no significant connection with the major Ranters of the early 1650s. Tany displays a beggared version of considerable arcane learning,

[24] Hill, *The World Turned Upside Down*, pp. 224–6.

[25] John Pordage, *Innocencie Appearing Through the dark Mists of Pretended Guilt* (1655), 22–9; Bodl. MS Rawl. D. 833, fos. 63–4. In his defence Pordage presents himself as a caring and considerate pastor.

[26] Bodl. MS Rawl. D. 833. fo. 64ʳ.   [27] Bodl. MS Ashmole 240, fo. 96ʳ⁻ᵛ.

[28] It has been assumed that this tract by M.P. was written by Mary Penington, wife of the Quaker Isaac Penington. However, in 1649 Mary and Isaac were not yet married. Mary Pocock's authorship is decisive because of the conjunction of her appearance in Pordage's defence in 1654 with the clearly Pordage-influenced *The Mystery of the Deity in the Humanity* (1649).

[29] Christopher Hill, B. Reay, and W. M. Lamont, *The World of the Muggletonians* (1983), 88.

some of whose organizing principles seem to be taken from Boehme. Tany's preference for direct inspiration leads to a descriptive vocabulary which resembles Boehme's, though Tany's actual concern with the signifying power of words goes beyond Boehme. Tany follows Boehme's central precepts and rhetorical organization: they provide part of a base for Tany's unique expression of hypostasy and Hebraic identity.

John Webster, the disciple of John Everard, read Boehme as part of a much broader concern with Neoplatonic occult and natural philosophy. His attack on orthodox university education in *Academiarum Examen* (1654) reveals him as the ideologist of a reformed science and knowledge in the radical Puritan way just as Bacon, Webster's idol, was the ideologist of empirical science.[30] For this reason, Webster has been accused of an imperfect knowledge of occult and mystical writings.[31] Despite this, it is possible to show Webster's comprehension and use of Boehme.

Finally Boehme is present in the writings of the Welsh Independent and Fifth Monarchist, Morgan Llwyd. He appears to have successfully adopted Boehme's imagery, especially that concerned with nature, merging it with his own dialectical and logocentric mythology which he expressed in a number of allegorical prose works and poems. Llwyd also translated two of Boehme's works into Welsh from English.[32] It may be that Llwyd introduced Peter Sterry to Boehme. Llwyd's interest in mysticism was certainly cultivated by his correspondence with William Erbery and John Saltmarsh.[33] His more orthodox Puritan use of dialogue and biblical symbol sets him apart from Pordage and Tany, but his debt to Boehme is probably greater.

II

Before Boehme's influence on the English sectarians can be explored in detail, it is necessary to analyse the nature of

---

[30] See Christopher Hill, *The Intellectual Origins of the English Revolution* (Oxford, 1965), 107, 112, 122, 298.

[31] Seth Ward, *Vindiciae Academiarum* (1654). See also Charles Webster, *The Great Instauration: Science, Medicine and Reform, 1626–1660* (1975), 188, 192.

[32] See Nuttall, *The Holy Spirit*, p. 16, no. 5; Hugh Bevan, *Morgan Llwyd y Llenor* (Cardiff, 1954), 36.

[33] *The Testimony of William Erbery* (1658), 95, 104, 111–12, 234.

Boehme's writings themselves as they occur in English translation. Boehme's ideas have been subjected to several penetrating
analyses in the third and fourth decades of this century, though
he has since fallen from fashionable and serious interest.
Alexandre Koyré in particular was able to reduce the vast length
of Boehme's *œuvre* to comprehensible order, without losing a
sense of the complexity of the elements which make up Boehme's
philosophy.[34] However, the extent to which the modern understanding of Boehme coincides with the seventeenth-century
radical religious understanding is a matter which remains to be
decided.

Throughout his work Boehme writes in a prophetic mode.
Nineteenth- and twentieth-century commentators have obscured
this by concentrating upon Boehme's mystical cosmology,
highlighting such aspects as the Fall of the Angels preceding the
creation of men.[35] This is undoubtedly important since it
facilitates a far greater measure of free will and liberty in man
than predestination theology does, making possible the idea of a
perfectibility attainable on this earth. However, this was not the
primary consideration of the English sectarians. They were more
interested in what Boehme had to say on revelatory process, even
though they were interested in perfection. First and foremost,
Boehme was seen to be prophesying a truth which was immanent
in the creation, if only each individual could come to a
sufficiently pure knowledge to see this. *The Third Booke of the
Authour* (1650), the text which John Webster used, refers to the
'sea of glass' from Rev. 4: 6, 15: 2 (p. 40) for instance, which
continually identifies Boehme's enterprise with apocalypse and
revelation.

Within this framework Boehme builds his essential picture of
divine immanence within all objects. It is not directly Neoplatonic though the notion of God as 'essence' and as 'centre' is
as axiomatic to Cusa as it is to Boehme. Similarly, the
description of God as the 'abysse' by Boehme is common to Cusa
and, before him, Pseudo-Dionysius. It is Boehme's cosmological
system, however, which makes him different. The 'abysse' exists

---

[34] Koyré, *La Philosophie de Jacob Boehme, passim*. The achievement of the work also
lies in its delineation of Boehme's developing ideas, according to the influences he fell
under, again without losing a sense of the theosophy as a whole.

[35] G. C. A. von Harless, *Jakob Boehme und die Alchymisten* (Berlin, 1870).

before the three principles which permeate the universe. The first and second principles represent the external nature, the spiritual principles upon which the universe is based. The first principle is God's wrath, or hellishness, which is opposed by the second principle, the light and angelical world. The third principle is the external world, the 'out-spoken visible WORD'. For Boehme there is no simple and historical act of creation by God; the three principles represent the creation as a continuing process of God eternally expressing himself. This system is tabulated in *Four Tables of Divine Revelation* (1654) (see Fig. 5). Nevertheless, Boehme's notion of God comes originally from the Bible:

Moses saith: the Lord our God is but one onely God. In another place is said; of him, through him, and in him are all things: in another am not I he that filleth all things? And in another: through his Words are all things made; that are made: say he is the Originall of all things, he is the Eternall unmeasurable unity.[36]

This passage from *The Clavis, or Key* (1647) is Boehme's own exegesis of *The Third Booke of the Author* which is itself an interpretation of his first work, *Morgenröthe*. As Boehme develops he extends his 'theosophy' so that it becomes both clearer (in that it can be represented as a table) but subject to an infinite regress of meaning, as Boehme makes his apprehension of divine essence and the three principles fit different aspects and qualities of the internal and external worlds. In *Morgenröthe*—or *Aurora*, as the English translation of 1656 was called—essence is extended into creation as emanating qualities which are in each object. God is a 'fire' in the world and in man.[37] The word 'fire' represents both the inner, spiritual operation and the external. It forms a link between the two, facilitating significant correspondences between inner and outer worlds, so that the latter gives an indication of the nature of the former, though it should be remembered that there are two different kinds of fire in the first and second principles respectively. Alchemical language was of great appeal here to Boehme since its symbolism operates in a similar way to Boehme's language, stressing the conjunction of spiritual and material potentialities in single terms. Boehme, however, stresses the inner and spiritual as compared with the alchemists. Here

---

[36] *The Clavis, or Key* (1647), 1.   [37] *Aurora* (1656), 52.

1 Table — *What GOD is without Nature & Creature.*

what God without Nature and Creature is, and what the Mysterium Magnum is: How God, by his breathing forth or speaking, hath introduced himself into Nature and Creature.	**I**	Abyss	
		NOTHING & ALL	
	Father **2**	VVill of the Abyss.	J E
	Sonn **3**	Delight or impression of the VVill.	H O
	Spirit **4**	Science or Motion.	V A
	5	GOD in Trinitie.	*Thus is* GOD *without*
	6	VVORD in GOD.	Nature *and* Creature *considered.*
	7	VVisdom.	

Begining of Mysterii Magni of the Eternal NATURE

		GOD *in* LOVE		GOD *in* WRATH				
Here beginneth Mysterium Magnum as distinction in speaking the WORD; where the WORD by Wisdom is made distinct, Natural, Sensible, Comprehensible, and Invensible.				**9.** *The First* principle				Spiritual
	8 *The second*	Principle			Moving,	Thinking		
				Dark,	Feeling,	Mind,		Nature
		V	**10** Tincture or	I	II.Prick	111	1V	
	II *Angel, Light, Love- fire.*	speaking of the Trinity.		Desire,	or Science.	Angush,	Fire,	
The Eternal begining of the Principles is here also understood, with Gods Love and Anger, in Light and Darkness.	*Angelical World Root of the four Elements.*	VI *Sound or Distinction.* VII *Essence, or essential wisdom.*		Austere,	Cause of Enmity,	Five root of heat.		
				Hard,	Hellish-life,	Hell,		Substantial
	Growing or Greening in the Spiritual World.	**12** *Pure Element.* **13** *Paradise.*		Sharpness cold fire,	Root,	Devill,		Essential
				SAL,	MERCU-RIUS,	SUL-PHUR		tial

14 *Begining of the external World.*

Here beginneth the external visible World, as the out-spoken visible WORD.	The third	Principle	
		15 *Heaven.*	
1 Is understood the good Life of the creature which stands in the Quint-Essence.	Starrs	**16** Quint-Essence	*Good Powers.*
2 The poyson and grossness of the Earth and Earthly Life. *3 The Reader understanding these, all Doubts and Queries cease in him: and Babel is left in Ignorance.*	The	**17** *The 4 Elements.*	*Devill's Poyson introduced.*
	Out spoken WORD.	**18** *Earthly Creatures.*	

FIG. 5. Jacob Boehme, *Four Tables of Divine Revelation* (1654), Sig. H5ᵛ

is *The Clavis, or Key* again, demonstrating the elaboration upon the initial work:

The first [quality] is the going upwards of the fiery will, the second is the going downwards, or the watery Spirit, *viz.* the Meekeness; and the third is the going out forwards of the oyly Spirit, in the midst, in the centre of the firey Spirit of the Will; which oyly Spirit is the Ens of the unity of God.[38]

Boehme makes this process fit the three principles, so that his system becomes perfectly closed: any one point can be seen in relation to the entirety of the whole, and layer upon layer of elaboration is built up in this way.

Boehme consistently divides immanent will into various categories, each of which is identified metaphorically with a particular sensory quality. This is the true nature of substance, which is permeated by the dualism embodied in the first and second principles. Thus, nature has the potential to be both good and evil, light and dark. In the external world, nature is identified with negative senses, signifying the fallen state, with the 'pure element' and paradise representing progressive states of perfection. Nevertheless, there are still good and bad qualities in all things, as represented in the 'MACROCOSM' (see Fig. 6). Boehme has a problem here in that he is seemingly making God the author of evil as well as good. He copes with this, somewhat unsatisfactorily, by stating that in the 'abysse' of God, the 'Mysterium Magnum', evil did not exist but was, as it were, compensated for 'through the sensibility and assumption of self-desire'. Boehme seems here to have made the essence of God like a perfect human who needs to recognize some degree of self-preservation in order to function.

Boehme explains the Fall as a psychological aberration within the first two principles. Having been engendered within the first principle, Lucifer wanted to rule by the power of the second principle: he wanted to become God himself. Since the human soul contains the imprint of the first and second principles, it must embody both the stamp of the serpent as well as the cross of Christ's atonement. The macrocosm has a corresponding micro-cosm for man (see Fig. 7). Once again, the alchemical and occult vocabulary is made to connect parts of the human anatomy with

[38] *The Clavis*, p. 15.

(n) Highnels
Hochheit.

and (n) celfitude. Thus is there a contrary in the *Eternal Nature*; that the Properties exifting therein, the love is known, and that there might be fomething to be beloved, wherein the Eternal Love of Gods Unity may work, and God may be praifed. For if the properties of life be penetrated with the Divine love-flame, then they praife the great love of God, & yield themfelves all again into the Unity of God. Such rejoycing & knowledge could not be revealed in the Unity, did not the Eternal will bring it felf into painfull moving properties.

The Seaventh Property, is that Effence, wherein all the other are effential; wherein they all act, as the Soul doth in the Body: wherein the Natural, Effential, Eternal *Wifdom* of God (as the *Myfterium Magnum*) is underftood; out of which the vifible World, with its Effence and Creatures, did arife.

Thus by this Table is underftood the hidden Spiritual world, as the Eternal manifeftation of God; from whence the Angels and Souls of Men received their exiftence; therefore may they turn themfelves to evill or good, for both lie in their Center.

This Spiritual world is no other than Gods revealed Word, and hath its being from Eternity to Eternity; for therein is Heaven and Hell underftood.

III. TABLE. The feven Properties of the vifible World, or external Nature. MACROCOSMUS	1 Ground	2 of	3 Nature	4 Pure	5 Element	6 Para-	7 dife
	Cold,Earth, Snow	Original of Air	Fire of Effence	Heaven	Light of Nature	Starrs	water
	Saturn the planet	Mercury the planet	Mars	Sol	Venus Soft	Jupiter	Luna
In this Table is fignified, how the hidden Spiritual, Eternal Word, (as the *Myfterium magnum*) by the motion of *Gods Word* iffued forth, and became vifible, manifeft, and Material; And how the inward Powers, through Gods working, have comprehended and fafhioned themfelves; how good and bad in every thing is to be underftood; and yet there was no evill in *Myfterium magnum*, but exifted through the fenfibility and affumption of felf-defire. Here alfo is fhewed what in the working iffued forth from every property, and which have the predominancy; according to which every thing is formed and governed.	Sal	Mercury thunder	Sulphur Flefh	Sal-niter	Oyl	Power	Body
	Black, Gray	Mixt-coiours	Red	Yellow	Green, and white within	Blew	white without within Red and Green
	Melancholy	Collerick		Sanguin		Pleg matick	
	Goffnefs of Stone	Metal, Stone	Ruft	Growing	Pearls	Jewels	Menftruum
	Lead	Quickfilver	Iron, Steel	Gold	Copper	Tinn	Silver
	Bone Wood	Herbs	Refin	Tincture in the Earth	Sweet	Bitter	Grafs
	Sour	Poyfon	...	Opening	Healing	Strengthning	Flefh
	Stopping	Smelling	Feeling	Seeing	Tafting	Hearing	Loathing of Nature
	Dying	Lying	Wrath War	Richefs	Noble	Reafon	Own poffeffion
	Lord	Craft	Force	Juftice	Faithfull	Truth	Simplicity
	Stealing	Deceiving	Lofing	Finding	Earthly Love	being friendly	Lightminded
	Obftinate Sad	Confounded Senfes	Carelefs	conftant	Pure	Joyfull	Ignorant
	Earthly	Beaft'y	Evill	Heavenly	Modeft	Senfible	Low
	elfe	Fox	Dogg	Lyon	Bird	Ape	Great Beafts
	worms	Venemous wormes	Evill Beafts	Good Beafts	Flying Beafts	Tame Beafts	Fifh.

FIG. 6. Jacob Boehme, *Four Tables of Divine Revelation* (1654), Sig. K1$^\mathrm{v}$

will flow, even to the end of this time; and therein the Separator, with the 7 *Properties*, is understood. In this Table we see what proceeded from the 7 *Properties*; and how the Spiritual power hath brought it self into a Material one (as in the *seven spaces* downwards appears) whereby we may understand whence Good and Evill sprung up in this World.

IV TABLE. *MICRO-COSMUS.*	Humane Ground before and after the FALL	1 T S ♄ Satur-day	2 I OU ☿ Wednf-day	3 N L ♂ Tuef-day	4 C E ☉ Sun-day	5 T SPIR ♀ Fri-day	6 U IT ♃ Thurf-day	7 R BODY ☽ Mon-day
In this Table MAN is held forth; What he hath been in Paradife; as also how the *Properties* in him (without affuming Self-defire) equally ftood in the Image of God: and what he is become through Satan's Deceit: what that Monfter of the Serpent (whereby he is become earthly and mortal) is in him. And then how Gods Word and LOVE came in to help him again, new born in CHRIST, daily deftroying that Serpentine Image: alfo in what danger & mifery he ftandeth in fuch an Image, either on the ground of Hell or Heaven. Alfo a fimilitude of Divine Revelation and Knowledg in the feven *Properties* according to *Time* and *Eternity*, formed out of all the *Three Principles*; for a further underftanding how he is wifely to regulate his Life; and unto what driving (impulfion) he fhould yield himfelf.	Adam *in* Paradife	Defire	Motion	Senfibility	Seeing	Loving	Rejoycing	Heavenly flefh
	Erring fp.	Sharpnefs	Anger	Pain	Bitter woe	Hating	Defpair	Paffion
	Chrift	Gods word	Life	Accep-tance	Sweet	Glorie	Power	Divine Effence
	Adam *in* Paradife	Simili-tude	Out going Spirit	Heating	High	Humble Will	Praifing	Unity
	Sathan	felf-feeking	Self-knowl.	Self-will	Dominiering	Pride	Reproaching	Folly
	Chrift	Gods unity	Refigna-tion	Suffering	Yielding	Defire	Equality of Power	Wifdom
	Adam *in* Paradife	Tafting	Thinking	Mind	Under-ftanding	Spirit	Speaking	E veftrum of Nature
	Sathan	Defire of divifion	Lying	Anguifh	Doubting	Fall	Stinck	Extru-ding
	Chrift	Baptifm	Law	Breaking	Hopeing	Humility	Believing	Genius or Type
	Adam *in* Paradife	Strength	Pentra-ting	Might	Holy	Modeft	Power-fall	Throne
	Sathan	Lord	Potent	Malice	Thirfty	Wanton	Mad	Self honor
	Chrift	Humility	Obedience	Mercy	Forgiving	Going	Generating	reverence
	Adam *in* Paradife	Angel	Officious	Mild	Friendly	Beauty	Vertue	Diligent
	Sathan	Devill	Perverfe	Theevifh mind	Murther	Belial's Whore	Poyfon	Earthly flefh
	Chrift	Chrift	returning	repentance	New life	Holy	Reftoring	Sophia
	Adam *in* Paradife	Heaven	Child like	Secret	Manifeft	Singing	Sounding	Paradife
	Sathan	Hell or Perdition	Strife	Torment	Ever fal-ling	Fantafie	Changing	A Den of the Deep
	Chrift	Chrifts Calling,	Teaching,	Diffolving,	New mind,	Rejoicing	Praying,	Springing.

FIG. 7. Jacob Boehme, *Four Tables of Divine Revelation* (1654), Sig. K2ᵛ

distinct spiritual values. The result is a physiological and alchemical allegory:

He [God] created *but One Man*, with the *whole Crosse in the Brainpan*, which signifieth the number Three: he was both Man and Woman, yet you are not to understand any woman, but a virgin wholly pure and chast; he had in him the Spirit of the Tincture of the Fire and also the Spirit of the Tincture of the Water *viz.* of Venus: he loved himselfe, and through himselfe [he loved] God: he could generate *Virgin-like* (out of his will, out of his essences, without pain, without tearing or dividing [his body]) such a Man as himselfe was; for he had all Three Centres in him.[39]

The three principles are here paralleled by the 'threefold life of man', whereby the qualities in the individual correspond to the archetypal experiences of Adam in Paradise, Satan or the 'erring spirit', and the redeeming Christ. The three centres refer to the Trinity which generate the figure of wisdom, the Virgin Sophia, almost a fourth element in Boehme's Godhead (see Fig. 5). Boehme's usage of Sophia in this way is the first in the English language. She embodies the potential and hope for regeneration: 'Deare Virgin of Wisdome remained starting in grief, till the *Word of the Lord* came againe, and looked upon her againe with the promise of the Seede of the Woman.'[40] Just as all objects emanate from essence, so Boehme's eschatological goal is a merging back with essence, to 'transmute themselves into *one* Body'.[41] The extension into creation uses the number symbolism not only of threes but also of sevens. For Boehme there are seven properties of eternal nature and seven of external nature, each letter of the word 'tinctur' representing one of the seven properties. In turn, each property is manifested in a different way in different faculties, forms and senses (see Figs. 6–8). Further amplification of the importance of seven is given in the seven

---

[39] *The Third Booke of the Authour* (1650), 165–6. Tincture (in the alchemical usages): spiritual principle whose character is infused into material things; active principle of a physical nature (*OED*).

[40] Ibid. Koyré, *La Philosophie de Jacob Boehme*, p. 473, suggests that Boehme's Sophia had some of her roots in Weigel's adoration of the Virgin Mary. The creation of woman symbolized the second principle which substituted the celestial virgin for Adam.

[41] *Aurora*, p. 168. For a comparison which makes clear the difference between Boehme and Sir Henry Vane (often seen as a Behmenist writer), see Vane, *An Epistle General, to the Mystical Body of Christ* (1662, 8⁰ edn.), 71–2.

II. TABLE.	AD	Father	Will	IE
	O	Son	Delight	HO
	N	Spirit	Science	VA
	A	Power	Word	Life
	I	Colours	Wisdom	Vertue

In this second Table, God is considered according to his Essence in Unity; what he is in Trinity without Nature and Creature, whereby he filleth all things, and yet needs no place.

TETRAGRAMMATON.

In this Table is consider'd the efflux of the Eternal Divine *WORD*; how the *WORD* through Wisdom brings it self from Unity into Separation and Multiplicity; as well in the Eternal Nature and Creature (according to which God calls himself angry jealous God, and a consuming fire; as well as a mercifull God wherein is understood the foundation of Angels & Soules, and how they may receive salvation or damnation.)

In the *Septenary* without by it self, is understood the *Mysterium Magnum*, as the 7. properties of the Eternal Nature.

In the *Novenarie* downwards, are signifi'd the properties of Life.

In the fourth Form, as in Fire, 2. Principles separate themselves from each other, as Darkness and Light.

Gods The	Wrath, first	or Dark Prin-	World ciple	Gods The	Love, or Second	Light Prin-	World ciple.
Simi-litude	1 T	2 I	3 N	4 C	5 T	6 V	7 R
E	Desire or Comprehending	Science or Drawing	Anguish	Fire	Light Love-fire	Sound	Essence
T	Dark	Feeling or Moving	Willing	Painful Life	Love-Life	Understanding	Working
E R	Austere Hardnes	Enmitie	Minde	Terror	Joy	Five Senses	Form
NAL	Sharpness	Elevating	Wheel of Life	Killing	Power	Love	Sperm
N	Furie	Pride	Despair	Hell	Glorie	Giving	Taking, or Comprehending
A	Greater Death	False will	Lesser Death	Souls ground Devill	Souls Spirit Angell	Praising	Increasing
T	Standing still	Breaking	From Original separating	Folly	Wisdom	Highnes	Humility
V R	Impotent	Self-will	Robbing	Fantasie	Knowledge	Strength	Throne

The second Table Expounded.

(a) Or expansion.
THe word ADONAI signifieth an (a) opening, or free motion of the bottomless Eternal Unity; how the Eternal generation, expansion, and effluence of the Trinity of God is in it self.

A;

FIG. 8. Jacob Boehme, *Four Tables of Divine Revelation* (1654), Sig. 12ᵛ

planets, angels, vials, and candles. It has been suggested that Boehme is using kabbalistic forms of interpretation here, though no specific source has been identified.[42] Like many Renaissance occultists Boehme was using a method which was thought to be kabbalistic, though he was using a particular and simplified version of it, which he in turn fashioned according to his own needs. Thus, he counts the symbolic number six four times, six for the form-qualities in each of the three worlds, and six for the form-powers in God's eternal nature. Altogether they make twenty-four, the number of letters in the German alphabet.[43] The radicals in England were similarly attracted by what they thought was kabbalistic symbolism, though their understanding of it was somewhat different from Boehme's, enabling them to modify Boehme himself through these different notions.

Boehme's tendency is to stay close to the Scriptures, expressing his most abstruse insights often in what appears to be orthodox biblical language. The presence of Sophia is usually described in terms of the traditional allegory of union in the Song of Solomon. The Pauline imperative is also prominent, just as it is in Paracelsus:

Christ the eternal Word of the Father, the most noble and celestial, proved, triune stone is dis-esteemed by the greater part of men in this world, and is (as 'twere) cast out of our sight . . . and therefore in 1 *Cor.* 3, it is accounted, especially by the wise ones of this world, for foolishness.[44]

Here Boehme is capable of constructing simple allegories, based around the fulfilment of God's Word in the Seed, and the dual nature of the Tree of Knowledge of Good and Evil, in a manner similar to Franck and Weigel, and the tradition of *Theologia Germanica*. It is this aspect of Boehme which is most often overlooked when explaining the popularity of Boehme with some of the English sectarians. So, the object of spiritual transmutation is to negate 'I, I-hood, selfe, or selfenesse', and *The Way to Christ Discovered* recommends resignation and poverty of ego in order to reach enlightenment.

Yet Boehme sets this within the understanding of Adam, the

[42] François Secret, *Le Zôhar chez les kabbalistes chrétiens de la Renaissance* (Paris, 1964), 12.

[43] Koyré, *La Philosophie de Jacob Boehme*, p. 275.

[44] *The Water Stone of the Wise Men*, in *Paracelsus His Aurora* (1659), 157.

original man and archetype, as androgynous: since God made Eve from the flesh and blood of Adam, they are really part of the same being. This was not an unusual notion at that time, but it becomes distinctive when Boehme extends the androgyny so that creation becomes permeated by masculi e and feminine principles or 'tinctures'. This enables desire to be expressed alchemically:

Suppose *two* young people of a noble *Complexion*, these being kindled in the Heat and fervour of burning Love one to another, there is such a fire as this; so that if they would creep into the Bodies and *Hearts* one of another, or transmute themselves into *one* Body, they would do it.[45]

At the same time Boehme develops the spiritual anthropology of the *Theologia Germanica* in these terms. The individual becomes a type for heaven and hell, as emanation endows all of creation with a typological significance:

Thou must not think, that they are there only as it were as a Type or shadow of things; *no*: for the Spirit sheweth plainly, that in the heavenly pomp in the heavenly *Salitter* and *Mercurius*, do grow *Divine* Trees, Plants, Flowers and all *sorts*, of whatsoever is in this World but as a type and resemblance: And as the Angels are, so are the vegetation and fruits, all from the *Divine power*.[46]

This, part of Boehme's earliest writing, displays an elaboration upon earlier explanations of the supernatural. The patristic notion of the nine types of angel is married with the idea of the emanating fiery spirits inside and around material objects: 'the gracious amiable love, which is the *fifth* fountain-spirit, in the divine power, is the *hidden* source fountain or Quality'.[47] The entire universe is interconnected in this way, so that fire and fountains are the sources (*Quellen*) which empower the course of the planets and the state of the individual:

when the Gall [secretion of the liver: bile] overfloweth, and runneth to the Heart, then it kindleth the Element of *fire*, and the fire, kindleth the Astral *spirits*, which *raign* in the *Blood*, in the veins and in the element of *Water*; and then the whole Body trembleth by reason of the wrath and the poyson of the Gall.[48]

[45] *Aurora*, p. 168. [46] Ibid. 104.
[47] Ibid. 162. [48] Ibid. 52.

The imagery of illumination and emanation was as appealing to the English sectarians as was the language of mystical self-negation. The action of emanation is itself contained within collocations popular with Boehme like 'day-spring'. The representation of essence and emanation extends into a variety of forms. One version is the visual, for instance a woodcut Calvert took for his 1656 edition of *Aurora* and had Wenceslas Hollar make from the German edition of 1635, printed in Amsterdam (see Fig. 9). The woodcut shows the Trinity as a triangle seated on a throne, while the prophetic aspect is emphasized in the presence of the seven vials and the kings from Revelation, with references to illumination from Isa. 9: 2 and Matt. 4: 16. The visual and phonic qualities of emanation are given parental relations, so integrating emanation into the simpler allegory:

thus it is; the flash is the *mother* of the light: for the flash genereateth the light, and is the *Father* of the fierceness, for the fierceness abideth in the flash as a *seed* in the Father, and that flash genereateth also the Tone or Sound.[49]

God is an *ens manifestativum sui*, reflecting himself in the mirror of Wisdom or Sophia, which is also the eye of divine perception. The essence spreads out its rays as a '*Fiat*' which moves creation. This penetrates outer and inner knowledge, nature and the human soul: 'the Mobility boyling springing and driving of a thing'.[50] Boehme's greatest debt to Paracelsan terminology is here in his utilization of the word 'Archaeus', the principle which rules animal and vegetable life:

The foure Elements doe flow from the *Archaeus* of the Inward ground; that is, from the foure properties of the Eternall Nature; and were in the beginning of time so outbreathed from the Inward ground, and compressed and formed into a working substance and Life: and therefore the outward world is called a Principle, and is a subject of the Inward World, that is, a Toole and Instrument of the Inward Master, which Master is the Word and power of God.[51]

Images of jewels and plants are also employed in this context, intensifying their particular symbolic value in the Bible, re-invested by the richness of Boehme's thought. For instance, the

[49] *Aurora*, p. 188.   [50] Ibid. 34.
[51] *The Clavis*, p. 21. The 'archaeus' was the Paracelsan term for the immaterial principle or vital force which produced and presided over animal and vegetable life. It was held to be situated in the stomach (*OED*).

FIG. 9. Jacob Boehme, *Aurora. That is, the Day-Spring* (1656), Sig. 12ᵛ

Lilly comes to stand as a metaphor for divine perfection and the power of Christ's redemption. In Boehme, perfection is a figure of speech:

> Wee goe into the Garden of Roses, and there are Lillies and flowers enough, wee will make a *Garland* for our sister, and then she will rejoyce with us: wee have a Round to dance, and we will hold hands together.[52]

Finally, Boehme's figural patterns and his Scriptural and occult interpretative methods are put to the service of finding words which will exactly describe the divine nature of the things they name. This is in part Boehme's definition of the 'language of nature' which is discussed in greater detail in Chapter 6. The clearest explanation of this is in *Signatura Rerum* (1651), where the signature is detected:

> with the Sound or Speech the Form doth note and imprint itself into the similitude of another; one like tone or sound catcheth and moveth another; and in the Sound the Spirit imprinteth his own similitude which it hath conceived in the Essence, and brought to form in the Principle.[53]

Utterance is itself subjected to this analysis, so that it becomes located in Boehme's enlivened universe as an emanation from the essence. After all, God is in the individual's soul as much as the individual's soul is in God, and speech is a manifestation of this. The analysis of physical speech acts seems quaint to us now, but for Boehme it points to the notion of a particular signifying power, or 'quality', being in a particular language, and determined by the *Archaeus* of the utterer:

Dein Reich Komme
Thy Kingdom come

49. *Dein*, there the poore soule giveth it self up againe into the will of God, as Gods childe.
50. *Reich*, heere the soule giveth it selfe into the vertue and Power of the Angelicall world, and desireth to come out of the Deepe of the Waters into the power of God.
51. *Komme*, in the syllable *Kom-*, it goeth in into the vertue and power, and apprehendeth it: and with the syllable *-me*, it maketh the Heaven be open, and goeth forth with the apprehended power,

---

[52] *The Third Booke of the Authour*, p. 192.
[53] *Signatura Rerum* (1651), 1.

into the Kingdome, as a sprout: for the *-me*, maketh the Lips be
open, and letteth the sprout of the will goe forth, and lets it grow
softly by degrees.[54].

In this way human utterance can partake of the divine voice, and
occasionally it is enforced by a series of liturgical effusions, '*Te
Deum Laudamus*',[55] so that a language of orthodox devotional
ritual is divorced from its original place within the mystical
epistemology.

Although English sectarians looked most to Boehme's model of
creation, they were also attracted by Boehme's voluntarism. This
was most probably the case with William Erbery, for instance,
who believed in universal redemption and rejected, like Boehme,
the idea of a limited atonement.[56] Since good and evil existed in
every person, the victory of good over evil, Christ over Satan, was
something which was permanently acted out within a godly
person. For Boehme the individual's liberty was defined by his
ability to make choices, to take responsibilities. This, together
with the knowledge of the three principles and the threefold life of
man, was the state of perfection. What became of this among the
English sectarians was either the eager assertion of felt perfection
in Pordage and Tany, or Llwyd's location of pious voluntarism
within the elect body of the Saints. Perhaps only Bromley
genuinely exhibits what Boehme considered to be true liberty.

III

A reading of *Innocencie Appearing* (1655), Pordage's elaborate
defence of himself after he had lost his living, suggests that he
appropriated parts of Boehme's thought in order to help the
expression of his own hypostatic experiences. The 'teutonick
philosophy' was most probably his starting point and inspiration, though he took it to greater extremes than Tany did by

---

[54] *The Third Booke of the Authour*, p. 261.   [55] *Aurora*, p. 262.

[56] *Concerning the Election of Grace* (1655), *passim*. Likewise Boehme put Llwyd's
understanding of the relationship between divine justice and mercy into doubt: letter
to Henry Jessey, July 1656, National Library of Wales, MS 11438D, letter 86, *ll.* 8–11.
At the same time Boehme could be used to stress or deepen an understanding of
relatively unproblematic theology, as in Henry Walker's citing of Boehme on the
names of God: *The Protestants Grammar* (1648), 1. See also N. I. Matar, 'Peter Sterry
and Jacob Boehme', *N&Q*, N.S. 33 (1986), 33–6 for Sterry's attraction to and
reservations on Boehme.

claiming to have actually seen angels. The central Behmenist tenet which obsessed Pordage was the existence of a 'fiery deity of Christ' in the centre of the soul, which burns up lusts and corruptions. Pordage had to answer the charge that this was a heresy, which he did by setting it at the centre of traditional Lutheran teaching, that the imputed righteousness of Christ was useless without such a purgation. Clearly Pordage could be speaking in terms of the generally accepted spiritual imagery of being refined by fire (Mal. 3: 2) and this is how it may have appeared to the members of the Committee for Plundered Ministers who examined him in 1651, and the magistrates before whom he appeared in 1654. This was in fact a version of Boehme's conception of the 'firey' Spirit which emanates in the individual, though for John Tickell, the young minister from Abingdon who was at both interrogations, the doctrine was baffling nonsense and an example of Pordage's propensity to maintain incongruous positions simultaneously.[57]

One of the witnesses who appeared against Pordage in 1654, John Lewin, accused Pordage of maintaining that Adam was male and female by himself.[58] This refers in a broad way to the kabbalistic myth, which we have already seen in Boehme, of Adam Kadmon, the archetypal man, who in one version of the myth had a male part representing the 'mental meeting of the angels' and a female part representing the 'animastic'.[59] There were several such allegories in sixteenth-century radical religious thought: for the Familist Hendrik Niclaes the male stood for the deity, the female for earthly humanity. Both together made up the humanity consubstantiated with the deity. Pordage is, however, more specific in his meaning here. In this first instance Tickell reported that Pordage had learnt from a rabbi that Gen. 1 could be understood figuratively, so that the male stood for the deity, the female the humanity, in a manner vaguely similar to Niclaes, whom Pordage might well have read. However, Pordage is insistent that a rabbi did indeed tell him that 'the Deity and the pure Humanity might be shadowed forth, which by union become one; the male representing the Deity, the

---

[57] Pordage, *Innocencie Appearing* (1655), 9, 36–8, 42–50.

[58] Ibid. 56. John Lewin was minister at Hampstead Norris.

[59] *Pauli Ricci in cabalistarum seu allegorizantium eruditionem isagoge* (2nd edn., Augsburg, 1515), trans. and printed in J. L. Blau, *The Christian Interpretation of the Cabala in the Renaissance* (New York, 1944), 70.

female the pure Humanity, or regenerated part of the soul, which by union is partaker of the Divine nature'.[60] Pordage probably did mean a rabbi, rather than Tany who claimed that he was *King* of the Jews. He was drawing on the kabbalistic understanding of the *shechinah*, the divine presence which was often seen as having female attributes, different from the notions of Niclaes, and which he was using to supplement his knowledge of Boehme.[61]

Pordage's other major appropriation of Boehme was his use of the first and second principles of the eternal nature as a basis for his visions. Before this is examined, though, it is worth exploring the way in which his description of symbol and vision as part of physical actuality was understood by the community he lived in, especially the hostile elements. It is a measure of the way in which the Behmenist roots of Pordage have become obscured. The fact that he claimed to see visions externally led his persecutors to portray him as a conjuror, though he was engaged in nothing more than a form of spiritual hermeticism. One of his followers, Mrs Flavel, was accused of seeing in a trance the philosopher's stone, which was taken as a symbol of the divinity in the humanity. Pordage did not deny that this had happened, but he did connect it to the whole body of hermetic writings, of which his enemies were suspicious.[62]

The witnesses against Pordage seem to have been confronted with confusing experiences which they could not understand. Their accounts demolished the barrier between literal and figurative, this world and the spiritual world, which orthodox Calvinism strictly maintained, as well as limiting speculation on the nature of the spirit world itself. Richard Seward entered the Bradfield rectory and heard a cry which lasted for a quarter of an hour. Pordage said that he had heard people at prayer. Whatever really did occur, *Innocencie Appearing* includes exaggerations and evasions by both sides—Seward was further confused when he

---

[60] Pordage, *Innocencie Appearing*, pp. 44.

[61] I am grateful to Dr D. S. Katz for help with this point. Another version is presented by Pico, 'Alia ratio huius literae ה: aditionis est: quia sicut in creatis est masculus & foemina: ita & in Divinis, Pater est thiphereth, mater uero, est malchuth, & quaelibet sephirah respectu suae superioris, dicitur mater', *Archangeli Minoritae Interpretationes in selectoria Cabalistarum Dogmata*, in Joannes Pistorius, *Artis Cabalisticae* . . . (Basel, 1587), 735–868 (p. 781). Niclaesian symbols were combined with Behmenist ones, however, in the woodcut prefixed to Samuel Pordage's *Mundorum Explicatio* (1661). [62] *Innocencie Appearing*, p. 29.

visited Pordage's brother, Francis, later on.[63] Francis was rector of the neighbouring church of Stanford Dingley, and he told Seward that the sound in Bradfield rectory was 'one in travel, and the pain was so extream, that h [ad] I [Seward] stayed there a little longer, I might have heard it as far as the Town, but now she was delivered of a man-child, and the travel was at an end'. Whether Francis Pordage was referring to genuine birth or not, he was using a form of expression which made out the cry to be the manifestation of a (spiritual) apocalypse coming upon the Bradfield community, the cry and the birth coming from the popular apocalyptic text of Rev. 12. The pamphlet does not finally make clear an intended meaning, though it is evident that both Pordage brothers saw the event as partly symbolic at least. This would have been encouraged of course by Boehme's writings, where an essential divine meaning was always perceived in natural events.[64]

There are other reports of such behaviour by Pordage in *Innocencie Appearing*. A doctrine of sympathies was being espoused when Pordage said that Daniel Blagrave was cold physically because he was cold to vanities. This is similar to the representations of Sarah Wight and Anna Trapnel (see above, Chapter 1, pp. 45–53). Indeed, Pordage held that flesh was a regenerated part of the soul and so could be interpreted in such a way as was opposed to the traditional view of the sinful nature of flesh.[65]

One Mrs Grip testified that Pordage had been visited by angels and a dragon. Pordage's explanation of this is rather more subtle. He explains the occurrence as a vision, but one which has a physical manifestation growing out of the purely mental aspect of the vision. Pordage says that he had a vision of (?William) Everard in his bedroom in 1649. Everard is usually assumed to be the Digger who visited Pordage during this time. He was known as a conjuror too, though for Pordage he is functioning as a symbol of approaching apocalypse. This was followed by a vision of a giant with a sword 'having the figurative similitude of a great Tree lying by him'. This is an angel guarding the tree of life. Pordage then reports a vision of a dragon. He interprets both giant and dragon as symbols of two invisible principles, *Mundi*

---

[63] Francis Pordage was a friend of Isaac Penington.

[64] *Innocencie Appearing*, pp. 10–19, 28–31.

[65] Ibid. 37, 80.

Ideales, which were manifested to him some time in 1650 and 1651.[66] These are the first and second principles in Boehme's system.

Pordage describes the *Mundi Ideales* as two spiritual worlds extending and penetrating throughout the whole visible Creation in which many particular beings were discerned, suitable to the nature of these worlds. The influence of Boehme is unmistakable:

these two Principles or worlds, seemed very different one from another, as having contrary qualities and operations, by which they work upon this visible Creation, which we see distinguished and differenced into varietie of Creatures, . . . according to the difference and contrariety in the internal worlds, upon which the External doth in som measure depend, as standing in them or rather proceeding from them.[67]

The first principle, or dark world, *Mundus Tenebrosus*, was represented by chariots (like those from the bottomless pit in Rev. 9: 9) drawn by six or four beasts each and attended by 'many inferior spirits' who served the 'Princes' (of darkness). The beasts were terrifying lions, dragons, elephants, tigers, bears, while the princes and attendant men were deformed with animal features. He says that they left visible impressions upon the window, chimney, and ceiling of his house—two globes and a coach and four horses on the chimney—which could be removed only by obliteration with hammers. Pordage also reports that both inwardly and outwardly, nauseating sulphurous smells were witnessed and 'strange' wounds were felt in a similar manner.[68]

The light world, *Mundus Luminosus* or second principle, corresponds point for point with the dark world in a positive and opposite way. This time Pordage sees a host of pure Angelical spirits 'in figurative bodies', transparent like crystal, like the host which Jacob saw at Mahanaim in Gen. 32: 1, 2. These 'manly' forms are full of beauty and majesty. They sparkle like diamonds, and, true to their Behmenist conception, they send forth a 'tincture like the swift rays, and hot beams of the Sun', which refresh Pordage and his followers. Moreover, it is the variety of colours of the Angels within their tinctures which causes Pordage to praise God most, and colour was a major signature indicator for Boehme. As opposed to foul smells, the Bradfield community now sense pleasant smells and tastes, they hear inward music, and are subject to a healing 'quickning vertue' and a 'burning tincture' from the light world in the sense of a 'spiritual contaction'. They are all rewarded with a vision of the world to come, though this is not described. Indeed Pordage dismissed as fancy the supposed vision which Susannah Day had at Pordage's house of the new Jerusalem descending from above as a 'City four square, with borders and precious stones'.[69]

The way to appreciate the essence of God was, for Pordage, to reject the lusting of '*Venus*' in the outward world and turn to the true Virgin life, having come through spiritual death. This Pordage explains in terms of Boehme's microcosm, and the acceptance of this life leads through persecution to self-annihilation, conformity to Christ's death and fixation in the love of the Holy Ghost, Love being the ultimate positive principle in Boehme's thinking:

This Life of Virginity was placed fore-right as to the inward eye of the minde, being that mark of persecution, at which we were to aym in our pressing toward the Resurrection of the dead. To this, Wisdom that eternal virgin (*Prov.* 8. 20, 23) as a leading star, invited us.[70]

For Pordage, as for Boehme, this results in a final merging with essence, which is imparted in a final prophesying speech printed in italics. Later on, in *Mundorum Explicatio*, Pordage's son Samuel was to elaborate on the light and dark worlds or principles at great length, and to set these as 'bowls', 'cups' or *sephiroth* which had emanated from the original essence at the pouring of the vials, according to the Lurianic Kabbalah.[71] Here though, Pordage yearns for union:

there is no satisfaction in man, or the things of man: therefore the spirit of thy servant flyes to thee, like a dove into the true Ark of rest, to be caught up into thy eye, and to be taken into thy heart, and bosom-love; for in such union oft lies union of hearts, union of wils and union of spirits, there is satisfaction only. O how my soul groans for after this union with thee, and presential enjoyment of thee O my God.[72]

An interesting version of Pordage's interpretation of Boehme exists in a pamphlet by one of Pordage's followers, Mary Pocock,

[69] Pordage, *Innocencie Appearing*, pp. 75–6, 90.   [70] Ibid. 77.
[71] *Mundorum Explicatio* (1661), 282.   [72] *Innocencie Appearing*, p. 133.

entitled *The Mystery of the Deity in the Humanity* (1649). The pamphlet's title bears the same phraseology as Pordage uses to express his sense of Behmenist and kabbalistic emanation. Mary Pocock spoke in Pordage's defence on the issue of the heretical 'fiery deity of Christ' in each invididual's soul, and Pordage describes her as a 'deeply experienced woman'. Her pamphlet represents an authentic appropriation of Behmenism for the sectarian spiritual meditation. On the title page she describes herself as a 'member of the body', the community of enlightened people, and she writes of the threefold life of man, the original 'Paradisical Form and Being of man', the fall and the restoration, all of which are internal states which are used to comprehend the individual, and, because of the political vocabulary, the rest of English society. The 'abysse' is clearly seen as responsible for its image in man:

Now behold this vaste motion of Eternity, the first principle; who in himself, through himself, from himself, delights to bring forth himself in his likeness, even in his image, man. The Godhead breathed the man from the Womb of Eternity; the man being the image of this Godhead, having his Being from the Godhead, returns to the Godhead. (pp. 9–10)

This is not strictly faithful to Boehme since for him God is anterior to any principles. Nevertheless, figurative Adam is androgynous and for Pocock a 'shadowing forth' of the ideal proper order of things in the state:

Here is now the soul in the body, the husband and wife, God and the man. This is the Representative, King and Parliament, whose happy condition is bound up in the enjoyment of each other, in the union of the manhood, in the power of the Godhead: And this is the glory of the King, in his paradisicall Kingdome. This is the figure of *Adam* in Paradise, in his beginning, when he had union and fellowship with God in the figurative Paradise, as he was breathed from God in the spiritual Form, being placed in *Eden*. (pp. 16–17)

The Fall occurs when the King, paradisal Adam, loves only himself, and self-seeing Reason, rather than dwelling with Eve, who represents divine reason (Pocock has altered here the original interpretation of the androgynous Adam). The result is, in typical English sectarian terms, an inversion of the proper relationship between substance and shadow, a desire to be God himself: 'This king being in love with it self, made it self the substance, and the substance the shadow, and so grew into earthly mindedness' (p. 19). Mary Pocock's use of political vocabulary in a figurative way allows her to achieve that interpenetration of internal and external whereby vision is coequal with church organization. Thus, putting on the garment of love and realizing the true meaning of emanation is 'true Independants indeed' (pp. 33–5).

Thomas Bromley's *The Way to the Sabbath of Rest* (1655) presents a heavily Behmenist meditational treatise in which the central motif is the journey of the soul towards spiritual rebirth. This, rather than the emanation-oriented side of Boehme, is prominent, which suggests that Bromley took as his model *The Way to Christ Discovered*, though he clearly knew much of Boehme.

In his preface, Bromley argues that some form of representational language, connected to human apprehension of the physical world, is necessary for the soul to begin its journey to the 'eternall world' by meditation.[73] As an apology, as it were, for Boehme and Pordage, Bromley complains that those who totally ignore 'forms' do not see the most obvious 'signatures' which God leaves for man to contemplate. Bromley's language is emblematically sharp: '*We part with darkness, vanity, and lust: We receive light, substance, and love*' (sig. A3^v). The goal of *The Way to the Sabbath of Rest* is to change the nature of the soul and the reader's perception, so that each sees beyond the mirroring function of human reason to the mirror of wisdom. Again, like Boehme, this is couched in a series of short epistles, each of which is punctuated with a brief, summarizing verse or hymn:

> Then let us pray for that true light
> Which gives a true and constant sight
> Of God, Christ, angells, who do lie,
> Much deeper than sharp Reasons eye;
> Which in the glasse of Phantasie
> A lively Picture may aspie
> But not the Essence of true verity.   (p. 23)

---

[73] Baxter conversed with Bromley. Though he found him to be very intelligent, he thought he confused the spiritual with the natural. Bromley would not dispute, claiming to have an 'Extraordinary Irradiation of the Mind', an intuition which was beyond human discourse. He also attacked propriety and *all* institutional, civil and familial relationships, as an impulse towards perfection: *Reliquiae Baxterianae*, ed.

Spiritual advancement is portrayed in terms of images, so that in its unregenerate state, the soul is unable to see itself as a piece of creation in the image of God, but as only in the image of the Serpent: 'bespattered with the dust of the earth, clothed with polluted rags, wrapt up in darknesse and hellish confusion, stained with the poyson of sin, centred in the fire of God'. The reverse, of course, is for the soul to find the good Seed, which requires a passage opposite to the progress of the Serpent, or dark world, by walking 'according to the Royall Law of Love and charity to cherish it' (sig. A3ʳ). Such perception is 'the exercise of the internal sences, we see spiritual objects, as the internal Light-World, visions of Angels, and visions of Representation' (p. 13).

This is set against or before the description of God, which follows Boehme's reorganization of the model of the universe as concentric and interconnected circles.[74] Where Boehme uses a diagram, like astrologers and Hermeticists, Bromley is content to use words: 'The centre is the Highest: the circumference the lowest. God is in the centre; being most Inward: Matter in the circumference, being most Outward, yet God is in the Outward, as his footstoole, but in the most Inward, as his Throne'.[75] God again occurs as light, but Bromley takes care to split up the functions of God. This is achieved by invoking Boehme's quasi-goddess of wisdom, so that as the soul approaches the 'eternall world', 'showrs [*sic*] of Love' rain upon it from 'God's heart' and the 'bosome of *Sophia*', while the soul itself is viewed historically, and so is seen to enter a new 'dispensation' (a word used by Pordage), thus matching the use of the 'internal sences' with the idea of the revealed Age of the Spirit. At this point, the pertinence of symbols begins to decrease: 'we come to slacken the exercise of the Crosse, upon imagination it selfe'. The imagination is to be subjected to the 'illuminated understanding'. Here, Bromley attributes considerable power to the re-born 'new man' whose spiritual 'eye' is capable of 'slaying' the 'old man': Behmenist illumination is made compatible with the familiar

Matthew Sylvester (1696), i, 78. See also letter from Baxter to Bromley's brother Henry, 30 May 1654: Dr Williams's Library, MS Baxter Letters 3, fos. 302–9.

[74] *Aurora* (1656), 242, 591: 'The whole Body of this world is as a Mans Body, for it is surrounded in its utmost Circle with the Stars, and arisen powers of *Nature*, and in that Body the *seaven* spirits of Nature, Governe, and the Heart of Nature, standeth in the Midst or Center.'

[75] Bromley, *The Way to the Sabbath of Rest* (1655), 9. This is glossed as Acts 7: 49.

Puritan sense of regeneration.[76] The final result is to make the soul a point of intersection in the complex universe of Boehme. Here, the characteristic verbs of penetrating action in the microcosm which intimate emanation are compounded with an extended metaphor of physical union. William G. Madsen claims that the late metaphysical poet Edward Taylor, an avid reader of Boehme, turned to an aesthetic which was rooted in Catholic sacramentalism, while more recent critics have been prepared to stress the use of sensory imagery for spiritual purposes among Calvinist writers.[77] With Bromley, however, the specific contribution of Boehme allows him to write a 'progress of the soul' which speaks the spiritual through sense impressions which Bromley believes are in touch with something sunk below the recesses of the imagination:

for Christ many times toucheth the soul with a piercing beame of love, which by this is suddenly drawne to a quick returne, and this gives freer passage for a New Impression, which more exciting the powers of the soul to a new Imbrace, opens the way more for the King of Glory to enter with that power and unutterable force of divine love, that the soul becomes filled, swallowed up, and transported into a kind of rapture, not being able to express those pleasures [, l]usts, imbraces, love-extasies, which then are p[ie]rced thorough it.[78]

IV

Thomas Tany's particular emphasis upon transcendent signification owes a considerable debt to Boehme's rhetoric of essence and emanation. The full extent of Tany's attitudes regarding divine languages is discussed in chapter 7. Tany did not read Boehme extensively and distil a philosophy from him which resembled the original in general terms. Rather, he appears to borrow particular parts of Boehme, along with scattered parts of other occult ideas, in order to speak with the absolute authority of a prophet. There is little consistency in his borrowings, no genuine contiguous set of insights which collectively could be said to constitute a cosmology. Instead, Tany sets side by side a

[76] Bromley, *The Way to the Sabbath of Rest*, p. 24. See also Pordage, *Innocencie Appearing*, p. 113.
[77] *From Shadowy Types to Truth: Studies in Milton's Symbolism* (1968), 171; N. H. Keeble, *Richard Baxter: Puritan Man of Letters* (Oxford, 1982), 48–68.
[78] Bromley, *The Way to the Sabbath of Rest*, p. 42.

series of linguistic features, aimed at realizing the transcendent knowledge, some of which are Boehme's.

Tany named one of his works after the first of Boehme's, *Theauraujohn His Aurora in Tranlagorum in Salem Gloria* (1655),[79] which emphasizes the threefold deity. It appeared in the year before the publication of *Aurora*, though Tany could have seen a German version. What is more likely is that he took the idea of the *Aurora* from one of Boehme's works which was already available, such as *The Clavis, or Key* (1647), or that he came across it through his acquaintance with Pordage.[80] However, Tany's notion of the divine presence in the individual does not display any specific Behmenist principles. Its language is common to the radical spiritualists:

> The spirit of man is nothing, as I said before, but imagery: and nothing is not God, for God is all things, and no name, all things is so called, is but names and not thing, therefore not God.[81]

Tany follows Boehme in the habit of organizing his visions into epistles, but he constructs a rival language to Boehme's for the presence of the divine in nature. Where Boehme is dependent upon occult vocabulary, Tany builds his language by writing Hebrew, Latin and Greek phrases in English, which are then interpreted according to their place in the doctrine of emanation and essence. Tany goes on to argue that his inspiration allows him to attack tithes, and to realize the Millennium by witnessing and calling for the return and conversion of the Jews.[82]

As with Boehme God is the essence for Tany, though he does not use this particular word. He does use 'centre', which is found in Boehme as well as other popular mystics. Tany also uses 'operation' and 'declaration' to intimate emanation, words which

---

[79] Tany dates this work 25 Feb. 1650, on p. 16, which suggests that it was originally published in this year, or in 1651.

[80] Coppe the Ranter and Tany are known to have stayed with Pordage, according to Christopher Fowler, *Daemonium Meridianum* (1655), 60. In his *DNB* article on Pordage, Alexander Gordon suggested that Coppe introduced Boehme to Pordage. However Coppe's overt use of Boehme is dubious and the Ashmole connection for Pordage is more likely (see above, p. 190). But Pordage did appear to defend Coppe at Reading in 1651, at about the same time that Coppe visited Bradfield. Evidence that John Dury ran errands for Pordage in Holland (a Behmenist centre) in 1641 is provided by G. H. Turnbull, *Hartlib, Dury and Comenius. Gleanings from Hartlib's Papers* (Liverpool, 1947), 220.

[81] *Theauraujohn his Theous Ori Apokolipikal* (1651), 20.

[82] *Theauraujohn High Priest to the Jewes* (1651), 8.

come from the popular Neoplatonism originally disseminated by Everard and Randall. Tany emphasizes the divine in every individual, the 'Perfect Truth' living in 'every Creature':

for I *Theaurau John* did behold and have seen the precious pearle, the souls delight, O the Apples of life that my soul thirsts after! oh the paradaical fruit, *o so aluah halalujah al*, oh the divine being is the ravishment of the soul, oh the evangelical injoyment in the paradaical essence![83]

Tany here stresses the light world, the second principle, at the expense of the dark world. There is a dualism present in his work, however, in the opposition between light and dark, 'hieroglyphically represented', but there is no explanation of God's relationship with the dark world. In fact, Tany strays markedly towards the monism of the Ranters:

Now know that the light is God, darkness is suffered by God, which lyes in these two great declaratives, of day and night; for the day is, the night is not, the night is, and day is not, this is to us; but to him that is both day night and day, all is but one; for light and darkness is but one unto the Lord. The two hieroglyphs of day and night were but looked upon with enlightened eyes, they hold all in them and so fully represent all things and contain under their hyroglyphacic whosoever is and is not.[84]

Tany's monism seems to derive from the Neoplatonic writings proper, and he is akin to Laurence Clarkson in his Ranter phase in this (see below, p. 235). So, Tany uses the Neoplatonic 'descension' in order to connect essence with creation, rather than image or *vestigia* as with Boehme. But, on the contrary again, the figure of Aurora itself exists as a metaphor for the transcendent world. As with Boehme, alchemical language points to the spiritual invigoration of natural objects. God is 'the Elixer and that Attrackt of beauty', while the familiar symbols of the Lilly and the Vine Branch recur in Tany.[85] With Boehme and the Neoplatonists, Tany emphasizes the divine presence in this world in terms of verbs of action. Thus, the fountain head is connected with the eye, and sight with light. Vision is a predisposition of union.

The obsession with grammar pervades Tany's writings. 'The proper compound word' is necessary to understand God's

---

[83] *Theauraujohn his Theous Ori Apokolipikal* (1651), 30–1.
[84] Ibid. 38. 　　　　　　　　　　[85] Ibid. 44.

conversation. As with Boehme, the Word is 'grafted' on to our souls, though, yet again, this word was often used by orthodox Puritans. For Tany, visions are accompanied by a dumbness in the recipient, but as a result of the vision, the ability to name, or rather re-name, results in a re-ordering of Biblical myths:

> *now Christ the first borne among many brethren*, this text is *wrong rendred;* for the *Antecedent* goes before the *relative,* as *hos in patroas* in a *legma in a saleph in rem fratris*, tis in his full *intendant*, he was the birth of the first *brethren* know that my *knowledge* transcends the *translated coppies*.[86]

Tany is here concerned to reduce all creation to the 'radax' (*sic*), the root of each word, which, as with the kabbalah and Boehme, embodies a centre for the emanating light, a *sephira* or at least part of a *sephira*. The term 'radicall' or 'radix' is common among seventeenth-century occultists to express an origin. With hindsight it is ironic that the Quaker James Nayler attacked an occultist, George Emmot, for using 'radix' to describe essence, given that the presence of essence is so central to Nayler's expression. For another Quaker, John Anderdon, writing in *One Blow at Babel* (1662), such sophisticated concepts elaborated by followers of Boehme are 'carnal conceptions, begotten in their Imaginations upon Jacob Behmen's Writings'.[87] While stressing his sense of the divine in terms of an emanating inner Light, Anderdon is repelled by what he sees as Papist elements: Boehme's supernaturally invigorated natural objects become '*Mediums* like Sacraments', while the spiritual pride in Boehme's conception of speech is sarcastically ridiculed: 'what advantage would it be to us if we were able to speak with the tongue of men and Angels'?[88] On the contrary, Tany stresses his angelic nature in the posture of an 'annointed mad-man', against the Ranters, who are for him devoid of the divine in that they are not true humans, '*Ante-no-men*'.[89]

V

Of the two Independent ministers dealt with here, John Webster was the more spiritually radical, since he thoroughly limited

---

[86] *Theauraujohn His Aurora in Tranlagorum in Salem Gloria* (1655), 17.

[87] Nayler, *A Foole Answered According to his Folly* (1655), 14; Anderdon, *One Blow at Babel* (1662), A1ʳ. John Perrot showed a somewhat more positive attitude towards Boehme: see above, p. 109.   [88] Ibid. 6, 3.

[89] *Theauraujohn His Aurora in Tranlagorum in Salem Gloria* (1655), 25.

sacraments and ordinances to strict Pauline practice, so that he may be truly called a Seeker.[90] Despite his Fifth Monarchist allegiance and his growing mysticism in the later 1650s, Morgan Llwyd still clung to the idea of the efficacy of sacraments and ordinances, much more so that many other Independents.[91] However, both display considerable debts to Boehme, though Llwyd's is more profound. Also, he is more devoted to making use of Boehme's perceptions for pastoral and soteriological purposes.

Webster's knowledge of occult and mystical philosophy is extensive, and Boehme is but one thinker he acknowledges within this field. Like Tany, Webster explores the notion of a perfect, divine language, in his attack on orthodox university education, *Academiarum Examen* (1654). Unlike Tany, Webster is more centrally concerned with developing Boehme's notion of the language of nature. Though, as Webster says, many regard Boehme's philosophy as 'fabulous, impossible, or ridiculous', the truth of the matter begins with Boehme's notion of the archetypal, protoplast Adam (p. 26). Adam spoke the language of the Father as it was out-spoken from the essence into the third principle, the external world. This eternal word which the unfallen Adam understood was characterized by the desire which lay at the heart of the Godhead: 'the *tongues of men and Angels*, which would profit nothing, if they were not spoken in, and from the eternal word, which is the love-essence'. This enables Adam to comprehend the variety of signatures and tinctures which are expressed by the 'outflowing *fiat*' (p. 27). That the word was 'radically and essentially one' with Adam meant that he had the true signatures of things in creation already planted as *Ideas* in his mind, including Eve (p. 29). Webster does not seem to register the Fall before the creation, that part of Boehme which is radically different from Paracelsus. Rather, he manifests greater interest in apprehending the entire expanse of knowledge and insight to be gained from Boehme's natural philosophy:

men not understanding these immediate sounds of the soul, and the true *Schematism* of the internal notions impressed, and delineated in several sounds, have instituted, and imposed others, that do not altogether concord, and agree to the innate notions, and so no care is taken for the

[90] See John Webster, *The Saints Guide* (1653), sigs. A3ᵛ–A4', pp. 17–19, 24.
[91] On Llwyd's attitudes to ordinances, see Nuttall, *The Holy Spirit*, pp. 98–9.

recovery and restauration of the Catholique language in which lies hid all the rich treasury of natures admirable and excellent secrets. (p. 32)

The perspective in Llwyd is immediately very different. He is not as apparently close to Boehme as is Webster. His most famous work *Llyfr y tri Aderyn* (*The Book of the Three Birds*) (1653) is set very much in the turmoils of the Interregnum, displaying an abrupt tension between a timeless divine world and the historically limited human timescale:

Dirgelwch frar-iw ddeall ac i eraill iw watwar, sef Tri Aderyn yn ymddiddan yr Eryr, a'r Golomen, a'r Gigfran. Neu Arwydd i annerch y Cymru. Yn y flwyddyn mil a chwechant a thair ar ddêc a deugain, Cyn Dyfod, 666.

A Mystery for some to discern, and for others to deride; namely, Three Birds in conversation together, the EAGLE, the DOVE, and the RAVEN—or an admonitory salutation to the Welsh in the Year 1653, before the coming of anti-Christ (666).[92]

The relationship between human and divine is, as with Bromley, interrupted by the imagination's propensity to create mirrors of the material world. Only spiritual regeneration can bring the mind to the proximity of the 'eternall world':

understand, O Eagle, that there are images in the mind of every man, and these are the likeness of every thing which the eye hath seen in the world; all of them appear in the mind as it were in a mirror, and these reflections will continue for ever, unless they be destroyed before the death of the body.[93]

This stems from a mature appreciation of Boehme's strictures on the nature of the Godhead '*without* Nature *and* Creature', as manifested in a letter from Llwyd to Richard Baxter:

None knowes the will before the revealed essence of God, knowe wee him (as immanent), then all is plaine, and the key is found, though philosophy could never well attend to the eternall word who is the only begotten Image and universall declaration of the wonderful everblessed Godhead and is God eternall.[94]

---

[92] *Llyfr y tri Aderyn* (1653), sig. A1ʳ; English trans. J. L. Parry (*The Book of the Three Birds*), in *National Eisteddfod of Wales, Llandudno 1896* (Liverpool, 1898), 192–275.

[93] Ibid. 241. The gloss here is Ezck. 4.

[94] Letter to Richard Baxter in *Gweithiau Morgan Llwyd*, 2 vols. (Bangor and London, 1899, 1908), ii, ed. J. H. Davies, 271.

For Llwyd, God as 'fountain head' and 'eternal essence' entails the concomitant use of traditional mystical language. The 'morning star' (Rev. 2: 28; 22: 16) becomes a symbol of spiritual regeneration and the realization of the Second Coming: 'But, as to the Jews, they are looking for a Morning Star, and are on the Eve of rising yet above the whole hills.'[95] The rose (Cant. 2: 1; Isa. 35: 1) and the veil are employed as symbols of *unio mystica*.[96] Llwyd stands out from other Fifth Monarchists in that his appropriation of Boehme leads him to stress the inner Millennium rather than a literal Second Coming. He appears to believe in an internal and an external return, a position taken by one of Cromwell's favoured ministers, John Owen.[97] In *Llyfr y tri Aderyn*, the balance between political critique and mystical revelation is almost equal: the inner life became more important as the 1650s progressed. So, in the poem '1648', Llwyd envisages all mankind becoming enlightened according to the process of purgation described in the imagery of Revelation. Singing represents the voice of a regenerating soul, inspired by the invigorating fire, and finding a response in the enlivened creation:

> Sing on a brittle sea of glasse
> Sing in a furne of fire
> In flames wee leap for joy and find
> a cave a singing quire.[98]

Once again it is difficult to see the overt presence of Boehme here. If this poem was written in the year of its title, it surely represents a Llwyd who had not yet fully incorporated Boehme into his work.[99] However, by the time of *Gair o'r Gair* (1657) Boehme's reading of Revelation is evident: 'By this, that which was like Glass is turned to Earth, and the Sun is darkened, and the radical strength is degenerated into weak, rotten flesh.'[100]

---

[95] *Llyfr y tri Aderyn*, in Parry (1898), 208.

[96] R. Tudur Jones, 'The Healing Herb and the Rose of Love: The Piety of Two Welsh Puritans', in *Reformation, Continuity and Dissent*, ed. R. Buick Knox (1977), 154–79 (p. 177).

[97] See B. S. Capp, *The Fifth Monarchy Men* (1972), 175, 223.

[98] *Gweithiau Morgan Llwyd*, i, ed. T. E. Ellis, p. 24. In the seventeenth century, Rev. 15: 2 was thought to represent the vitrification of the sea.

[99] Presumably, '1648' was not written before the date of the title.

[100] *Gair o'r Gair* (1657). Trans. Griffith Rudd as *A Discourse of God the Word* and published 1739. All quotations are taken from this edition. The present quotation is from p. 47.

Taking another perspective, the Dove in *Llyfr y tri Aderyn* is a mouthpiece for realizing the difference between humanity and essence: 'I dare not utter words of mine own self (they must emanate from One above)'.[101] The Dove proceeds to explain man's emanation from, and eventual return to, the Eternal. The angelic spirits are never far away here. 'Christ's Army' (a veiled reference to the New Model Army) is endowed with one vast energy, as it 'hath two wings and diffring colours all', just as with Boehme's angels.[102] The powers of the second principle, the light world, are merged with the glory of the Saints.

Most of Llwyd's more metaphysical statements which are influenced by Boehme come with regard to the logocentric nature of creation and incarnation. In Behmenist terms this is part of the language of nature. Unlike Webster, who demonstrates how the language of nature works in the natural world and how it was generated through the agency of Adam, Llwyd looks to the oneness being hinted at in silence, the angelic language:

There is with GOD, who is three in one, but one Language; and with his intelligent Angels but one peculiar Dialect; and in that they glorify GOD, and converse with one another, and with the Saints, without the Noise of Tongues or Sounds of Words; but silent and heavenly in his Presence.[103]

To know this is to have one's foundation in God and the understanding of this language is the key to worship with one consent. The disunity which is a result of non-comprehension is the estrangement of Soul and Word, a fault which Boehme's archetypal Adam enacted, but which is still present in man as an elemental defection: 'This is the radical Cause why GOD has no Delight in any man, or in any Thing but through the Coelestial Water in his Son.'[104] Here, Llwyd follows precisely Boehme's model of divine essence, which places Christ as the 'Delight or impression of the Will' after the Father, the 'will of the Abyss' (see p. 194, Fig. 5); 'a Word is the Delight of the Will, if it be perfect, and they are but one; the Light, Heat, and Form of a

---

[101] *Llyfr y tri Aderyn* in Parry (1898), 220. R. Tudur Jones. 'The Healing Herb', 177, maintains that for Llwyd God is essentially different from man: the light in the individual's heart is divine light, but it is not an emanation, since God is objective for Llwyd, even though he is within. In the light of the passage quoted here, Llwyd's position cannot be as certain as Jones indicates.

[102] '1648' in *Gweithiau Morgan Llwyd*, i. p. 24.

[103] *A Discourse of God the Word*, p. 1.   [104] Ibid. 24; see also 1, 3.

Candle burning before you is but one'.[105] It has been suggested
that Llwyd's metaphors and analogies do not describe eternal
verities, but are merely representative of states of mind and
emotion in Llwyd's reader.[106] However, while this is true for
much of the traditional symbolism and biblical imagery, as with
the candle in the quotation above, the adherence to Boehme's
theosophy must mean that Llwyd believed that the imagery
which describes universal processes, especially the essence,
emanation, the three principles and the threefold life of men,
does exist as a representation of eternal forces and realities. Quite
often the two types of usage are mixed, and indistinguishable
without careful consideration, because of the complex way in
which Boehme's eternal reality is constructed through several
interlocking systems of metaphors.

More simply Llwyd follows Boehme in attributing to God an
immanence in nature: 'the Spirit of the Creation is the Life of
Nature, but GOD is the Spring of that Life'.[107] Likewise, Llwyd
says that the creation was inside God before he created it, while
Christ wears nature as a garment.[108] In this way it is possible for
some to be known by Christ through their insights into nature
without knowing the Bible. The Spirit is the key to nature,
though obviously knowledge of the Scriptures can do no harm. In
fact Llwyd looks to an uncomplicated first-hand knowledge of the
Word through Hebrew, which is part inspired and part learnt.
Since Hebrew was the first language, it contains more of the
language of nature in it, that language of nature being perfectly
understood in Eden.

The Scripture finds an echo in the individual's conscience
according to the operation of the Word in the individual. Again,
this puts inspiration and perception over the Letter. Yet, like
Bromley though unlike Pordage, Llwyd cannot but take his
points of reference from the Bible. The frequent reference to the
new creature comes from Gal. 6: 15: 'For in Christ Jesus neither
circumcision availeth any thing, nor uncircumcision, but a new
creature', and the presence of the eternal Will in man from Rom.

---

[105] *A Discourse of God the Word*, p. 23. The same context applies to the will and self-shouldst place thy own Will in the Will of GOD, uniting to him, by forsaking and denying thy own Will, as a River pours itself into one sea, giving thyself up to his Will to lead thee in every Thing' (p. 55).

[106] R. Tudur Jones, 'The Healing Herb', p. 169.

[107] *A Discourse of God the Word*, p. 6.   [108] Ibid. 7, 25.

10: 8; 'The Word is nigh thee, *even* in thy mouth, and in thy heart: that is, the word of Faith.' In fact, Llwyd allows Boehme's notion of essence and imprint in the individual to reconcile spirit and Scripture with apparent parity: 'look with great Reverance in the Face of the Spirit of the Scriptures; and suffer the eternal Word to look in the Face of thy Mind through the Conscience, as at thy first coming to thyself.'[109] When this is put inside the repetitive rhetoric of devotional exhortation, the effect is emotionally awesome, as in 'Where is Christ?':

He is stiled the brightness of the fathers glory, because in the eternal still liberty he maketh a glance, which taketh its original out of the sharpness of the eternal nature. He is called the love of the Father, because the Fathers first will to the genetrix [female parent] of nature, desireth only this his most beloved heart, and this is the best beloved above nature, and yet is the Fathers own essence. His name also is called Wonderful, because he is the creator of all things, by whom all things out of the Center of the essences of the Father are brought to light and being, so that the nature of the Father standeth in great wonders.[110]

Llwyd is most remarkable for his mixture of styles, rhetorics, and registers. There is no doubt that this ability to blend is partly facilitated by the imagistic and descriptive dexterity of Boehme, which Llwyd inherited. The achievement of *Llyfr y tri Aderyn* is to use animals with various symbolic values to construct a rich political and religious allegory. The Dove is a messenger of the inner millennium and a voice of the illuminated, described as having been in flight since Noah's day. The Raven is a repository of sloth and unenlightened 'carnality', an adherent to pure 'formal religion', as well as being a political sceptic. In the middle is the Eagle, who consistently speaks against the Raven's condemnation of the Dove, but who does not seem to be sufficiently self-denied to understand all of what the Dove has to say. At the same time, the Raven is clearly identified with the episcopal church, the Dove with the Independent churches and congregations, and the Eagle with Cromwell, who holds all the power and destiny, but who is not properly and consciously connected with the One. The struggle is set almost in epic fashion between good and evil *Will*, as we are told that the Eternal has willed the creation, 'the water of divine beatitude'

---

[109] Ibid. 55.   [110] 'Where is Christ?', in *Gweithiau Morgan Llwyd*, i, 302.

into being. Each bird possesses a distinct type of allegorical language. It is clear that the language of the Dove is divinely inspired and prophetic. By contrast the Raven speaks an allegory merely of the political nation. Without a king the nation is 'headless' and anarchistic, as the wild activities of the Doves or separatists implies:

Raven. These Doves fly about in every kingdom, and that is an unfavourable sign for the stability of kings. There are many of them in Holland, some in France, and a few in Spain, and I do not like to see them everywhere flying to their dove-cots; they are, too, so swift that no hawk is able to catch them.[111]

The Raven sees the Dove's speech as 'threats and dream', and the Eagle fears that the allegorical language of the Dove (generally the Independent interpretation of the Bible, but also Llwyd's employment of Boehme) will scare the Raven away, so mirroring the alienation of some Protestants from the sublime language of the sects. The Dove speaks in a dense allegory, using natural imagery from the Bible to stress inner rebirth. This could be characteristic of any spiritual Puritan, but the vividness of the images is generated partly by Llwyd's comprehension of Boehme's insights into biblical symbols:

Let not the spirit of the creature hold thee captive, but swim away to the Spirit of the Creator. Consider the good that is before thee as a pearl, and the work that thou has[t] done as dirt. Sweet to the flesh is the sugar of the devil, but do thou eat of the mystic manna. Lucifer is a hog indwelt in man's flesh. His cauldron is an impure heart boiling on the fire of hell. The lusts of the flesh are the horses of war; dismount them and delay not. The reasonings of man are a bush of thorns, and whoso denyeth himself wil escape out of it.[112]

Here is Llwyd's use of epigram and adage to lodge the phrase inside the reader's memory as sure as God's imprint, light and dark, is inside every person. But there is also an irony here in a secondary sense: the Eagle is unable to understand all of the Dove's utterances. When the Dove says that the Pope will be 'amongst Quakers', he does not perceive the Dove's meaning, that at the Judgement Day all will tremble in the presence of

[111] *Llyfr y tri Aderyn* in Parry (1898), 207.   [112] Ibid. 207.

God, rather than the popular identification of Quakers with Papists.[113]

The sectarians were silent on the finer points of Boehme, those inconsistencies which were later to occupy Schelling and Coleridge. But this does not mean that they did not think seriously and deeply about the 'teutonick philosopher'. A close reading reveals, especially in the cases of Pordage, Pocock, Bromley, and Llwyd, an attempt to make Boehme's thought enlarge the exhortative, prophetic, and the epistemological capacity of English radical Puritan literature. Partly because of the greater availability of Boehme's writings, in German or in English, the extent of Boehme's impact upon sectarian discourse and thought was greater than that of Everard and Randall's translations, and of the Familist writings. None the less, we should not forget that the tracts of Niclaes and his disciples were read in radical Puritan and sectarian circles. If a closer look is taken at sectarian thought about the creation, the Godhead, and the relationship between divine and human languages, the spiritualist and mystic presence can be seen still at work, helping to shape a distinctive and extraordinary response to the nature of knowledge and of language.

---

[113] Ibid. 207. See also Nuttall, *The Holy Spirit*, p. 182.

III

The Theory and Practice of
Radical Religious Language

6
'Chambers of Imagery' *

I

RADICAL Puritan and sectarian writing, like that of Puritanism as a whole, was concerned with the 'whole man', with registering the changing spiritual state of the self. Instances where natural imagery is used to describe sanctified believers have already been discussed. More than this, however, in their desire to describe the perfect state and the way in which the divine worked in the universe, the religious radicals elaborated a series of allegories and images based upon words which name natural objects and qualities. The result was a metaphysical system which accounted for physical objects, human bodies, and natural objects themselves, in terms of a fixed set of metaphors for transcendent realities. The chief feature of these metaphors is the habit of making no distinction between moral and cosmological realms. In the more extreme cases, such systems were fashioned in order to construct an authentic theory of knowledge from first principles for the purposes of bolstering the authority of a sectarian stance. Knowledge of God was a precondition of salvation, and to know God was to partake of his nature.

Several critics have stated that radical religious writing, especially that of Gerrard Winstanley, should be read as visionary poetry. They refer to the allegorical aspects of sectarian prose, and assert that such allegories and also obscure myths need to be decoded in order to reveal the social and political determinants of the writer, and the social and political statements which the writer is making.[1] Indeed, contemporaries talked of enthusiasts as types of poet. But, of course, none of the radical religious writers had a pre-conceived notion of such a 'poetic' enterprise with which to invest their work. Nevertheless, critics are right to draw attention to the peculiar allegories of the sectarians, specifically the way in which biblical episodes and

* Ezek. 8: 12.

[1] Gerrard Winstanley, *The Law of Freedom and Other Writings*, ed. Christopher Hill (1973), Introduction, 54–9; T. W. Hayes, *Winstanley the Digger* (Cambridge, Mass., 1979), *passim*.

events are simplified and made to apply to the internal state of the individual. As has been seen, sectarian religion aggressively eschews outward forms of religion and concentrates upon the inner state of the believer. The radical religious writers wrote with this *theological* preconception, and so 'poetry' refers to the manner in which radical religious language represents the internal, largely beyond the categories of covenant theology.

More significantly, the radicals were constructing a system of describing God's operation in the universe both internally and externally, over and against 'carnal' learning. Among the sectarians, inner experiences and processes are ordered by means of strict allegories which enable the writers to understand themselves, the universe, and the divine, and the relationships between all three. In their own terms, the discourse which they produced to achieve this aim becomes charged with the authority of the truth they are describing. Since the rejection of external forms by the most extreme sectarians is so total, it may also be conjectured that the very rigidity of the sectarian allegories replaces outer rituals with an inner certainty in divinely instituted processes which take place within the individual and within every natural object. In Winstanley's case, such language lays the foundation for his social vision in a mysticism which merges each person with creation.

The allegories are based upon simple dualistic myths which are themselves derived directly from the Bible, and which are common in much seventeenth-century devotional discourse. However, the extent to which these dualisms are regarded as universals is remarkable in radical religious writing. For instance, the universe is described as a series of clouds and veils which hide the reality of God.[2] The image occurs in several manifestations: in *The Smoke in the Temple* (1646), John Saltmarsh talks of truth being obscured by clouds (sig. **1ʳ). There is also the sense operating behind the text 'He made darkness his secret place' (Ps. 18: 11), as well as the Platonic sense of God the reality hiding behind the shadows of material objects. For the sectarians the notion is a historical one in the sense that the Millennium is described as God revealing himself, while individuals describe their sense of falling away from an achieved grace as God hiding himself again, as in the case of the Ranter Joseph Salmon in

[2] See Isa. 3: 23; 27: 7; Matt. 27: 51; 2 Cor. 3: 13–16; Heb. 6: 19; 9: 3; 10: 20.

Heights in Depths.[3] In an earlier pamphlet, *A Rout, A Rout* (1649) Salmon's God hides in the 'form' of Monarchy, so that the allegory comes to explain the political order:

In this form of Monarchy God hath vailed his beautiful presence with a thick cloud of darkness: He hath made darkness his secret place, and his pavilions round about him have been thick clouds of the Sky. Though the image and brightness of God have dwelt in it, yet under such black darkness that man could never discern it. Tyranny, persecution, opposition, wil[l], nature and creature, hath been (as it were) that vail betwixt God and man in this dispensation.[4]

This type of discourse had its immediate origins in the political critiques of the army chaplains, Saltmarsh, William Erbery, and especially William Sedgwick. The mystical element is apparent where God is envisaged as the omnipotent and indifferent driving force behind the political state of the nation, and this sense is enhanced by the fact that Salmon makes no explicit judgement upon monarchy: he merely lets the reader feel an implied sense of its awesome menace. Also of note here is Salmon's vocabulary since it throws light upon the figuration which operates in the allegory. Salmon identifies natural objects, human beings, and animals ('nature' and 'creature') as impediments to God's true manifestation, even though he has used a language of natural qualities to describe the way in which God operates. The abstract qualities of darkness and brightness represent the power of God, unknowable to man in the rational sense, so that the images are evocative of what can only be felt or intuited by the spirit. Natural objects (as well as selfish and oppressive qualities—tyranny and persecution) restrict the purity of the divine, yet words which are associated with the description of natural objects are necessary to describe the immanent and transcendent divine. The idea of 'form' allows different spheres of reality to be connected, making sense of them in terms of the overall sectarian epistemology.[5] In this light, though Austin Woolrych is correct in maintaining that Ranters did not participate in the political process, this does not mean that they did not comprehend the political in their own terms.[6]

---

[3] *CRW*, p. 212.   [4] Ibid. 193.

[5] See Sedgwick, *Letter to Fairfax* (1649), sig. A3ʳ: for 'form', see Rom. 2: 20; 6: 17; Phil. 2: 20; 2 Tim. 3: 5.

[6] *From Commonwealth to Protectorate* (Oxford, 1982), 393.

It is now accepted that the historical scheme employed by the radicals is not directly derived from the system of the twelfth-century abbot, Joachim of Fiore, despite the apparent close similarities. Joachim said that God manifested himself in three ages or dispensations, a prophecy developed from Jer. 31: 31. The first Age,—that of the Father, and corresponding to Jewish history as chronicled in the Old Testament—was when God 'vailed' himself in 'Jewish ceremonies' and when divine authority was accepted from the Law of Moses. This was followed by the Age of the Son as recorded in the New Testament, when divine teaching was to be taken from the example of Christ. This Dispensation had lasted until the present, at which point God was gradually coming to dwell inside the body of every man, so that each individual would receive direct inspiration from God. This was the third and final dispensation, the Age of the Spirit. The presence of ideas like this is reasonably common among radical Puritans. Saltmarsh, for instance, believed that the Age of the Spirit had been growing by gradual revelation since the time of the New Testament. Only Dell, however, makes specific reference to any of Joachim's writings.[7] Joachim's works were known to sixteenth-century English reformers, Foxe, Bale, and Knox in particular, for whom Joachim was primarily a victim of Papal vigilance. However, in the mid-seventeenth century the case seems to be that in the excitable environment these ideas were circulating spontaneously without any specific connection with Joachim's ideas.

Salmon's myth of cosmic activity operates on a local level as well, so that the historical progress of God from one form into another can take place within an individual, and in infinitely variable amounts of time: 'this Power (God) hath a dayly [that is, constant] motion out of one dispensation spiritual into another'.[8] At the same time the concern with the metaphor of 'vailing' is extended so that there is a concentration upon the way in which the immanent God 'clothes' himself. There are two

---

[7] Marjorie Reeves deals with the problem of the circulation of Joachite texts in the sixteenth and seventeenth centuries, and on the relative nature of the historical or a-historical third ages in *Joachim of Fiore and the Prophetic Future* (1976), 136–65. She is even more sceptical of Joachim's influence in Marjorie Reeves and Warwick Gould, *Joachim of Fiore and the Myth of the Eternal Evangel in the Nineteenth Century* (Oxford, 1986), 18–26. See Saltmarsh, *Sparkles of Glory* (1647), 52; Dell, *A Plain and Necessary Confutation of Divers Gross and Antichristian Errors* (1654), 17–18.

[8] *CRW*, p. 192.

related senses here. First, and obviously, God is within the object, institution, or sequence of events, while there is a simultaneous imperative for all things which pertain to the divine to transcend 'form', to cease being God's 'clothes', and to become 'power' or part of the divine itself. For Salmon, God is continually 'vailing' himself because that is the nature of his original perfection: 'this divine Power (or Mystery) admits of no eternal habitation in any thing below it self'. It is a doctrine of correspondences. God is veiled in all things, in some more darkly than in others, though all reflect him to some extent. Thus God's progression of his residence from within Monarchy to within Parliament is seen as a change in form though not in power:

> The power and life of the King, and in him the very soul of Monarchy sunk into the Parliament, and here it lost its name barely, but not its nature; its form, but not its power; they making themselves as absolute and tyrannical as ever the King in his reign, dignity and supremacy; yet the Lord ascended a little nearer himself, by taking off this form (the Parliament) and hereby made way for his after-design. (ibid. 193)

Similarly, in the microcosm of the individual, God follows his footsteps out of man 'into a more compleat image or likeness of himself'.[10]

The metaphor of the veil is inextricably linked to the moral impulse in Salmon's critique. The 'darkly' veil is the oppressive powers of persecution, tyranny, and personal selfishness which lie in Monarchy and Parliamentary power alike, a carnal and arbitrary power which shall be consumed in the apocalypse as the New Age comes on. Here the veil is 'clouds of bondage' and both Salmon and Winstanley employ the popular Puritan identification of the English with the Hebrews, who shall escape from their bonds of oppression in fleshly Egypt and proceed to the new Jerusalem.[11] Also, by casting political institutions into the mould of the veil metaphor, Salmon is able to predict an apocalyptic end for Monarchy and Parliament, and all 'fleshly regality'. So the veil is part of an apocalyptic interpretative

---

[9] Ibid.   [10] Ibid. 193.

[11] Winstanley, *The New Law of Righteousness* (1649), sig. A2ᵛ. See also the 'Egyptian' bond of 'self and flesh' in Jacob Bauthumley, *The Light and Dark Sides of God* (1650) in *CRW*, 236. Such language probably had its immediate origins in the preaching and publications of William Sedgwick and John Saltmarsh: see Laurence Clarkson, *The Lost Sheep Found* (1660), in *CRW*, 177.

system and its application to any earthly subject guarantees an eventual inner apocalypse for that subject: 'God (having hitherto walked under this form) is now (and hath in these last days) come forth to rend this vail in pieces, to shake this form, to lay it waste, and clothe himself with another'.[12] The roots of this explanation lie in the widespread Parliamentarian notion of the power of Providence on their side: Salmon enhances his appeal by developing his metaphysic of the 'mystery' from this premiss.

Significantly there are other metaphors of concealment. Coppe sees the hypocrisy of religious orthodoxy as the 'cloak of fleshly holiness and Religion' and the 'Shell of Episcopacy'. Likewise there is the 'husk' which surrounds the 'kernel' of spiritual excellence, as with Winstanley: 'Well, your word Divinity darkens knowledge: you talk of a body of Divinity, and of Anatomyzing Divinity: O fine language! But when it comes to triall, it is but a husk without the kernall'.[13] As with the veil, the husk and kernel dualism is common among radical religious writers, though again it is quite popular with more orthodox Puritans.

The metaphors centre upon the individual as much as the entire creation or the Scriptures. The light and dark powers of God are seen to operate everywhere:

Every Dispensation under Heaven hath its Light and its Darkness. There is a Day and a Night to man, in every state, whereinto he is cast: And all under every Dispensation walk either in the light or dark part of that Dispensation.[14]

For John Reeve, most men are 'dead . . . from inward dark-ness',[15] while Winstanley employed the dualism to illustrate the moral inversion made by those who have the Serpent within them:

This is the darknesse, that hath covered the Earth, and the curse that destroyes all things, this is he that calls light darknesse, good evill, and

---

[12] *CRW*, p. 193.

[13] *The New Law of Righteousness* (1649), 118. For biblical references to 'husk', see Numb. 6: 4; 2 Kings 4: 42; Luke 15: 16, and for 'kernall' see Numb. 6: 4.

[14] Isaac Penington, *Severall Fresh Inward Openings* (1650), 6.

[15] 'The Prophet Reeve's Epistle to his Friend', 24 Sept. 1654, in *A Volume of Spiritual Epistles* (1820), 8.

evill good: and while this power rules in mankind, mankind is in prison and bondage within himselfe and sees no Light.[16]

For Winstanley even more than for Salmon the dualism of light and darkness yields an almost Manichean vision, analogized at one point as a battle: 'Light fights against darknesse, universall Love fights against selfish power: Life against death: True knowledge against imaginary thoughts.'[17] In this way Winstanley builds up a series of analogies all of which are part of his mythic universe, so that a dialectic is constructed through various associations. Of course Winstanley's universe is only Manichean in a limited sense, because there is always the promise of the Second Coming when darkness is defeated. The progress towards the new birth is registered in Winstanley by a successive 'casting off' of 'fleshly Form', so that the clothing metaphor enhances that of light and darkness. For Laurence Clarkson, in *A Single Eye All Light, no Darkness* (1650), the perfect creature is already able to see that darkness is the same as light since both emanate from the same source, God; while Winstanley reinforces his dualistic vision by juxtaposing different pairs of opposites with that of light and darkness. Clarkson first admits the duality of light and darkness, but subverts it by referring to Scriptual exegesis which finds contradictions in points of grammar: 'From hence you may observe the connexion hereof run in the plural, not Power, but Powers; a Power of darknesse, a Power of light, a Power in the wicked, a Power in the Godly; yet you have held forth in the same Scripture but one God'.[18]

Clarkson is peculiar in that he admits the absolute truth of neither dualistic myth nor Scripture, as all is subordinated to his impulse to regard any act, good or bad, as an emanation from God: the term 'evil' is thus a creation of the human imagination only. However, when Clarkson looks back at his career as a Ranter he says that at this stage he had no faith in Scripture because it was so contradictory, 'though I would talk of it, and speak from it for my own advantage', but he extends the idea of God as a power or powers in the universe so that the myth or allegory becomes a description of the actual ground of being. There is no God 'but only nature' and 'that which was life in

[16] *Fire in the Bush* (1650), 10.
[17] Ibid. 11. [18] *CRW*, p. 167.

man, went into that infinite Bulk and Bigness, so called *God*, as a drop into the Ocean, and the body rotted in the grave, and for ever so to remain'.[19] The author of *Divinity And Philosophy Dissected* (1644) states that the allegory is necessary in order to overcome the problem of contradictory Scriptures: 'Therefore, O man, looke not thou on the history of the Scripture, but upon the mystery which is hidden [there]in since thy wicked world began, for these are all holy and sacred mysteries which are hid from all fleshly and sinful hearts' (p. 41).

Even so, other radicals, not necessarily less extreme, though certainly with a greater rational and literalist aptitude, were not prepared to see the meaning of light drift as far as Clarkson took it. For Robert Everard the Baptist, Putney debater, and later Catholic convert, light in the Scriptures meant wisdom and neither the essence nor the image of God. Everard does seem to identify biblical light with natural light. His point is that Adam had no supernatural light to guide him. His 'light' was equivalent to that which all men before Christ were born with, so that all have the potential to exercise free will in coming to God.[20] Natural images are used carefully by Everard in a discourse which is devoted equally to defining human and divine will in contractual terms.[21] A similar critique of Quaker imagery was made by John Jackson in a series of pamphlets throughout the 1650s which demonstrated the failure of Quaker terminology to name parts of divine reality accurately and specifically. Far from partaking of physical reality, such words, especially as they occur in the Bible, are words of 'faith'. Jackson's interpretation of Scripture was of a scholarly and sceptical nature which refused the simple elaboration of personal knowledge in rigidly harnessed imagery, even though he was regarded by some radicals as a fellow traveller.[22]

The allegories of the self are centred upon the radicals' response to the Fall. The Quaker James Nayler, like Joseph Salmon, sees the decay of man in the Fall as the separation of man the image from his true resemblance to the divine.[23] This

---

[19] *The Lost Sheep Found* (1660) in *CRW*, p. 185. It was this combination of allegorization and literalism which George Fox abhorred in the Ranters: see *The Journal of George Fox*, ed. J. L. Nickalls (1952, rev. rpr. 1975), 47.

[20] Robert Everard, *The Creation and Fall of Adam Reviewed* (1649, 2nd edn., 1652), 3, 15–17   [21] Ibid. 46, 127, 161.

[22] John Jackson, *Hosannah to the Son of David* (1657), 10, 46 and *passim*.

[23] *A Discovery of the First Wisdom* (1653, repr. 1656), 23.

further allowed the sectarians' myths to transcend the historical. Most sectarians regarded the Fall as a historical event, part of the 'history', but they also took the 'mystery' to be the allegorical re-enactment of the Fall inside every individual. The allegory also permitted the regeneration of the individual, the internal re-birth of the second Adam, Christ.[24] Every unregenerate indivi-dual contains within him or her (and so he or she is the image of) the first Adam, the 'natural man', who is divorced from the spiritual life. Re-birth is achieved by the succession of the second Adam, the 'spiritual man', or Christ within the individual. With typical verbal assurance Winstanley describes this myth in terms of a visual pun: Adam is 'A-dam'. The first Adam 'appears in every man and woman: but he sits down in the Chair of Magistracy, in some above others: for though this climbing power of self-love be all in all, yet it rises not to its height', though the work of the dam can be turned the other way by the second Adam; 'Christ, the restorer, stops or damnes up the runnings of those stinking waters of self-interest, and causes the waters of life and liberty to run plentifully in.'[25] To hope to 'build' in the first Adam, who has no spiritual discernment, is illusory, as Henry Pinnell says, it is 'a meere *Eutopia*, a world in the Moone, a *Chymaera*, a Castle in the aire, having existence only in supposition, notion, and a deluded fancy'.[26] Yet again the distinction between the natural and the spiritual man is not uncommon in seventeenth-century religious literature, deriving as it does from Paul (1 Cor. 2: 14), and it crops up for instance in the Baptist Thomas Collier's works, though not so frequently as in the Antinomians and Quakers.[27]

Another popular myth which comes from the story of the Fall is that of the Trees of Life and of the Knowledge of Good and Evil. The ambiguous nature of knowledge for the benefit of man, especially man's spiritual well-being, had been made plain by Sebastian Franck in *The Forbidden Fruit* (see above, pp. 114–25). As we have seen, Franck's work was based upon Cornelius Agrippa's *De incertitudine & vanitate omnium artium et scientiarum*, though he also wrote under the influence of Erasmus's *Encomium*

---

[24] Which was open enough to suggest forms of regeneration from the free grace of the Independents to the perfectionism of the Ranters.

[25] Winstanley, *The New Law of Righteousness*, pp. 5, 7.

[26] *A Word of Prophesy, concerning the Parliament, Generall, and the Army* (1648), sig. A5ᵛ.

[27] See Thomas Collier, *The Marrow of Christianity* (1647), 120.

Moriae which he had translated. The influence of Franck upon the radicals is unmistakable here. It extends from Henry Pinnell's borrowing, 'What a stage of Vanity is this world, where every Art and Science is made up of madness & folly' to Isaac Penington's *Divine Essays* (1654) which appears to follow the general organization of *The Forbidden Fruit*. Penington follows the structure of opposing contraries, setting speculative against experimental knowledge. Beginning with the Tree of Knowledge of Good and Evil, Penington shows that it has three parts, natural, spiritual, and divine knowledge, which correspond to the human faculties of sense, reason, and spiritual perception. In the world of men the powers of light and dark bring each other forth in a never-ending dialectic while, just as in Franck, it is necessary to 'vomit' up the Tree of Knowledge in order to attain pure spiritual knowledge.[28]

The Trees of Knowledge of Good and Evil and of Life are planted in the heart of every individual, just as the light and dark sides of God are in every individual. Again, the drama acted out in Eden is internalized in the heart of each man. For Winstanley the Tree of Knowledge, covetous 'fleshly wisdom' (2 Cor. 1: 12), is balanced in every man by the Tree of Life which is identified as the soul of man, part of the primordial life-giving force of the universe. For both Winstanley and James Nayler both of the Trees form 'branches' which bind all mankind together for better or for worse. The sense of this mythic design dominates any reading of these authors.

Metaphors of action concerning the Trees generally come from the root biblical passages. George Fox, for instance, refers to the eating of the Tree of Knowledge as the pursuit of fleshly wisdom, which is the literal action of Adam in the Garden of Eden. Similarly John Lilburne, freshly converted to Quakerism, sees his own past temptations in terms of an image of his own soul eating the Tree of Knowledge.[29] In the Bible the Tree stands for knowledge which is not commensurate with man's proper place in the order of things, and this is the attitude adopted by most of the radicals, including Lilburne. Here knowledge is primarily evil, instituted by the devil and associated with selfishness and

---

[28] Pinnell, *A Word of Prophesy*, sig. A8ᵛ: Penington, *Divine Essays* (1654), 7.
[29] Fox, *Newes Coming up out of the North* (1654), 27; Lilburne, *The Resurrection of John Lilburne* (1656), 3.

covetousness. Little is said of any good knowledge. On the other hand some religious radicals, under the influence of alchemical and occult theories, are concerned with what they define as the Tree of Knowledge's good knowledge. For Paracelsans the knowledge contained in this Tree contained the worldly secrets of knowledge on creation so that man would be perfect on earth by knowing this.[30] Henry Pinnell, translator of Crollius and Paracelsus, argues that even pre-Fall Adam's knowledge was imperfect and 'natural' because, if he had known about the Tree of Knowledge, Christ, and God, he would have been immortal.[31] Adopting yet another position still, Clarkson condemns the dualistic potential of the Tree of Knowledge. In *A Single Eye* he seems to imply that belief in the myth of the Tree itself is a state of mind generated by 'imagination' rather than by spiritual perception, which was Adam's 'sin': 'there is an appearance in thee, or apprehension to thee, that this act is good, and that act is evil, then hast thou with *Adam* eat of the forbidden Tree.'[32] Similarly, but still slightly different, in the anonymous Ranter tract, *A Jvstificajon of the Mad Crew* (1650), which closely resembles both Clarkson's *A Single Eye* and Coppe's *A Fiery Flying Roll*, 'innocent, holy upright man' divides the original unity implicit in the concept of the Tree of Knowledge of Good and Evil, thereby imposing untenable moral judgements upon the world (p. 7).

There is further flexibility in the use of the Tree myth. Thomas Tany sees the interpretation of the myth as typological rather than allegorical, which seems to stress the historical nature of fallen man over the eternal, transcendent divine: 'The Fruit typed out by that Forbidden Tree'.[33] Winstanley uses the myths as rhetorical divisions for his argument. In *Fire in the Bush*, within the general frame of the garden, or man's heart, the Trees are smaller frames or spaces for the battle between serpent and seed to take place. The actual mention of both Trees is almost entirely restricted to chapter headings (numbers 2 and 3), within which the dialogue and struggle between reason and imagination takes place. Here Winstanley works out the process of Daniel's and

---

[30] See British Library, MS Sloane 3991. fos. 110ʳ–124ᵛ, 'Of Spirituall mumy & the tree of knowledge of good and evile', esp. fo. 114ᵛ. This translation belonged to Dr Daniel Foote, and is dated 2 May 1654.

[31] Pinnell, *A Word of Prophesy*, p. 46.   [32] *CRW*, p. 169.

[33] *Theauraujohn his Theous Ori Apokolipikal* (1651), 12.

John's prophecies according to his own exegetical system. The trees exist as general symbols as well as specific allegories: 'slauish fear within them keepes [them] the way of the tree of life' (p. 14), while the existence of the Trees as chapter headings, within which internal, spiritual processes take place, produces a tension. The Tree is both *within* man but also the *container* of the spiritual process, so that the reader's apprehension of the allegory is challenged and he or she is made to see the distance between the myth and symbol of the Tree and what it actually represents. This paradox returns again and again in radical religious writing as a spatial representation of divine mystery: 'The heart lives in God, when God lives wholly high in the heart: Now here is the mystery. This God lives in us, he cannot live out of us.'[34]

The distinction between natural and spiritual man is closely connected to the genealogical metaphor of the Seed, a figure which is more important for the radicals than that of the Trees. The seed is the positive power which runs through mankind. It is immortal and incorruptible, and bears within it the promise of redemption, based upon the divine prediction of Gen. 3: 15: 'the Seed of the Woman shall bruise the Serpents head'. The godly are often described as the seed of Israel, as in the Independent Jeremiah Burroughes's *Jacobs Seed: Or the Generation of Seekers* (1643). There is also a less common tendency to talk of a positive seed, that of Abel, and a negative one, that of Cain, the spirit and the flesh, the light and the dark. So, Henry Pinnell talks of the seed of the spirit gaining the upper hand when he undergoes divine inspiration. Even though the Seed was a promise and guarantee of liberty, for Isaac Penington it was but a copy of God's liberty. So Penington follows the notion of reflection of the divine in the human, which has already been seen in the Quaker James Nayler. The Quakers seem to put this distance between man and God even though they have a doctrine of an inner divine presence (the light within) like the Diggers and Ranters. But for the Muggletonians it was the Quaker habit of dissociating spirit from what John Reeve defined as substance which was the fatal error in their metaphysics.[35]

---

[34] Ibid. 37.
[35] Pinnell, *A Word of Prophesy*, p. 5; Penington, *Severall Fresh Inward Openings*, p. 82; John Reeve, *The Prophet Reeve's Epistle to his Friend* (1654), 12.

The seed for Winstanley, as for many other radical religious writers, is primarily a genealogical metaphor for the presence in mankind of the force which will defeat evil and bring on the New Age. In fact Winstanley suggests an equation between seed and spirit, while other radical writers combine the seed image with other genealogical myths: Pinnell describes Satan as the 'Father, man's heart the Mother of all evill'.[36] George Fox refers to Quakers as 'sons and daughters' who are part of the seed, so stressing the special nature of the sect. Other biblical stories were resorted to in this way. Coppe sees himself as the heir of Isaac, the son of Abraham by the free woman, not Ishmael, the son of Abraham by the bondwoman (Gen. 21: 9–20). He identifies the free-woman with Jerusalem, and her son as the spirit and a 'Libertine', which implies that the bondwoman is Babylon, and her son is clearly identified as flesh and form. The two sons are permanently at war, even though the 'Libertine' is above persecution: 'the Israel of God, the seed of the Lord, that Spirit, which the whole seede of the flesh, *Ismael* (in the lumpe) and forme (in the bulk) would quench and kill'.[37]

Winstanley makes a further series of identifications. The seed is Christ and the spirit of Christ in each believer. George Fox agrees, following Rom. 8: 10–11. For Henry Pinnell, the Seed is also that of God's love: it guarantees the death of the Old Man. The pure seed, says Fox, is threatened by the ungodly, and England is the historical place where the seed is under threat.[38] The illuminist element is stressed by Penington, developing the myth of dissemination and inheritance from Matt. 13: 31:

Christ explains to them in another place, it was in them like a Grain of Mustard-Seed; it was the least of all the Seeds in their hearts. There are many great seeds of darkness there, but yet there was also one little Seed of Light. It was there, as well as the rest (though less then them all) and did sometimes cast some glimmering of light, and of its shining in the darkness, though the darkness could not comprehend it.[39]

Similarly, for Winstanley, there are two scriptural seeds, one of Cain, and the other of Abel. A more contemporary and

[36] Winstanley, *Fire in the Bush*, pp. 12–13; Pinnell, *A Word of Prophesy*, p. 31.

[37] Fox, *Newes coming up out of the North*, 12–13; Coppe, *Some Sweet Sips, of some Spirituall Wine* (1649) in *CRW*, p. 55.

[38] Winstanley, *Fire in the Bush*, pp. 5–6; Fox, *Newes*, p. 16; Pinnell, *A Word of Prophesy*, sig. A7ʳ; Fox, *Newes*, pp. 3, 5.

[39] *The New Covenant* (1660), sig. A2ᵛ.

immediate application was made by the Fifth Monarchist, Christopher Feake, who referred to the Army as the Seed, or the bearer of the Seed, so that the promise of regeneration is contained within the actual force of reformation, the force of which will make the Millennium possible.[40]

The opposite of the seed of Christ and Abraham is that of the serpent, so that they are characteristically perceived as being at war with one another inside each individual:

> The Seed of the Woman is but one in all generations, and the Seed of the Serpent is but one, which ever was, is ruling and reigning in the Children of Disobedience, who are disobedient to the Light of God within them, and betwixt these two Seeds is Enmitie, the one against the other, each Seed is known by its fruit: the old bottle pours out old Wine, the new bottle new Wine; therefore all people sink down to within, and call in your wandering thoughts, imaginations and affections, and desires, and see which seed is head in you.[41]

The tension is heightened in Winstanley's *Fire in the Bush* by the use of a dialogue where the seed speaks its displeasure against the soul, which is wooed by the perfidious imagination or serpent. There is a considerable degree of animation here, as the seed speaks in a firm but friendly voice of admonition, the imagination in a snivelling, self-piteous and tormented tone. So speaks one part of imagination, 'fear of poverty': 'goe; get what thou canst, by hooke or by crooke, lest thou want, and perish, and die miserably' (p. 17). Here, the dialogue constitutes a drama of salvation which takes place during the space of a day, and where the battle is interrupted by the 'parleys' which reveal the state of the inner components of man, or which comment upon that state.

Though Winstanley has his seed speak against the serpent, dragon, or Satan, his opposing speaker is imagination. Conversely for the Ranters, the evil force, which represents the concentration upon outward things no less than in Winstanley, is allowed to speak. Whatever the hierarchies of gender in the supposed sexual rituals of 'My one flesh', Coppe's incarnation for iniquity undoubtedly has a female form. Winstanley's 'proud imaginary flesh' and Nayler's 'Serpentine wisdom that rules in the outward'

---

[40] Winstanley, *Fire in the Bush*, p. 67; Feake, *A Beam of Light* (1659), 34.

[41] Edward Burrough, *A Warning from the Lord to the Inhabitants of Underbarrow* (1654), 18. The marginal glosses here are to Gen. 5: 9–21; Gen. 3: 15; Matt. 12: 39. The reference to old and new wine is from Matt. 9: 17.

becomes for Coppe the 'holy Scripturian whore', an internalized version of the whore figure in Rev. 17, and a representation of the hypocritically selfish behaviour of sectarians who do not see the need for social charity.[42] She is outwards-emphasizing, but she rides inside Coppe, rather than upon the horse, as she does in the Apocalypse (Rev. 17: 3). Within Coppe also is the absolute altruistic selflessness of the 'Divine Majesty', but the woman stands for the conventions of social propriety: sixpence is quite enough for a squire to give to a poor man, who is a sinner anyway because he cannot afford to look after his own family, she says, after the self-regarding dictum 'True love begins at home.' The pragmatism becomes worse as she warns Coppe that he should have a care for the main chance since he does not take tithes, and himself depends upon a certain amount of charity. Significantly the Ranter lets evil speak from within him as well as God. Clearly this is a version of the imaginary powers of fear and fear of poverty which we have seen in Winstanley's work. Coppe's picture is rather more vivid however: the woman is portrayed in terms of a language which suggests sexual innuendo and illicit seduction, and of course, she is a character in a dramatic encounter. The 'WEL-FAVOURED HARLOT' 'flattereth her lips' with words 'smoother than oile'. She is a '*quondam mistris*'. Because the beggar cannot change a shilling for sixpence, he receives no money from Coppe, whereupon the 'rust of his silver' rises up in judgement against Coppe, his flesh is burnt, the imperatives to share wealth from James 5 thunder in his ears, and he gives all his money to the beggar.

Joseph Salmon paints a similar picture of the whore within. Like Coppe, he refers to the dangerous deceiving harlot of Prov. 7, though Salmon expands upon the mysterious and mythopoeic qualities of the whore. Her human qualities are none the less fearful, as Salmon describes a vicious licentiousness which he feels is part of human nature. The Protean appearance of the whore is most evident, since she appeals to men with a semblance of religious nonconformity. Using an image of *pathos*, Salmon describes her as both a 'passive Mother' and an 'active Babe' in subverting Christ. She makes men fail to interpret the myths of nature correctly, so that under her influence men take the fruit for the tree, the stream for the fountain, the emanation

---

[42] *A Second Fiery Flying Roule*, in *CRW*, pp. 102–3.

for the essence, the outside for the inside. If such men looked in a mirror they would see the whore as their reflection, though it is her deceptive servility which enables her 'fleshly wisdom' to dominate man. The text from Prov. 7: 12 facilitates the internal, illicit meaning:

This *Mother of Harlots*, thy fleshly wisdom wil propose herself to be all to thee, that so She may draw thy affections after her; Shee will tell thee that she can supply all thy wants and relieve al thy necessities, and therfore thou needst not to bee beholden to God for any thing: She will tell thee with *Adam*, that She can give thee the knowledge of good and evill: and she can open thy eyes, & She it is that gives thee any thing.[43]

Still, the reader is not allowed to forget that the whore is the personification of a force inside mankind. She is called the 'spirituall Serpent', and as well as the whorelike qualities of 'opposing' and 'exalting', she has the four names of Anti-Christ, Babylon (from Rev. 17: 5; 18: 2), the Wicked One (from 2 Thess. 2: 8), and the Mother of Harlots (from Rev. 17: 5). To emphasize the spiritual allegory as well, Salmon denies that she is either the Pope or any particular state, which distinguishes him from orthodox Protestant interpreters.

The Serpent also has a place in the genealogical myth, so that the figures of both worm and inheritance are mutually enhanced, as in James Nayler: 'Now wouldst thou but look back, and search the Scriptures, thou shouldst find thy generation all along from *Cain* to thy self, for all particulars are of that Serpents brood'.[44] The sense of the great degree of belief which the radicals had in these myths is clearest however when the myths are broken down into individual elements, in order to explain a particular event. In this manner does Coppe interpret Mrs T. P.'s dream (see above, pp. 100–2), and in making the myth appear in any event, the assurance and the authority necessary for enthusiastic excitement are found.

II

Behind the internalized biblical symbols and characters there also occur in radical prose a number of descriptive models of

---

[43] *Anti-Christ in Man* (1647), 19.
[44] *A Discovery of the First Wisdom*, p. 19.

physical creation based upon the idea of the circle. The circle can have a figurative use, so that models of circularity permeate other observations. Thus, William Sedgwick refers to the '*Egge* of Reformation'.[45] Egg, of course, suggests origin, which links with seed and another circular shape, the womb, though the circle also corresponds with the globe, and the shape of the universe. In *Heights in Depths* Salmon's world is a circle 'including nothing but emptiness' while worldly wisdom is sceptically defined as a 'womb of Wind', 'whose wringing Pangs, pretend the birth of pure Substance, but in times revealing Order it am [*sic*] its nothing, except travel for sorrow, whose high aspires, do cursorily expire into an airy notion',[46] as the womb itself is a metaphor, in the radical religious imagination, for the matrix of divine regeneration.

There is some similarity with Renaissance models of harmony and perfection here, which go back, by way of the Neoplatonists, to Plato's description of the World-Soul in the *Timaeus*: 'in the centre he set a soul and caused it to extend throughout the whole and further wrapped its body round with soul on the outside: and so he established one world alone, round and revolving in a circle.'[47] It is not known precisely what Salmon read though he does seem to have appropriated a consistent Neoplatonic system, juxtaposing the perfect and the imperfect, time and the eternal. He talks of the earthly world as a place where beings exists only in 'variety' and 'appearance', rather than in 'Unity'. The material world is but an 'endlesse Labyrinth' where the 'scattered spirits' are lost. On the contrary if they ascend into their 'original center', they find themselves 'where we were, before we were'.[48] In an earlier pamphlet Salmon had even spoken of fleshly wisdom, the 'Strumpet', having her own 'proper sphere and *center*' in which men would know her truly, so that the image is not only used for positive truths.

Henry Pinnell makes a similar distinction, using the precise timetable of recorded events to recount how the divine operates in the material world by giving him a vision, which empowered him to remonstrate with Cromwell, though he frames this with an appeal to the return of the Second Adam

[45] *The Leaves of the Tree of Life* (1648), 21.   [46] *CRW*, p. 207.
[47] *Timaeus* 34B, trans. and ed. F. M. Cornford (New York, 1959), 23–4.
[48] *CRW*, p. 207.

Christ, who was in existence before the First Adam, and by an evocation of the eternal spirit of life in the vision of the wheel in Ezekiel 1 and 10.[49] The interpretation of the wheel in Ezekiel in this way is aligned with a tradition which is rooted in Joachim of Fiore.[50] Because of Pinnell's learning, it seems likely that he developed his imagery from Paracelsan sources. The problem of identifying a source or influence still remains with Salmon, though the similarity between part of his meditation in *Heights in Depths* and John Everard's translation of Hermes Trismegistus is remarkable, especially concerning the womb:

And as much Mater as there was laid up by him, the Father made it all into a Body, and swelling it, made it round like a Sphere: endued it with Quality, being it self immortal, and having Eternal Materiality. The Father being full of IDEAS, sowed Qualities in the Sphere and shut them up, as in a circle.[51]

It is also significant that a manuscript copy of another Ranter pamphlet, Bauthumley's *The Light and Dark Sides of God* (1650), copied from the printed edition by an early Quaker, Benjamin Antrobus, is bound up with a Neo-Hermetic treatise, 'The Figure of the Philosophique Globe or Eye of the Wisdom of the Wonders of Eternity in a Looking Glass of Wisdom', which would suggest a common readership of Ranter 'pantheism' and 'pansophie' proper.[52]

Winstanley gives no hints, through a similarity between his images and those of occult philosophy, as to what his reading might have been, if at all. The task of detection is made harder by the fact that the phrases in which Winstanley casts his imagery are typical only of himself. The circularity of the cosmic order is implied in the language, rather than in the visual appeal of the images. There is the impression of simultaneous rising and falling in the juxtaposition of 'running up' and 'wearing away' to

---

[49] Pinnell, *A Word of Prophesy*, pp. 5–10, sig. A6ʳ, pp. 40–1.

[50] See Marjorie Reeves and B. Hirsch-Reich, *The Figurae of Joachim of Fiore* (Oxford, 1972), 224–31.

[51] *The Divine Pymander of Hermes Mercurius Trismegistus* (1650), 203.

[52] BL, MS Sloane 2544, fos. 1ʳ–53ᵛ and 55ᵛ–59ᵛ respectively. The copy of Bauthumley is dated 1655. The further influence of this philosophy is detectable in Antrobus's poetry, *Some Buds and blossoms of piety* (1684). It is not known precisely when Antrobus became a Quaker, though he did shelter Fox towards the end of the latter's life: *The Journal of George Fox*, ed. J. L. Nickalls (1952, rev. rpr. 1975), pp. 745–6.

underline the sense of spiritual death followed by rebirth, even though it might be expected that the rising should follow falling rather than vice versa for the parallel to be accurate: 'But for the present state of the old World that is running up like parchment in the fire, and wearing away.'[53] The impression of circularity is compounded with a sense of purgative refinement as the image of curling up precedes consumption by flames. In *The New Law of Righteousness* (1649) the rising of the seed is enhanced in a description where lowness in oppression is compounded with participles which suggest rejection, suppression and obliteration of the younger brother, Jacob, but which is followed by a repetition of 'rise', and a reversal of the previous oppressive relationship. That this circular, overturning motion takes place within each individual, but which also makes the individual part of a greater whole is implied in the use of 'in you' and 'from you', which represent opposite motions though they are part of the same action:

He lies hid in you, he is hated, persecuted and despised in you, he is Jacob in you, that is and hath been a servant to Esau *a long time; but though this* Jacob *be very low, yet his time is now come, that he must rise, and he will rise up in you that we are trod under foot like dust of the earth; he will glorifie himself both in you and from you, to the shame and downfall of* Esau. (sig. A2ᵛ)

The myth-permeated cosmos of the radical religious imagination is also shot through with analogies and metaphors of emanation which intimate the penetration of the divine into every part of life on earth. There is no biblical source for this image, surprisingly, though it is extremely common among radical religious writers. Emanation is used here in a general sense. There is the important theological point to be made since an emanating beam from God in the heart of the believer does not necessarily make the believer himself an emanation or beam, though this was certainly the fear of Baxter.[54] In the broadest sense of the word, all material creation becomes subject to permeation by the spiritual life, of which emanation images are a visual and sensuous analogy. The image of the beam of light is, of course, common in much Christian writing, let alone that of the Neoplatonic variety, and the employment of such imagery is

---

[53] *The True Levellers Standard Advanced* (1649), 7.
[54] Baxter, *Plain Scripture Proof* (1651), 147.

particularly associated with the relationship between man and God. The popular Puritan preachers prior to 1640, especially Richard Sibbes, had used such imagery, while emblem books, such as those of George Wither and Francis Quarles, gave frequent pictorial representations of God's eye looking out of a cloud and emitting rays down to earth. W. P. Ingoldsby has demonstrated how such imagery prevailed in the writings of the Nonconformist Calvinists who rose to power under Parliament's and Cromwell's patronage, though it should not be forgotten that a Royalist tract, the *Eikon Basilike* (1649), used beams of light on the frontispiece woodcut to illustrate divine-right kingship theory.[55] Those Puritan divines who were familiar with Neoplatonic emanation theory proper, such as Peter Sterry, presumably let their knowledge of man *as* emanation from essence exist within the more usual representation without challenging it.[56] After all, the notion of an ever-watchful, all-penetrating God who acted *upon* mankind was central to Calvinist theology, and so such beam or emanation imagery was well fitted to it. But for the radicals, who stressed a divine who acted primarily *within* mankind, emanation imagery was used in a different though no more entirely consistent sense.

If some of the radical writings are carefully scrutinized, fine distinctions can be made with regard to the generation of each individual's use of emanation imagery. In a tract by the Baptist Army officer and preacher, Paul Hobson, *A Garden Inclosed* (1647), the 'Divine Beames' are openly identified as metaphors for Christ's perfect qualities:

Even of himselfe, Nay of his Father; and they are so inclosed in the heart of him, that there they live in the midst of all his Loves: They are comprehended, within the Divine beames of his eternall delights, loves and content. And this is the second ground, why they may be called Christ's Garden: because as they are planted by him, so they are inclosed in him. (p. 32)

Note here that the beams are metaphors which *envelop* man, and that they are combined with another figure for the placing of man inside God, the garden, which will be discussed later. In

---

[55] W. P. Ingoldsby, 'Some Considerations of Nonconformist Sermon Style: 1645–1660' (B.Litt. thesis, University of Oxford, 1973), 109–11.

[56] See, for instance, Sterry's contemplative writing at Emmanuel College, Cambridge, MS 294, fo. 259.

Saltmarsh's mind, beams are identified with an angelology which he derives from Augustine and Luther.[57] The angels are functions of God's will, but they are described figuratively as beams of light. Not surprisingly Saltmarsh, aware of the figurative nature of his language, stresses the empirically indescribable nature of this 'aphorism of light', a privilege for the enlightened person. Though angels may be represented by beams, Saltmarsh also implies that enlightenment by beams makes human beings more like angels: angels perceive by means of visions, and individuals may be experiencing visions, a direct communication from God, when they are penetrated by beams, 'soul-quickning Rayes'. The beam then is a visual analogy for spiritual communication and perception, which has a rather more specific field of reference than the cosmic dualism of light and darkness.

Nevertheless, beams are part of that universal light for Laurence Clarkson, and it is the tension between the essential light, and the light emitted by combustion, which is axiomatic to the argument in *A Single Eye*. Clarkson is concerned with problems of the original oneness of God, and the extent to which God is 'descensive' throughout creation. He finds a scriptural contradiction in that God is said to have made both light and lights.[58] Since God is ubiquitous (all is 'in him, of him, to him'), and since he is light, he is simply repeating himself in his creation of sun, moon, stars, fire, and candle. But, says Clarkson, if God is light, by virtue of his original scriptural contradiction, God is also lights, by which it follows that God is many gods, as many gods as there are light-emitting objects. Here, Clarkson returns to the paternal myth that God is the Father of lights (James 1: 17), and draws an analogy with the sun as the original essence emitting beams. When the beams are in the sun they are the sun, but when they are emitted they are distinct by 'divers appearance'. Just so, the bodies of the sun and moon are 'divers appearances' of the 'one Father'.

More than logic, though, is at work here. Clarkson is seeking to achieve the reader's acceptance that God's light is everywhere so that it may sanction any act made in the conscious acceptance that that light is everywhere. Clarkson proceeds to say that

[57] *The Smoke in the Temple* (1646), 2. See also Henry Pinnell, *Nil Novi. This Years F[r]uit, From the last Years Root* (1654), 19.
[58] *CRW*, p. 166.

although it can be argued that there is a distinction between physical light and 'a divine and spiritual light, by which a creature beholds and enjoy[s] God',[59] both are 'appearances' of the light which is God, since 'though Lights, yet but one Light with God'. Effectively Clarkson does not admit the distinction between physical and spiritual light, which is an important example of the way in which the Ranter imagination reduces all definitions and distinctions into a positive, transcendent essence, the monistic impulse which brought the Ranter prophets under the accusation of Gnosticism. The Muggletonians, providing yet another alternative, use the figure as a way of connecting substance with spirit, as the source of all emanations is substantial and material; sun, fountain and body.[60]

This observation is exemplified when Clarkson moves from his characterization of God as the father of lights to the analogy of God as sun, a figure which is based upon the same quality, the emanation of light, as that which Clarkson is using the analogy to explain. Thus again, the distinction between two different characters tends to disappear, especially to the unwary reader, by virtue of the prevalence of 'light'. The critical reader, however, may also be forgiven for seeing Clarkson's choice of his beam analogy as part of a mental structure which actively collapses distinctions and categories of figurative meaning. It is a form of intuition which wishes to have and know light in its essential state and to do this it aims to appreciate every form of light in its 'divers appearance'. The total sum of 'divers appearances' is gathered into essence by the intuitive 'reason' of the Ranter, who operates by the 'light' within him. This is so say that the inspired individual uses the knowledge of the divine within to effect types of argument and deduction which defy logic. Humanists commonly stated that the sun was a natural metaphor for God, but whereas the orthodox maintained a clear distinction between symbol and referent, the Ranters make the symbol the thing, so that 'light' is not at all strictly defined.

Nevertheless, light imagery continues in the radicals to represent Christ, who, for Saltmarsh, is a sparkling mirror and a crystal, a refractor, and a reflection of God's original divine

---

[59] *CRW*, p. 166.
[60] See, for instance, *The Ranters Recantation* (1650); Reeve, *The Prophet Reeve's Epistle to his Friend*, p. 130.

emanations.[61] For Winstanley, Christ is the 'Sun of Righteous-ness' (Mal. 4: 2), with the obvious pun on sun/son. Though he is by no means the only radical religious writer to use the image, he is especially fond of its redemptive connotations to the extent that it becomes a leitmotif in his work.[62] When Winstanley refers to the sun by itself, it is usually as a metaphor for God the Father: 'And if at any time God was pleased to let a beam of light and peace shine into me, and gave me enlargements of heart, then I thought my self to know God, but when this sun was clouded again, then I was in bondage again'.[63] On the other hand, the more common description of Christ among the radicals is as the 'day-star' of 2 Pet. 1: 19. In John Saltmarsh's version Christ the '*morning-star*' (Job 38: 7) will rise within the individual, which is more commensurate with the Antinomian position than the externalized notion of the 'sun of righteousness'. No particular preference is given to any of these images, and it seems that the radicals were more interested in the cumulative effect of several emanation analogies as a means of registering enthusiastic attachments and inspired exhilaration. So Henry Pinnell writes of the 'Day-star; that bright or Morning-Star, Jesus Christ, the *Sun of Righteousness*; when they depart from the fountain of light, life and living waters, they digge and drinke at the *broken Cisternes* of earth'.[64]

Eye imagery is also commonly preferred, and it is closely inter-connected with the other images of perception. With the eye (the spiritual or 'single eye' of Matt. 6: 22), two senses are imparted. As God's eye it is the centre of all vision, something which the individual should come to look at, by means of spiritual enlightenment. At the same time, the eye is also that which enables God to see, and indeed, like the beam, to penetrate the individual. And like the beams again, the eye enlivens the universe, as much as it facilitates vision. 'Sight' or 'perception' here is achieved through the acquisition of 'power', so that the eye is a function of spiritual perception. Again, Neoplatonists

---

[61] Saltmarsh, *The Smoke in the Temple*, p. 65.

[62] *The Saints Paradice* (?1648), 28–31, 39.

[63] Ibid. 11. Henry Walker makes his distinction between signifier and signified very plain, unlike Winstanley: 'we may see Emblems of the Trinity in the Sun', בראשית א, *The Creation of the World* (1649), 18.

[64] Saltmarsh, *The Smoke in the Temple* (1646), 37; Pinnell, *A Word of Prophesy*, sig. A4ᵛ.

were fond of the image, especially those with a Hebraic interest, since the eye was used by Talmudic writers. Peter Sterry provides one such example:

Men and Angels. They have only a transient, no permanent Being. No eye ever takes in twice the same beam of Light. No man standing upon the bank of a River sees twice the same water present with him. Before he can cast his eye upon it the second time, it is past by and gone: So is no Creature in appearance the same two moments.[65]

Among the Antinomians Paul Hobson begins to explain the mystical perception of the eye: 'It is not the glory that we view in God that covers our eyes, but rather the thick myst that intercepts our view of that unchangeable object', and he returns to sun imagery by comparing this obscure vision to an eclipse of the sun: the sun in all its glory is always there, but our eyes are intercepted by an '*Earthly substance*'.[66] The difference between Clarkson's and Hobson's sense of vision is registered by the fact that Hobson takes care to explain the limits of his analogy, to highlight its figurative status, whereas Clarkson does not. Isaac Penington, however, equates eye with essence, emphasizing the Apostolic roots of the image. In Matthew and Luke the single eye is an analogy for the power of the spirit in man, an analogy for the myth of light: 'The light of the body is the eye: if therefore thine eye be single, the whole body shall be full of light' (Matt. 6: 27). Penington refers to this as the 'spiritual eye' which is associated with the spiritual region of Christ. The '*true eye*' sees beyond the '*creaturely eye*'.[67] This, though, does not entail a divorce of flesh from spirit because to have the true eye is to partake of God's vision, which is defined as any part of God's creation: 'Flesh is Gods eye, an eye of his making, and therefore it can be no disparagement to God to have it see the things of God in its own Religion.'[68] To gain the 'single eye' then requires a change in spiritual attitude. So, given that Christ is both eye and light, a knowledge of Christ involves seeing Christ's nature with one's own eyes. In other words it is necessary for the individual to make his own 'eye(s)' perceive the divine 'eye' or light, so that

---

[65] *A Discourse of the Freedom of the Will* (1675) in V. de Sola Pinto, *Peter Sterry: Platonist and Puritan* (Cambridge, 1934), 156.

[66] *A Treatise Containing Three Things* (1653), 8.

[67] *Light or Darknesse* (1650), 4. 'Single' in this sense means simple, one-fold (*simplex*).

[68] Isaac Penington, *Divine Essays* (1654), 57.

both senses of eye are brought together, if not entirely reconciled, in the act of enlightenment. A similar process of merging two definitions is apparent in Thomas Tany's definition of the divine as a self-reflexive 'eye that sees itself', while for Winstanley, the New Man is granted new vision: 'Well, the eye is now open.'[69]

The action of emanation can also be represented in the fountain image as well as in beams from the sun. As the sun pours out its rays or beams, so the fountain pours out the waters of God's goodness. Indeed the two images are often confused or conflated. John Saltmarsh juxtaposes the image of the fountain of life with the apocalyptic image of the 'light of the world' from John 8: 12; 9: 5, while the sun is often described as 'pouring' forth its beams, the verb being borrowed from the action of flowing water.[70] For Laurence Clarkson, when he was a Ranter (or so he later claimed), this natural image was utilized to explain a genuine pantheism based on a belief in 'onely nature' over the Scriptures: 'for I understood that which was life in man, went into that infinite Bulk and Bigness, so called *God*, as a drop into the Ocean, and the body rotted in the grave, and for ever so to remain'.[71] Edward Billing, the Quaker, adopts what appears to be a position like Clarkson's, though his God is not so clearly a ground of creation only. Billing sees the hand of God in the sun and the flux of the seas, though he resorts to the figurative to describe God as the 'Fountain of life' (Ps. 36: 9; Prov. 13: 14; 14: 27).[72]

The metaphor enables Clarkson, in *A Single Eye*, to transcend the scriptural contradictions which rigidly confine his monistic impulse. Here the genealogical myth is turned back on its origins, just as the 'two Powers' of light and darkness, good and evil, Esau and Jacob, come from the same womb, flesh and nature, 'of the self same Nature of God', so they are as two streams which run in different directions, though from the same fountain. It is only a seeming opposition, just as the tide strives for victory from the rest of the ocean.[73] Here, coming from the same fountain, sin and darkness are made the same as purity and

---

[69] Tany, *Theauraujohn his Theous Ori Apokolipikal*, p. 14; Winstanley, *The Law of Freedom in a Platform* (1652), 73.

[70] Saltmarsh, *The Smoke in the Temple*, p. 20.

[71] *The Lost Sheep Found*, in *CRW*, p. 185.

[72] *A Faithful Testimony For God and my Country* (1664), 1. See also Winstanley, *The Saints Paradice* (?1648), sig. A4ʳ. [73] *CRW*, pp. 167–8.

light. The process of identification becomes quite subtle here. The central analogy is of saffron converting milk into its own colour, just as 'sin, hell, and devil' will flow into the fountain of life converted into the fountain of life's own 'nature and light as it self'.[74] The treatment of sin is also contained within the action of the dying image. Sin must not be cast out. Rather, it should be 'cast within' the vat to be dyed the colour of perfection. Here the vat becomes the body of the believer where the divine light dwells and where the fountain of life pours forth.

As we have seen with Clarkson the fountain image is used as a vehicle for the Christian Platonic doctrine of filiation, by which human beings are derived by 'descensions' from God.[75] The theory relies upon a genealogical metaphor for its expression. Indeed the theory *is* a metaphor. Neoplatonic theory proper, as it is found in Cusa, is fairly sophisticated, 'filiation' being divided into 'abstract' (the creation in general), and 'particular' (individual human beings). However, in *Copp's Return to the wayes of Truth*, there is a general, unspecified use of 'filiation', though Coppe is trying to impart the sense that men's souls are part of God (p. 153). Connected to this is the notion of the 'sonship' of all believers, described by Henry Pinnell in *A Word of Prophesy* specifically in the sense of the 'filiation' of man. Adam is made in the image of God, but *nullum simile est idem*. Neither is Adam the son of God. Instead, he is described as a 'descension from God, by successive propagation; the fountain of which life was in God'.[76] Winstanley alters the co-ordinates of the emanation of the fountain, however, so that it becomes a part of his mythology of resurrection of the Digger Utopia. In *The Law of Freedom in a Platform* (1652) Winstanley defines five fountains 'from whence all arts and sciences have their influences', so that any person who is an 'actor' in any or all of the five parts (which are concerned with husbandry, artisanal skills, agriculture generally, industry and natural philosophy) is a 'profitable' son of mankind. The fountains are therefore flowings forth from nature, wherein God dwells; they are 'descensions', the products and benefits of nature, and it is for men to participate in these

---

[74] *CRW*, p. 172.

[75] See Ernst Cassirer, *The Platonic Renaissance in England*, trans. James P. Pettegrove (New York, 1953, repr. 1978), 137–8.

[76] Pinnell, *A Word of Prophesy*, pp. 38–9. See also Christopher Hill, 'The Religion of Gerrard Winstanley', *Past and Present Supplement*, 5 (1978), 12.

emanations (pp. 69–70). Through his 'pantheism', then, Winstanley closes the gap between spiritual and material emanation, the gap which Clarkson felt the Bible prevented. In effect, both writers are reconciling the orders of nature and grace. This framework remains in Winstanley's image of society, providing the representation of the freedom (through unity with God in nature) which degrees· of coercion are supposed to encourage or protect.[77] Here, nature and culture are merged, under the auspices of grace.

There is a consistent concern with the source of the emanating light or fountain. It is the essence, the 'being' or 'center'. Winstanley sees the New Man as the locus of such a source: 'We find the streaming out of Love in our hearts towards all; to enemies as well as friends.'[78] For Clarkson spiritual regeneration, the personal apocalypse which perfects the individual, is just such a return to this source:

Now it is damm'd and ramm'd into its only Center, there to dwell eternal in the bosom of its only Father: This, and only this, is the damnation so much terrifying the Creature in its dark apprehension, that it shall be robbed and carried it knows not whither, cryeth out I am damned, I am damned, being carried out of its former knowledge, now knoweth not where it is, therefore lamenting, *Master, Save me, I perish* [Matt. 14: 30] perished in its own Apprehension, yet saved in the essential.[79]

Here is the Ranter slogan 'ram me, damn me', where some Ranters claimed that 'ram' stood for God.[80] As the phrase reveals, enlightenment involves a collapsing of inner and outer: though the individual is reduced to the centre, which comes to be within the heart of the individual, such a process also involves an immersion *in* God. As has been shown, both Clarkson and Winstanley challenge the distinction between object and image, and the attitude is no different concerning the 'center'. Clarkson takes the 'center' tó be substantial. The Father is the Light, the 'Center'. However, it is the lack of a distinction between spiritual and figurative on the one hand, and physical on the other, which

[77] For a discussion of the coercive nature of Winstanley's utopia, see J. C. Davis, *Utopia and the Ideal Society: A Study of English Utopian Writing 1516–1700* (Cambridge, 1981), 169–203.   [78] *The True Levellers Standard Advanced* (1649), 18.

[79] *A Single Eye All Light, no Darkness*, in *CRW*, p. 172.

[80] Ramming and damning seems to have been a Cavalier phrase, parodied, and adopted by Ranters and several other perfectionists (see below, p. 337).

leads his opponents to challenge his notion of essence. For the Presbyterian John Tickell, Ranter and perfectionist descriptions of the creation were merely words in the mouth or on the page, 'Chambers of Imagery', with no anterior reality, physical or metaphysical.[81] Viewed this way, images of light and the ocean are finally self-exposing metaphors for the spirit, the soul, and the divine reality. To the sceptic or biblical literalist, the metaphors tend to imply that there is no more to them than their place in a sophistical argument. The affective potential of the images remains invigorating by virtue of the visual appeal: 'even as a stream from the Ocean was distinct in it self while it was a stream, but when returned to the Ocean, was therein swallowed and become one with the Ocean; so the spirit of man while in the body, was distinct from God, but when death came it returned to God'.[82] A similar critique was made of *Divinity And Philosophy Dissected* (1644) by Robert Baillie.[83] The tract has a metaphysic which is indebted to the occult tradition, and in addition to the specialized vocabulary, mystical imagery is compounded by verbs of increase, 'groweth' and 'bloweth', and the constellation of names of the spiritual essence:

A spirit is that internall fire, life and motion of all things, as the spirit or fire, and life of herbes, and trees, which is named the [v]egative spirit that manifesteth it selfe to the world and all other spirits. Now there is another spirit or fire that groweth and bloweth it selfe up into one organ, and feeleth any thing that toucheth it, and its name is the sensitive spirit. There is another spirit, eye, light or fire, that groweth and bloweth it selfe up into an organ, whose name is called the rationall spirit or eye of capability and judgement, which discerneth all things in their order and place, and this is the man. (pp. 21–2)

However, to the author of the tract, his explanation of the cosmos is real enough. Like Clarkson and Salmon he states that God the essence is more perfect than the 'lower changeable elements' (p. 37), while his version of the fountain metaphor is based upon an interpretation in the first instance of Ecclesiastes 3 and Hebrews 1. Clarkson had used the former passage to justify his sexual licence, but this author takes Ecclesiastes 3: 11 as a

---

[81] *The Bottomles Pit Smoking in Familisme* (Oxford, 1651, 2nd edn., 1652), 46.

[82] Clarkson, *The Lost Sheep Found*, in *CRW*, p. 182.

[83] *Anabaptism, The True Fountain of Independency, Antinomy, Brownisme, Familisme* (1647), 99–104.

justification of the internalization of the biblical creation myth: 'he hath set the world in their heart'.[84] Solomon goes on to say that God has done this in order to make His ways an entire mystery to man. However, the author of *Divinity And Philosophy Dissected* attempts to decode the mystery, with the assumption that God also created at least two worlds (Heb. 1: 1–2):

> Now the creation of Gods first world in Man, is Man and God joyned together from eternity: and this was that deep silence and waters that God moved or brooded on, and he separated the waters from the waters, for God is that light and holy spring, and Man is that darke and blacke water. (p. 1)[85]

III

The crux of natural imagery for the religious radicals lies in the problem of the extent to which God is held to live in nature. Natural imagery and myths utilizing natural imagery are used to describe divine operations, but if those divine operations are inside nature then nature (signified) and natural imagery (signifier) are one. The clearest statement of God's presence in natural objects comes in Jacob Bauthumley's *The Light and Dark Sides of God* (1650): 'I see that God is in all Creatures, Man and Beast, Fish and Fowle, and every green thing, from the highest Cedar to the Ivey on the wall; . . . and hath his Being no where else out of the Creatures' (p. 232). It is an extreme statement, since by 'creatures' Bauthumley means not just animals and humans, but also inanimate creation, though he does stress that God in nature puts man and beast on the same level. It removes the capacity for the expression of divine operation as natural analogy. Bauthumley still manages to state the medieval view that the trees and herbs are for the use of man, but he does not exclude God from them.[86] As in Clarkson God is one entire 'Being' of which all objects are 'distinct Beings', while the womb is identified as the ground of being wherein all things are conceived and brought forth.

---

[84] Clarkson, *The Lost Sheep Found*, p. 181.

[85] There seems to be no conflict in this work between the assertion of a world in constant flux (p. 37) and a finite world (p. 45).

[86] See Keith Thomas, *Man and the Natural World: Changing Attitudes in England 1500–1800* (1983), 17–25.

Winstanley, however, stresses the greater presence of God in man, which makes him perfect: '*the Spirit, or Father, which as he made the Globe, and every creature; so he dwells in every creature, but supremely in Man; and he it is by whom every one lives, and moves, and hath his being*'. More so than in Bauthumley though, Winstanley implies the sense that the life of the spirit is *elsewhere*, even if God is inside earthly objects. 'Perfect Man' must 'see' and 'declare' God, and when perfect he is 'taken up' into the Spirit even though that Spirit is within him. Again, as with some examples of emanation imagery, God lives within the individual, but the individual in Winstanley correspondingly lives inside the 'light of reason'.[87] Earlier Antinomians were not sure how much of the divine was actually in nature. Though for Winstanley it is the Father or Spirit, for John Saltmarsh it is specifically Christ's image which is in everything, which is really an extension of the basic Antinomian doctrine of the redemptive free grace of Christ living within each regenerate believer. Isaac Penington posits a union with the divine which is not pantheistic since it relies upon a distinction between 'thing' and 'spirit', rather than a union between the two.[88]

In any event, whatever the extent of God in nature, the focus of the religious radicals is primarily upon the self. Christ or Satan within corresponds to the relative state of freedom or bondage in the individual, while the union with nature, through the proper respect for it, is defined as the state of freedom: 'the Word of God is Love, and when all thy actions are done in love to the whole Creation, then thou advancest freedome'.[89] In Winstanley nature represents a state of grace. The effect of this elevation of nature is a negation of man's egotistical, acquisitive and fanciful faculties ('imagination'), in favour of 'reason', and intuitive faculty which makes decisions, is the true centre of cognition. 'Reason' perceives by virtue of a direct communication with God, and a communication with God through nature. Elsewhere in Winstanley, Reason is identified as God himself. Winstanley says that he prefers to use the word Reason since the term God is

---

[87] *The Saints Paradise*, sig. A3'. These notions are in Winstanley's earliest pamphlet, *The Mystery of God in the Creation* (1649), 2, where God is the 'uncreated', man the 'created' being.

[88] Penington, *Concerning the Sum or Substance of our Religion* (1666), 7.

[89] Winstanley, *A Watch-Word To The City of London, and the Army* (1649), sig. A2'.

used by formal, 'fleshly' professors.[90] For the Muggletonians, even reason was vain in the eyes of God.

The metaphorical treatment of Reason has some peculiar consequences in Winstanley. First, as a means of showing how God/Reason is present inside nature, the clothing metaphor is re-introduced so that nature becomes secondary, merely the clothing God wears:

> The whole Creation of fire, water, Earth and Aire; and all the varieties of bodies made up thereof, is the clothing of God: so that all things, that is A substantiall being, looked upon in the lump, is the fullness of him, that fills all with himselfe: he is in all things, and by him all things consist.[91]

But this is complicated by another metaphorical verb of envelopment. God is in natural objects, his clothes, and so he is possessor of creation, but then Winstanley speaks of the imminent time when the 'restorer' Christ is coming to 'draw up' all things to live in him. By contrast again, the dark power, 'imagination', 'comes into' man when he is in his fallen state.[92] Yet there are also a number of puns connected with the clothing metaphor (whether they are intended or not is impossible to say), so that while God is 'clothed' with 'creation', those ruled by imagination are spiritually 'naked' though being rich in worldly treasures. The allusion is to Adam's guilt in Eden: 'and when you have all these, which you thinke or imagine to have content in, presently troubles follow the heels thereof; and you see your selfe naked and are ashamed'.[93] In the same context George Fox talks of the individual 'hiding in mountains and green trees until the Lord makes all naked'.[94]

The clothing metaphor is sufficient to dismiss the claim made by Hill, and disputed by Knott, that Winstanley establishes a

---

[90] For a discussion of this aspect see G. E. Aylmer, 'The Religion of Gerrard Winstanley', in J. F. McGregor and B. G. Reay (edd.) *Radical Religion in the English Revolution* (Oxford, 1984), 91–119 (esp. 96–8).

[91] Winstanley, *Fire in the Bush*, 1. The most striking similarity with Winstanley known to me is in *Astrologie Theologized (1649)*, the translation of a work falsely attributed to Valentin Weigel, and published by George Whittington. For instance, 'The Firmament is put in us, and we are put and placed in the Firmament' (p. 8).

[92] Winstanley, *The Law of Freedom*, pp. 58–9.

[93] Winstanley, *Fire in the Bush*, p. 4.

[94] Fox, *Newes Coming up out of the North*, sig. A1ʳ.

'materialist pantheism'.[95] Nature and man are the clothes for the *spirit* of God. The reader is, however, presented only with the picture of nature in the first instance in *Fire in the Bush*. The exploration of the workings of the spirit in man comes later, so that it is possible to read only half of Winstanley's exposition. Nevertheless, the connection is made between God inside nature and the spirit inside man. Here Winstanley states that his figural language, when it is based upon specifically biblical and allegorical nature imagery, does refer to the inner state of man, for 'the Kingdom of God that is within you' (Luke 17: 2). Man is conceived of as a garden of creation. In the garden are five rivers (unlike the four in Eden), the senses of 'hearing, seeing, tasting, smelling, feelings', and it is they who keep the creation refreshed and invigorated.[96] Within the figure of the garden Winstanley makes a connection between man and nature itself. Winstanley seems to assign both man and nature to 'creation' as the 'five Rivers or senses'.[97] For Winstanley there is a continuity between man, nature, and God based upon the figure of the Garden, while he would seem to be implying that the 're-invigoration' of man is his perception and enjoyment of nature, which is as much to say that perfection is achieved when man returns to his original relationship with nature, when material and spirit are one:

In the beginning of time the whole Creation lived in man, and man lived in his Maker, the spirit of Righteousnesse and peace, for every creature walked evenly with man, and delighted in man, and was ruled by him; there was no opposition between him and the beast, fowls, fishes or any creature in the earth: so that it is truly said, The whole Creation was in man, one within, and walked even with him; for no creature appeared to be a visible enemy to him: for every creature gave forth it self, either for pleasure or profit of man, who was Lord of all; And man lived in his Maker the Spirit, and delighted in no other: there was an eveness between man and all creatures, and an evenesse between man and his Maker the Lord, the Spirit.[98]

Biblical echoes of Eden and of the garden in the Song of Solomon (Cant. 5: 1; 6: 2, 11) were strong in most imaginations in the seventeenth century, an image of a lost perfection.

---

[95] Christopher Hill, *The World Turned Upside Down* (1972), 142; J. R. Knott, Jr., *The Sword of the Spirit: Puritan Responses to the Bible* (Chicago, 1980), 101. For Hill's qualification of this earlier position see 'The Religion of Gerrard Winstanley', p. 18.

[96] Winstanley, *Fire in the Bush*, p. 3.

[97] Ibid. 7.   [98] Winstanley, *The New Law of Righteousness*, p. 2.

Increasingly for the radicals, however, it was a figurative statement of a perfect relationship for the believer to obtain with God. The allegory of the first and second Adams is placed in Eden so that Henry Pinnell expresses the view, taken from the German spiritualists, that the first Adam did not have perfect knowledge in Eden. Though Pinnell is unspecific regarding the distinction between historical and allegorical Adam, he allows the allegorical *schema* to predominate, so that Adam in Eden is purely a natural, rather than spiritual man, and he combines this with the argument that if Adam knew all about the Tree of Knowledge of Good and Evil, Christ and God, he would have been immortal.

Near to Pinnell's position were a number of other arguments, one of which involved an open attack on Winstanley's interpretation of Eden. In *Adam Unvailed, And Seen with open Face* (1649), William Rabisha disputed Winstanley's idea of the Fall, because the first Adam was 'earth earthly', entirely natural, and so had nothing to lose. A beast originally, it was the eating of the Tree of Knowledge of Good and Evil which gave Adam his natural knowlege, since it contained the law of nature. In the Tree of Life was the law of the spirit and life in Christ (p. 2). Nevertheless, the eating of the fruit brought Adam closer to the spiritual, so that Rabisha, taking Gen. 3:22 quite literally, describes a god-like Adam being driven from Paradise.

A close scrutiny of this tract reveals a greater degree of unusual interpretation. Rabisha holds that Adam was not created in Eden. Relying upon a crude empiricism, Rabisha asserts that Adam must have been a child originally, and that he was not made by God but 'grew out of something by the Providence of God' (p. 38). He was not created in Eden, but was put there to till the ground 'into pleasure and delight'. Behind this are two theories. First, the notion that there were men before Adam. Second, a rather idiosyncratic picture of Rabisha's mode of symbolic interpretation begins to emerge. Tilling the soil is connected with bringing up good seed (from Jer. 4: 3), which, says Rabisha, is the condition of all men from the age of six upwards. So biblical figures are in some respects representative of human universals, though literal perspectives are never entirely discounted. For Rabisha biblical figures may represent several aspects at the same time. Allegorically Adam and Eve may be taken on two different levels, the 'personal' and the 'spiritual', the 'type' and the 'anti-type', both of which are but images. The 'personal' describes invisible and incomprehensible matters which are nevertheless outward, whereas the 'spiritual' refers to the image of God in respect of 'holiness, righteousness, wisdom' (p. 13). God always tends towards the spiritual and anti-typical.

When applied, this rather cumbersome system leads to a severely misogynistic conclusion. Spiritually Adam and Eve are both the image of God, while in the type or 'person', Adam is the second man, Christ, Eve the church. In this latter form Genesis presents the serpent's temptation (says Rabisha) through the eyes of the woman, and not according to God. Hence, death is perceived in its literal and not figurative sense. The sin is in the desire and not in the actual eating of the fruit. This sin is of Eve only, representing the church, while Adam as Christ remains passive in this transgression, though in the sense that Eve 'holds forth' both Adam and Eve as 'creatures' (here the allegory slides again), both contain that part of humanity which quenches the spirit and carries away the inward captive. Rabisha's curiosity, which leads him to see contradictions in Winstanley's description of Eden, is no more successful in describing a consistent system, but his attempt to read Genesis as a typological figuration of Pauline theology is remarkable in radical religious writing for its ingenuity. One distinct effect is to divorce entirely the divine from any substantial presence in human thought or language, which can only ever represent:

Adam the type was prohibited from eating of the one tree in the midst of the Garden, upon the penalty of death: So in the like manner is *Adam* the antitype which is all flesh, prohibited from power in themselves, and commanded in the word of God, not to go to make themselves perfect by their owne righteousnesse, which is the tree of knowledge of good and evill in the substance; which tree, mans righteousness, or the Law, is in the midst of the garden, that is, of all the delights and shelters that are: This is one of the chief, even placed in the very heart of man (pp. 40–1).

There were other images of the garden to be derived from the Bible. As Stanley Stewart has shown, the allegorical interpretation of the Song of Solomon as the wooing of the Church by Christ had an enormously popular appeal to the seventeenth-century mind.[99] Paul Hobson provides the simple and central image of *A Garden Inclosed* (1647) as a frame in which his reader would come to know his or her true relationship with the divine. Similarly the figure of the garden provides his speaker with a means to talk of the spiritual enlightenment of others, drawing upon the Song of Solomon 8 and Isa. 60: 1–3, 17. Coppe attempts to exhort enlightenment in the reader, as he impersonates the lover: 'It is the voyce of my beloved that knocketh, saying, Open to me my *Sister*, my *love*, my *dove*, for my head is filled with dew, and my locks with the drops of night . . . For brass, I will bring gold, and for iron I will bring silver.'[100]

Later, Coppe expands his appropriation of biblical cultivation by utilizing the vineyard (Jer. 12) as a symbol for the soul or the life of the spirit, which has been exploited by 'Husbandmen', who are selfish, unfriendly, and concerned only with outward things: 'Thus my *Fathers* Vineyard goes to wrack, while it is let out to Husbandmen. But it is yet but a little while, and behold, the Lord of the Vineyard cometh, and will miserably destroy (& that very suddenly) the *Husbandmen*.'[101] The husbandmen are in fact 'formal' priests who do not cultivate the soul properly. Here, the gloss on Jer. 12 in the Geneva Bible may be in the back of Coppe's mind since it interprets the passage as a prophecy of the return of Christ and the true prophets to the Church. Indeed, Coppe concentrates upon the spiritual apocalypse rather than extends the cultivation imagery. By contrast James Nayler does exactly that at which Coppe halts, having more faith in the suggestive power of the image to enhance the sense of the Fall:

And as the *light* ariseth the Creation is seen, and how the enmity hath spread over, and how the lust hath defiled it, and how that which was planted as a vineyard is become as a Wilderness for barreness, grown over with thorns, and bryars, Sturdy Oakes, and tall Cedars, for want of the Vine-dresser; and where the Lilly should grow, its grown over with weeds, thistles and Nettles; so that GOD walks not there because of the great abomination; and that is the cause of all your woe, even his absence.[102]

---

[99] Stewart, *The Enclosed Garden* (Madison, 1966), 3–30.

[100] *Some Sweet Sips, of some Spirituall Wine*, in *CRW*, pp. 51–2.

[101] Ibid. 54. The reference here, however, is to Matt. 21: 3. Throughout this tract, Coppe conflates the language of Jer. 12 and Matt. 21. Anna Trapnel walked in gardens in order to gain spiritual strength and to communicate with the Lord: *Anna Trapnel's Report and Plea* (1654), 5, 12.   [102] Nayler, *Love to the Lost* (1655), 5.

Winstanley, also in contrast to Coppe, is prone to extend the use of this imagery in accordance with his metaphor of man as a garden: in the cool of the day, the battle between flesh and spirit declines, so that God walks with delight in the middle of the garden ('mans heart').[103] It may not have made any difference to Winstanley himself, but his analytical perspective and his vision are made possible by a man–nature connection which neglects referential boundaries. The great 'oneness' is rooted in part in this use of metaphor. Mankind, for instance, is portrayed as the earth, the living earth, and the 'shattered earth' in his unregenerate state, as opposed to the divinely cultivated garden. Here, the allegory subtly extends to present Winstanley's critique of the oppressive and appropriative social and religious hierarchy. The churches become 'enclosures' which constitute a corruption of the original garden or vineyard. To live out of the garden in the enclosure is to 'live out' of oneself in selfish outward forms. Since God lives inside the garden, it is also to 'fall out of one's maker'. 'Out' here is used in the sense of being 'outward', rather than of actually falling out, though for the reader the two senses contained within 'out' (being outward and falling out) impart a simultaneous sense of action and stasis. The extent to which Winstanley's metaphorical visions extend to his later works, where he proposes a communal utopia, has been much debated, and despite the emphasis in *The Law of Freedom* (1652) upon social organization, the allegories are still employed: the five rivers, for instance, become the major skills which will make society flourish.[104] Even if the concentration of the allegory upon the nature of the individual and the natural world, rather than upon its reconstruction, is maintained, Winstanley still applies his allegorical perceptions to social organization, again emphasizing the two conjoined treasures of the earth:

So long as such are Rulers as cals the Land theirs, upholding this particular propriety of *Mine and Thine*; the common-people shall never have their liberty, nor the Land ever freed from troubles, oppressions

---

[103] Winstanley, *Fire in the Bush*, p. 16. See also Richard Russel, *The Spirit of God in Man* (1654), 4 for a similar use of the garden image.

[104] In 'Winstanley: A Case for the Man as He Said He Was', *JEH* 28 (1977), 57–75, Lotte Mulligan *et al.*, argue for the continued visionary perspective in *The Law of Freedom*. Winstanley's modernism and increased concern for the legal aspects of social organization is maintained by J. C. Davis, *Utopia and the Ideal Society: A Study of English Utopian Writing 1516–1700* (Cambridge, 1981), 169–203.

and complainings; by reason whereof the Creatour of all things is continually provoked.[105]

The natural world also comes to suggest degrees of perfection in a loose, typological fashion. For Winstanley weeds become symbols of self-love, pride, covetousness, honours, pleasures, imagination, outwardness, joy of envy, hypocrisy, evil surmisings, and grudgings in the garden of the spirit of man, while 'sweet flowers and herbs' represent joy, peace, love, humility, self-denial, and so-forth.[106] In *The Saints Paradice* (?1648) this symbolism is connected with the genealogical myth as grass becomes representative of 'tender sons and daughters that Christ hath newly called out of the earth' (p. 81), while the components of creation are examined in their post-Fall situation, to show how man's selfish influence is manifested in nature. Winstanley implies that the way in which man has treated nature suggests how natural symbols should be read. Just as man's selfishness causes a corresponding selfishness in creatures and bodies, so man going 'out' of his maker causes the creatures to go 'out' of man. 'Out', then, intimates here the disruption of the proper order of things:

And this now is the curse, Man is gone out of his Maker, to live upon objects; and the creatures are gone out of man, to seek delight in pushing and devouring one another, and the whole Creation of fire, and water, earth and air; and all bodies made of these are put out of order, through man's rejecting the Spirit to live upon objects.[107]

Perspectives not dissimilar to Winstanley's existed in circles less extreme than the Diggers, those with far larger memberships. Robert Everard published two pieces which argued for the dissociation of an untainted nature from fallen man. The first, *The Creation and Fall of Adam Reviewed* (1649), was published in 1652 with the 1651 'Faith and Practice' of the midland (General)

---

[105] Winstanley, *The New Law of Righteousness*, pp. 6–7.

[106] Winstanley, *Fire in the Bush*, sigs. A4^r–A5^v.

[107] Winstanley, *The New Law of Righteousness*, 3. John Jackson displayed remarkable clarity of perception in seeing what this language led to: 'This new birth presupposeth a new Life, which holds similitude and proportion with the first Creation', *Hosannah to the Son of David* (1657), 27. The tendency to think in these metaphysical terms would support the similarity between Winstanley and the Quakers at an earlier stage than has usually been supposed, if we accept the evidence of Edward Burrough: Friends House Library, MS Caton, 3/63.

Baptist churches appended. Using a vast array of Pauline texts, Everard makes a distinction between sin and nature. The 'book of creation' is for man to understand the 'eternall Power and Godhead'. Man was sinful in himself, and against nature since Adam was a natural man before the Fall. With the Fall came the Law of God, whether graven in stone, or the Law of Nature, that makes wicked men the children of wrath by the appointment of God'.[108] And before the Fall, Winstanley's interpretation is again reversed using the very images that he had employed:

Now *Adam* had not such a cup of water in all his foure Rivers which passed through his garden, neither any such Flowers to smell of in the garden, that he might breath into his nostrils any spiritual life; he could not savour the voyce of a resurrection from the dead; for the goodnesse of a Saviour must be resented by those that are lost: but *Adam* knew no such need, so could not be in any such distresse, so uncapable to participate of the knowledge of the Saviour.[109]

In some cases, then, the fascination with biblical keywords and symbols enabled some radicals to produce versions of the creation myth and the presence of the divine in the universe which were not merely crude derivations from the New Testament *topoi* in the Pauline epistles and in Revelation. Through a series of imagistic and logical transformations, the radicals, Winstanley and Clarkson in particular, were able to establish epistemologies which broke down the barriers between God, man, and nature, setting knowledge alongside power. The significance of this lay not only in the hostile attention it brought from the more orthodox ministers, but also in the controversy which it produced among other radicals. Knowledge of creation was as important a factor in the competition for authority as knowledge of the means to salvation, and just as controversial in the struggle for the discovery or assertion of truth. As is now well known, the Muggletonians went on to construct their own original cosmology which certainly served as one of their articles of faith. The other radicals remained more speculative. In

[108] Robert Everard, *Nature's Vindication* (1652), 26. On p. 44 of this work Everard connects this defence of nature on biblical grounds with a political theory of natural law: the true ground of magisterial power is the preservation of nature, even if that means war; necessity and nature are bedfellows. This is significant in the light of Everard's participation at Putney. Forthcoming work by Kent Gulley deals extensively with Everard's General Baptist and Leveller involvement.

[109] Robert Everard, *The Creation and Fall of Adam Reviewed* (1652), 122.

Winstanley's case in particular, his facility with metaphor defines the possibilities as well as the limitations of his vision.

One theme throughout this chapter has been the extent to which extreme sectarian knowledge systems were produced by men who were unlearned if literate. The gap between orthodox university education and the ways in which the unlearned came by what they knew provides a similar context for the radical religious understanding of the connection between divine language and human language, and between God's Word and its interpretation in the world. Here, the central focus is not so much upon the representational capacity of certain images, as upon the extent to which human language, as speech and as writing, can be said to represent the spirit, and the degree to which the 'creature' can apprehend the language of God. To this subject it is necessary now to turn.

7

Theories of Divine Signification

I

THE dualisms which the radicals developed and elevated in order to explain the relationships between God, man, and nature also had a central bearing upon radical religious attitudes towards language, both divine and human. The sense of transference from flesh to spirit, from form to power, resulted in an impulse to leave behind the trappings of mere earthly speech and writing (notably grammar) in order to partake of regenerate or even divine language. Language was central to the radicals because it was the medium of communication between God and man, either through the Scriptures or through the inner speech of inspiration and prophecy. In fact the radicals took the major current debates about the nature of language and education, and assessed them in the light of their developing theologies. The result is a rich spread of responses which took sectarian ideas of language and of inspiration to their respective extremes.

One of the most central metaphysical concerns for puritans if not for Christian theology generally was the logocentric nature of God, creation, and the divine intervention. The λόγος, or Word, according to John 1: 1–2, is identified with God, throughout all time: 'In the beginning was the Word, and the Word was with God, and the Word was God. / The same was in the beginning with God.' At the same time and by extension from this, God was held to have 'spoken' the world into creation. The act of creation then was an act of simultaneous making and naming. In Genesis the jussive subjunctive, 'And God said, Let there be a firmament' for instance (1: 6), is coupled with naming, 'And God called the firmament Heaven' (1: 8), by means of making: 'And God made the firmament' (1: 7).

Most Puritans accepted this, together with the notion that the Word had been transmitted down to them through history as the transcendent manifestation of the divine. Where they parted company was over the definition of the Word: how did God's Word communicate with humanity? In which human faculty was the Word perceived? More orthodox Puritans accepted that the Word was encapsulated within the Bible entirely, whereas radical Puritans and sectarians were more prone to accept the transmission of the Word through dreams and visions as an equal or superior authority to the Bible. For the radicals the Bible was the word, rather than the Word, the letter, rather than the Letter.

There are many varied viewpoints expressed within this general framework. John Saltmarsh, for instance, ignores the distinction between Word and word. Word becomes for him a linguistic vehicle, or collection of linguistic vehicles, which bear the transcendent truth. There is no transcendent Word, while dream and vision are also assigned the non-transcendent status of Word:

A *word*, as the New Testament is, may be as well a Way and dispensation to an *infinite God* to make out himself by, as any other, either of *dream* or *vision*, or *revelation* or *Oracle*, all being but ways of a *naturall* strain and *condition*, no more then the *Word*.[1]

This radical divorce of the transcendent divine from human language had ·its roots in the emphasis in popular Puritan preaching upon the necessity of engaging with the Spirit, as exemplified in the New Testament, over against the claims of the Law in the Old Testament.[2] Fierce in his adherence to Pauline practice, another radical divine, John Webster, echoes Saltmarsh in defining Gospel language as no less divinely endowed: 'The weapons and instruments of a minister of the Gospel are of a more transcendent and sublime nature, than those that one man can furnish another withall', even if it is a purely natural phenomenon.[3]

Most sectarian understanding of language is based upon the dualisms which explain the presence of the divine in the human, and which were analysed in the last chapter, though the more learned radicals, like John Webster, did elaborate upon the simple dualisms by incorporating occult theories, such as those of Boehme. In his collection of sermons, *The Judgement Set* (1654), Webster nevertheless makes a series of typical radical statements

---

[1] John Saltmarsh, *The Smoke in the Temple* (1646), 28 (wrongly paginated as p. 22).

[2] See Saltmarsh, 'Shadows Flying Away', in *Reasons for Unitie, Peace and Love* (1646), repr. in D. M. Wolfe, *Milton in the Puritan Revolution* (New York, 1941), 428.

[3] *Academiarum Examen* (1654), 5.

regarding the transcendent. He does not dwell here upon the difference between fallen and unfallen, perfect language, as he does in *Academiarum Examen* (1654). The implication here is that idolatry, concentration upon worldly forms, is the fallen means of interpretation of the divine, whereas transcendent concerns represent an approximation to the original, unfallen interpretation and expression of the divine. Still, Webster distinguishes between Christ's divine and earthly manifestations in terms of a theory of copies:

There are usually two things in the way of Christ which oftentimes in the world are mistaken, and taken for one another: there are, I say, the *heavenly things* themselves, and there are the *Patterns* of them: now the *Pattern* is not set forth for it selfe, but in *reference* and *relation* unto *the thing* of which *it is a pattern*; And a *copy* or *exemplar*, it is not *for it selfe*, but in relation to what we should act, imitate, or doe by it: so there are the *heavenly* things themselves, and the *patterns*, or *types*, or *similitudes* of them.[4]

Clearly, by this explanation, earthly *types* are not idolatrous but simply the necessary earthly manifestations of the divine. Webster does not say whether it is possible for man to understand the heavenly, and so the status of the earthly type remains obscure.

The radical Puritan position regarding the spirit/letter opposition is somewhat easier to delineate. The language of the letter is a veil which the spirit either dominates or encapsulates. In the words of the Independent, Joshua Sprigge:

Election containes *sanctification* of the Spirit, and faith in it; but in the *manifestation* and bringing downe of things to us, the *latter act* still gathers up and comprehends the former; yea, swallowes it up as the *Rationall* life containes the *Sensitive* in it selfe eminently; so the *Spirit* comprehends the *Letter*, and the *Mystery* comprehends the *History*.[5]

For orthodox Puritans, however, the mystery was something which would never be revealed to any human. This was exactly why it was called a mystery. Placing the Scripture over the spirit, the defender of learning, Thomas Hall, felt that it was essential to maintain distinctions in Scripture between the literal and the

[4] John Webster, *The Judgement Set* (1654), 101.
[5] *A Testimony to an Approaching Glory* (1649), sigs. A7ᵛ–A8ʳ.

figurative.[6] Given that it was the treatment of biblical language
as figures which led to the interpretation of the mystery, Hall is
at the very least limiting the claims of the spirit by juxtaposing it
with the literal, the history. The opposite is the case with Hall's
opponents. Coppe speaks of his discourse in *Some Sweet Sips, of
some Spirituall Wine* (1649) as an attempt to provide a 'Clavall'
hint to the mystery (p. 49). This was the attitude taken by radical
Puritans and sectarians whether they were rationalists, like
Winstanley and Henry Pinnell, believing at least to some extent
in inspiration by intuition, or like Coppe, a spiritualist and
mystic, where a spiritual hermeneutics was applied to the second
Scripture of inspired babblings and whisperings.[7]

The debates which the sectarians held with others, and
sometimes among themselves, regarding the relationship of
Spirit and Scripture centred upon attitudes towards the divine
signifying power of language itself. The capacity of human
language to signify the divine rested upon the rhetorical and
metaphorical procedures employed during composition, given
that in the first instance the Bible was written by men who were
divinely inspired. The sectarians looked towards a transcendent,
spiritual meaning in each word. So baptism becomes a spiritual
initiation expressed by 'anointing', while for the Familists, the
sense of regeneration and perfection within the special community of the Family of Love was captured in the phrase
'Godded with God'. Typically this was accompanied by the
rejection of the significance of any outward or physical signification in symbolic words like 'anointing' or 'circumcision':

Now indeed there was a kind of truth in it, that they were the *fleshly seed*
of *Abraham*, and they had submitted to *Circumcision* and to those external
rules commanded: and this seemed to be somewhat, as to outward
appearance, as if they were the *true seed* of Abraham: but that was not it:
and they had the *Circumcision*, and yet were not *Circumcised in heart*;
neither were they his *true* seed.[8]

Thomas Hall's plea for a strict division of literal and figurative
readings is rejected for a total concentration upon the transcendent truth which is supposed to dominate the consciousness of

---

[6] '*Centuria Sacra*', in *Vindiciae Literarum* (1654, 2nd edn., 1655), 80.
[7] For the sixteenth-century continental application of these terms, see G. H.
Williams, *The Radical Reformation* (1962), 829.
[8] John Webster, *The Judgement Set*, p. 170.

the regenerate individual. The most extreme position was taken by John Pordage in *Innocencie Appearing* (1655) where Christ himself becomes the type and shadow of the divine substance (pp. 81, 99).[9] This, then, is by no means to reject the divine signifying potential of figurative language. Rather, it is to limit the significance of particular referents.

The sectarians tend then to define the essential Word in terms of inspiration, so that prophecy itself becomes a metaphor for ineluctable essence extending itself: the Word is received from the Lord in terms of a figure of the body, linking mind and mouth. In the writings of the Seeker, John Brayne, this is supported by the use of breathing as a metaphor for divine condescension. In *The Unknown Being of the Spirit, Soul and Body; Anatomized* (1654), Brayne argues that soul and spirit are one, that the Word is light, and that the Word as spirit is breathed into all, so that regenerate man becomes πνευματικός (pp. 2, 3, 7, 8).[10] At the same time, there is an attempt to come to terms with the precise status of the essential Word. The Welsh radical Walter Cradock points directly to the self-defining nature of the divine essence and states that its representation as 'Word' is apt because of the self-reflexivity involved here on the figurative level. The 'Word' is an 'elogie', or descriptive inscription, which defines God: it is a word which refers to itself as much as it refers to the transcendent essence.[11] In more sophisticated terms, according to pseudo-Weigel's pamphlet *Astrologie Theologized* (1649), the Word is 'pre-signified' and 'pre-lucidated' (p. 3).

Morgan Llwyd offers this position a subtle perspective. He was prepared to accept the 'letter' as long as it was permeated with the Bible.[12] By this alignment of definitions all discourse, spoken and written, should resemble biblical language. This is a somewhat less radical position than Saltmarsh's, since Llwyd

---

[9] Making Christ a type was the easiest way of inviting the charge of Familism.

[10] Brayne was roundly attacked for making such an identification by Clement Writer in *Fides Divina* (1657), 107–8.

[11] *The Saints Fulnesse of Joy* (1646), 3. This is related to the notion, common among Congregationalists, that the Scripture as container of the Word, is a perfectly, self-authenticating, self-sufficient body of truth, which had passed untainted through human history. This was termed αὐτόπιστος by Calvin: *Institutes*, 1. 7. 5. For a similar view which is more critical of translations, see John Goodwin, *The Divine Authority of the Scriptures asserted* (1648), 17–36.

[12] *A Discourse of God the Word* (1657), trans. Griffith Rudd (1739), 36.

does not appear to give any credence to the power of inspiration (though he does so elsewhere in his writings). The important point is that Llwyd's statement is part of a general sectarian distrust of rhetoric, of fallen human discourses, as opposed to the spiritual inner communication.

Llwyd's equation between Bible and godly speech allows him to invert the relationship between language and mind. The implication is that God cannot be expressed directly, but only pointed to through metaphor and godly language. Given that the sectarians felt that Christ worked within the mind as well as the spirit or soul, the sectarians returned to the Bible or book as a metaphor for the inner experience. For instance, in a letter to William Erbery, Llwyd wrote 'Flesh is burning so fast with us here, and elsewhere, that I cannot transcribe what is written for the present.'[13] To push the analogy home, Erbery himself talks of the internal as the 'little Book' of the heart.[14] For all the Seekers, the metaphor was an index of the way in which 'experience' led to a clearer communication with the divine, though of course the concern with books and readership as a godly activity exists in orthodox Puritanism at large.

However, the more radical sectarians did move beyond human language, both literally and as a metaphor. Transcendency results in the final abolition of metaphor. So, Coppe's enthuasism in *Some Sweet Sips* exceeds the 'notional' bounds set by the precise limits of moving from Type to Truth. The Familist Hendrik Niclaes had expressed this as the passage beyond the veil to the heart which the Presbyterian Samuel Rutherford identified as Niclaes's 'conferences with Angels'.[15] For the pseudo-Weigel and for Coppe, this is to partake of the *ens* or being of inspiration, that is, God. For the Quakers this union is what the prophetic state amounts to. In fact George Fox states that the true prophetic voice, which the regenerate in the present possess, antedates the confusion of languages.[16] The pure language is generated by inspiration though, as we shall see, for some sectarians perfect speech lies increasingly in the realms of solipsism.

---

[13] Letter to Erbery, in *The Babe of Glory*, in *The Testimony of William Erbery* (1658), 95.

[14] Erbery, *Nor Truth, nor Error*, in *The Testimony of William Erbery*, p. 7.

[15] *A Survey of the Spirituall Antichrist*, 2 parts (1648), i. 55.

[16] *Astrologie Theologized* (1649), 21; Coppe, *Copp's Return to the wayes of Truth* (1651), in *CRW*, p. 138; Fox, *A Battle-Door for Teachers and Professors* (1660), 22.

Eventually, by the late 1650s, various sectarians, notably the Quaker Samuel Fisher, felt able to dispense with the problem of the Word and word dualism altogether. Fisher's great critique, *Rusticus Ad Academicos* (1660), is a reply to several Puritan divines, notably John Owen, who had published his *Of the Divine Originall, Authority, self-evidencing Light and Power of the Scriptures* in 1659. Owen's work is an appreciation of and adumbration upon Brian Walton's 1657 Polyglot Bible. The Torah is defined as a piece of direct inspiration placed in the mind of Moses without any medium. The word becomes the Word: 'the Authority of the *written Word*, in its selfe and into us, is *from* it selfe, as the Word of God, and the *eviction* of that Authority unto us, is by it selfe' (p. 35). Though Owen says that the Word operates through power rather than as a naked word (from 1 Thess. 1: 5) he describes the Word as having its own inner light. In effect he subsumes what is the dominant Quaker term for divine presence into the literal. Although Owen seems at one point (p. 106) to keep the supernatural *Word* away from the historical acceptance of the Word in the Scripture, he distinctly refers to Scripture as the Word. On both counts this is a crime of logical inconsistency for Fisher. If belief only in the transcendent and immanent light is the central religious tenet, as it was for the Quakers, then there is no need to cling to any fine and discerning distinctions. Accordingly sectarians tend to become radical nominalists (the transcendent 'Thing' is the important factor) while all attempts by others to justify the mediation of Word by word appear ridiculous and self-contradictory.[17]

In the first instance Fisher sees an ambivalence in Owen's simultaneous use of light imagery and his attack on the Quakers. Assuming from the Quaker position that the Scripture can only be the letter or simple human language, even if spoken by holy men, Fisher enforces the form and content dualism (where content or matter is the transcendent Word) so that his opponents appear to be confused among themselves:

they plainly enough confess the Scripture to be neither the *Word of God* nor the *Rule*, witnesse T[homas] D[anson]'s words, who, when told

---

[17] The term 'radical nominalist' is used in the sense that true naming is only possible for the transcendent essence, the origin or root, of the material object. In terms of the earlier debate between realists and nominalists, the realists allowed the material to partake of the real.

what the *Scripture is* viz. τὸ γράμμα, ἡ γραφή **בתב** the *letter,*
writing that the holy men wrote, replies *you cannot think us so silly* sure *as to*
affirm the Scripture in that sense (which yet is the only sense in which it can
properly be called *Scripture*) *to be the Word of God, but we mean the matter*
contained in the scripture (which is another matter then the Scripture)
whether that be the Rule of faith or no.[18]

John Webster extended this critique to a theory of proper
naming: 'And whereas names should truely express notions, and
they be congruous to things themselves, the *Aristotelian Philosophy*
leads us into an endless Labyrinth, having nothing in manner
but *Syllogisms*',[19] the name being ideally co-extensive with the
thing, since both are connected by the *Idea* in the mind; 'yet did
he [Adam] immediately give unto her an adaequate name, suiting
her original, which most significantly did manifest what was her
nature, and from whence it came, and doubtless the name being
exactly conformable, and configurate to the *Idaea* in his mind'.[20]
In other words, the proper use of language, as in Paradise,
involves the inevitable naming of the transcendent, given that all
material creation is a shadow of the transcendent thing.

II

Inevitably the different stances taken in the debate regarding
the relative claims of transcendent and literal truths led to different attitudes towards the significance of original biblical texts.
The general Reformation attitude that the Scripture contained the
absolute authority of the Word, when interpreted through
the power of the spirit, was coupled with a return to the Hebrew
and Greek originals in order to escape from the dominance and
what were felt to be the faults of the Vulgate translation. Mid-
seventeenth-century Puritans felt that the sophistication of pre-
Reformation learning, rhetoric, and translation had corrupted
the original sense of the Bible. Webster's opponent, the Calvinist
Aristotelian Thomas Hall, stressed that learning was necessary
in order to recover the original language, circumstances and
contexts of specifical biblical passages. Hall goes as far as to
categorize biblical language in terms of classical rhetoric in order
to enhance clarity, even though he is writing seven years after

---

[18] *An Additionall Appendix* to *Rusticus Ad Academicos* (1660), 17. See also pp. 32–3.
[19] *Academiarum Examen*, p. 67. [20] Ibid. 30.

Jeremy Taylor had intimated the final impossibility of finding the correct sense.[21] Hall then is still interested in determining some sort of transcendent meaning: 'not the bare words, but the meaning of the law is the Law'. The Scripture is both a text and a gloss unto itself, while 'words of knowledge imply affection and practice', so that the comprehension of scriptural originals becomes a moral prerequisite.[22]

The sectarians did not reject this framework. Rather, they took the anxiety regarding the corruption of the original text a stage further, even though for some the power of the inner light negated any final worry over scriptural accuracy. This resulted in a type of return to the roots of the Reformation: several radicals preferred Dutch translations of the Bible. Vavasor Powell's metrical psalms contain several variant translations from Dutch Bibles, while George Fox describes the Dutch as 'true men who translated the Bible'.[23] Another early Quaker, Henry Clark, compares the earliest Worms Bible with John Hollybush's 1538 translation of the Vulgate, so reclaiming old glosses and apocryphal texts.[24] From a rational point of view Clement Writer (possibly he was a Seeker) echoed Taylor in claiming that the problem of translation was so great that no final solution could ever be reached. In *Fides Divina* (1657) he exemplified this by accusing John Brayne of faulty translation from the Greek so that Brayne could make the identification of soul with spirit which was so essential to his theory of divine emanation (p. 108). As Christopher Hill has intimated, Writer's significance lies largely in the fact that he connected continuing corruption with the continuing influence of particular institutions.[25]

Despite the considerable prevalence of statements by radicals,

---

[21] Hall, *Vindiciae Literarum*, pp. 75–77, 151–83; Taylor, ΘΕΟΛΟΓΙΑ ΕΚΛΕΚΤΙΚΗ, *A Discourse of the Liberty of Prophesying* (1647), 64–9.

[22] Hall, *Vindiciae Literarum*, pp. 77–8, 84–5.

[23] Powell's poetry is appended to תצפר בפה or *The Bird in the Cage* (1661), sigs. H1^r–16^v; Fox, *A Battle-Door*, sig. D2^v. Powell may have used Theodore Haak's *The Dutch Annotations upon the Whole Bible* (1637, English trans. 2 vols., 1657). He agrees with Haak on Lam. 4: 1, but not on Lam. 4: 3, however: Powell, *The Bird in the Cage*, sig. 12^v.

[24] *A Rod Discovered* (1659), sig. A1^v. The Worms Bible was Tyndale's translation, published by Peter Schoeffer in 1526. This interest is most significant because highly unusual for Quakers.

[25] *The World Turned Upside Down* (1972), 265–6, 268. For Writer's possible connection with Seekers, see his entry in *DNB*.

such as Walter Cradock's assertion that the source for union and
'onenesse' with the Father and Son is 'seldom' in the Scripture, a
level of literalism did persist in the sects not in the critical sense
of Writer but in a positive sense. The Baptist Thomas Collier
accused the Quaker James Nayler of regarding the Bible as vain
jugglings and conceits, as an allegory which makes God out to be
a liar.[26] The letter as much as the Word conveys the truth for
Collier, who often quotes Hebrew and Greek originals to bolster
his arguments. John Rogers searched for the spirit in the
Scriptures but to do so he learnt Chaldaic, Samaritan, Syriac,
Arabic, Persian, and 'Aetheopian' during his imprisonment at
Carisbrooke on the Isle of Wight. Such extremely erudite
enterprises were not uncommon among Independent pastors,
but Morgan Llwyd most clearly relates this to spoken discourse.
He was prepared to accept the 'letter' as long as it was permeated
with the Bible.[27] In other words, all discourse, written and
spoken, should resemble (spiritualized) Biblical language,
following the imperative of letting the spirit act upon the
individual so that God's ordinances are registered in human
speech. This is the same position reached by John Saltmarsh,
though the two take different routes to arrive there: Llwyd takes
Bible into the category of spirit while Saltmarsh replaces Word
with spirit to the exclusion of word. Both are still trapped within
logocentric definitions.[28]

The concern with the status of original Biblical languages
resulted in the sectarians' also engaging in the widespread
seventeenth-century debate on the nature of Hebrew as the
original language. It was assumed that the language spoken by
Adam and Eve in Eden before the Fall facilitated a perfect degree
of communication with the divine as well as expressing an innate
knowledge of the natural world. The latter was exemplified in
Adam's innate ability to name objects in Paradise, so that 'the
imposition of their names was adquately agreeing with their
natures'. Generally, as has been well documented, the observation

---

[26] Cradock, *Gospel-libertie* (1648), 117; Collier, *A Looking-Glasse for the Quakers*
(1657), 5, 12.

[27] Rogers, 'A High Witnesse, or a Heart-Appeale', p. 13 in *Jegar-Sehadvtha: An
Oyled Pillar: Set up for Posterity* (1657); Llwyd, *A Discourse of God the Word*, p. 36.

[28] The result of John Owen's rational approach to Hebrew as an original is to
reduce its status as a supernaturally endowed entity. See N. Smith, 'The Interior
Word', 315–18, n. 35.

tied in with the seventeenth-century distrust of the power of language to signify more than the thing or quality to which a word referred.[29] Empiricists like Hobbes believed that the proper understanding of man and of the natural world could not proceed until the one-to-one relationship between words and things was once again established, but more idealistic thinkers felt that a return to the original language would re-establish perfection on earth, and salvation for all.[30]

At this point the original language concern touched upon another issue of linguistic reform. This was the search for a 'universal character', or language which would enable all peoples of all races, nations, and languages to communicate. The promulgation of Hebrew as the original language was one possibility within a series of further options for a universal character such as mathematical symbols. The concern with original languages here is significant, since they were felt to contain the most perfect, universal, and effective signifying power: all languages had in some sense derived from the original. Towards the late 1650s Chinese was posited as the original in a challenge to Hebrew. In fact the complications in the historical development of Hebrew eventually resulted in its discrediting as a potential universal language by Restoration linguists.[31] This dismissal was related to a problem which did face the sectarian position regarding Hebrew. Firstly the question was asked: if Hebrew was spoken before the Fall, was it Hebrew as seventeenth-century man knew it or was it some more powerful, transcendent spiritual language? Generally it was assumed, as we have seen already, that Hebrew was corrupted after the Fall. In fact it was held by most that Hebrew was a post-Fall language which was the *only* language (with a few dialectal variations) spoken until the confusion of Babel when many other languages appeared. While the linguistic reformers rejected Hebrew because of its complicated history and uncertain origins, the sectarians were faced

---

[29] Webster, *Academiarum Examen* (1654), p. 29. For the two most recent contributions to this area see Murray Cohen, *Sensible Words: Linguistic Practice in England, 1640–1785* (Baltimore, 1977) and M. M. Slaughter, *Universal Language and Scientific Taxonomy in the Seventeenth Century* (Cambridge, 1982).

[30] Hobbes, *Leviathan* (1651), ed. C. B. Macpherson (1968), 100–1.

[31] See David S. Katz, *Philo-Semitism and the Readmission of the Jews to England 1603–1655* (Oxford, 1655), 43–88. Henry Jessey among others believed that Hebrew would be universally spoken in the Millennium: E[dward] W[histon], *The Life and Death of Mr. Henry Jessey* (1671), 62.

with the prospect of discerning the original unfallen spiritual language which would ensure communication on the supernatural level.

Most of the sectarians' attitudes towards the original language stemmed from their epistemology of the Spirit, but the attitudes of some of the early Quakers have roots which might more accurately be described as ideological, in that they were concerned with the role of languages in particular cultures, and how these languages expressed the morality of the cultures, rather than with the divine origins of a language. For instance, Richard Farnworth and Thomas Aldam maintained that since Pilate wrote in the languages of Hebrew, Greek, and Latin, none could be original or signifying of the divine. Likewise, for the Seeker Henry Hasselwood Latin is the 'stammering tongue' of Isa. 33: 19.[32] In his famous broadside against classical education, *A Battle-Door for Teachers and Professors* (1660), George Fox identified what he saw as the major linguistic blemish in English—the use of 'you' for the second person singular instead of 'thou'—as an inheritance from the Roman Empire (p. 16). Proper English should follow the biblical rule: 'Thou' to 'One', 'You' to 'Many'. In fact Fox holds that language is a wholly natural creation. It was formed by man and has no connection with the divine:

This is a whip, and a rod to all such who have degenerated through the pride, and ambition, from their natural tongue, and Languages, and all Languages upon the earth is but Naturall, and makes none divine, but that which makes divine is the Word, which was before Languages, and Tongues were. (sig. A2ᵛ)[33]

For other sectarians human languages were at least originally connected with the divine. This led to some distinct conclusions being reached regarding the extent of linguistic signification, both human and divine.

According to the Paracelsan and Behmenist version, Hebrew was a corruption of the original Adamic 'natural language', the knowledge of which held the key to the secrets of nature and the spirit. When God created the world, he spoke the 'characteristical word' which man 'stood' in, 'and so spoke in, from, and through

[32] Farnworth and Aldam, *The Priests Ignorance* (1656), 4; Hasselwood, *Doctor Hill's Funeral-Sermon*, 2 parts (1654), i. sig. B3ʳ.

[33] See also George Fox, *The Lambs Officer* (1659), 14–15.

this outflown language of the father, which is the procedure of the all-working *fiat*, . . . in which all things live stand, operate'.[34] This constitutes the 'language of nature', which was 'innate and implantive' in Adam, 'radically and essentially one with him', 'dative from the Father of Light', rather than 'inventive or acquisitive'. The sense units, as it were, of the language of nature are the 'signatures' or characters divinely inscribed upon each object of the creation, making them unique, and defining their relationship with the divine. As John Webster explains, '*ideal-signatures*' were originally contained in the divine essence, but with the expansion of the 'serviceable word' the signatures became part of the 'Womb' of the 'generative and saetiferous [bristling] word' from which sprang the 'seminal natures', so that ideal signature is transformed into true signature in the created world.[35] Put together, all the signatures constitute a harmony which is likened to music:

like so many *Harmoniacal* and *Symphoniacal* voices, or tones, all melodiously singing, and sounding forth in an heavenly consort, the wisdome, power, glory, and might of the transcendent central *Abysse* of unity, from whence they did arise, and all speaking one language in expressing significantly in that mystical *Idiome*, the hidden virtues, natures and properties of those various sounds.[36]

However, sound is not merely an analogy for the language of nature. Also it is part of that language, as the voices of birds and beasts are seen to express animals' 'passions, affections and notions', even though they appear inarticulate to humans. Thus, the crying of babies when born is part of the universal 'natural' sign of grief. Later on Webster recommends particular scientific disciplines to study the 'Caelestial signatures' in natural objects, which may be made known in part through the study of 'light, colour, motion, and other affections', with the ultimate aim of discovering the height of alchemical knowledge, the 'three great *Hypostatical* principles of nature, *Salt, Sulphur*, and *Mercury*, first mentioned by *Basilius Valentinus*'.[37]

---

[34] Webster, *Academiarum Examen*, p. 27. 'Characteristical': 'inscribed with magic emblems' or 'that serves to indicate essential nature'; 'Fiat': 'authoritative sanction or pronouncement; command of creation'.

[35] Ibid. 29. 27.   [36] Ibid. 27–8.

[37] Ibid. 76–7. See also John Everard's metaphor of Christ as a redemptive alembic in *The Gospel-Treasury Opened* (2nd edn., 1659), ii. 398, 470.

The notion that sounds are natural signs allows Webster to reconcile the doctrine of signatures, the sectarian spiritual epistemology and the idea that words or signs are commensurate with the notion or thing which they signify. So, 'the mind receiveth but one single and simple image of every thing, which is expressed in all by the same motions of the spirits, and doubtlessly in every creature hath radically, and naturally the same sympathy in voice, and sound'.[38] Such sounds are the utterings of the soul, which man cannot understand since he has lost the ability to match perfectly signs with notions. Originally, however, Adam did understand the language of nature, the 'internal and external signatures' of things, so that 'the imposition of their names was adequately agreeing with their natures'. It is absolutely essential that there should be this congruity, since 'names are but representations of notions, and if they do not exactly agree in all things, then there is a difference and disparity between them, and in that incongruity lies error and falshood'.[39]

The language of nature does not need any formal lexical, grammatical, or syntactical components in order to operate. Rather, it is akin to a network of symbols and diagrams, the 'true *Schematism* of the internal notions impressed' in Webster's words,[40] which signifies simultaneously by means of association of similar patterns (which are in turn representative of the divine) as opposed to the contiguity of sense-signifying units offered in human language. In one sense the language of nature could be associated with the way in which astrologers interpreted signs and symbols in order to predict future events and the eternal presence of the divine. Indeed, in a way similar to astrological method, the Seeker William Erbery found anagrams which expressed the ever present immanent divine world, while Abiezer Coppe noted that the 'Dominicall letter G' was given by astrologers to signify every Sunday for the year 1649, G signifying for Coppe not only 'God' but also 'give' and 'give up'.[41] Thomas Hall put together the language of nature with astrological interpretation, identifying both as '*Magia Diabola*' which William Perkins had warned against, though Hall was

---

[38] Ibid. 32.   [39] Ibid. 29.   [40] Ibid. 32.
[41] '*Christiana Regina Sueciae*' becomes '*Hic est in virgine Caesar*' in Erbery, *The Babe of Glory*, in *The Testimony of William Erbery* (1658), 95; Coppe, *A Second Fiery Flying Roule*, in *CRW*, p. 101.

prepared to admit that the Bible contained symbolic numbers.[42] However, the identity of the two for John Brayne was wholly positive:

Out of the Word, *Astrologie* and other natural Philosophy, may be deduced, with Tropes, Metaphors and Figures; *Geographie* &C, by which men may be better acquainted with the Word, then now they are. This is the wisdom of a people, and not the knowledge of the custom of Heathens, which onely tends to make men such, and justifies them.[43]

By seeing a connection between the language of nature and the Scripture, Webster scandalized Hall. The doctrine of signatures is built upon biblical texts, not only Genesis but also, for instance, Psalms 19: 1–14: 150: 6: '*the heavens declare the glory of God, and the firmament sheweth his handy work*' and '*every thing that hath breath prayseth the Lord*', and 1 Cor. 14: 10, which becomes an 'oracle of mysteries': there are '*so many kinds of voices in the world and none of them mute, or without signification*'.[44] The connection between God's Word and *schemata* which represent the language of nature is, in fact, total in Webster. In *Academiarum Examen*, he expresses an interest in the use of astrology, while Boehme's works, by which Webster was so heavily influenced, often contained kabbalistic *sephiroth*, diagrams of the divine inter-pretation of the universe, so that the simultaneous and non-contiguous signification of the language of nature is enhanced in its pictorial representation here.[45] The *sephiroth* themselves were supposed to represent divine emanations from the original essence, so that they are intimately related to the notion of logocentric creation. It should be stressed that the type of signification associated with the kabbalah was not only the preserve of occultists or sectarians interested in occult thought. Kabbalistic interpretation had been introduced to European thinkers in the sixteenth century, and many learned men at least knew vaguely of what it consisted.[46] If other theologians were not so prepared to use it openly, they did use pictorial diagrams to

---

[42] Hall, 'Histrio-Mastix: A Whip for Webster', in *Vindiciae Literarum*, (2nd edn., 1655), 205, citing the first volume of Perkins's complete works (Cambridge, 1626), 39, 43–4.　　　　　　　　　　　　　　　　　　　　　　[43] *The New Earth*, p. 90.

[44] *Academiarum Examen*, pp. 27–8.

[45] Boehme, *Four Tables of Divine Revelation* (1654), sig. H3ʳ. See also *Astrologie Theologized* (1649), 26.

[46] See G. Lloyd-Jones, *The Discovery of Hebrew in Tudor England: A Third Language* (Manchester, 1983), 86–110, 144–74, 180–272.

interpret biblical symbols, the most famous example being Joseph Mede's deciphering of the seven vials.[47]

A slightly different view of the doctrine of signatures, in particular the way in which it operates through human language, came from the pen of John Cole-venman in a single sheet, entitled, *A True Alarm, In Weakness, unto Babel, from God*, which Thomason dates 12 April 1654. The author urges his readers to re-comprehend the meaning of letters and individual syllables in order to understand God's original meaning in them. Cole-venman says that he had elaborated a fuller explanation of this system in a previous tract entitled *A Voice From Heaven* but this does not seem to have survived.

The work begins with the voice of the Lord instructing Cole-venman to put pen to paper, which is rendered with a characteristic pun, '*Thus saith the Lord, Thou art well come Pen to Paper.*' Having attacked excessive riches and 'gay clothing', Cole-venman maintains that God confounds humans because they simply do not understand the true meaning of language. Every name has a nature to which it should directly correspond or reflect. Mankind is still under the curse of Babel and subject to the 'deceiver'.

The letters and syllables have a meaning which may be derived from what amounts to an associative, punning logic, and which results in the re-spelling of words. Thus, the signatures put by God into the word 'spirit' may be detected by re-spelling the word as 'spi-right'. 'Spi' is the perceptive faculty from God, the 'single eye' which facilitates the comprehension of the distinction between light and darkness, between the seed of the soul and the seed of the body, between truth and lies. With a stress on the authoritative power of the rhyme which is reminiscent of Coppe, the '*spi-right*' '*doth a ly defy*'. Cole-venman claims to know what the twenty-four letters of the alphabet really mean, both as 'single letters' and as 'compacted word'. The Gospel is a collection of falsely spelt words, which vain minds falsely understand. In effect they steal from other men's experiences for their own advantage with an intent to deceive. For Cole-venman though, words come to mean more than they usually do. By extension from 'spi-right', 'spiritual' becomes '*spi-right to all*', so

---

[47] See the diagram in Mede's *The Key of the Revelation* (2nd edn., 1650), between p. 26 and p. 27.

extending the sense of immanent inspiration. 'Of' becomes '*ouf*', combining the senses of 'of' and 'out' to imply 'out of', which mirrors the idea of the signature of the thing or 'nature' being contained within the sound: 'The unfallen Angels, that never did deceive, nor ever was deceived, will have the government ouf the vailed soul, from the deceit they are vailed with, by subjecting ouf the deceiver.' Cole-venman finishes his single sheet by asking readers to hang it up in a public place or in their houses, so that his mystical etymologies can have a popular forum. They become literally the writing on the wall.

Within this context, words, letters and even sentences became for the sectarians hieroglyphs or speaking pictures, where the material, visual, and graphic qualities of words signify as much as, or in place of, their linguistic sense. Words can only ever represent the signature, rather than be the signature, so that the cure for confusion must come in the discovery of the correct word for each signature. Thus, in the fallen world, there is, says Webster, only one notion or ideal-signature for 'man', but several different words for 'man' in different languages, 'Ανθρωπος. Homo, Un Home, Der Mann, Un Hombre, Man.[48] Hence the need for a universal character. Moreover, the comprehension of hieroglyphs and the language of nature rests not at all upon a merely rational, analogical and verbal understanding: 'alas! who spells them aright, or conjoyns them so together that they may perfectly read all that is therein contained?' Instead, the individual requires experience of the divine, so that the 'unsealed Book of God' where 'every creature as a Capital letter or character' forms 'one word or sentence of his immense wisdome, glory and power' is transformed into 'preaching *Symbols*' of 'the light of *Abyssal* glory and immortality'.[49] In other words, divine knowledge requires a shift in the operation of signification.

The Hebrew language did play a significant role here. It was felt that the secrets of nature were contained in the Hebrew character. Coppe explained at length in his preface to Richard Coppin's *Divine Teachings* (1649) how the letter A, Aleph, or Alpha expressed in its appearance several transcendent qualities. In fact Coppe is closer to Webster here in that he is interested in the transcendent qualities behind several languages rather than in one particular language, though elsewhere Coppe spells his

---

[48] Webster, *Academiarum Examen*, p. 26.   [49] Ibid. 28.

name in Hebrew characters, so that he endows himself with superior, divinely signified qualities associated only with the Hebrew.

Coppe's preface, entitled '*An Additional* and Preambular Hint.—As a general Epistle written by ABC', consists of two parallel texts, one of which is a series of biblical riddles and allegories, the second of which is a gloss upon the first text. It attempts to explain the 'mystery' hinted at in the first text. Seen by the 'immortal eye', 'A' breaks down into four lines, two in 'rectitude', two in 'obliquity' which are named as in Fig. 10.

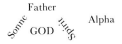

Fig. 10. Abiezer Coppe, '*An Additional* and Preambular Hint', in Richard Coppin, *Divine Teachings* (1649), *CRW*, p. 73.

'*An Additional* and Preambular Hint', in *CRW*, p. 73. Possibly there is a pun on 'obliquity' as, in addition to the sense of geometrical rectitude, there is a secondary sense of a divergence from moral rectitude and also, in the grammatical sense, a case inflexion. Coppe's identification of himself as hieroglyph belongs to a more accessible tradition than the Hebrew: 'Man is man's ABC: There is none that can / Reade God right, unlesse he first spell Man'; Francis Quarles, *Hieroglyphes of the Life of Man* (1638).

The 'A. Alpha' then stands for 'Trinity in Unity', and it symbolizes the reduction of all to the original essence. Coppe then proceeds to show a 'further hint' of the A in the Hebrew figure for A, **א**, Aleph. The English, Greek, and Hebrew all signify the same truth, the 'inward ground', the original 'out-breathing', or emanation of the divine. Coppe takes Aleph's *linguistic* sense to be 'one', and he proceeds to compound this with its hieroglyphical signification, which is defined as one 'obliquity', and a 'tripple semicircularity', named as in Fig. 11.

Fig. 11. Abiezer Coppe, '*An Additional* and Preambular Hint' in Richard Coppin, *Divine Teachings* (1649), *CRW*, p. 75.

In its circularity the aleph, perhaps more than alpha, suggests Omega, which is defined as the 'eye or globe of eternity, where the end makes towards and meets the beginning, and makes up a heart full of love, and all's swallowed up into Unity'. Finally Coppe enhances the symbolic power of A with a rather complex pun upon 'aspiration'. In the first instance 'aspiration' suggests the desire to return to the original, but it also means 'exhalation', that is, 'out-breathing'. Thirdly there may be an ironic pun at the expense of formal grammar, since an aspiration is a notation of pronunciation in Greek, ' ' ', which often precedes alpha.

Since the hieroglyph is pre-grammatical as a signifying unit, it embodies the pre-rational, the transcendent, for the sectarians. For Lodowick Muggleton, however, the elaboration of such diagrammatic interpretations were part of the 'seed of reason'.[50] Muggleton posits here the total impossibility of capturing any trace of the transcendent upon the written page, which is to go even further than Winstanley in the elaboration of transcendent allegories.

In the Renaissance many humanists were antipathetic towards the kabbalah, but both alchemical and hermetic *magi*, and humanists, were attracted by hieroglyphs. The concern is best exemplified in the work of the French Protestant poet, du Bartas, as Martin Elsky had shown, where words become receptacles in which the created world and its spiritual significance are held together as one.[51] Resemblance is important here: in George Herbert's poem 'The Altar', which is literally shaped like an altar, the central image is of the heart. Heart and Altar share a spiritual significance, derived from the similarity of their respective positions in body and church. The shape of the poem serves to enhance the sense of the poem, though in terms of the type of representation presented in this particular case, it is a question of a *similarity* between shape of altar and image of heart which must rely upon a *difference* between the two objects in order to avoid a complete *identity* between the two. Still, there is another close connection between graphic qualities and sense. In the Hebrew grammar published by the Berlin Jew Christian Raue, who taught Hebrew to the Baptist, Hanserd Knollys, there

---

[50] 'To Ellen Sudbury', 17 Feb. 1661, in *A Volume of Spiritual Epistles* (1820), 38.
[51] 'George Herbert's Pattern Poems and the Materiality of Language: A New Approach to Renaissance Hieroglyphics', *ELH* 50 (1983), 245–60.

are precise details on how to form the strokes which go to make up particular characters, so that the act of forming the letter becomes part of the signifying act, and the visual again becomes part of the meaning signified in the word.[52]

This last notion was derived from kabbalistic attitudes towards the Hebrew language. In the Christian era Rabbis had conceived of the Hebrew language as one which signified the divine, one which had supernatural power. Hebrew scribes were implored to copy characters exactly, otherwise they would be destroying the supernatural power of the words. In this way scribes came to have a sacred function (though, as has been shown, sceptical Renaissance commentators did dismiss this claim). The kabbalists also developed complex allegorical interpretations of Hebraic texts. The Torah, for instance, was seen as an explication of, and commentary upon, the Name of God, which could itself be subjected to infinite later interpretations to reveal literal, allegorical, hermeneutical, and mystical levels of meaning (the kabbalists were influenced by the Christian four-fold method of interpretation). Hebrew became a divinely signifying allegorical language where the visual appearance of characters amplified or allegorized the already constructed allegory in the text.

Poets like Herbert who employed hieroglyphical configurations in their own English poetry believed that the signifying power of Hebrew on this level was transferred into English. In the sects this attitude partly continued, though it was confused by several issues. Many sectarians, like Vavasor Powell and Hanserd Knollys, seem to have revered Hebrew characters because of their initial search for original scriptural accuracy. They say nothing of the power of hieroglyphs, though their quoting of Hebrew sometimes implies that they would allow a hieroglyphical reading.[53] Coppe is ambiguous in a different way. He is prepared

---

[52] Christian Raue (Ravius Berlinas), *A discourse of the Orientall tongues* (1648). By the same token George Fox's *A Battle-Door* (1660), 58–60 contains instructions for the correct pronunciation as well as the reading of Hebrew, Chaldaic, and Syriac.

[53] For instance, see Henry Walker, 'We expresse what is in our mindes by writing, as well by words; and so the Egyptians did the like by *Hereglifixes*: And men by their lives and conversations thus speake what it is in their hearts and mindes: And therefore saith the Prophet *David*, Psal. 94: 4. יתאמרו כל פעלי־און (jithammeru col pongale aven) which our English translation renders thus. *All the members of iniquity boast themselves*, speak themselves, their hearts speak by their works.' *The Creation of the World* (1649), p. 24.

to use Hebrew characters to enhance his own prophetic identity, and to show the superior signifying power of Hebrew over formal, Classically derived grammar, but he sees hieroglyphical qualities operating in all languages, Greek and English, as well as Hebrew. John Webster takes a similar attitude, stating that divine patterns may be seen in all languages though, as in Coppe, these are merely signs of the transcendent idea or spirit. Samuel Fisher the Quaker goes so far as to deny any divine signifying power at all in any language, including Hebrew, since the divine can only be known through the inner light, the internally perceived allegories of the two seeds and of light and darkness.[54]

In the sects the attitude also prevailed that the transcendent language could be understood at least in part through the physiological mechanics which created speech. The emphasis in Boehme upon the divine significance of particular pronunciations and mouth shapes has already been discussed (see above, p. 204). This led John Webster to posit the notion that the receptacle of truth in language lay not in grammatical rules but in the 'natural' acquisition of speaking ability through experience. Therefore people would learn language better without rules. The 'signatures' in natural objects and events were sufficient to suggest their proper names. Webster combined this with the utilitarian notion that 'practical' experience of speaking a language, that is, living in the country where a particular language is spoken, is the best way to learn a foreign language. For Webster words, names, and things should be learnt together.[55] From Thomas Hall this brought the accusation that Webster wished to teach children without grammar.[56] However Webster in fact implies that he wishes to relocate grammar, the necessary formal rules in human language, closer to the reality of the divinely interpenetrated nature. This also has the effect, in *Academiarum Examen*, of subsuming the search for a universal language into the search for the re-discovery of the natural language. Perfection would be achieved when all spoke a language which was universal, original, pre-Hebraic, natural, and transcendent, in that it would be above fallen human languages.[57]

---

[54] *Rusticus Ad Academicos* (1660), 142.

[55] *Academiarum Examen*, p. 21.

[56] Hall, 'Histrio-Mastix: A whip for Webster', in *Vindiciae Literarum* (2nd edn., 1655), 198–200.   [57] Webster, *Academiarum Examen*, 32.

III

Such linguistic idealism found ready targets in the well-known sectarian attack upon university education. Here, various forms of satire were the result of the engagement of radical Puritan and sectarian aims and procedures of thinking with the modes of language acquisition, grammar, and logic, by which orthodox learning was conducted. The list of those who explicitly attacked formal education is extremely long, including not only Webster but also Dell, Winstanley, Henry Hasselwood, Coppe, Clarkson, Salmon, Bauthumley, and many of the early Quakers. The characteristic image for knowledge which is not derived from or through the spirit is to speak 'parrat' fashion. 'Formal' preachers speak 'like a Parot in a Cage' for Coppe, while Webster inverts the charge that the inspiration of the spirit is mere 'babbling' by applying that term to 'Parrat-like' Scholastic syllogizers.[58]

The sectarians' ire here did not stem from specific attitudes to language and learning, though that is where the debate was centred: the sectarians saw the universities as the historic centre for the production of the orthodox established clergy and doctrines, the 'stumbling block' to lay religion, and before the Reformation, to lay language. However, the sectarians, as we have seen with Clarkson and Webster, did not wish to abolish learning. They wished to reform it according to the claims of the spirit and, as R. L. Greaves has said, to remove what they felt was a hindrance to the accumulation of true knowledge.[59] Their critique is, not surprisingly, an extreme version of non-sectarian Puritan complaint. So, while Winstanley wanted to put the knowledge derived from his intuitive 'reason' to the service of the Digger utopia, John Webster was able to refer back to the imperatives of his old teacher, the radical Puritan John Everard, who desired that scholarship in Greek and Latin translations of the Bible should prove the necessity of 'brotherhood'. Webster also referred to Everard's favourite, the doctrine of ignorance of Nicholas of Cusa, and Descartes's scepticism, to prove that in the final instance only the holy spirit can teach: 'if I should subject

---

[58] Coppe, *A Remonstrance of The sincere and Zealous Protestation* (1651), in *CRW*, p. 121; Webster, *Academiarum Examen*, p. 40.

[59] Greaves, *The Puritan Revolution and Educational Thought* (New Brunswick, N.J., 1969), 123–4.

them to the examination of my weak reason, and whosoever did attend the handling and interpreting of those things, did seem to me in need of the peculiar grace of God for that work.'[60]

The criticism of the established clergy on this account is no less severe. George Fox feels that the clergy have traditionally kept the people ignorant of grammar in order to foist biblically untenable doctrines upon them.[61] It is clear that here the most basic level of formal education is at issue. Laurence Clarkson's earliest pamphlets indicate that he could hardly express himself: the syntax is awkward and the grammar sometimes fails.[62] The emphasis in the universities upon eloquent rhetorical competence, either ornate or plain, excludes this side of sectarian writing. Joseph Salmon's warning in *A Rout, A Rout* (1949) could be aimed at the Aristotelian, the Baconian, or the Ciceronian: 'the form, method and language invites not the curious and nice spirit of anie man.'[63]

John Webster, of course, would not have agreed with this. Again, Coppe provides the ambiguous example, though he and Webster have similar starting points. Webster reveals the limitations of Aristotle's theory of modes in *De Interpretatione*. In this theory Aristotle states that moods modify the proposition, that is, 'how the praedicate is in the subject', and that these moods can only be of four types: necessary, possible, impossible, contingent. Taking the extreme nominalist position again, Webster argues that, since all descriptive words modify the subject in that they have each distinct meanings, all adjectives are moods unto themselves. Coppe, however, does not redefine terms. He parodies by comparing the formal and grammatical with the transcendent index in *Some Sweet Sips, of some Spirituall Wine* (1649),[64] the result being rather more comprehensive criticism than Webster's. At the beginning of Epistle III. ch. 2, Coppe initially inserts the subtitle: '*Being a Christmas Caroll, or an Anthem, sung to the Organs in Christ-Church at the famous University of . . .*'. The music is a synonym for the operation of the spirit while Christ Church, Oxford is ironically juxtaposed with Coppe's idea

---

[60] Webster, *Academiarum Examen*, citing Descartes's *A Discourse on Method* on p. 11 and Cusa's *De Doctrina Ignorantia*, on p. 12.   [61] *A Battle-Door*, p. 16.

[62] *A Generall Charge, or Impeachment of High-Treason, in the name of Justice Equity, against the Communality of England* (1647).   [63] *CRW*, p. 200.

[64] Ibid. 60–2.

of the universal church of spiritualized men, modelled on the early apostolic community. Then the Bible is juxtaposed with the Book of the '*Creatures*' (the natural world): both are 'the *Sword* of the *Spirit*', though orthodox Puritans characteristically took this phrase to mean the Bible only. The effect is to elevate unlearned sectarians to the same status in terms of divine knowledge as University men. The confusion of academic and sectarian trappings, both in clothing and in language, results in a comic release of laughter. Coppe's personal sense of exhilarated wonder at this upheaval enhances the reader's sense of the strength of the operation of the spirit, though the passage also reads as if Coppe were engaging in self-parody, in which case the academics are ridiculed by means of deflation: 'Tanners, Tent-makers, Leathern-aprons, as well through University men,—Long-gowns, Cloakes, or Cassocks; O *Strange*!'[65]

The parody continues with reference to the spirit in Latin as well as in English, '*Verbum Dei, in verbis diei, noctisque sermone*', while Coppe compares orthodox scriptural scholarship with inspiration. So *Some Sweet Sips* becomes a 'Primer' which should be read 'not by roate' but 'plainly and perfectly' for its sense and more importantly as a hieroglyph which symbolizes the universal presence of the divine, in Hebrew as much as in English, in an octavo edition as much as in a respectable, scholarly folio. The parody of parallelism is hilarious in its deliberately boring nature, suggesting the dullness of the liturgy or academic senility:

that can reade him within book, and without book, and as well without book, as within book: that can reade him downwards and upwards, upwards and downwards, from left to right, from right to left: that can reade him in the Sun, and in the Clouds, and as well in the Clouds, as in the Sun.[66]

This is followed by the picture of rebellion in which the spiritualization of individuals results in the leaving of 'pedagogues' who put people *sub ferula*, and the burning of books, akin to the metaphor of the burning of the flesh for spiritual regeneration.

The climax comes when Coppe describes spiritual regeneration in terms of grammatical components, moods, tenses, and parts of speech. Being in a hypostatic state is the '*Indicative*' state since it

[65] Ibid. 60.　　[66] Ibid. 61.

is a sign of inspiration. The calling out of oneself into God is the '*Imparative*', the state of union: 'He is in the *Imparative Moode*, and so are you: For thus saith the Lord, Ask me of things to come concerning my sons, and - *command ye Me*.'[67] Then the optative, potential, and subjunctive are passed through to express the desire, the possibility, and the certainty of enlightenment for all, culminating in the union of all in heaven, the infinitive. The parody is compounded here by actual conjugations of the particles of the Latin word for wishing: '*Utinā, si, ô, ô, si, utinam*' which supports the case for the optative, while the optative is still shown to be operating in the infinitive: 'by this time I am so far besides my self, as to add an *Interjection* unto an Adverb in the *Optative* line (*now*) *ha, ha, he*.'[68] The effect, given the unifying rather than categorizing operation of the spirit, is to recall the musical motif so that the particles become sounds, part of the babblings of the spirit rather than grammatical components. Finally accidence is redefined so that it becomes the point at which Christ and his spirit are born in history and in the soul of every individual in the mystery: '*Et hoc accidit dum vile fuit*'. It is necessary to describe this small parody in detail because, while learning is ridiculed here, the length and subtlety with which the parody is employed shows the hold which learning had over the Oxford-educated Coppe's mind at this time.

Webster's critique is directed against the syllogism, which he associates entirely with Aristotelian logical procedures. It is vain and an example of the fallen human imagination since it distorts truth or creates falsehood by not relying upon inductive reasoning and *a posteriori* observation.[69] Aristotle's description of the creation is challenged in Webster's sermons, while the syllogism itself is seen to be part of the forbidden Law.[70] In fact Webster's critique of Aristotelian logic is largely moral, which is one reason why several modern historians have found it difficult to extract any positive method from *Academiarum Examen*.[71] What we have seen elsewhere in the work, repeated imperatives to diminish human invention in the light of God's knowledge, appears with regard to logic, this time using Chrysostom on

---

[67] *CRW*, p. 62. [68] Ibid. [69] Webster, *Academiarum Examen* (1654), 14.
[70] *The Judgement Set* (1654), 291, 306.
[71] Greaves, *The Puritan Revolution and Educational Thought*, p. 100; Charles Webster, *The Great Instauration: Science, Medicine, and Reform, 1626–1660* (1975), 199.

Paul: 'Non veni syllogismorum captiones, non sophismata, non aliud quiddam hujusmodi vobis afferens praeter Christum crucifixum' (p. 16). This is coupled with constant ridicule of Aristotle, featuring strings of abusive words to describe the syllogism's divorce of word from thing through too great a concern with its own procedure, and fierce mockery of Aristotelian trivialization:

> *Therefore it behooves the respondent not to take the business grievously, but by putting those things which are not profitable to the position, to signifie whatsoever doth not appear.* O excellent and egregarious advice of so profound and much-magnified a Philosopher! (p. 33)

Nevertheless there is a careful use of Bacon, Gassendi, and other empiricists by Webster, which has been discussed already by Allen Debus.[72] More interesting for this argument, Webster draws upon the sceptical mysticism of Cornelius Agrippa to show how the divisions in syllogistic method distort truth. It may be argued that Webster's discourse is self-defeating on two accounts. Firstly Webster describes the Aristotelian habit of disputing about the art of disputing as like someone trying to see the vision of their own eye, that is, the act of seeing itself, but it is that very type of eye imagery which is used to describe God's vision in the Neoplatonic works which Webster professed. Secondly Webster describes Aristotle as guilty of 'battology', the needless repetition of the same thing, a charge often made against radical religious preachers. Though Webster would not have thought of himself as a 'battologist', Coppe was one who associates 'battology' with inspired 'babbling'.[73]

Webster also openly displays his learning as a token of his fitness to speak. While *Academiarum Examen* is packed with references to scientists, alchemists, and philosophers, with a notable concern for early Christian writers like Tertullian, Irenaeus, and Nazianzen, which occur elsewhere in radical religious writing, *The Judgement Set* includes references to Lucian, Cervantes, and Horace (p. 288). This, together with the fact that Webster writes in a discernibly sectarian style, led Hall to label Webster as a hypocrite in that he develops his own sophistical

---

[72] *Science and Education in the Seventeenth Century* (New York, 1970), 40.
[73] Webster, *Academiarum Examen*, sig. A4^{r-v}, 3, 35; Coppe, *Some Sweet Sips, of some Spirituall Wine*, in *CRW*, p. 60.

rhetoric, his own 'Iddle and Addle conceits'. In particular, his rhetoric is seen as 'πλαστοῖστ λόγοις, fictitiis verbis quia more plastis ac figuli multa configunt, ut haeresis suae idolum velent, vestiant & ornent'.[74] Hall is critical of the radical religious tendency to argue for the existence of divine elements in man by means of analogy. All judgements should rather be subjected to the analogy of faith. Hall literally cannot comprehend the connections which Webster makes: they appear to him as *non sequiturs*, while Hall maintains that Webster cannot genuinely disprove Aristotle's logic because he initially refused to define categories.[75] Webster and Hall look at each other across an epistemological divide, the former replacing logical divisions with Neoplatonic imagery, both mystical and empirical: 'So humane knowledge is good, and excellent, and is of manifold and transcendent use, while moving in its own orb; but when it will see further than its own light can lead it, it then becomes blind, and destroyes it self.'[76]

Seth Ward said that Webster should have attacked the grammar schools rather than the universities, and elsewhere sectarians did criticize the use made of the classics in earlier stages of education. Generally the critique was moral again. John Brayne felt that Aristotle, Plato, and Ovid were corrupt and obscene. He wanted a scheme for Hebrew learning (in order to enhance scriptural interpretation) to be instituted by Parliament.[77] George Fox echoed this moral revulsion, though Quaker historians have not really shown how this attitude was shared with other sects.[78] Fox imposed a form of censorship upon Quaker publications after 1660 to enhance the purge of Classicism, so that language would become even more pure and godly. The most worrying aspect was children's books. Classical languages are innately depraved for Fox, as he expresses rage at both the obscenity and insignificance of a primer's phrase: 'Where does a fox fart?'. 'A little above the hams.'[79]

Fox's criticism was not, however, wholly negative. The

[74] Hall, *Vindiciae Literarum*, p. 200.
[75] Hall, 'Centuria Sacra', in *Vindiciae Literarum* 79; 'Histrio-Mastix', in *Vindiciae Literarum*, pp. 202, 226.
[76] Webster, *Academiarum Examen*, p. 3.
[77] *The Unknowne Being of the Spirit, Soul, and Body; Anatomized* (1654), 2–3.
[78] See L. M. Wright, *Literature and Education in Early Quakerism* (Iowa, 1933), *passim*.
[79] *A Battle-Door*, 9th pagination series, p. 2.

Quakers wanted to restore language, which for him was natural in the sense that it had no connection with the divine and certainly could not bear divine 'signatures' from the natural world. Language should reflect the purity of the scriptural original, as interpreted by the inner light. This seems a surprising statement given the stress placed upon the working of the spirit within, but the early Quakers saw proto-types for themselves and the experience of the inner light in biblical heroes, especially in the New Testament. This is one origin of the demand for the reform of the second person singular from 'you' to 'thou'. Of course Fox's argument here rests upon the particular words chosen in biblical translations and the ways in which words found their way from Hebrew into English. In *A Battle-Door* Fox accuses teachers of wilfully neglecting true grammar, unlike Webster and Coppe who deny formal grammar altogether, and Fox goes to great lengths to show how different languages have two forms for the second person singular and plural.[80] This includes Latin, even though other Quakers felt that linguistic corruption emanated from Rome, both before and after the Popes. Fox is ultimately trapped by the inability of languages to match each other in practice and in meaning: even though other languages might have two different forms for each second person, there is no proof that 'tu' means 'thou' or 'you'. Custom defeats linguistic idealism.[81]

It might be argued that Fox selects random examples of languages to justify his case, but his duplication of instructions for correct grammar acquisition in first the modern European, then the Celtic, and finally the Hebraic dialects does reveal a historical concern for justification by reference back, eventually, to the original tongue. Significantly, Fox attacks not only those books which use traditional grammar (Richard Bernard's translation of Terence (1598), Cicero, and Samuel Purchas's *Purchas his Pilgrimage* (1619) for instance), but also the universal character movement in the shape of Comenius's *Janua Linguarum* (1631, ch. 3), which John Webster had previously praised:

---

[80] Ibid. *passim*.

[81] In '*Thou* and *You* in Early Modern English: Brown and Gilman Re-Appraised', *Studia Linguistica*, 37 (1983), 107–25 (esp. 119–20), Kathleen M. Wales argues that the stigma associated with 'thou', because of its archaic, liturgical, and socially unacceptable associations (since used by Quakers), contributed to its decline.

Scis numerare utique? Now tis *scis*, knowest *thou*, not *scitis*, know you, in the *plural*. But this Non-sencical way is commonly used by all our National Priests and Teachers; so also in the same Book.[82]

With hindsight there is a further irony at Fox's expense. A letter from John Stubbs to Fox in 1661 reveals a large amount of errors in *A Battle-Door*, the corrections for which were endorsed only in 1664, possibly with the help of a Polish Rabbi, Samuel Levi Ben Asshur.[83]

Though scriptural practice provides a worthy example of pure language for the Quakers, the absolute divorce of the Word or inner light from language does give extra sanction to the use of satirical language against the ungodly. So, while the search for accurate Hebrew and Greek originals is pointless in the final instance, those who engage in that search are justifiable targets for ridicule. In Samuel Fisher's writing there is, as much as in Ranter writing, a free play of argument and association in order to mock the search for original truth by logical disquisition and especially the acquiring of Rabbinical knowledge.

In *Rusticus Ad Academicos* Fisher employs the technique of presenting his enemies as self-defeating *personae*. John Tombes and Richard Baxter become monstrous aberrations, unnaturally conceived, and excreting pamphlets:

In the nine Sermons of *John Tombs*, B.D. which came piping hot from the Press, while this of mine to you two, is coming to it, put out by *R. Baxter*; which pair of blind Brethren, as much enmity, threatning, and Thunder without Lightning, as hath been between them hitherto against each other, are it seems, like *Herod* and *Pilate*, now made friends together against *Christs* Light, so as to make one Head, though two Horns, wherewith to thrust it down if they could, for which a Rod, a Rod in the Lords hand, is already ready for the back of *Baxter*, who, and his once Heretical and Heterodox, but now Reverend and Orthodox Brother *Tombs*, as two Twins that tumbled both out of one Belly, even one and the same womb of that *Babylonish Bawd*, are both to be tumbled into one and the same *Tomb*. (Sig. Bl[v])

The satire functions also by means of puns. For instance, there is the affirmation of the 'Fox-like strong' which carries the double sense of identifying the Quaker readership with both John Foxe

[82] Fox, *A Battle-Door*, 7th pagination series, p. 6. See Webster, *Academiarum Examen*, p. 22.

[83] This letter was printed on a single sheet by George Crosfield (Liverpool, 1842).

and George Fox. There might also be the hint of a juxtaposition with the wolf, the symbol of Roman Catholicism or episcopacy.[84] The pun facilitates a form of knowledge superior to contiguous logic. This is the impression Fisher intends to create, given that, like John Webster, the placing of all divine knowledge in the category of the spirit enables him to disregard the validity of any role which reason might play. Hence, to Fisher, John Owen's distinctions appear as absurd flexibility, 'the Lesbian rule' (a mason's rule which could be bent to fit the curves of mouldings). Also, the power of association enables Fisher to depict an Owen unable to make clear distinctions and differences. At the same time Fisher supports his anti-rational authority by juxtaposing an explicit defence of autodidactism with the parody of a learned controversial text:

Howbeit, I have answered them hitherto with no other then sober silence, partly because the first is captivated already from doing so much mischief as it was designed to, and both before and behind too well besieged to do any great Execution against the truth, being, *a Priori*, beset by a Book of *R. Hubberthorns* which it gives (as it saith it self, *p.* 34) a short Answer to, & *a Posteriori*, by a Book of *G. Whiteheads*, in which it is as soberly and sufficiently replyed to, and partly (if not principally) because, as J.O.'s *three Treatises* have one with another, as he saith, *Arctissimum materiae seu Doctrinae consortium.*[85]

The puns extend to physical characteristics, though they are not in any sense hieroglyphs. Fox's work for linguistic reform, *A Battle-Door*, has a border design on each page which mimics the shape of the battledore, or horn-book, which was used in schools to teach elementary grammar and the alphabet. There are also several associated meanings here. A proverbial phrase for illiteracy in early modern England was 'not to know a B from a battledore',[86] while a battledore was also the name given to an instrument used in washing clothes. Fox insinuates that his readers are both in need of literate training and in need of cleaning. The puns operate across different languages with the emphasis upon the spirit providing a meaning which subverts the pomposity of learned Latin. Both Fisher and Coppe ridicule

---

[84] Fisher, *Rusticus Ad Academicos*, sig. B4ᵛ.   [85] Ibid. 1.

[86] According to *OED*, the phrase was employed by John Foxe in his *Acts and Monuments*, ii. 474; A battledore was also used to hit a shuttlecock and Fox may have been making an oblique reference to the lightness of orthodox grammar and learning.

rhetorical procedures in this way. At the beginning of *Some Sweet
Sips, of some Spirituall Wine* there is a contents list of spiritual
discoveries contained in the tract, which is punctuated by 'Cum
multis aliis, quae nunc perscribere longum est'.[87] For Fisher also
this is '*De quibus haec fabula verè narratur*'.[88] For both Ranter and
Quaker here the parenthesis, which had been an elegant means
of stating a complicated position with economy, becomes a
means of expressing the multifarious workings of the spirit: 'the
Lord should lend me strength, life and leasure (not in my own,
but the Gospels Right, which now I saw must suffer, if I were
silent).'[89] Coppe also used learned references from classical
sources which appear monstrously out of place in the enthusiastic
context and would therefore probably have offended staunch
learned readers, episcopalian, Presbyterian, or Independent.[90]

For Fisher, Owen's 'Enthusiastical spirit flows with contradiction' so much that it renders the discourse as nonsense. In
addition to the portrayal of Owen as a man who is slowly
engulfed in a quagmire,[91] Fisher employs the dominant figure of
circularity, similar to Joseph Salmon's 'womb of Wind' in *Heights
in Depths* (1651).[92] Owen is seen to adopt all sides of an
argument:

Though I.O. who sayes elsewhere, the *Scripture*, is *without need of other
helps or advantages, or revelation by the Spirit, or Light within* (per se sola
sufficiens) *living, absolute, full of power and efficacy to save souls*, and yet rides
the Rounds so here, as to say that *without the Spirit the word* (and thats more
than the *Qua*: dare say, howbeit he means thereby but the *Scripture*) is a
dead letter, of no efficacy to the good of souls.[93]

Owen is seen then to adopt even more radical positions than the
Quakers do, while the circle figure is extended to become that
other round, the snare or trap.[94] The contradictory sense is
emphasized on the verbal level through the utilization of the
popular slang for argue, 'argle', a word which Marprelate had

[87] *CRW*, p. 46.
[88] *An Additionall Appendix*, p. 26. The Latin is from Horace, *Sermones*, I. 1. 70.
[89] Samuel Fisher, *Christianismus Redivivus* (1655), sig. A2ʳ.
[90] *Some Sweet Sips, of some Spirituall Wine*, in *CRW*, 46, 55, 59, 62; *A Fiery Flying Roll*,
in *CRW*, pp. 89–90.
[91] *An Additionall Appendix to Rusticus Ad Academicos* (1660), 20.
[92] *CRW*. p. 207.   [93] *An Additionall Appendix*, p. 23.
[94] Ibid. 30–1.

previously made much of.[95] The final attribution of folly comes in the verse suffixed to the *Appendix*. This is doubly ironic since one poem is in Latin and bears the appearance of learned satire:

> *Ebriaris sic, titubasq; 'grotas,*
> *Haud dubes nunc, nunc dubitas,* Εϱωτας,
> *(O Sacerdos)* δος *modò* ποῦ στῶ? Εϱῶτας.[96]

This is punctuated by a palindrome 'ROTAS/OPERA/TENET/AREPO/SATOR', underlining Fisher's inventive authority, while Owen's dithering is identified with the interminable wrangling of the Rabbis (Fisher attacks the Talmuds on p. 28) in a vignette which resembles a kabbalistic diagram and which suggests endless repetitions:

Fig. 12. Samuel Fisher, *An Additional Appendix* to *Rusticus Ad Academicos* (1660), p. 47.

It should be remembered that, despite the humour, Fisher was finally taking part in an important European debate over the nature and strength of scriptural authority. At least once in *Rusticus Ad Academicos* he uses the commentaries of Arias Montano (p. 88), one of the most advanced humanist commentators on the Bible, while it has recently been demonstrated that Spinoza translated Fisher and other Quaker authors into Hebrew.[97] The final influence of radical religious biblical criticism was not all negligible and certainly not confined to the Quakers.

IV

Though the pamphlets of Thomas Tany have already been discussed in respect of the influence of Jacob Boehme's thought

[95] Ibid. 25: *OED* cites Marprelate's *Hay any Work for Cooper* (1589) as the nearest example of the use of 'argle' to Fisher.

[96] Ibid. 48.

[97] Richard H. Popkin, 'Spinoza's Relationships with the Quakers in Amsterdam', *Quaker History*, 73 (1982), 14–20.

upon them, they deserve consideration in this chapter because Tany takes to an extreme the attitudes to language which we have already seen among radical religious writers. His attitudes to language stem from his assertion that in seven days God told him how to translate the Bible properly. It soon becomes clear that for Tany there is very little difference between translation and interpretation.

At first glance Tany's writing appears to be like other sectarian works. He maintains that Scripture which is written by men points only to a higher discovery, the transcendent essence and the calling of the Jews. This latter is for Tany, however, the prime coming event in this world, which directly precedes the return of all objects into essence, including Jews and Gentiles. Tany's philo-semitism is a significant factor in his attitudes towards language, as we shall see. Nevertheless, the radical religious dualisms persist in Tany though perhaps with a freer elaboration upon standard images. So in *Theauraujohn his Theous Ori Apokolipikal* (1651) the symbol of the two Edenic trees is reduced and transposed upon the spirit/letter distinction, so that we see the necessity to peer through the 'bark' of language (p. 15). Similarly the word 'Ty' is associated with 'Type', compounding a sense of bondage within with the confines of the material shadow or corrupt language: 'blasphemy is onely the tye in the soul of man, loosed from its principle of obedience, and from that looseness comes a dissoluteness in life' (sig. A2ᵛ). Tany also appears to have a sharper awareness of inspirational experience. Whereas Coppe, for instance, expresses clearly the images which come into his head during inspiration, Tany goes a stage further by fitting experience directly into his metaphysic: 'when the truth is, the speech is broken by the inside spirit, as it is essencied in the eternal being' (p. 35). Accordingly the representation of the divine becomes strictly self-reflexive—God is glorious in the transcending of himself (p. 15)—while the Bible is more than an allegorical mystery as it is for most sectarians, it is a 'microcosm' to the world (p. 70).

Tany suffers from the same ambiguity which we have already seen regarding the power of naming. Words are nothing compared with the transcendent truth, yet specific words in particular languages signify the supernatural, as hieroglyphs as much as sense-signifiers. Whereas Coppe never brings the two attitudes together in one work—they are in fact representative of different stages in his thinking—Tany is able to let both exist side by side with no apparent sense of contradiction.

In the first instance names given by God have talismanic qualities. Tany's Hebrew names, which God sent directly to him, set him apart as a prophet, and signify his power: 'Theauraujohn/ Tanniour/Allah al/Sabbah Skribahjail' (sig. A3ʳ), which Tany translates as 'the Lords Hi-priest, and holy writer [that is, divinely appointed scribe] of the Law which is love'.[98] The important factor is that the names are not English but a divine language which has a superior signifying power to English. Naming is also a means of creating distinction: 'for he that gives that name confers himself into that new thing named by himself' (p. 6). This is the 'practical' part of the 'Theos-logi', corresponding to 'outward' activity. With the 'inner', however, naming is associated with God, so that the divinely named object becomes a 'distillative' by descension from the One:

for God is union, yet distillative into three persons, but from and into unions Deity, so to be named by God, the name causes the named to be turned into a distillative, that this name hath received, the effects that flow, is love, else not new named.[99]

In the event this results in a reversion to original names. The English have been deceived by the name 'Jesus' because they do not necessarily know that it derives from the Hebrew—'*chevah*' or '*Massah*' which means 'all-saving, the all, his things' (p. 33). He proceeds to invent new names for Christ. Tany here returns to a kind of literalism: he says that the Greek for Christ, *kristos*, is true since originally it derives from the Hebrew *kopf* [kaph].[100] He denies that there is any hieroglyphical significance here, but what matters in any case is that the spirit may signify in the shapes of any language. As far as theories of divinely signifying language go, Tany clearly wants to have his cake and eat it.

Still, there is a predominant concentration upon hieroglyphs, which have the power to reduce names: 'the number of names of things are all but the Hieroglificy of One thing, in which that one

---

[98]   *Theauraujohn His Aurora in Tranlagorum in Salem Gloria* (1655), 11.
[99]   Ibid.
[100]   *Theauraujohn Tani His Second Part of his Theous-Ori Apokolipikal* (1653), 85. Tany prefers Polycarp to Augustine, because the former wrote in hieroglyphs: *Theauraujohn His Aurora in Tranlagorum in Salem Gloria* (1655), 37–8.

delighteth; in the goodness of beholding his things made: One more, Heaven, Earth [,] all things, are but a case for the Divinity to operate or act forth in' (p. 5). Hebrew, claims Tany, was originally written in order to signify in a purely hieroglyphic and 'virgin state'. It was given 'roots', and so sense signification, by Moses. Three 'radaxes' form any word in creation, so enhancing the implicit connection between words and things.

Naming can be negative, if divorced from the divine: 'the Gospel is not a lying name, but an over-powring and commanding thing' (sig. A2ᵛ). Hieroglyphs signify essential truths always: 'Now **ם** Sambah [properly *sāmekh*; Paradise for Tany] stands on her soul intire, as **ש** doth, but she is closed and barred upward, I speak as they are Hebraically wrote in their first Apparition: *Let there be light, and it was so*' (p. 13). Here, it is the shape of the characters which is important, though elsewhere, sound is as important: **ש** [*shîn* or *sîn*] signifies to Tany the English 'sin', so that while it is the Hebrew character which is the signifying component only, its meaning is comprehended entirely in the English language. Clearly Tany's hieroglyphs are not entirely divorced from earthly languages.

From another perspective Tany wants all languages to be spoken in order to gain the maximum spiritual knowledge, given that all languages are pale reflections of the divine (p. 31). In order to expand from the condensed sense of Hebrew words, Tany explains that he may insert Latin words into his pure language, so that we may have a language somewhat closer to English.[101] In his study of seventeenth-century English philo-semitism, Dr D. S. Katz claims that Tany's knowledge of Scripture and Jewish philosophy was 'less than nothing'.[102] Perhaps this is too extreme a view. Tany may not appear to be formally learned or to display any references to learned texts, but this does not mean that he did not use original scriptural texts to build up his own metaphysical systems. Robert Bacon reports that he came across the Ranter John Robins in a house in London. Robins was sitting in bed, clapping his hands and speaking glossolalia. At the same time his follower Joshua Garment seems to have been attempting

---

[101] *Theauraujohn His Aurora*, p. 16. Unlike Jessey and Rogers, Coppe and Fox wrote Hebrew without pointing as a means of signifying their return to purified speech, condensed without vowels. ·

[102] *Philo-Semitism and the Readmission of the Jews to England 1603–55* (Oxford, 1982), 110.

to follow his speech in a Hebrew Bible.[103] Likewise, Tany may
have been familiar with Hebrew texts, even though he claimed
that his knowledge of tongues came directly from God.[104]
Whichever text he had, Tany was able, for instance, to identify
Hebraic dialects. Thus, extending his English mediation, Tany
articulates Isa. 8: 10: 'read from the original root in the Caldean
tongue, *Ousono oon a sabat olemus mem devata abbat alus beneal sabat
allu phene solamo as inter apti sagat men*' (p. 20). In the original this
reads as:

עצו עצה ותפר דברו דבר ולא יקום כי עמנו אל'

Inite consilium, & dissipabitur: loquimini verbum, & non fiet;
quia nobiscum Deus'. It is the sounds which seem to count, and
so Tany is removing the obstacle of unfamiliar characters for his
readers. This would seem to be Tany's solution to the loss of
signifying power incurred through translation into English. Tany
seems to regard signification moving from pure sound (identified
with the spirit) through pictures to sense signification as it
became progressively more corrupt.

Tany seems to have known a little Greek: he claims to return
scriptural translations to their true meanings. 2 Cor. 4: 3 in the
Authorized Version is ridiculed for using the word 'gospel'
instead of 'light' (as in κεκαλυμμένον). He claimed to
know an 'Indian Greek' language which was the missing link
between Hebrew and Greek. So, Matt. 28: 19 can actually be
reduced to a perfect original, which contains the Hebrew letters
לטקין. Searching back this way, Tany decides that the English
translation's 'baptise' at this point should really mean 'knowledge'. Once again, the gnomic, in order to enhance the prophet's
personal power, is to the forefront.[105]

The 'radaxes' look like large versions of Hebrew letters. In the
example above, kaph is immediately recognizable. The letters
have different moral qualities. Daleth is an 'impeade', and

---

[103] *A Taste of the Spirit of God* (1652), 42. For Tany's glossolalia, see Hugh Ormsby-
Lennon, 'The Dialect of Those Fanatick Times: Language Communities and English
Poetry from 1580 to 1660' (Ph.D. diss., University of Pennsylvania, 1977), 372.
Garment's prophetic self-naming collapses prophetic and divine names in his own
work, *The Hebrews Deliverance at Hand* (1651), 7: 'So I, *Josherbah, tanquam, tanquan,
pistauvah, Jah, pashtauvah, Jah, achor, ab, sha, bah, Jah.*' This is different from the
monosyllabic words which George Foster sang when he wrote his *The Sounding of the
Last Trumpet* (1650), 10.
[104] *Theauraujohn Tani His Second Part of his Theous-Ori Apokolipikal*, p. 35.
[105] *Theauraujohn His Aurora*, pp. 12, 35.

prevents us from understanding the true nature of Adam. Hence
he is called 'Hamah'. Tany however is the Lord's 'gimmel', ℷ, which
together with what he calls Greek 'kion' and the English E are
key words to knowledge and power. Likewise, Tany reassigns
some English letters (x becomes k for instance) so that English
begins to approximate to the original language. Tany proceeds to
spell in some conformity with this reformed alphabet.[106]

The concern for language is still intimately theological. Tany
is prepared to compare his own inspired writings with those in
the Koran (p. 2), while one Bha. Jones questions Tany's
association of his 'Theos-logi' with mortalism (p. 1). Characteristically the soul is conceived as the divine breath of God in man
and free will is defined as obedience to Christ (pp. 3, 5). It is the
notion of naming in the original languages which allows Tany to
develop his re-interpretation of the Bible. Like Laurence
Clarkson in *A Single Eye All Light, no Darkness* (1650) he moves
towards an allegorization of the Scripture. This starts with a
ridicule of the Vulgate's literalism: 'Joseph's son the Carpenter,
and the Virgin *Mary* (thank the Popish translation for that if it be
worth it)' (pp. 7–8). Then Adam's Hebrew name is returned to,
Hamah, which builds upon the notion of the first and second
Adams, the second being a restored version of the original unified
perfection: '*Hamah* is Jesus, Jehovah, Eloal, L, The all of all, and
in all things' (p. 7). Note that Tany fashions Hebrew names in
his own spellings, so that *Elohim* becomes *Eloal*. *Hamah* is an
essential principle of stability. On the other hand woman is
rendered as *Hevah* (properly *chevah*), the principle of weakness.

Tany develops several ideas here which may betray some
familiarity with kabbalistic thought in its Christianized form.
Firstly Christ is identified as a virgin, the virgin itself coming to
stand for the 'womb' in which all souls are grounded (p. 8). The
implication here, if we can temporarily put aside the different
layers of symbolism, is that in the original state of perfection and
'hieroglificy', male and female are one. The uniting principle also
functions: *Hevah* is the virgin Mary just as *Hamah* is Christ. The
illuminated one becomes part of the substance of all these
entities. We cannot really suppose that Tany read Reuchlin or
Postel, and his only reference to this type of thought is the
unhelpful 'the Prophets Cabalasterial inclue' (p. 51). The most

[106] *Theauraujohn His Aurora*, sig. A2ᵛ, p. 16.

likely source would again be Boehme. As we have already seen, Tany's work abounds with Behmenist vocabulary, 'infolding', for instance. Here, natural phenomena become hieroglyphs according to Tany's own system: 'the whole mystery lyes in the Sun, and Moon, of which the creation ciphereth out, and are in their center heroglyphicks temporal of the trines celestial' (p. 17). This is a version of the language of nature, where the doctrine of descension is described in terms of 'declaratives', of the divine, or 'influs' emanating from God.

Tany extends the bounds of natural signs from objects to historical or legendary figures. Thus, Boadicea is a 'declarative' or emblem of England because she is lukewarm (as in 'lukewarm Laodicea', from Rev. 3: 14–16), neither hot nor cold, which Tany sees as the root of England's problems (p. 38). The important distinction to be made here between Tany and the other radicals is that while Webster, say, explores the ramifications of the language of nature to some degree, as we have seen, Tany is prepared to extend that which signifies divine nature, though there is no elaboration of the character, function, or meaning of that signification. So night and day become simple exemplars of the light and darkness symbols in the Bible. Alchemical and astrological elements are compounded as emblems for the same end. God is, in the first instance, the 'Elixer and that Attrackt of beauty' (p. 44), while secondly, Christ's placing himself in man is connected with a 'composure of Olymet under the equinoctial' (p. 40). Tany either assumes that the hieroglyphs express perfectly his own version of sectarian theology or that they are communicating something which man cannot yet understand. So Enoch's hieroglyphs are given an obscure place according to Hebrew astrology: 'in the clue of the Moon, under *Saturn*' but 'at length we shall see this product produced' (p. 54). Here Tany may be referring to the problem of the long lifetime of Enoch as a hieroglyph. Some contemporaries took the years referred to as lunar years but Tany's reference is too obscure to determine any definite sense. Nevertheless, the 'radaxes' or Hebrew radical letters refer to planets, and are to be interpreted accordingly. One other effect is that Tany also reverses at will the distinction between history and mystery, so that the literal reading prevails, paradoxically preserving the mystery. This is how Tany takes up the social imperative in James 1: 27:

To visit the fatherless and widows in their adversity, and to keep himself unspotted of the world. Brethren this is a metaphorical expression, but I will give you the literal meaning, that is this: the fatherless hold in it all that are in need. (Sig. A3ʳ)

Tany's tendency to see all objects as hieroglyphs (which removes the need for extended cogent argument) and his *goût* for autochthonous vocabulary entirely subverts logic. Clausal abbreviation leads to cryptic phrases: 'Thus he fell, how? Not by eating an Apple, but by being nothing, That is, he is nothing, and nothing can be nothing, Thus, he was not at first: was, not he' (p. 9). 'Tie' reappears, this time presumably with the sense not of holding back inner development, but paradoxically of negating negation in order to attain union: 'the Negation doth tie up the Affirmation' (p. 4). Things as opposed to names do not require reason to articulate them. Rather, by implication of the hieroglyph, they are simultaneously apprehended. This breaks down the capacity for the sense of contiguous thought, a crisis which Tany expresses in metaphors of physical and mental purging, or refashioning, similar to Coppe's discourse in *A Fiery Flying Roll* (1649):

The time of visitation hastens, *O se, o se, o se*, O thy self! oh thy self! oh thy self! is thy own ruine, yet these words will not print in thy spirit, but when afflictions have made naked thy vains, then thy lancing is near, then the plaister will be seasonable, but not before. (p. 4)

With his claim that the printed word destroys the capacity for hieroglyphical signification, Tany's reason verges on solipsism, something which we have seen in Coppe, but which here is pronounced not merely in obscure expressions but in the differently spelt vocabulary ('in origim') which sometimes is obscure: the 'Creterrised noise' (pp. 62, 63).[107]

In absolute terms the spirit exceeds the signifying power of 'radaxes' or originals but still some 'radaxes' are more accurate clues than others.[108] ‭ד‬ phe (?800) is preferable to ‭כ‬ (?2 or 3)

---

[107] As in κριτὴς ἐνυπνίων, 'interpreter of dreams'.

[108] Ormsby-Lennon, 'The Dialect of Those Fanatick Times', p. 373, maintains that Tany derived his 'radaxes' from the work of Francis Lodwick. But Tany's usage is specifically his own and is meant to imply more than Lodwick's use of the term as the roots for his language conventions; Lodwick, *A Common Writing* (1647), in Vivian Salmon, *The Works of Francis Lodwick* (1972), 187–97, 200. Tany simply draws upon a general trend in seventeenth-century thought.

because it is a 'golden number'. Tany admits that there are first-, second-, and third-state radicals, each of which represents a further stage of distance and corruption from the original. The Tartarian tongue, which Tany identifies as that which comes from east Armenia, is at a third descent from the original. There is no notion of these ancient languages modifying in time, so for Tany the Hebrew spoken by seventeenth-century Jews is the same as that spoken since the time of Babel and no different from Old Testament Hebrew. Significantly, when Tany deals with the original of the key sectarian concept of self-negation, one Greek word, *Othroas* (according to Tany's orthography) translates as 'a departing, a detraction, a diminution, then annihilating or a falling away', but a better Greek word, *Euseieel*, is based upon the Hebrew פ, *kof in morphe*, which directly means 'self-lessening', the importance being the actual negation of self (pp. 47–8). Yet Tany also said that sometimes he knew what his original language meant but he had no way of making its meaning plain in English or any other national language. Clearly Tany had taken pains to establish his own pattern of linguistic descent which has no small degree of sophistication, if equally no small degree of dishonesty.

There is no doubt either that Tany's writings and behaviour represent an extreme version of radical religious attitudes to language, in which the autonomous claims of prophetic witness resulted in an attempt to manifest an individual language which was divine and perfect, however cynical our judgement might be today. But along the route to Tany's position, there are many complex qualifications manifesting two opposite responses to the notion of a divine language: that human language can actually become part of divine expression; and so may signify in more powerful ways than ordinary language, and that human language cannot possibly be divine, so leading to a modern-seeming rational and sceptical critique of biblical language. If these two positions seem odd bedfellows (and for the Quakers, they were definitely conjoined principles), we should not be too surprised, since they were together making manifest the same paradox of the desire yet still the impossibility of expressing the divine. Similar contradictions exist in the discursive systems and literary styles adopted by the radicals.

8
From Rhetoric to Style

I

THE search for divine speech left the radicals in a dilemma. All speech seemed to leave traces of carnality, however reformed or pure. Reason's capacity as a guide for at least some comprehension of divine purpose was not trusted. With radical religious attitudes to language made in an explicit way, as in the last chapter, the problem is not hard to isolate, the thought close to the surface of their discourse. Yet no area was more vulnerable to the paradox than the actual organization of spoken and written discourse, which, of course, had to have a 'form', however offensive this was to the radicals. In this respect radical religious language attempted to modify the established forms of Puritan discourse, ultimately to let the spirit speak in full freedom and power, so the radicals maintained. The significance of the modification of order in soteriological discourse and the elevation of features like rhyme and songs cannot be overstressed, especially since they have received little or no attention from historians. Here, written and spoken discourse is most obviously continuous with other aspects of behaviour, starting with practices of worship, but expanding to include every aspect of life, so that finally, it is possible to show how the radicals were spiritualized men and women in the sense that they were assuming, in a pervasive way, habits of behaviour, gesture, and expression which were taken to reflect perfection and to have a potential greater than mere forms.

William Perkins's *The Arte of Prophesying* (1592) summarized Puritan preaching and catechism practice since the early 1570s and incorporated reforms in rhetorical theory made by Ramus. Perkins was to have an enormous influence in the next century on all Puritan discourse. He described an affective language which combined the proper interpretation of scriptural texts with a profound moving of the individual towards a sense of salvation. Comparison of texts according to the analogy of faith was matched in 'application' by the emotional power of the spirit operating through the preacher. This encouraged the listener to make a *voluntary* submission of the will in him or herself, the preacher functioning as Ciceronian orator, hiding worldly speech in order to attain self-persuasion at the point of audience persuasion.

Several other types of soteriological discourse were used effectively by Puritans, from Perkins's comprehensive statement, *A Golden Chaine: Or The Description of Theologie* (1600) to more simple dialogues and catechisms. Employing similar methods of division, extrapolation, and exhortation to the sermons, these discourses displayed the same marriage of doctrine, rhetoric and psychology (understood in Aristotelian terms). The popularity of writers like Richard Sibbes and Arthur Dent rested upon their use of simple affective registers, and the sophisticated analogies of 'preparation' in writers like Robert Bolton gradually fell off in more radical versions of Puritan writing.[1] Perkins's work has been admirably assessed by Perry Miller, though others have accused Miller of stressing the rational as opposed to the emotional component in Puritan writing.[2] However, the influence of these theories and practices upon the radicals remains unexplored.

II

Radical Puritans and sectarians continued to apply rhetorical patterns which were derived from the mainstream tradition, especially in respect of dialogues and catechetical patterns. In part, the ideal was embedded in a more orthodox tradition: John Saltmarsh's meditational *Holy Discoveries and Flames* (1640) is heavily influenced by George Herbert's aesthetics and embodies the ideal of clearer communication through the structured oscillation between glorification and purgation, symbolized by vignettes of hearts and flames (successively alternating) at the beginning of the chapters, the opposition of Emotion and Reason:

He that is only a seeing *Christian, hath his salvation meerely in perspective: and such is but Ethiopian holinesse, that hath a bright* Eye *in a darke body: the* Heart

---

[1] See Bolton, *A Discovrse about the State of Trve Happinesse* (1611) and *A Three-fold Treatise* (1634).

[2] Perry Miller, *The New England Mind: The Seventeenth Century* (Cambridge, Mass., 1954), 300–62 (chs. XI and XII); Patricia Caldwell, *The Puritan Conversion Narrative* (Cambridge, 1983), 36.

then is the part must be affected as well as that; and this must not be barely
enlightned, *but* enflamed. (sig. A6ᵛ)

Although this work belongs to the period before Saltmarsh's
change to radicalism, he took this type of rhetorical organization
with him into his later writings.

Such an adherence is not surprising. The expression of
individual inspired experiences, the widespread speaking of the
'free spirit' was a feature which became predominant in the sects
only in the last two years of the 1640s. Before then it was but a
part of a larger body of discourse, most of which was much more
rigidly designed to induce patterns of salvation in the reader, and
to communicate a particular theology. The organization of
sermon exposition, dialogue, and catechism was expected to
control reader responses in this way. Nevertheless, the roots of
inspired speech are evident here, in the first instance in the
Puritan preference for lay reading of the Bible and the potential
for 'expounding' in worship. Whether the Bible was interpreted
literally or allegorically, the appropriation of biblical phrases by
individuals who would then repeat them as part of an inspired
speech, so that they could claim that this was God speaking
directly through them, is another feature of the 'free spirit'.
Memory clearly played a major role here in this automatic
recounting of divine biblical speech, and there are the significant
examples of Coppe learning up to nine chapters of Bible every
day when an adolescent, and John Rogers's memorization of
catechisms which he would then repeat at night in order to ward
off evil spirits.[3] Still, even in the 1650s sermons and catechisms
played a major role among the sects while, as has been shown
previously, 'experiences' and 'prophecies' were made to follow
certain conventions.[4] Indeed, there are clear connections between
'experience' and sermon organization in intention if not in
practice. Just as John Rogers took from Bernard the notion of
every soul becoming a violet through experience, so Knollys
refers to Aristotle's *De Anima* and named the souls of believers as
florem delibatum.[5] The inspirational and the mnemonic were
curiously interlinked.

[3] Coppe, *Copp's Return to the wayes of Truth*, in *CRW*, p. 134; Rogers, *Ohel or Beth-shemesh. A Tabernacle for the Sun* (1653), 421–2.
[4] Henry Walker's *The Protestant's Grammar* (1648), esp. pp. 18–19, sought to enable believers to match their experiences with the Scriptures.
[5] Preface to Thomas Collier, *The Exaltation of Christ* (1646), sig. A2ᵛ.

Those clergymen held to be responsible for the outbreak of Antinomianism after 1640, specifically Tobias Crisp and John Eaton, pursued what seem to be orthodox Puritan preaching procedures and persuasive practice. In Crisp's collected sermons, *Christ Alone Exalted*, published posthumously in three volumes, in 1643, 1644, and 1648 respectively, propositions are set forth clearly and consecutively. Indeed, in volume iii of 1648, edited by Henry Pinnell and prefaced by Pinnell and the influential Independent, George Cokayne, the contents list provides a detailed breakdown of subjects considered. Crisp does not neglect proofs:

That you may the better therefore dive into the mysterie of this Propitiation, you must understand, that the word in the originall ἱλασμός, is of the same originall and signification with the word the *Septuagint* translation doth use, when they do interpret the Hebrew word that is rendred by Mercy-seat, for Mercy-seat is here Propitiation.[6]

In Crisp, the marriage of doctrine and exhortation is such that it is impossible to separate the one from the other: 'Ask your hearts this question: Was this sin brought into the agreement of reconciliation, or was it left out? Did God accept of the reconciliation when this transgression was in the agreement?'[7] The point is that Crisp is beginning to concentrate upon the exhortative element, so that while the basic pattern of Perkins's rhetoric is adhered to, the insistence upon free grace becomes unremitting:

So, beloved, your hearts are drie things, there is no sap, no moisture, no life in them. Christ must first be poured in, before you can get any thing out. Wherefore then stand you labouring and tugging in vain? Oh stay no longer, goe to Christ; It is he that must break thy rocky heart before the plough can come over it, or at least enter into it. As I told you before, you must consider Christ as freely given unto you by the Father, even before you can believe.[8]

For the more orthodox this sort of writing constituted a frightening neglect of doctrine and analysis of the Scriptures in favour of sensory images, similitudes, and analogies.

The emotionalism of Crisp and John Eaton exists also in the

---

[6] *Christ Alone Exalted*, iii (1648) 288–9.
[7] Ibid. 300.
[8] *Christ Alone Exalted*, i (1643) 214–15.

sermons of the Independents and Baptists stressing 'free grace' in the 1640s and 1650s, though the theologies of Antinomianism and 'free grace' were somewhat different. In fact a detailed analysis of radical Puritan rhetoric exposes the relationship between what have hitherto been supposed as different and distinct theological positions. Where Eaton's Antinomianism is characterized by an emotional rejection of legalism, Crisp puts justification before faith but also says that faith is converted into a good work upon which eternal life is conditional unless justification comes before it. By this argument it would be possible for most to become saved.[9] Within Puritan rhetoric is the capacity for the two opposite sides of the predestination coin to be contained, a feature which helps to explain the popularity of Crisp's sermons in the period. Perkins's insistence upon one single 'literal' meaning becomes, for John Bachelor, a single insistence upon free grace felt spiritually by each believer:

First, if you consider this grace in the *effects*, which it *selfe onely* is *causall* and *influentiall* to, *viz.* those *supernaturall* and most *precious* operations of *it* in the Saint [s'] *hearts.* Some have fancyed pure gold in the veynes under ground to be nothing else but a condensation of *Sunne-beames* concocted by the *influences* which *themselves* brought with them: which opinion, though very absurd and ridiculous, yet may serve to *illustrate* the thing in hand. For what are those holy dispositions in *renewed* hearts?[10]

The single meaning is significant in that it is another version of the gnomic conclusion which John Everard reached through his compounding of Perkins's rhetoric with the mystical and Neoplatonic tradition (see above, Chapter 3, p. 135).

The use of rhetorical models, conventions, and registers by the radical Puritans is widespread. In terms of defending himself against hostile attacks, Saltmarsh is prepared to engage in the satirical discourse which had become an accepted decorum in ecclesiastical controversy. So Thomas Edwards is referred to as a 'brother' by Saltmarsh, which has a biting irony since both are clergymen, and despite Edwards's attack Saltmarsh is actually suggesting a toleration of all reformed churches.[11] The simple point-by-point clarity by which Saltmarsh sets out the beliefs of different religious factions is matched in other areas by other

[9] See Dewey D. Wallace, Jr., *Puritans and Predestination: Grace in English Protestant Theology, 1525–1695* (Chapel Hill, 1983), 119.

[10] Χρυσάμμος (1647), 12–13.   [11] Saltmarsh, *Groanes for Liberty* (1646), *passim.*

radical Puritans. Henry Denne, a Baptist with Antinomian tendencies, constructs his entire discourse in *Anti-Christ Unmasked* (1645) according to an oscillation between argument and response. In the more mystical works such organization becomes a sense of preventing the worldly, human imagination from dominating the apprehension of heaven and angels. Such is the function of the insistent questions in Thomas Bromley's *The Way to the Sabbath of Rest* (1655). Rhetorical organization therefore functions as an instrument for the inculcation of the divine in the individual believer. Similarly Everard's disciple, John Webster, organizes his *The Saints Guide* (1653) upon a series of queries where truth is attained through a process of positions or arguments, propositions, and confutations. Fluidity between the sections is maintained by the frequent employment of conjunctions which begin sentences. So even with someone like Webster who stressed the operation of the spirit over formal ordinances the reading congregation still needs contiguous order to comprehend the full implications of that operation of the spirit. Similarly Samuel Petto provides numbered significant observations at the end of each inspired experience in his collection 'Roses from Sharon', in *The Voice of the Spirit* (1654).

The connection between theology and rhetoric was most sharply realized by Saltmarsh in his dialogue *Free Grace* (1645). Here Saltmarsh argues that justification (Christ's atonement) precedes faith, but that free grace is granted only to the elect, the believers. Conversion to membership of the saints is to become such a believer, so that believing becomes a spontaneous act of free will, though it should be stated that Saltmarsh denied free will and, as we have seen, advised intense contemplation of Christ's divine nature before making a profession of belief.[12] In the first instance he makes clear that this type of believing (free grace experienced through an individual act of will) is contained within orthodox English Calvinist thinking, and quotes widely from English Calvinists at the end of *Free Grace* to justify himself. Secondly his specified point is that many have kept preparation and qualification away from the act of believing (p. 97). It is precisely these two terms which the rhetoric of *Free Grace* attempts to put back into the act of contemplative worship.

[12] See L. F. Solt, 'John Saltmarsh: New Model Army Chaplain', *JEH* 2 (1951), 69–80 (esp. 72–3).

If the rhetorical expectations of the orthodox pre-1640 Puritans remained in the sects, they were modified also by the sectarian propensity for extreme and profuse biblical allusion. Henry Denne intersperses his sermons with large conglomerations of the texts he has used before embarking upon his exposition again.[13] Another feature is extensive marginal glossing.[14] It is not one text which is dissected, as with the sermon, but a constellation of several condensed together, to imply the necessary glorification, instanced here in the Baptist Robert Purnell's *Good Tydings for Sinners* (1649):

1. The word in generall. To all that are truly godly, for now to you I speak, *even to you my fellow members, and brethren in Christ*, Awake, awake, Put on thy strength O *Sion*, put on thy beautiful garments O *Ierusalem, thou holy City* Isa. 52.1. *Arise my beloved, and come away*, Can. 10. 13. *For the day is dawning, and the day-star arising in your hearts*, 2 Pet. 1. 19. (p. 20)

Taking a more general perspective, the rhetorical organization of Puritan discourse does produce distinct experiential patterns which the reader or listener undergoes. However, the pattern derived from sermon rhetoric is not necessarily the same as that which characterizes the recounting of personal 'experiences'. Broadly speaking this latter has been typified as enacting a process from bondage or restraint to release and freedom, a reflection of the casting out of sin and the onset of religious liberty through conversion and the arrival of grace.[15] Though the Antinomian sermons do dwell upon the nature of sin, both Crisp and Eaton spend more time defining the way in which the believer's saved state acts upon the process from restraint to release. Crisp combines fierce emotional exhortation with a speaking voice which is full of rational good sense and calm confidence. A sense of optimism remains all the time, while in one sermon, the *topos* of Christ as lawyer, counsel for the believer, is continually raised, so that redemption is continually present:

That he is an Advocate, is cleer enough; how he doth deale with God in the execution of it, is more obscure.

---

[13] *The Doctrine and Conversation of John Baptist* (1642), 3, 6, 21–2.

[14] Samuel Gorton, *Simplicities Defence* (1646), 11. For the extempore procedure of Baptist writing, see A. S. Langley, 'Seventeenth-century Baptist disputations', *TBHS* 6 (1918–9), 216–43.

[15] Caldwell, *The Puritan Conversion Narrative*, pp. 135–7.

. . . and yet, beloved, I must be bold to goe a little further in respect of the persons whose cause Christ doth plead, and in whose behalf Christ is an Advocate; I say, it is for all sorts of Believers; nay, I goe further, it is for more then present Believers.[16]

Though John Eaton's *The Honey-Combe of Free Justification* (1643) is not a sermon or a distinct soteriological form like a dialogue, it does display many elements incorporated from them. Like Crisp, Eaton dwells largely upon the benefits of free grace. There is less of the union of doctrine and 'application' than in Crisp, though the book builds up to a sustained climax in the final chapter: not so much Miller's charge of doing away with propositions as the constant dwelling upon grace. The importance of schematic diagrams here is paramount, since they make the message plain after some complex exegesis. Whereas the diagrams in Perkins's works always stress the potential for backsliding into sin, Eaton's schemata deal only in definitions of the believer's justification and sanctification. The reader is defined in the former category as subject to the atonement and the inescapability of wearing Christ in gloriousness, while in the latter category sin is inevitably mortified daily as the believer walks sincerely and zealously in the light. Justification and sanctification are inseparable. Unlike the open reliance upon biblical texts for this type of affirmation, as in Denne, '*He that beleeveth and is baptized*',[17] Eaton and Crisp rely upon the accumulation of stock affective imagery. Believers must 'cleanse', 'mortifie' and 'purifie' to put on the 'wedding-garment of Christ's perfect righteousnesse':

A Christian is truly said to see purer and whiter than snow; Yea, rather purer than the Sunne, and the Starres; notwithstanding the spots of the spirit, and of the flesh, doe cleave unto them; because they are covered and abolished from before God, with Christs cleanesse and puritie, which wee attaine by the hearing of the Word, and by Faith.[18]

This elaborate contrived language was not seen by the learned sectarians as in any way in conflict with the attack on 'eloquence' and 'dispute'. Indeed, John Webster makes it plain that it is not human reason which has anything to do with '*the things that are freely given to us of God*'.[19] Still, his rhetorical organization in this

---

[16] Crisp, *Christ Alone Exalted* (1648), iii, 169, 175.

[17] Eaton, *The Honey-Combe of Free Justification* (1643), 9.

[18] Ibid. 24, 33.   [19] *The Saints Guide* (1653), sig. A2ʳ.

pamphlet is extremely precise, with repeated exaltations and prayers, and a series of distinct 'queries'. Webster does not say so directly, but he seems to imply that his rhetorical organization is determined by the divine alone. Eventually this leads to a type of rhetoric which is controlled by the sense of a sublime operation of the spirit. It is characteristic of more extreme Seekers and Ranters, though these items were in fact articulated in theoretical terms by John Saltmarsh in 1645. Characteristically the definition is an attack upon fleshly 'forms', under whose influence scriptural allegory is as mistaken 'as *Philosophers* upon *Moral vertues*'. In fact the allegory exists in order for the fleshly to understand spiritual truths. The spirit is, for Saltmarsh, divorced from the allegory entirely but 'formalists' 'do bring down the spirit into the very Allegory, and so allegorize and incarnate or make *fleshly* the *things* of the *Spirit*: And so do many, both preach and write of the regeneration as a work of nature'.[20] The allegory in fact demands no 'right division', it simply speaks the divine rhetoric through the inspired speaker, though strong traces of orthodox Puritan rhetoric remain.

Seekers generally retained order through the consecutive discussion of doctrines, but expounding is not made according to any preconceived tripartite method. Instead William Erbery, for instance, literally 'seeks' the Scripture for passages which suggest his line of explanation. The precepts have become much more Erbery's own set of mystical relationships, his internal 'ordinances', rather than the accepted soteriological conclusion, though it should be noted that elsewhere Erbery does expound a text in the more orthodox manner.[21] Exegetical seeking involves a literal chase after principles, as in this definition of Christ and the Trinity:

follow him who is our forerunner, and gone before into the Holiest into the fulness of the Godhead with him; then we are said to overcome and inherit all things. God is our God, and we are his sons, then this shall be manifest; for *Rev. 22. 3* we shall see his face, and his name shall be in our foreheads.[22]

The alternating pattern of 'Objection' and 'Answer' in order to explain points of doctrine remains, at least through to Ranter

[20] *Groanes for Liberty*, p. 72.

[21] e.g. *The Woman Preacher: Or, The Man of War*, on Ps. 68: 11. 30 in *The Testimony of William Erbery* (1658), 146–51.

[22] *Nor Truth, Nor Error* in *The Testimony of William Erbery*, p. 16.

writings. This was akin to the form of the popular dialogue. For the radicals then, this was one 'form' which could be tolerated since, according to Saltmarsh, it was either necessary or it did not qualify as an outward 'form' at all since the spirit was operating within the godly speaker. Very effective use had been made of the dialogue by earlier separatists.[23] The potential for subtle manipulation of the reader in order to effect persuasion was not lost on the mid-century religious radicals. The positive, almost over-willing response of the addressee in Saltmarsh's *Free Grace* (1645) does not display the accomplishment of Dent, but it does identify closely with the reader, taking him or her down Saltmarsh's path of soul-saving:

Quest.

But did you not seem to be satisfied in the doing of those, as if all were well betwixt God and you, having done something that was commanded you in Gods Word?

Answ

Yes, I thought all was well, till I brake the bonds and vows I had made, and then I was full of terrours and checks again. (p. 3)

Saltmarsh comments upon each of the dialogue sections with 'observations', which make the theological import of each interrogation clear without losing any of the insistent tone, while the reader is moved from sympathy with the addressee to agreement with the observer, thus acquiring godly authority, having previously been judged by it: 'And in a *Religion* or *form of godlinesse* of this nature, there goeth alwayes a *spirit of bondage* or fear with it, which shews such to be *children* of the *Bondwoman*, not of the *free*' (p. 9).

In Vavasor Powell's *Saving Faith* (1651) the emphasis is equally upon achieving a sense of true obedience by employing the character of the publican, the traitor to the Jews, as a type of sinner. Further character types follow, including the Pharisee and the doubting believer, the latter making the transition for the reader between the gospel past and the present. The dialogue form could also be used to define a doctrinal position in the public forum. For instance, the enormously popular defence of Free Grace, *The Marrow of Modern Divinity* (1645) contains a dialogue between EVANGELISTA, a Minister, NOMISTA, a 'legalist',

---

[23] See John Robinson, *A justification of separation from the Church of England* (Amsterdam, 1610).

ANTINOMISTA, an Antinomian, and NEOPHYTUS, a young Christian (p. 1).[24] The minister resolves the opposition between
legalist and Antinomian largely by asserting that free grace
does not mean freedom from guilt of sin, while showing that the
two views do not occupy contradictory territory. The legalist
makes the Commandments the law of Christ and rule of life to
the believer, while the Antinomian asserts that the Commandments as the law of works are not the rule of life. The point is to
achieve a resolution compatible with orthodox Calvinism, so that
Free Grace is rescued from accusations of lawless libertinism.

Vavasor Powell's **חצפר בפח** *or The Bird in the Cage* (1661) was
written during Powell's imprisonment, as a help and assurance
to his church, and it employs the entire range of persuasive
and affective soteriological devices which the radicals took
from Puritanism.[25] Much of the work concerns advice on the
interpretation of 'experiences', but the stressing of covenant
theology, assurance, and self-denial is made through a series of
objections and answers, followed in each case by analogies,
'comparisons', which make the concepts clear. So some saints
unwittingly do wrong when they try to persuade in terms which
they do not themselves understand, even though they are all
travelling to the same place: 'As a man that is Exceedingly wel-
hors'd, travelling with others that are but meanly hors'd, drives
too hard for his Companions' (p. 61). The denser biblical
references in Powell, as opposed to the example of the earlier
Calvinists, give greater scope here for the frequent appropriation
of biblical phrases, with their accompanying tones of authority:
'2. He is *unbottomed*, and *broken* off from himself, he hath no
confidence in himself: his *Birth, Education, Parts, Performances*, and
best works are impure, and imperfect in his own sight, *Phil*. 3. 3.
Isa. 64: 6' (p. 94). At the same time, however, in exactly the same
fashion as Perkins, Powell ends his work with an inclusion of
piety through verses, a Jeremiad and lines on the idea of
Christian pilgrimage, so compounding his earlier analogies.
Again, there is no divergence from orthodox rhetoric in an earlier
pamphlet, *Christ Exalted* (1651), originally a fast sermon preached
before Parliament in February 1649, which proceeds by means of
a three-fold division, explanation, and statement of positions.

[24] This work is now thought not to be the work of Edward Fisher.

[25] 'rightly dividing the Word [2 Tim. 2: 15], to every one a portion'; Edward
Bagshaw, *The Life and Death of Mr. V. P.* (1671), sig. A4ʳ.

Nevertheless, more extensive alterations to orthodox rhetorical forms are apparent in more mystical and illuminist writers. As well as encouraging the publication of lists of queries, George Fox clearly saw a use for the catechism in the establishment of the Friends, even though the Presbyterian Provincial Assembly's *An Exhortation to Catechizing* (1655) blamed a decline in catechizing upon the emergence of thirteen·sects in the previous years. Fox makes the catechism fit perfectly the simple notion of the inner light. Fox's devastatingly straightforward first principle is just that truth does not lie, so that the rest of his points seem to follow without objection since they are perceived as true.[26] Answers in the dialogues become simple 'yeas' which enhance the sense of assertiveness. It is more than the affirmation in the soteriological pattern, as with Saltmarsh. Rather, it is an open acceptance at the expense of debate and the possibility of sin operating in the believer. As in Clarkson the Ranter, the light and not the Scripture dominates the conceptual logic of the catechism:

Q: *Where is the way where I may be kept from out of all distraction, and distemper, and drunken thoughts, and imaginations, and conceivings and my own reasonings?*
A: Heed the light, and stand still in that name that discovers all this, and there thou shalt receive power, to overcome all that, from him that hath given thee a light, to see all that which is contrary to the light. (p. 53)

Thomas Bromley's *The Way to the Sabbath of Rest* (1655) adopts a complex organization which maps out the enlightenment of the individual's soul according to mystical and Behmenist symbolism. In sixteen sections, each of which has a small instructive poem suffixed, the reader passes from regeneration, to mystical union with Christ, to the death of the soul in Christ, through spiritual visions, the 'circumcision' of the heart, the annihilation of all thoughts, a passage through further inward spiritual death and the experience of hell as selfishness, to a blessing of the soul and its transposition into the eternal world, where it finally 'lives in the habitual springings-up of the love in the Centre of its Spirit, Where the work is near finished' (p. 45). Nature imagery concentrating on the growth of plants suggests seasonal patterns,

---

[26] *A Catechisme for Children* (1657), 1. See Ian Green, ' "For Children in Yeeres and Children in Understanding": The Emergence of the English Catechism under Elizabeth and the Early Stuarts', *JEH* 37 (1986), 397–425.

which implies a correspondence to the actual life of the believer, or at least an engagement with a linear pattern of development which contains within it cycles of growth and decay, progress and relapse (p. 6). This pattern of oscillation is significant in that, despite the emphasis upon some kind of perfection in this life, the foregrounding of sin which occurs in orthodox Puritan rhetoric is still somewhat retained. One further example here is the near Ranter, Richard Coppin's *Mans Righteousnesse Examined* (1652). The pamphlet is an exposition of 2 Pet. 2. Coppin dispenses with the three-part exposition and imposes his own allegorical interpretation, but the shape of the work proceeds so that the first three chapters are concerned with sin, the next three with salvation and Christ, then a pivotal chapter on Christ, three more on immorality, three on an explanation of angels and allegories with moral consequences, and a final chapter on people who slip back into sin. Even here the oscillation between bondage and release is present, as it is in the recounted 'experiences', and it is the pattern of 2 Pet. 2 as Coppin sees it. So, despite the professions of perfection, the awareness of sin is retained in the rhetorical organization.

To take yet another case, in *The Saints Travel to the Spiritual Land of Canaan* (1650) Robert Wilkinson employs an organization of successive false and true rests to impart a sense of spiritual progress which has been termed 'Familist' because he moves eventually towards the realization of Christ as a clear manifestation of God within the individual.[27] However, it is more correct to say, as is customary with radical spiritualists in this period, that he compounds several elements, redefining several key theological definitions, to arrive at his own illuminist mixture. There are seventeen false rests which range from simple restraint from the committing of 'grosse evils' (p. 1) through obedience to the law, zeal for the truth, the '*outward* holinesse' of Sanctification (a radical redefinition by excluding it from any inward meaning), the notion of free grace, visible Church communion, gospel faith, experiences, and the gifts of the spirit. On the way, the use of fancy and imagination is rejected, together with forms, the appeal of the letter of the Scriptures, and appearances of God in

---

[27] G. F. Nuttall, *James Nayler: A Fresh Approach* (1954), 6, recognizes 'Familist' tendencies in Wilkinson's pamphlet, but while there are some instances of similarity in organization and vocabulary Wilkinson seems closer to other English perfectionist works than to Niclaes's rather different strategies.

either visions, forms, or administrations. It is the substance of God which is possessed in the heart that is important, so that the individual reaches the true *center* of the soul. Spiritual death or annihilation is achieved through an 'unbottoming' by God, akin to the notion of God as an abyss, where the creature moves from realizing the unalterable and unutterable Godhead outside itself to realizing it within, a 'carrying forth, of creature, out of creature, into the place where he had his first being', so that both are co-existent, 'to live for every [*sic*] in him who is now become his manifested being' (p. 114). Man becomes interdependent with God, by the 'centering up of a spirituall man in a spirituall place, not made or created, but a being of himselfe' (p. 117).

A different example of the co-existence of the spirit and formalized discourse is 'holy violence', appropriate as a register in which to vilify the ungodly, without losing the sense of direct inspiration from the divine. Robert Purnell writes with more than the intention of constructing a physical analogy for the appreciation of sin in the reader. The effect is emetic and terrifying, taking off from the point at which Coppe was to cast himself as an agent of transgression:

I see him falling upon his necke, that is, he hugg'd and embraced him, how? fall upon his necke? who would not have beene loath to have touched him? yea, to come neare him? Is he not in his loathsome stinking rags? Smels him? yea, to come neare him? Could a man come neare him without stopping his Nose? Would not a man bee ready to cast up his Stomach, upon such an embracement. (Ezek. 16: 4, 5, 6)[28]

Henry Denne follows a similar strategy in *The Man of Sin Discovered* (1645), compounding the references to vomiting with a fulsome impression of the sinner as a Bacchus figure. The psychology behind 'holy violence' becomes significant in another way when it is applied to religious opponents of the radicals. John Webster uses violent language to hurl back the arguments and actions of his opponents: 'throwing dirt upon us and hotly raging in persecution against us'.[29] It is as if violent expression is necessary in order to protect the tender inner man from persecution. At the same time sinners speak a form of violent language, so to speak against sinners in something akin to their language is to answer them in their own terms and to

[28] *Good Tydings for Sinners* (1649), 13.
[29] *The Saints Guide*, sig. A3ᵛ.

externalize sin in verbal expression, expelling it from the believer by attaching it to the ungodly.

Curiously enough another type of 'holy violence' is registered in more extreme religious radicals which is not employed in such an overtly affective way. Simply to evoke a piece of violent language from the Bible is sufficient for it to have a condemnatory effect, within the controlling framework of ecstatic spiritual rhetoric. Both Richard Coppin and Laurence Clarkson use the phrase from Isa. 66: 3, 'as if he cut off a dog's neck', without any attempt to enhance its appeal. They appear to rely on the reader's knowledge of the Bible: the context is God's denunciation of idolatry. The phrase is successful because it is so vivid, and the delivery becomes almost nonchalant:

> *as if we slew a man, or cut off a dog's neck*: and therefore dear friends, know this, that there is no love nor peace to be procured of God by any thing that we can do for him, or towards him.

> the censures of Scripture, Churches, Saints, and Devils, are no more to me than the cutting off of a Dog's neck.[30]

Violent rhetoric for the Ranters arises partly from their adherence when necessary to registers of denunciation. This is the case with Coppe in *Copp's Return to the wayes of Truth* (1651) where the recantation proceeds in patterns of repeated denunciation done to the point of exaggeration: 'Also I once more, disclaim, declaim, and protest against all other Errors, and blasphemous opinions therein insinuated, &c.' (p. 151). The verbs here belong to the formal vocabulary of recantation, and the sentence is repeated at each error, while Coppe increases the emotional force of each one by presenting himself as increasingly more penitent: 'to him I refer my cause who Registers my groans, and hears the sighing of the prisoners' (ibid.), 'never any man hath lien under the wrath and heavy displeasure of God for sin, than I have done' (p. 152). Repeated denunciations not of the self but of one's enemies become a favourite preoccupation with the New England Antinomian Samuel Gorton, who employs the same portrayal through vivid verbs of action as John Webster, but whose condensed phrases are far more intense:

[30] Richard Coppin, *Divine Teachings* (1649, 2nd edn. 1653), 93; Clarkson, *A Single Eye All Light, no Darkness* (1650), in *CRW*, p. 164.

Even so the passions of sin, which are by the law, having force in your members, you going about with great labour and industry to satisfie them by your submission unto the Word of God, in your fasting, and feasting, in contributing, and treasuring, in retirednesse for study, and bowing of the backs of the poor.[31]

Generally radical Puritan rhetoric displays a structure of oscillation between a sense of salvation and of damnation, which is assertive and derived from a sense of the indwelling spirit first, rather than any reliance upon the exposition of a particular text. Still this is partly indebted to orthodox Puritan rhetoric. The control of the narrator's questions in Denne's *The Man of Sin Discovered* (1645) achieves the oscillation by subtly inverting the dialogue convention so that it is only after the reader has taken in the answer that he realizes he has read ungodly words:

Ans . . . And we have the revelation of God that the price is not onely payd, but that also the *Father is well pleased*, Matth.3. the *new Covenant is ratified* from the time of the death of the Testator. That such things as these should come from *Rome*, that the hot *climate* of *Africa* should breed snakes and serpents is no wonder: But who could thought to have found such in *England*? (p. 22)

This pattern in Richard Coppin's *Divine Teachings* betrays not so much conscious control as a genuine habit of mind. Coppin's interpretation of biblical imagery has an effortless control which diminishes some of the brutal roughness of the vocabulary so that the final conclusion of restraint is reached through a steadily climbing tension. The mastery of the rhythms implies the assured, saved, 'free' nature of the speaker:

1. That by Dogs is meant carnal men, such whose nature is doggish, and dwells in them, as to be alwayes barking, biting, snapping, and snarling, as persecuting, reproaching, slandering and back-biting their fellow-creatures, catching at what they can, either in words or actions, that they might have to accuse them, as the Pharisees did by Christ, and so bring them into bondage or under contempt of the world. (p. 4)

Oscillation between the allegorical reading of the Bible and open exclamation or denunciation provides the central tension in Coppe's second recantation, 'And yet go away no more justified then the worst of Publicans and sinners. / But for my part I will

[31] *Simplicities Defence* (1646), 11.

not justifie any of these in my self, or in others',[32] while a few
pamphlets, I. F.'s *John the Divines Divinity* (1649) and Mary
Pocock's *The Mystery of the Deity in the Humanity* (1649), for
instance, are sufficiently short and simple to provide a deceptively
comfortable sense of definition: 'The fire of misery is greatned by
sin; its the fuel of the fire: *The sting of death*, but not the
fountain.'[33] In fact this entire pamphlet is built upon such
aphorisms, while Mary Pocock's work enhances the sense of
solidity by following a biblical order of subjects.

However, the polish of this spiritual and uneducated rhetoric
does break down for two reasons. Firstly the extremities of
Antinomian experience demand more than the circular, oscillating
structures, just described, can contain in an eloquent way.
Secondly these extreme experiences themselves return to more
orthodox rhetorical requirements in order to find expression,
though these requirements themselves also fail to satisfy the
demands of the spirit. The result is an ambiguous debt to public
and sermon rhetoric.

In the first instance, the demand to engage directly with a
biblical text led Samuel Gorton to become sidetracked, as it
were, from his description of the spirit's control:

The occasion of the Ark pitching upon this place, which me-thinks looks
like *Elim* in this wilderness, where there are twelve fountains of water,
and 70. Palm-trees, Numb. 33. 9. For our Apostle writes of the twelve
Tribes out of which we may draw plenty of the water of life.[34]

The rejection of learning and the lack of it lie at the root of this
problem. Those radical Puritan and sectarian writers who were
not educated at least put pen to paper, and this seems to have
forced them to confront rhetorical and doctrinal expectations.
None the less, the interesting case of the other New England
Antinomian, Anne Hutchinson, has been recently documented.[35]
Hutchinson was the daughter of a Puritan minister. She had
never been taught to write, and certainly had no knowledge of
Perkins's Ramist-influenced theories of exposition. She had

[32] *Copp's Return to the wayes of Truth* (1651) in *CRW*, p. 150.
[33] I. F., *John the Divines Divinity* (1649), 6.
[34] *Saltmarsh Returned from the Dead* (1655), sigs. *3ᵛ–4ʳ.
[35] Patricia Caldwell, 'The Antinomian Language Controversy', *Harvard Theological Review*, 69 (1976), 345–67. For the rather different situation of Anna Trapnel, see above, pp. 49–53.

heard many sermons and prophesyings, the result being that she imbibed the general notion of free grace without the qualifying mechanisms which would have allowed her to set it within the orthodox doctrines of Calvinist New England. Moreover, she broke down the division between inner experience and external behaviour which is so much a feature of Ranter and early Quaker experience. The case, however, is not so clear-cut with Samuel Gorton, who was literate. In *Simplicities Defence* Gorton takes the word associated with the notion of self-denial and applies it to the crucifixion and atonement itself. The usage is ironic, since he is exploring doctrine in a vocabulary which is not directly associated with it, something which would have been obvious error and blasphemy to an orthodox Puritan minister. Coupled with the awkward syntax (an aspect which will be examined later in this section), the effect is a parody of Puritan rhetoric:

So that you plainly crucifie to your selves the Lord of glory, and put him to an open shame so that as you know not how Christ conversing with his Father in heaven is found on the earth amongst the true worshippers, no more do you know how in his conversing with *Nicodemus* on the earth he concludes himselfe to be in heaven with his Father; on this foundation hangeth the whole building of your doctrine, concerning the sufferings of Christ, you annihilate the Crosse, then the which the Saints have no other consideration. (p. 12)

Ranter pamphlets go further in merging reason, logic or 'formality' with the totalizing moment of illumination. The reliance upon forms of disputative order, especially in the recantations, is itself a symbol of conformity. The recantations of Coppe and Salmon include point-by-point refutations of particular doctrines, an order which is determined by the order of the Adultery and Blasphemy Acts themselves.[36] The ambiguity of these recantations is enhanced by a sense of acute embarrassment at having to adhere to this form of order. So, while Henry Pinnell's dedication of *A Word of Prophesy* (1648, sig. A2^r) to Lady Anne Aston lies within the accepted conventions of dedication decorum (even though it might appear to be overdone to the modern reader), Coppe's praise of Marchamont Nedham is too fulsome. Nedham is addressed not only as an equal, but as Coppe's '*much Honoured friend*'.[37] The tone does not fit with the

---

[36] See *CRW*, pp. 133–6, 148–66, 218–23.

[37] Coppe, *Copp's Return to the wayes of Truth*, in *CRW*, p. 156.

manner of humble supplication which Coppe is expected to write, while paradoxically Coppe's letter proceeds as if it were still following successive points: 'By deleating . . . / By altering . . . / By explicating . . .'. Coppe is attempting to make himself as appealing as possible to Nedham by presenting himself as a worthy Christian and Commonwealth man while making the formal sense of recantation as full as possible.

A similar attempt to enhance authority occurs earlier in the same pamphlet when Coppe uses John Dury's very words in order to refute the accusations which Dury makes against him: again, paradoxically, in order to avoid the sense of ambiguity here, it is best to use the very same terms as one's opponents. The short, one-sentence paragraphs also occur in Salmon's recantation, *Heights in Depths*, where they create the impression of progression by successive points, though they are also intended to correspond to the organization of biblical verses. The prophetic and doctrinal in this pamphlet have the same form, so that it is difficult for the reader to distinguish between Salmon's own inspired statements and the requirements of the recantation. Both gain authority from their similarity to biblical texts. Likewise Saltmarsh's pamphlet *England's Friend* (1649) contains letters to Fairfax which are intended to look like prophetic admonitions. Before his recantations Salmon also displays a true embarrassment different from Coppe's in his use of the exordium, though it is coupled with a clear sense of his inspiration: 'Dear Hearts, / *I know it will be a wonder to some of you, to behold this Frontispiece faced with my Character: and truly it is as much my wonder as yours.*'[38]

Ideally Ranter discourse would dispense with all forms of order imposed by convention. Coppe begins *A Second Fiery Flying Roule* with an attack on Formalists, a word which for most Puritans meant anyone who stressed external ritual and sacraments, but which Coppe redefines as anyone who ignores the indwelling 'divine majesty' for the sake of biblical literalism. In a similar but less fierce vein Jacob Bauthumley would like to dispense with biblical citation altogether, otherwise '*I would lose, or let passe what was spiritually discovered in me, I was willing to omit the*

---

[38] *A Rout, A Rout* (1649) in *CRW*, p. 191. For an exploration of the roles of address in pamphlet and trial in the period see Gillian Alexander, 'Politics of the Pronoun in the Literature of the English Revolution', in R. Carter, ed., *Language and Literature* (1983), 217–35.

outward viewing of them in a chapter or verse', though *The Light and Dark Sides of God* (1650) does in fact contain several citations as well as overt biblical phrases in Bauthumley's inner language.[39]

On the other hand, when a formal disputation is adhered to, it is very difficult for enthusiasts to appear in an entirely convincing way since their methods of explanation and interpretation do not entirely meet orthodox requirements which were followed by literalists. The case in point is a debate between Richard Coppin and John Osborn, a Presbyterian (according to Anthony Wood) who nevertheless published in 1659 an attack upon tithes. Coppin's imposition upon Job of the notion of inner regeneration from natural to spiritual man yields an entirely different interpretation from the literal one:

Cop. *That he shall see, God was true, but the place and time was not true: he spake not aright according to the time and place as to the thing, that he should see God was true, but that it should be after he had laid down his body, that was not true: and accordingly he did see him, but in his natural life before he died.*

Osb. That the sight expected *ch.* 19. was accomplished before his death you onely affirm, without one reason or Scripture to demonstrate it; your bare assertion must be of no weight or consideration with me, so long as I have the text so plainly and fully speaking the contrary, let me hear what you say to this, that *Jobs* sight of his Redeemer was not expected to be accomplished until his skin and bones were destroyed with worms. What say you to this?[40]

Coppin's answer is to extend the notion of the analogy of faith, so that under the notion of regeneration, Job. 19: 26 is verified as spiritual rebirth according to Isa. 26: 18: 'Thy dead *men* shall live, *together with* my dead body shall they arise.'[41]

This attempt to expand the parameters afforded by discursive and interpretative rules would always leave the radicals open to the rational objections which were made by men like Osborn and John Jackson. Indeed, such procedures gave these critics a wide target in radical discourse, given that they were also objecting to the radicals' use of image and analogy. Finding a response to the radicals' manifestation of spirit in their style, in the very construction of their sentences and symbols, was a rather different matter.

---

[39] *CRW*, pp. 220, 253.
[40] John Osborn, *The World to Come* (1651), 61.
[41] Ibid. 63.

III

Radical Puritan and sectarian prose style followed the general Puritan imperative, taken from Paul's words in 1 Cor. 2: 4, that the godly should speak 'not with enticing words of man's wisdom, but in demonstration of the Spirit and power'. In so far as exhortation was employed, short clauses which constitute a staccato cascade of questions are inherited directly from sermon style. Here is Crisp:

Whence comes this believing? where is the root of it? Is Christ the root? then have they first union with Christ, that they may receive it from him; then must they first be united unto Christ, and made one with him, receive this faith as a fruit of that union.[42]

The similarity with Coppe's prophetic exhortation in *Some Sweet Sips, of some Spirituall Wine* (1649) is immediately apparent.[43] In Salmon the short clauses intimate a sense of reducing the inner and essential principles of being to their bare essentials in terms of verbal representation, 'essence' indeed in tension with 'variety': 'God is to us light in darkness, glory in shame, beauty in deformity, liberty in bondage, we possess nothing, yet enjoy all things.'[44]

Here, there is some sense of deliberation, and however strong the imperative towards the plain style, there is a clear sense of the need to organize syntax and punctuation in order to exert the maximum effect upon the reader. Salmon is exemplary through his steady rhythm and symploce: 'When you see this way of conquest, you will throw your swords behind you in an holy despite and scorn; you shall lay all your honor in the dust, and by that sweet spirit of meekness shall destroy and subdue your enemies.'[45] However, whereas the clausal stuttering of Crisp and Coppe belongs to a tradition of deliberation, the syntax of the ostentatiously unlearned 'tub-preacher' Samuel How attempts to mirror the plain man's thought processes. Short clause sequences are intertwined with ungainly longer ones, while repetition is based upon components of the initial biblical phrase. Double negatives confuse clarity, as does the attribution of two verbs to

[42] *Christ Alone Exalted*, p. 277.
[43] See *CRW*, pp. 51, 53.
[44] Salmon, *A Rout, A Rout* (1649), in *CRW*, p. 196.
[45] Ibid.

one subject. Finally phrases are denied parenthetical status, adding further confusion:

For God who knows the hearts of all men, knows that it was not my intent at all at that time to have medled in this Argument, nor with this Scripture, not till the night before I spake of it, and all because I knew if I did, it would be offensive, as it hath proved; and what I did herein it was by the advice of Friends, but now I see that *Gods* hand was in it, and I doubt not but for good: though it is, and may be my portion deeply to suffer for it: and for men to be offended at the *truth*, and such as declare it, is no new thing, even for the *builders* themselves to stumble at.[46]

Not quite such extreme features are evident in the constructions of Henry Walker, the so-called 'Ironmonger', in his *Sermon* of 1642.[47] The emphasis on the performance of being godly is achieved by the insistent present participles and the relative denial of pronouns:

Wishing in heart, and hoping it will be great, that so they might shuffle in, amongst the multitude; but not caring truly to learne, or when they are directed, obediently to follow, and walk in that path, which will, though it be narrow, lead them unto life. (sig. A3ᵛ)

There is an element of parody here, not blatant in the sense of Coppe or Samuel Fisher (see above, pp. 290–2, 296–9, 343–7) but in a more obscure way signalled through the deliberately crude appropriation of the orthodox clausal units associated with the 'plain style'. This aspect becomes ironically obvious in Samuel How when it is used to articulate an attack upon the clergy's monopoly of (religious) truth:

I will speake of some few things that are in different among them and us. You know it is usually objected against us because of our departure, out of the words of *Peter* to our saviour being these, *Whether shall we goe thou hast the words of eternall life?* from whence is concluded against us, if the text be not perverted, then we in leaving with them doe forsake Jesus Christ, where they take it for granted that he is with them, and not with those that forsake them.[48]

---

[46] Samuel How, *The Sufficiencie of the Spirits Teaching* (1640; 2nd edn., 1644), sig. [A]3ʳ.

[47] There are at least two and possibly three Henry Walkers in the 1640s. Whether the Ironmonger is the same as the leader of the Independent congregation of the 1650s is not decisively known. On Walker the 'Ironmonger''s *A Gad of Steele* (1641), Thomason wrote that he was ordained by Archbishop Laud.

[48] How, *The Sufficiencie of the Spirits Teaching* (1644), sig. F4ᵛ.

More openly still, the logic carried by the syntax of Thomas Tany appears to operate by means of parataxis and ellipsis. The reader is expected to make considerable leaps in argument which are either not stated at all, or are expressed merely by conjunction:

> Now, how could man Fall, having three persons in himself: Thus he fell, how? Not by eating an apple, but by being nothing, That is, he is nothing, and nothing can be nothing, Thus, he was not at first: I was, not he; he is by me: O Lord how wonderful is thy marvellous hidden depths.[49]

The other feature is sentence length. Given that seventeenth-century conventions of punctuation operated in such a way that semi-colons functioned as stops, so that sentence length is not a factor in the definition of clear sense, Laurence Clarkson's sentences are still extremely long. What is more significant is that the logic of these sentences operates by means of obscure connecting words, conjunctions or definite articles, which are used to introduce clauses whose sense is not always continuous with the sense of the previous one:

> That you the said Communality of *England*, have chosen and maintained an assembly of men, as cruell enemies to Justice-equity as ever any, these you have approved of & all their actions & proceedings to be just; insomuch, that when they had spent you many thousands, they brought to birth a child without life, created of the self-same substance of its Grandfather (*to wit*) the Directory, the Grand-child of the Booke of Common prayer: this at their command you suffered to be proclaimed in Church and Chappell for your God, and thereupon fall downe and worship it; an act detestable, yea contrary to the direction of the Law of Justice Equity.[50]

In one way this is a language of the spirit and the grammatical features signify it as such. Clarkson's language is not dissimilar to that of the dying speech of John Kayes, a minister from Kent whose last words John Saltmarsh published with a commentary in *A Voice from Heaven* (1644). Dying men's words were supposed to be prophetic, since they were coming close to the divine. What is more, their role as memorial rhetoric for

---

[49] Tany, *Theauraujohn his Theous Ori Apokolipikal* (1651), 8–9.
[50] *A Generall Charge, or Impeachment of High-Treason, in the name of Justice Equity, against the Communality of England* (1647), p. 8.

radical Puritans is pointed to by Kayes who said that he wanted his words to replace a funeral sermon. The speech consists simply of a series of extremely brief clauses in breathless succession. Kayes is literally running out of breath and the emotionally heightened anguish represents the spirit speaking in Kayes. Personal pronouns and exclamations perform the main connecting role: 'You see here a dying man, I know I must die, I shall only live till morning, you may conceive what you will, but it is all in vain, I shall continue thus as you see me till morning, but I shall then die, oh, I shall go down to the grave and be no more, oh, I shall die' (p. 1).

An increase in the syntactic prominence of personal pronouns is an index of the increasing importance of prophetic identity, and the desire to communicate the power of prophecy to the readers or audience. In Clarkson's early pamphlet, *Truth Released from Prison* (1646), a simple 'I' and 'You' does not contain a sufficiently strong signifying value for the difference between Clarkson and the people of Preston: 'saying I (yea I) a poore despised *Prophet*, am not the troubler of *Israel*, &c, but thou (yea thou) *King Ahab*, art he that troubleth *Israell*' (sig. A7ʳ). The effect is to assert paradoxically the actual identity between Clarkson and his home-townspeople since the constant fore-grounding of the two separate identities makes them appear inseparable: '*notwithstanding your displeasure herein, I dare not, I cannot*; but what I have seene and heard, declare unto you, (*yea you*) my Countrymen' (sig. A3ᵛ).

The short clauses with the enormous lists are derived from biblical syntax. In John Webster it is a conscious appropriation, though in writers claiming to be directly inspired it was to be seen as the work of the spirit, as we have seen:

Now *the works of the flesh are manifest, which are these; adultery, fornication, uncleanness, lasciviousness, idolatry, witchcraft, hatred, variance, emulations, wrath, strife, seditions, heresies, envyings, murders, drunkenness, and such like. But the fruits of the Spirit are love, joy, peace.*[51]

Webster lists his reference as Gal. 5: 19, 20, 21, 22, 23. The biblical tone, rhythms, and parallelisms remain when the biblical references are introduced by means of marginal glosses rather than in direct quotation.

[51] *The Saints Guide* (1653), 11.

In Winstanley the incantatory or exhortative rhythms stay, but the swift successive clauses now function directly to communicate a number of concepts in as short a space as possible. It would be wrong, I think, to agree with Olivier Lutaud's statement that Winstanley maintains simultaneously a litany and an exhortation since there is no such formal creed in Winstanley's work.[52] Questions of belief exist on the epistemological level, while Winstanley's syntax upholds the all-embracing nature of his vision:

But this Kingly power is above all, and will tread all covetousness, pride, envy, and self-love, and all other enemies whatsoever, under his feet, and take the kingdom and government of the Creation out of the hand of the self-seeking and self-honouring Flesh.[53]

Clearly this procedure is applicable to both political and religious fields, partly because Winstanley sees no difference between the two spheres. This is the operation again of Winstanley's intuitive Reason, so that clear, straightforward syntax is a sign of godliness and inexorable righteousness: 'they cry who bids most wages, they will be on the strongest side, for an Earthly maintenance; yea, and when they are lifted up, they would Rule too'.[54]

Turning from the incantatory to the openly musical, inspired singing seems to have generated a balance between the need for order and liberty. It is hard to see intention not being present here, even though the form is supposedly extempore. The gift of singing came to the Baptist Katherine Sutton in February 1655 as the voice of God or Christ within. She delivers her verses as prophecies:

> *Didst thou not hear a voyce from on high,*
> *Deny your selves (take up the crosse) or verily you shall die?*[55]

The simplicity, the crudeness, the lack of metre, and the obvious rhymes bely the spontaneity of the song, but what makes it remarkable is the parallel 'd' and 'v' sounds, modulating yet sustaining the feeling of deep sublimity. This is aided by the

---

[52] Lutaud, *Winstanley: Son œuvre et le radicalisme 'Digger'*, 2 vols. (Lille, 1973), i. 670.
[53] *A new-Yeers Gift for the Parliament and Armie* (1649), 2.   [54] Ibid. 6.
[55] Katherine Sutton, *A Christian Womans Experiences of the glorious working of Gods free grace* (Rotterdam, 1663), 16. Another Baptist with the gift of singing adhered to iambic pentameters: see Susanna Bateman, *I matter not how I appear to Man* (1657).

vowels on the ends of the lines, changing from 'i' in the first, to 'e' ('verily'), while the centre of both lines contains 'o's (of different types), yet this brings together the theology of the prophecy, as word, 'voyce', and atonement, 'crosse', are connected.

In genuine ecstasies the pattern is familiar to Kayes's dying words. Anna Trapnel's inspired speeches in *The Cry of a Stone* (1654) were taken down as she spoke them, addressing both people and God in prayers, and the sequence of clauses does correspond to that which Saltmarsh took down from Kayes, even if Trapnel's clauses are somewhat longer. The exclamations are again abundant, 'Oh do thou fill their pools . . . Oh fill all places', (p. 24), while the repeated statements of desire are matched by an intensity of pronoun usage similar to Clarkson's:

Thou hast a few names that are cloathed in white [Rev. 3: 4], whom thou dost abundantly delight in, and they delight in thee; they commit their way unto thee, and thou wilt not destroy them, though they live in *Sodom*; thou hast many precious lights in this Nation, in this City, or it would be suddainly burnt with fire. (p. 24)

The desire to bend the will of God is thus strong, and it is compounded elsewhere by the frequent repetitions, another prophetic gesture. Coppe's *A Fiery Flying Roll* is often remembered for its use of God's words in Ezekiel 21: 27: 'Thus saith the Lord, *I inform you, that I overturn, overturn, overturn*' (p. 86). In fact the phrase is used in several tracts. Coppe is most probably following William Sedgwick in *Mr. William Sedgwicks Letter to his Excellency Thomas Lord Fairfax* (1649, sig. A2^v). Indeed, Coppe believed that he had the altruistic spirit of Sedgwick within him, while the context of Sedgwick's usage is as prophetic as Coppe's.[56]

The phrase is also used by Vavasor Powell in *Christ Exalted* (1651, p. 51) though without the sense of an indwelling God as in Coppe. Indeed, the phrase was identified as socially subversive in a direct sense as well as being prophetic: later on, Francis Higginson, in an attack on the Quakers, saw the Baptist Thomas Collier as responsible for passing on to them the Levelling phrase, 'overturn, overturn, overturn'.[57] In fact, God's voice is distinguishd by its repetitive qualities: '*Vengeance, vengeance, vengeance, Plagues, plagues, upon the Inhabitants of the earth;*

---

[56] Coppe, *A Second Fiery Flying Roule*, in *CRW*, p. 109.
[57] Higginson, *A Brief Relation of the Irreligion of the Northern Quakers* (1653), 23.

Fire, fire, fire, Sword, sword.'[58] The origins of this are arguably to be found in a more rational method of scriptural exposition. William Dell uses repetition of scriptural phrases in order to establish clearly the precise meaning of several words from John 4: 23: 'worship the Father in Spirit and Truth, for the Father seeketh such to worship him. God is a Spirit, and they that worship him must worship him in Spirit and Truth.'[59]

Repetition is a means of maintaining the emotional power of particular exclamations or vocatives. The intention and the effect is to make present again the particular sense and emotions associated with specific words: Robert Purnell's 'Come, come, come' plays exactly the same role in calling down Christ as Coppe's *'overturn, overturn, overturn'* does in threatening the levelling apocalypse.[60] The spirit operating inside the speaker also attempts to grasp all thoughts at once, to 'overgo' what the human brain is capable of under normal circumstances.

Repetition in Quaker literature is a somewhat more sophisti-cated matter. Quakers tended to identify sermons with pro-phesying: Quaker ministers were not allowed to write down sermons before they were delivered. From the few sermons which were written down, it seems that Quaker prophets relied upon the frequent repetition of stock scriptural phrases.[61] In Quaker tracts this method becomes transposed into powerful elabora-tions on particular biblical keywords which are developed by free association upon semantic connections. For example, George Fox in *Here is Declared the Manner of the Naming of Children* (1658) performs a stunning piece of scatology, based upon 'vomit' from Isa. 28: 8, Prov. 23: 8; 26: 11, 2 Pet. 2: 22 and Jer. 48 and 'drunk' from 1 Thess. 5: 7, building up a relentless verbal and pictorial impression of the clergy choking upon their own vomit, that is, their pamphlets. It is an endless process of corruption:

That which one spews out, & vomits out in their Books & Pamphlets, that another priest he takes the same up, & he eats the books, & vomits

---

[58] Powell, *Christ Exalted above All Creatures By God His Father* (1651), 83.

[59] *Uniformity Examined* (1646) in *Selected Works of William Dell* (1773), 60.

[60] Purnell, *Good Tydings for Sinners* (1649), 9; Coppe, *A Fiery Flying Roll*, in *CRW*, p. 86.

[61] All Quaker sermons which survive were delivered after 1660, however. See R. Bauman, *Let your words be few: Symbolism of Speaking and Silence among Seventeenth-Century Quakers* (Cambridge, 1983), p. 76. Henry Clark the Quaker said that the psalmodists Sternhold and Hopkins were mere poets: *A Description of the Prophets* (1655), 21.

it up again, till the whole Nation is filled with their vomit: And this hath been the state since the dayes of the Apostles, in the apostacy. (p. 7)

The action is transferred to God who spews out of his own mouth the drunkards, who for Fox are the entire collection of outward, formal churches, separated or otherwise.

One way of registering more than one thought at any one time is through the use of parenthesis. Though parenthesis for the Ranters is a means of exploring prophetic identity in relation to the speaking subject in each pamphlet, parenthesis exists in less radical sectarian pamphlets in order to make plain a sense of heightened imagination. Vavasor Powell uses parentheses to indicate his awareness of rhetorical nicety and to foreground his memorial control of significant biblical echoes: '*I now humbly present it to you, with a small portall (or short Epistle) for the Edifice it selfe, (being so little, and built with so many unhewne stones,) deserves not a great* Porch *or Gate before it.*'[62] As with John Webster in *The Saints Guide* the use of memory to call up a biblical echo is explicit rather than an example of sublime 'pouring forth'. Similarly, in Coppe, parentheses facilitate the expression of more than the syntax can usually accommodate. In each case the sense is continuous with the primary clauses: 'But thou shalt (first) drink a bitter cup', 'various streames of light (in the night) which appeared'.[63]

It should be noted that the parentheses also allow Coppe to comment upon his possession by the Divine Majesty, but this other usage is more frequent and suggests a thought process in which the impetus is to enact statement and the qualification of that statement simultaneously: 'for (as I live) it is the day of my vengeance'; 'It is my good will and pleasure (only) to single out the former story'; '*For I was (really, in very deed) besides myself*'; '*and NO FLESH (no not the FLESH of FOWLES which sore aloft) can stand before it*'.[64] In fact, in this latter tract Coppe is aware of his entirely parenthetical discourse, not just in terms of clauses but in terms of whole digressions, and his mention of it is a means of control, so that he can return to the formal order of the recantation.[65] By contrast, Winstanley uses parentheses as a means of building up

---

[62] *Saving Faith* (1651), sig. A1ʳ.
[63] *A Fiery Flying Roll* (1649), in *CRW*, p. 82.　　[64] *CRW*, pp. 99, 105, 129.
[65] Ibid. 121. It should be remembered that parentheses were often used as commas.

the power of his condemnation of the rich. His analysis of the
landed order's confiscation of common freedoms is repeatedly
prefaced by an '(I say)', but the final condemnation is delivered
as a common voice, where the exclusive parenthesis has been
broken down by the weight of community: 'Therefore we the
Commons say, Give us our bargain.'[66]

The 'babble' for which the more extreme sectarians were
notorious is in one sense, as has been shown above, a
manifestation of prophetic performance. On the other hand there
are instances where the frenzy and disorder involved would
appear to suggest genuine madness or mental imbalance. At the
very least the Ranters often appear as if their minds have outrun
their capacity for expression, even beyond the bounds of the help
which parentheses can give. Ungrammatical syntax and punctuation are the most common sign of this. Since no original
manuscripts of Ranter tracts have been discovered yet, it is
impossible to tell just how far this is due to poor compositing.
Salmon uses the first person indicative of the verb 'to be': 'but in
times revealing Order it am [*sic*] its nothing, except travel for
sorrow'.[67] It may be that the compositors simply misread the
copy, which would be understandable with tracts written in
prison conditions. Loose punctuation would be explained by a
habit of oral delivery, as well as the sense of inspiration, although
Quakers were forbidden to write down sermons beforehand since
they were meant to be as spontaneous as prophesyings.[68] There
is a considerable degree of flexibility of interpretation for the
modern reader here. In Coppe, sentences remain unfinished,
degenerating into an 'etc', notably in *Copp's Return*, though this
could be the consequence of someone taking down Coppe's
words:

But sure I am, this express hath (hundreds of times) wounded me to the
very heart; and hath (for many years) stuck as a dagger in my soul; and
hath cost me hot waters, even many, many showrs of tears; and
innumerable sighs and groans, &c.[69]

The reader is expected to know what is coming next. Here, in the
case of the recantation, it is the expected denial of errors
contained in the Blasphemy Act or what reads as a stock

---

[66] Winstanley, *A new-Yeers Gift*, p. 21.
[67] Salmon, *Heights in Depths* (1651), in *CRW*, p. 207.
[68] Bauman, *Let your words be few.*   [69] *CRW*, p. 150.

response to and account of mortification and sinfulness. The authority of the sentence, whether original or cited, is subjugated to the awareness triggered in the reader by the writer, a movement towards a shared silence of meaning and experience. Equal to silence is the elevation of all into pure sound, without any distinguishing sense between words. So, in Coppe, the exchange of sound between phonic similars in the same sentence serves to confuse meanings. The result is a registering of the Almighty in extravagant echoes, where the phonetically and semantically similar follow one another: 'Omnipotent, Omnipresent.'[70]

If there is a consistent denial of the verbally rational, there seems also to be a considerable degree of rhythmic intention in Ranter discourse. Coppe's discourse wavers between the poetic and the prosaic, each signalling a different response from the Divine Majesty within. There is a dramatic intensity as the wrangling syntax is interrupted by the spare simplicity of Coppe's renunciation of possession. Impeccable authority is intimated in the orderly distribution of vowels, as the hurriedness of 'But we brethren are perswaded better things of you &c. / Her's some *Gold* and silver' is cut short by the pious 'But that is none of mine. / The drosse I owne.'[71] There are rhyming phrases which function as *leitmotifs* of Antinomian experience, 'my *love*, my *dove*' being repeated throughut Coppe and Salmon, the more ferocious 'rod of God' in Salmon, and the popularly recognized Ranter slogan, 'ram me, damn me', where ram was supposed to stand for God.[72]

There is a sense of playfulness, of divine folly realized, as the rhymes border on doggerel, which is another familiar characteristic of Familist writing: '*Each Beggar that you meet / Fall down before him, kisse him in the street.*'[73] It is as if, having gone beyond biblical literalism, the Ranters search for some form of symbolic representation of what is beyond the Word. For Thomas Tany verse in English helps to capture what is lost when his original inspired language is translated:

---

[70] *A Remonstrance of The sincere and Zealous Protestation* (1651), in *CRW*, p. 119.

[71] *Some Sweet Sips, of some Spirituall Wine* (1649), in *CRW*, p. 47.

[72] William Sedgwick, *The Spirituall Madman* (1648), 14, talks of 'ramming' and 'damning'. *A Jvstifjcajon of the Mad Crew* (1650), the anonymous Ranter pamphlet, contains the reference to ramming and damning on pp. 2–4.

[73] *A Fiery Flying Roll*, in *CRW*, p. 90.

> *'Tis the Lilly, 'tis* Aarons *Rod;*
> *'Tis the Sparkling glory in that skie,*
> *'Tis inhabited withal all unitie,*
> *'Tis the* Aurorau, *'tis the morn*
> *'Tis the inclue our birth our born.*[74]

Dance was also a divine signifier, part of the Ranter interest in gesture though this time collective and ritually celebrative rather than individual and prophetic, and opponents of the Ranters did portray this wrongly as a Bacchanalian rite.[75] There is a simple authority rather in Clarkson's rhyming couplets: 'Though called God, yet that is not my Name, / True, I be both, yet am I not the same: / Therefore a wonder am I to you all. / So that to titul'd Gods ye pray and call.'[76] For Coppe, a similar effect is achieved by imitating biblical prose style, specifically parallelism and repetition. Here the model is Rom. 3: 10–13:

As it is written, there is none righteous; no, not one;—there is none that doth good; no, not one. Their throat is an open sepulchre; with their tongues, they have used deceit. The poison of asps is under their lips.[77]

Coppe may have had to suppress the voice of God within him, but this did not remove the precise style of divine voice.

Gestural and linguistic folly or play brings one full circle to the more extreme forms of prophecy which were documented in Chapter 1. The language usages here were direct manifestations of forms of prophetic style in behaviour and gesture. It would be appropriate to see such language as expressive of, or implicated in, displays of self or the body which may be described as prophetic and, in the case of the Ranters and early Quakers, transgressive. Yet this would be but a partial account of matters. The symbolic codes of gestures adopted by these sectarians were always connected with other discursive (especially printed) attempts to make the truth manifest. Human language, however simple, was always a bond upon the spirit but, as has been shown, no radical Puritan or sectarian ignored the potential or necessity offered by particular forms of rhetorical organization or accepted social register. It was not a case of simple opposition between liberty of the spirit and the repressive order of language:

---

[74] *Theauraujohn his Theous Ori Apokolipikal* (1651), 11.
[75] Samuel Sheppard, *The Joviall Crew, or the Devil turn'd Ranter* (1650), 10.
[76] *A Single Eye All Light, no Darkness* (1650), in *CRW*, p. 162.
[77] *Copp's Return to the wayes of Truth*, in *CRW*, p. 136.

in most cases the two principles are bound up with each other. The need to communicate, to proselytize, and to justify, led to such a series of practices among the sectarians, so that, however solipsistic individuals might become in their pursuit of prophetic authority, the operation of radical religious discourse at large justifies in some sense Milton's claim that each church constituted a spiritual *demos*. At this rather microscopic level there is no greater or clearer demonstration of the extremes of liberty and authority, freedom, and obedience than in these attempts to reconstitute the primitive Christian churches in the midst of revolutionary England.

Conclusion

Before 1640 religious separatism in England was a small though vocal and controversial phenomenon. The events which took place between 1640 and 1660 consolidated this extreme Puritanism by providing a context in which gathered churches and other groups could meet relatively free from persecution, and by fuelling the debates and sentiments which led to sectarian growth. Consequently these twenty years saw the emergence of other radical religious groups, each of an increasingly more extreme hue. The debates between religious radicals caused continual fragmentation and dissension: battles for authority within churches or sects were paralleled by individual claims for sole prophetic authority. At the same time the dominance of Puritan opinion in the Interregnum governments meant that some religious radicals influenced national rule, while others felt sufficiently involved in the plight of the nation to criticize and to remonstrate with governments, largely within the terms defined by their own religion.

This flourishing of early dissent produced its own culture, literature, and language-usages, as diverse, syncretic, and mutually interactive as the radical churches and sects themselves. Such a phenomenon occurred not merely because of the use of devotional literature in the functioning and dissemination of radical religious worship, but because special notions of the acts of speaking and writing were at the heart of radical theology. The end of sectarian theology was to make human language, in its attempt to embody the divine, behave in a way entirely different both from commonly spoken and written or printed language. In several ways, especially for the Quakers, speaking and writing, bearing witness to the personal experience of the divine in the individual, were central components of conversion and belief.

It is here that the Coleridge sentence quoted at the beginning of this study becomes so apt and perceptive: 'Enthusiasm . . . implies an undue (or when used in a good sense, an unusual) vividness of ideas, as opposed to perceptions, or of the obscure inward feelings'. In experiential discourse and the construction of prophetic identity lie a variety of colourful revelations of self, connecting inner conscience, external action and the sense of divine inspiration. These writings extend from the disruption of a sense of normative time and space in confessions of experience to the direct inhabitation of biblical prophetic figures and texts in the more extreme examples. Clearly the confessional narrative, ordered to suit the requirements of radical Puritan soteriology, crucial in the politics of individual congregations and determined by the outlook of those congregations, was very different from the more autonomous prophecy. Yet it would be wrong to divorce these two categories: they were intimately connected, continuous in the minds of the radicals. In the writings and prophesyings of the women prophets in particular, the claims of both may be seen. Indeed it is this mixture of genres in the writings of the women prophets which reflects both the extent to which their behaviour defied gender divisions in English society and the degree to which they were still contained by the claims of church and male ministry. Behind both the experiential and the prophetic lies a response to biblical narrative and symbolism. These different responses to biblical language define the degrees of religious radicalism and contain the tensions and contra- dictions within radical religion. In the more conservative experiences the potential for the expression of a glorified self, a free spirit, or at least a sanctified soul is compromised by the dependence upon 'externals', ordinances, and duties as forms of assurance. Even in John Rogers's congregation the sense of urgency and immediacy in many of the experiences is a reflection of the leadings of the free spirit being held in check by the claims of the visible church.

If these writings had not been produced in a volatile and politicized religious climate, they would without doubt have lacked much of what is interesting in them. The politics of the congregation and the politics of the nation were the causes of the striking claims of personal, divinely ordained authority which we have seen in Sarah Wight, Anna Trapnel, Abiezer Coppe, and George Foster. Moreover, the combination of the symbolic body of the prophet, the dream or vision, and the inspired rhapsody exists now as a record of the perception of Interregnum politics as much as of sectarian propaganda and performance. Both aspects together enable us to see how the prophets carefully constructed their images, so that the codes of their behaviour and utterances could not be missed (though they were mis-interpreted). Comparing Wight and Trapnel, the similarity of representations in the domestic sphere and in the political sphere is striking. Prophecy, the defeat of temptation to suicide, the overcoming of domestic subordination, and the final vision of the divine working in the family, in the nation, and in the world enabled the prophet or prophetess in the congregation to unite the inner and the outer, the individual and the group. The same authority and capacity was evident in Quaker writings, even though the means of prophetic utterance were comprehended in different ways.

However the concerns of radical religious literature did not stop here. Beyond the meetings of the radicals was a need for some to find a sense of illumination in a linguistic exploration of the way the divine operated in the self and the natural world. In this respect the interest in works belonging to the mystical and occult traditions was not only a sectarian obsession: it was part of the devotional make-up of Western Europe in the seventeenth century. The potential for a self-sufficient and personal sense of deification, the obliteration of ego to become one with the godhead, was a strong feature in the Reformation and the Counter-Reformation. The presence of such concerns among religious radicals should remind us not only of the links between the radicals and the rest of English and continental society, but also of the way in which the interest in the mystical and the *via negativa* was a continuing presence in, or threat to, what are usually though wrongly thought of as the rather more imagina-tively restricted avenues of Nonconformist Biblicism, especially those associated with the Baptists.

For learned and unlearned alike, engagement with these writings in the original or in translation was a question of sensitivity to new vocabulary inherited from continental sources. The religious history behind particular texts and words is often as revealing of their state as their subsequent circulation among English religious radicals. Finally, however, the result for the English radicals was a considerable expansion of concept and vocabulary, facilitating, in the case of their adoption of Boehme, a mythologizing of inner regeneration in terms of gender difference. Such patterns of vocabulary, metaphor, and myth, be they Neoplatonic imagery or kabbalistic *sephiroth*, were generally appropriated by radicals in order to expand or support their understanding of fundamental concepts, like the creation or the godhead itself. This notion of expansion is true even when we find a source (as with Boehme) modifying an author's sense of predestinarian theology. However there is one notable exception here. Though the writings of Hendrik Niclaes and other Familist literature were republished and are known to have circulated reasonably widely across the sects, no direct imitator of H.N. emerged. His complex forms of allegory, though indicative of radical religious interests in the Interregnum, belonged to another age. They were comprehended in the 1650s, but as a practice which was popular enough to be imitated they had been far surpassed, partly by the superior illuminative discourse available in Boehme and more significantly by the very idea that there could be an authentic, non-allegorical language for the self which also expressed eternal verities. Quaker discourse, especially that of Fox, Nayler, and Perrot, with its combination of the experiential and the cosmological is just such a language.

Most of the radicals lived with the English language, rather than inhabiting the continental material. The impulse to discover the truth of extreme outwardness in cosmology and extreme inwardness was vast and was facilitated by the fact that the same language was used to express both internal and external universes. The internal universe was a counterpart to the external universe and both shared the same terminology. Such an affinity led some, most significantly Winstanley, to envisage that interpretation of man, nature, and God in which those universes were merged. It was indeed the basis for his experiment in utopian living. If other radicals were not driven to this particular extreme, they were still prone to turn keywords in Old and New Testament language into names for universal processes which were taking place or could take place within all people. A new hermeneutic dimension had been found in England which enabled people to relate the 'sword of the spirit' and the 'book of the creatures' to the 'new man'. No doubt it is because such language also played a role in theologies and discourses which were hostile to radicalism—especially when Presbyterian heresiographers found the linguistically generated errors of the radicals to be a repetition of earlier heresies—that the attack on the radicals was at its most intense in this area. This was especially so as simple changes in the use of particular imagery seemingly altered the fundamentals of reformed Protestant religion.

However, the radical religious understanding of divine language, the place of the Scriptures, and the relationship of these two to human language are the most exciting and original contributions of the radicals. Though the final result, especially in the case of Thomas Tany, was one of baffling nonsense in the eyes of many witnesses past and present, it is equally possible to see the theory lying behind it as the assertion of an extreme nominalism. The search for the Adamic language may have ended in solipsism, but on the way to this lay many understandable choices with regard to the limits of signification, as well as the revelation of much about the construction of sectarian authority through grammar. In many ways this was the stopping point of the radical religious literary enteprise, for there was no way beyond speaking about the unspeakable except for the recourse to solipsism or to silence. The redefinition of allegorical interpretation, the role of the spirit, and the penetrating satire on orthodox learning and scriptural interpretation came as a product of the concern with language. In the general history of Nonconformity they must be counted as remarkable contributions.

This study has taken as its chronological finish 1660. The Restoration of the Monarchy was certainly an important date for the development of radical religious writing, as it was for the place of Nonconformity in English society, but it was not the watershed that it is often taken to be. The forms of expression analysed in this book continued to develop and modify, often subject to the restrictions placed upon Nonconformists after 1660. They were also influenced by the developments within individual churches or sects. The Quakers, for instance, became a formidably organized society, unlike the volatile and disparate association which existed during the Interregnum. The regularization of writing, and the censorship of material considered by Fox to be too perfectionist and detrimental to the need for public respectability, are features of this later period. The extreme perfectionist writing of Nayler and others was tamed as Fox's authority took hold. The image of the Ranters which was used to exclude or vilify the more extreme Quakers had actual roots in the pamphlets of Coppe, the early Clarkson, and Salmon, as well as in Nayler and Perrot. In this way the image of the more flamboyant prophets was generated within as well as outside the sects. In the 1650s the opportunity for publication and the exchange or juxtaposition of claims and statements was far greater than it was to be in later years. As a consequence the capacity for stereotypes to solidify was less during the Interregnum than was the case after 1660.

Turning to the less extravagant manifestations, confessions of experience and prophesyings continued to be published, though they were sometimes 'toned down' in order to satisfy the needs of the gathered churches in dangerous times. Of course these narratives tended to take in a longer expanse of time, including the Restoration. The pattern, however, was set in the congregations of the late 1640s and early 1650s, as Bunyan's testimony, *Grace Abounding* (1666) and other examples reveal.[1]

The literature of enthusiasm was still there. Men like Robert Bacon, with connections across the sectarian spectrum, learned and well-travelled, maintained communications at home and abroad with sectarians, mystics, and speculative philosophers. It is probably the case that the more extreme form of prophecy and expression did not receive the same interest that it had in the late 1640s and 1650s, but it was still produced across the social spectrum, from the artisanal Muggletonians to the somewhat more well-to-do Philadelphian society, of which John Pordage was a founder. Recent research into the fortunes of Restoration political radicalism is drawing a finely detailed picture of intimate connections between dissenters, ex-Commonwealth radicals and Whigs, which suggests a far stronger continuinty between pre- and post-1660 radicalism than was hitherto thought possible.[2] This may well be the case for radical religion too, especially since the kind of covert connection and transference of information current in the Restoration is very similar to the

---

[1] See Sarah Davy, *Heaven Realised* (1670); Hannah Allen, *Satan his Methods and Malice Baffled* (1683); Agnes Beaumont, *The Narrative of the Persecution of Agnes Beaumont* (in 1674), ed. G. B. Harrison (1929).

[2] See Richard Ashcraft, *Revolutionary Politics and Locke's Two Treatises of Government* (Princeton, 1986), 149–65.

way in which radical religious connections operated before 1640, during the earlier period of constraint. Moreover, radical books can be found in several libraries of Restoration men, some of whom had not been active in the Interregnum, though they certainly had radical religious connections.[3] The question to be asked here is: what use was made of these books after 1660 among other books of very different natures? Were there ways in which radical books had a specific role to play in libraries not generally radical, and read by owners who, though perhaps Nonconformists, were by no means extremists?

In some cases the literature of the Interregnum formed traditions of reading in the Restoration. John Everard was clearly very widely read and preferred by Quakers, as William Penn's grateful praise makes clear.[4] Robert Rich's list of spiritual radicals forms a very extensive genealogy of continental and native talents.[5] His own use of Cusa and the mystics puts him in line on the one hand with Everard and Randall, and on the other with late seventeenth-century sceptical philosophy. Sometimes the re-publication of mid-century material could be controversial. This was the case with Samuel Crisp's publication of the works of his father, Tobias: the spectre of Antinomianism could still frighten in the 1690s.[6]

Yet it is also the case that radical religious literature was close to more orthodox Puritanism in its continued use of particular forms and divisions of rhetoric and logic. This was not just the desire of the radicals to continue to proselytize in the areas where the catechism, the published sermon, and controversial literature found a readership. The necessary reliance upon some degree of rationality and the 'right dividing' of Scripture and experience establishes the continuity of the foundations of the radical religious imagination or expression with more orthodox Puritanism. Both shared habitual patterns of division and of the ways of recording the development of feeling. If anything, the more pronounced reliance upon the Spirit in the Baptists and those beyond them leads to a preference for popular poetic and song

---

[3] Benjamin Furly, *Bibliotheca Furleiana* (1695).

[4] William Penn, *The Invalidity of John Faldo's Vindication* (1673), 247–8.

[5] Robert Rich, *Love without Dissimulation* (1666), 6.

[6] Tobias Crisp's *Christ Alone Exalted* was published again in 1690. His son, Samuel, published *Christ exalted, and Dr. Crisp Vindicated* in 1698.

forms—nursery rhymes and ballads—in order to provide a form. It was a sanctifying of popular culture which orthodox Puritans in the years before 1640 had been encouraging in the chapbook market. The situation in the high years of sectarian controversy, between the mid-1640s and 1660, perhaps obscured this picture somewhat, while the claims of experience and prophecy led to very unsecular forms of expression in Independent, Quaker, and prophetic writing itself.

'Forms' crept in after 1660 in a more extensive way. Perhaps the best illustration of this is the uneasy yet certain adoption of hymns by the Baptists, the first Baptist hymnal being produced by Benjamin Keach. What does not seem to have reappeared was the proliferation of extreme theories of divine language and signification. As an extension of prophetic performance and insight, these notions exist now as monuments of the extent to which, in various ways, religious radicals could claim to be divine. In his autobiography Richard Baxter accused the Ranters of pushing together the light of nature with the new light of the Gospels. Coleridge annotated Baxter, reproving him for separating the two lights: 'The source must be [the] same in all light, as far as it [is] light.'[7] For the radicals, there was no doubt that it was light. The striving, the anguish, and the disappointment lay in articulating the conviction that the light linked man, natural world, and godhead. The glory was in speaking forth that sublime sense of the Word which flowed through creation. From that feeling stemmed the extraordinary products of the radical religious imagination.

---

[7] Annotation to Baxter, *Reliquiae Baxterianae*, Copy B, in *Marginalia*, 1, Abbt to Byfield, ed. George Whalley, being *The Collected Works of Samuel Taylor Coleridge*, xii (1980), 296.

BIBLIOGRAPHY

1. MANUSCRIPT SOURCES

Aberystwyth

National Library of Wales
MS 11438D, letter 86: Morgan Llwyd to Henry Jessey, July 1656.

Cambridge

Cambridge University Library
MS Dd. 6. 70: Sermon notes by Tobias Crisp (*c.* 1634).
MS Dd. 6. 90: English translation of Hendrik Niclaes, *Evangelium Regni*.
Ms Dd. 12. 68: Translations by John Everard:
    fos. 2–49: Sebastian Franck, *The Tree of Knowledge of Good and Evil*.
    fos. 51–90: *Theologia Germanica*.
    fos. 91–8: Extracts from Tauler etc.
    fos. 99–122: Nicholas of Cusa, *De Visione Dei*.
    fos. 123–4: Pseudo-Dionysius, 3rd, 4th, and 5th Chapters of the
        Mystical Divinity.
MS Ff. 6. 41: *The Cloud of Unknowing*, prepared by William Parish, 1647.
MS Add. 2641: English translation of Niclaes, *The Second Exhortation*.
MS Add. 2801: English translation of Niclaes, *A figurative Description of the True Tabernacle*.
MS Add. 2802: English translation of Hendrik Jansen van Barrefelt, *The Mysterie of the Eternitie of Christ*.
MS Add. 2803: English translation of works by Niclaes entitled *A description of the Inquitie*.
MS Add. 2804: English translation of Barrefelt, *An Eternall Testament*.
MS Add. 2805: English translation of Niclaes, *A Singular Description with an effectuall Resolution*.
MS Add. 2806: English translation of Barrefelt, *A Declaration of the Revelation of John*.
MS Add. 2807: English translation of Niclaes, *The Second Exhortation*.
MS Add. 2809: English translation of Barrefelt, *Fourth Epistle*.
MS Add. 3436: English translation of Niclaes, *Several Pieces*.

London

British Library
MS Sloane 601: Copy of Benet of Canfield's *The Rule of Perfection*, in English; made by Daniel Foote, 1652.

MS Sloane 648,
> fo. 10: Letter by Joachim Poleman, 1659–60, with references to Jacob Boehme, John Pordage, and Abraham von Frankenburg's 'De Via Veterum Sapientum'.
> fo. 173: 'Theologia Mystica est successive mysteriorum traditio a deo Mosi Primum, ad hoc deinde posteris revelata, et alio nomine Hae brevis appelata Cabala'.

MS Sloane 872: English translation of Tobias, *Mirabilia Opera Dei*, made from printed edition, signed John Burt, 1660. Made in 1655.

MS Sloane 2175, fos. 145–7: translation by John Everard of Basilus Valentinus, *Practica, una cum XII clavibus et Appendice*, from M. Maier *Themis Aurea* (1618).

MS Sloane 2538: English translation of Castellio's version of *Theologia Germanica*.

MS Sloane 2544, fos. 1–53: copy of Jacob Bauthumley, *The Light and Dark Sides of God* (1650), made by Benjamin Antrobus, 1655:
> fos. 53^v–54^r: Poem.
> fos. 55^v–59^v: 'The Figure of the Philosophique Globe'.

MS Sloane 2608: English translation of Barrefelt: *A Short Instruction according to the Being*.

MS Sloane 3991: English translation of Andreas Tentzel's version of Paracelsus, 'Of Spiritual mumy & the tree of knowledge of good and evile'. Owned by Daniel Foote.

MS Stowe 549, fo. 9^v: Warrant for seizing John Everard's papers, based on confession of Giles Creech.

Friends House Library
MSS Swarthmore: Early Quaker Letters.
Dictionary of Quaker Biography (in process of compilation).

Lambeth Palace Library
MS 869: Familist Hymnal.

Dr Williams's Library

MS Baxter Letters 3, fos. 302–3: Letter from Richard Baxter to Henry Bromley (Brother of Thomas Bromley), 30 May 1654.

Oxford

Bodleian Library
MS Ashmole 240, fo. 96: Letter by Jacob Boehme 'ad amicum'.
MS Ashmole 1440,
> fos. 196–8: Translation by John Everard of Hermes Trismegistus, *Tabula Smaragdina*, signed 9 Aug. 1640.
> fos. 200–4: Translation by John Everard of 'Aphorismes or Canons Hermeticall' ascribed to Basilius Valentinus in L. Zetzner, *Theatrum Chemicum*, iv (1613), signed 16 Aug. 1640.

MS Ashmole 1499, fo. 279: Letter by Jacob Boehme.

MS Laud Misc. 11: English translation of Hendrik Niclaes, *The Second Exhortation*.

MS Rawlinson A. 21, fos. 325–6: Account of Anna Trapnel's Prophesyings, by B.T.

MS Rawlinson A. 354: John Pordage, 'A Tract of Christ's Birth and Incarnation'.

MS Rawlinson A. 382: English translation of Niclaes, *The Second Exhortation*.

MS Rawlinson C. 249: English translation of Niclaes, *The First Exhortation*.

MS Rawlinson C. 250: English translation of Niclaes, *The First Exhortation*.

MS Rawlinson C. 554: English translation of six chapters from Niclaes, *The Glasse of Righteousness*.

MS Rawlinson C. 599: English translation of Niclaes, *Dicta H.N.*

MS Rawlinson D. 106: 'The Life and Character of Mrs Mary Carleton' (daughter of Tobias Crisp), by Samuel Crisp, her brother.

MS Rawlinson D. 399, fo. 196: 'Certain fifty erronious opinions gathered from the mouth of Bryerley and his hearers'.

MS Rawlinson D. 1347, fos. 317^r–318^r: Another copy of the errors contained in MS Rawlinson, D. 399: fo. 196.

MS Rawlinson D. 833, fos. 54–67: Accounts of the origins and rise of the Philadelphian Society.

MS Rawlinson D. 828: Records of Peter Chamberlen's Baptist Church at Lothbury Square, London, 1652–4.

MS Tanner 67, fos. 143, 149, 187: Interrogation of John Everard by Ecclesiastical Commissioners, 1638–9.

Worcester College

MS Clarke 18: Army Letters:

    fos. 17^v–19^v: From William Sedgwick.

    fo. 22v: Ranter poem by Valentine Sharp to John Radman.

    fo. 22^v: Another Ranter poem.

    fo. 23: Ranter letter to William Robinson (?Rawlinson).

    fo. 24: Abiezer Coppe to Joseph Salmon and Andrew Wyke, between Apr. and June 1650.

    fos. 25–27^r: Andrew Wyke, Ranter, to Mayor and Aldermen of Coventry, Apr. 1650.

2. UNPUBLISHED THESES AND DISSERTATIONS

ADAMS, S. L., 'The Protestant Cause: Religious Alliance with West European Calvinist Communities as a Political Issue in England, 1585–1630' (D.Phil. thesis, University of Oxford, 1972).

COPPINS, ANNE, 'Religious Enthusiasm from Robert Browne to George Fox: A Study of its Meaning and the Reactions against it in the Seventeenth Century' (D.Phil. thesis, University of Oxford, 1983).

GRAHAM, JOHN K., ' "Independent" and "Presbyterian": A Study of Religious and Political Language and the Politics of Words During the English Civil War, c. 1640–1646' (Ph.D. diss., Washington University, 1978).

HUNT, PAUL R., 'John Everard: A Study in His Life, Thought, and Preaching' (Ph.D. diss., University of California, 1977).

INGOLDSBY, W. P., 'Some Considerations of Noncomformist Sermon Style: 1645–1660' (B.Litt. thesis, University of Oxford, 1973).

JONES, R. TUDUR, 'The Life, Work, and Thought of Vavasor Powell (1617–1670)', 2 vols. (D.Phil. thesis, University of Oxford, 1947).

KERR, W. N., 'Henry Nicholas and the Family of Love' (Ph.D. thesis, University of Edinburgh, 1955).

LAURENCE, ANNE, 'Parliamentary Army Chaplains, 1642–1651', 2 vols. (D.Phil. thesis, University of Oxford, 1981).

LAYDON, JOHN PATRICK, 'The Kingdom of Christ and the Powers of the Earth: The Political Uses of Apocalyptic and Millenarian Ideas in England, 1648–53' (Ph.D. thesis, University of Cambridge, 1976).

McGREGOR, J. F., 'The Ranters: A Study in the Free Spirit in English Sectarian Religion, 1648–1660' (B.Litt. thesis, University of Oxford, 1968).

NELSON, BYRON C., 'Play, Ritual Inversion and Folly among the Ranters of the English Revolution', (Ph.D. diss., University of Wisconsin–Madison, 1985).

ORMSBY-LENNON, HUGH, 'The Dialect of Those Fanatick Times: Language Communities and English Poetry from 1580 to 1660' (Ph.D. diss., University of Pennsylvania, 1977).

PENRHYS EVANS, N. H., 'The Family of Love in England, 1550–1650' (MA thesis, University of Kent, 1971).

REAY, B. (G. [BARRY]), 'Early Quaker Activity and Reactions to It, 1652–64' (D.Phil. thesis, University of Oxford, 1979).

TROUT, P. A., 'Magic and the Millennium: A Study of the Millenary Motifs in the Occult Milieu of Puritan England, 1640–1660' (Ph.D. diss., University of British Columbia, 1975).

3. SELECT PRINTED SOURCES

A. REFERENCE WORKS

ADAMS, H. M., *Catalogue of Books Printed on the Continent of Europe, 1501–1600, in Cambridge Libraries*, 2 vols. (Cambridge, 1967).

Calendar of State Papers, Domestic Series, James I, Charles I, Interregnum, Charles II.

Dictionary of National Biography, 19 vols. (Oxford, 1921–2).

FORTESCUE, G. K., *Catalogue of the Pamphlets, Books, Newspapers, and Manuscripts relating to the Civil War, the Commonwealth and Restoration, collected by George Thomason*, 2 vols. (1908).

FOSTER, JOSEPH, *Alumni Oxonienses: the Members of the University of Oxford, 1500–1714* (Oxford, 1891–2).

GREAVES, R. L., and ZALLER, R., *A Biographical Dictionary of British Radicals in the Seventeenth Century*, 3 vols. (Brighton, 1982–4).

Journal of the House of Commons, 34 vols. (1742–92).

MATTHEWS, A. G., *Calamy Revised* (Oxford, 1934).

—— *Walker Revised* (Oxford, 1948).

NUTTALL, G. F., *Early Quaker Letters from the Swarthmore MSS to 1660, Calendared, indexed and annotated* (1952). Typescript deposited in major libraries.

PLOMER, H. R., *A Dictionary of Booksellers and Printers . . . 1641–67* (Oxford, 1907: repr. 1968).

POLLARD, A. W., and REDGRAVE, G. R., *A Short Title Catalogue of Books Printed in England, Scotland and Ireland and of English Books Printed Abroad 1475–1640* (1950); rev. edn. of vol. ii, *I–Z*, by K. F. Pantzer (1976), and of vol. i, *A–M*, by W. A. Jackson and F. S. Ferguson, completed by K. F. Pantzer (1986).

A Transcript of the Registers of the Worshipful Company of Stationers, from 1640–1708, A.D., 3 vols. (1913–14).

VENN, J. and VENN, J. A., *Alumni Cantabrigienses . . . to 1751*, 4 vols. (Cambridge, 1922–7).

WING, D. G., *Short Title Catalogue of Books Printed in England, Scotland, Ireland, Wales and British America and of English Books Printed Abroad, 1641–1700*, 3 vols. (New York, 1945–51, 2nd edn. rev. and enlarged: i, 1972; ii, 1982).

WOOD, ANTHONY *Athenae Oxonienses*, 2 vols. (Oxford, 1721).

B. PRIMARY WORKS

Each entry begins with the reference number from the appropriate short-title catalogue. Unless otherwise stated, dates given after the year on title-pages (in brackets here) are those noted by George Thomason on his copies. Unless otherwise stated, the date given is that of the first edition of each work.

18553   AINSWORTH, HENRY, *An Epistle Sent Vnto Two Daughters of Warwick from H.N. . . . With a refutation of the errors that are Therein, by H.A.* (Amsterdam, 1608).

A1025   ALLEN, HANNAH, *Satan his Methods and Malice Baffled* (1683).

A3082   ANDERDON, JOHN, *One Blow at Babel* (1662).

A3507   *Anti-Quakerism, or, A Character of the Quakers Spirit* (1659).

N1122   *An Apology for the Service of Love* (1656), 15 May.

A3614   ARCHER, JOHN [HENRY], *The Personall Reign of Christ upon Earth* (1st edn. 1641, 3rd edn. 1642), Jan. 1642.

795   ARTEMIDORUS, *The Judgement, or Exposition of Dreams* (1606).

A3988   [ASHMOLE, ELIAS], *The Way to Bliss* (1658), 27 Apr. Marginal notes by John Everard.

W1255   *Astrologie Theologized* (1649), 2 July.

A4127   ATKINSON, CHRISTOPHER: Whitehead, George; Lancaster, James; Simmonds, Thomas, *Ishmael, And his Mother, Cast out into the Wilderness* (1655), 12 Mar.

A4195   AUDLAND, ANNE, *A True Declaration of the suffering of the innocent* (1655), 3 Mar.

A4272   AVERY, ELIZABETH, *Scripture-Prophecies Opened* (1647), 8 Nov.

B210   B., W., *Experiences and Tears* (1652), 1 July.

B253   BACHE, HUMPHREY, *A Few Words in True Love* (1659)

B1073A   BACHELOR (BACHILER, BATCHILER), JOHN, Χρυσάμμος: *Golden Sands* (1647), 22 Dec. 1646.

B370   BACON, ROBERT, *The Spirit of Prelacie* (1646), 24 Apr.

B368   —— *Christ Mighty in Himself and Members* (1646).

B369   —— *The Labyrinth the Kingdom's in Yet Working* (1649).

B371   —— *A Taste of the Spirit of God* (1652), 6 July.

B418   BAGSHAW, EDWARD, *The Life and Death of Mr. V. P.* (1671).

B452   BAILLIE, ROBERT, *Anabaptism, The True Fountain of Independencie, Antinomy, Brownisme, Familisme* (1647), 28 Dec., 1646.

B533   BAKEWELL, THOMAS, *A Faithful Messenger sent after the Antinomians* (1644), 4 Apr.

B776   BARKER, MATTHEW, *Jesus Christ the Great Wonder* (1651).

S4998   BARREFELT, HENDRIK JANSEN VAN, *A Spiritual Journey of a Young Man, towards the Land of Peace* (1659), 2 Mar.

B986   BARTLET, WILLIAM, ἸΧΝΟΓΡΑΦΊΑ *Or, a Model of the Primitive Congregational Way* (1647), 25 Mar.

B1097   BATEMAN, SUSANNA, *I matter not how I appear to Man* (1657).

1583   BATMAN, STEPHEN, *The Golden Booke of the Leaden Goddes* (1577).

B1169   BAUTHUMLEY, JACOB, *The Light and Dark Sides of God* (1650), 20 Nov., in *CRW*.

B1344   BAXTER, RICHARD, *Plain Scripture Proof of Infants Baptism* (1651).

B1219   —— *A Christian Directory* (1673).

B1370   —— *Reliquiae Baxterianae*, ed. Matthew Sylvester (1696).

B1517   BAYLY, WILLIAM, *A Collection of the Several Wrightings of . . .* (1676).

    BEAUMONT, AGNES, *The Narrative of the Persecution of Agnes*

Beaumont, ed. G. B. Harrison (1929).

BENET OF CANFIELD, (Fitch, William), *A Bright Starre Leading to, & Centering in Christ our perfection*, trans. Giles Randall (1646).

1946   BERNARD, RICHARD, *The Isle of Man* (1627).

B2879   BIDDLE, JOHN, *Twelve Arguments Drawn out of the Scripture* (1647), 6 Sept.

B2900   BILLING, EDWARD, *A Faithful Testimony For God and my Country* (1664).

B3065   BLACKBOROW, SARAH, *A Visit to the Spirit in Prison* (1658), 10 June.

B3063   —— *Herein is held forth the Gift and Good-will of God* (1659).

B3064   —— *The Just and Equal Ballance* (1660).

B3212   BLOME, RICHARD, *The Fanatick History* (1659), 26 July 1660.

B3425   BOEHME, JACOB, *Two Theosophicall Epistles* (1645), 2 May.

B3408   —— *XL Questions concerning the Soule*, trans. John Sparrow (1647).

—— *The Clavis, or Key*, trans. John Sparrow (1647).

B3426–7   —— *The Way to Christ Discovered*, trans. Humphrey Blunden (1st edn., 25 Oct. 1648; 2nd edn., 1654; 3rd edn., 1656).

B3409–10   —— *Mercurius Teutonicus* (1st edn., 5 Feb. 1649; 2nd edn., 1656).

B3404   —— *The Epistles of Jacob Behmen*, trans. John Ellistone (1649).

B3422–A   —— *The Third Booke of the Authour*, trans. John Sparrow (1st edn., 1650; 2nd edn., 1656).

B3419   —— *Signatura Rerum*, trans. John Ellistone (1651), 22 July.

—— *Four Tables of Divine Revelation*, trans. Humphrey Blunden (1654), 29 Sept.

B3411–2   —— *Mysterium Magnum*, trans. John Sparrow and John Ellistone (1st edn., 1654; 2nd edn., 1656).

B3398–9   —— *Concerning the Election of Grace*, trans. John Sparrow (1st edn., 13 Nov. 1655; 2nd edn., 1656).

B3397   —— *Aurora: That is, the Day-Spring*, trans. John Sparrow (1656), 17 Oct.

B3427A   —— *Yr Ymroddiad*, trans. Morgan Llwyd (1657).

3228   BOLTON, ROBERT, *A Discovrse about the state of Trve Happinesse* (1611).

3255   —— *A Three-fold Treatise* (1634).

B3833A   BOULTON, SAMUEL, *Medicina Magica Tamen: Magical, but Natural Physick* (1656), 21 June.

B3844   BOURNE, BENJAMIN, *The Description and Confutation of Mysticall Antichrist* (1645), 10 Aug. 1646.

B4330   BRAYNE, JOHN, *The New Earth* (1653), 3 Oct.

B4333 BRAYNE, JOHN, *A Treatise of the High Rebellion of Man against God in Blasphemy* (1653), 5 Jan.

B4334 —— *The Unknowne Being of the Spirit, Soul, and Body; Anatomized* (1654).

B4455 BRIDGE, WILLIAM, *Grace and Love beyond Gifts* (1649).

B4445–7 —— *The Works of William Bridge*, 3 vols. (1649), Nov. 1648.

B4621 *A Briefe Rehearsall* (1575, 1656).

B4659 BRIERLEY, ROGER, *A Bundle of Soul-Convincing, Directing and Comforting Truths* (2nd edn., 1677).

W1173 BROMLEY, THOMAS, *The Way to the Sabbath of Rest* (1655), 6 Nov.

B4941 BROOKS, THOMAS, *Gods Delight in the progresse of the Upright* (1649), 26 Dec. 1648.

B5014 BROWN, DAVID, *The Naked Woman, or a rare Epistle sent to Mr. Peter Sterry, Minister at Whitehall* (1652), 17 July.

B5016 —— publisher, *Two Conferences Between Some of those that are called Separatists & Independents* (1650), 21 May.

3910 BROWN, ROBERT, *A Treatise of reformation without tarying for anie* (Middelburg, 1582).

  BROWNE, SIR THOMAS, *The Major Works*, ed. C. A. Patrides (1974).

  —— *Pseudodoxia Epidemica*, ed. Robin Robbins, 2 vols. (Oxford, 1981).

  BUNYAN, JOHN, *Grace Abounding to the Chief of Sinners* (1666), ed. Roger Sharrock (Oxford, 1962).

  —— *The Pilgrim's Progress* (1678), ed. Roger Sharrock (1965).

B6057 BURROUGH, EDWARD, *A Warning from the Lord to the Inhabitants of Underbarrow* (1654), 15 Apr.

B6048 —— *A Trumpet Of the Lord sounded out of Sion* (1656), 12 Apr.

B6005 —— *A General Epistle to all the Saints* (1660).

B6147 BURTHALL, RAUNCE, *An Olde Bridle for a Wild Asse-Colt* (1650), 31 Oct.

B6163 BURTON, HENRY, *The Grand Imposter Unmasked* (1644), 10 Jan. 1645.

  BURTON, ROBERT, *The Anatomy of Melancholy* (1621), ed. H. Jackson, 3 vols. (1932).

A894B BUTTEVENT, SAMUEL, *A Brief Discovery Of a threefold estate of Antichrist* (1653).

C321 CALVERT, THOMAS, *The Blessed Jew of Marrocco* (York, 1648).

  CALVIN, *Commentaries*, trans. Joseph Haroutunian, in collaboration with Louise P. Smith (1958).

  CANNE, JOHN, *The Necessity of Separation* (1634), ed. Charles Stovel (1849).

C737   CARY, MARY, *The Little Horns Doom & Downfall* (1651), 17 Apr.

C812–3   CASAUBON, MERIC, *A Treatise Concerning Enthusiasme* (1st edn., 11 Nov. 1654; 2nd edn., rev. and enlarged, 1656).

C1936   CHANNEL, ELINOR, *A Message from God* (1653).

C3832   CHIDLEY, KATHERINE, *The Ivstification of the Independant Churches of Christ* (1641).

C3833   —— *A New-Yeares Gift* (1645).

C4453   CLARK, HENRY, *A Description of the Prophets* (1655), 7 Dec.

C4457   —— *A Rod Discovered* (1657), 10 Oct.

C4585   CLARKSON, LAURENCE, *Truth Released from Prison* (1646), 5 Mar.

C4578A   —— *A Generall Charge, or Impeachment of High-Treason, in the name of Justice Equity, against the Communality of England* (1647), 7 Oct.

C4584   —— *A Single Eye All Light, no Darkness* (1650), 4 Oct., in *CRW*.

C4579   —— *Look about you, for the Devil that you Fear is in You* (1659).

C4582   —— *The Quakers Downfall* (1659).

C4583   —— *The Right Devil Discovered* (1659).

C4581   —— *A Paradisical Dialogue Betwixt Faith and Reason* (1660).

C4580   —— *The Lost Sheep Found* (1660).

C4988   COKER, MATTHEW, *A Prophetical Revelation* (1654), May.

C4989   —— *A Short and Plain Narrative of Matthew Coker* (1654), May.

C4990   —— *A Whip of small Cords, to scourge Antichrist* (1654), 29 June.

C5062   COLER, RICHARD, *Christian-Experiences from Scripture-Evidences* (1652), 4 Sept.

C5097   COLE-VENMAN, JOHN, *A True Alarm, in Weakness, unto Babel, from God* (1654), 12 Apr.

C5281, 84   COLLIER, THOMAS, *The Exaltation of Christ* (1st edn., 27 Apr. 1646; 4th edn., 1651).

C5290   —— *A Looking-Glasse for the Quakers* (1657), 13 Dec. 1656.

C5441   COMBER, THOMAS, *Christianity no Enthusiasm* (1678).

15078   COMENIUS, JAN AMOS, *Janua Linguarum* (1631).

C6008   COOK, FRANCES, *Mris. Cooke's Meditations* (1649), 5 Jan. 1650.

C6031   COOK, JOHN, *What the Independents Would have* (1647), 1 Sept.

C6022   —— *A True Relation of Mr. John Cook's passage by Sea from Wexford to Kinsale* (1650), 5 Jan.

F39   COPPE, ABIEZER, Preface to I. F., *John the Divines Divinity* (1649) in *CRW*.

358 Bibliography

C6096   COPPE, ABIEZER, 'An Additional and Preaumbular Hint' to Richard Coppin, Divine Teachings (1649), in CRW.

C6093   —— Some Sweet Sips, of some Spirituall Wine (1649), in CRW.

C6087   —— A Fiery Flying Roll (1649), 4 Jan. 1650, in CRW.

C6091   —— A Second Fiery Flying Roule (1649), Jan. 1650, in CRW.

C6089   —— A Remonstrance of The sincere and Zealous Protestation (1651), 3 Jan., in CRW.

6090   —— Copp's Return to the wayes of Truth (1651), 11 July, in CRW.

D1721   [——] Divine Fire-Works (1657), 21 Jan.

C6086   —— A Character of a True Christian (1680).

C6096   COPPIN, RICHARD, Divine Teachings (1649), 18 Sept.

C6102   —— Mans Righteousnesse Examined (1652).

C6104   —— Saul Smitten for not smiting Amalek (1653), 1 May.

C6101   —— A Man-Child born (1653), 25 Dec.

C6097   —— The Glorious Mystery of Divine Teachings (1653). This is the 2nd edn. of Divine Teachings.

C6105   —— Truths Testimony (1655), 3 Mar.

C6094   —— A Blow at the Serpent (1656).

C6094   —— Crux Christi (1657).

C6103   —— Michael Opposing the Dragon (1659).

C6512   COULING, NICHOLAS, The Saints Perfect in this Life (1647).

C6513   —— A Survey of Tyrannie (1650), 9 Aug.

C6736   CRAB, ROGER, The English Hermite, or Wonder of the Age (1655), 23 Jan.

C6735   —— Dagon's Downfall; or The great Idol digged up Root and Branch (1657), 19 Sept.

C6738   —— A Tender Salutation (1659).

C6737   —— Gentle Correction for the High-Flown Backslider (1659).

C6764   CRADOCK, WALTER, The Saints Fulnesse of Joy (1646), 21 July.

C6762   —— Gospel-libertie in the $\left\{ \begin{array}{c} Extension \\ Limitations \end{array} \right\}$ of It (1648), 24 July.

C6759   —— Glad Tydings from Heaven (1648).

C6757–8   —— Divine Drops distilled from the Fountain of Holy Scripture (1st edn., 21 Dec. 1649; 2nd edn., 1650).

C6760   —— Gospel-Holinesse (1651).

C6917   CRISP, SAMUEL, Christ exalted, and Dr. Crisp Vindicated (1698).

C6955, 58, 59   CRISP, TOBIAS, Christ Alone Exalted, 3 vols. (i, 22 July, 1643; ii. 1644; iii. 1648).

C6989   CROFTON, ZACHARY, Bethshemesh Clouded (1653), 1 Dec.

C7204   CROOK, JOHN, An Epistle of Love (1660).

D1983   DAVIS (DAVIES, DOUGLAS, AUDELEY), LADY ELEANOR, The Day of Judgements Modell (1646).

D1987   —— The Excommunication out of Paradise (1647).

D2006 —— *The Lady Eleanor her Remonstrance to Great Britain* (1648).

D1986 —— *The Everlasting Gospel* (1649).

D2012B —— *Sions Lamentation* (1649).

D1976 —— *The Benidiction* (1651).

D1995 —— *Hells Destruction* (1651).

D2007 —— *The Restitution of Prophecy* (1651).

D1978 —— *Bethlehem* (1652).

D1969 —— *Apocalypse*, n.p.; n.d.

D1988 —— *Ezekiel*, n.p.; n.d.

D444 DAVY, SARAH, *Heaven Realiz'd* (1670).

D939 DELL, WILLIAM, *The Way of True Peace and Unity* (1649), 8 Feb.

—— *Select Works* (1773).

DENCK, HANS, *Schriften*, ed. Georg Baring, 3 vols. (Stuttgart, 1955–60).

6608 DENISON, STEPHEN, *The White Wolfe, or A sermon preached at Pauls Crosse* (1627).

D1017 DENNE, HENRY, *The Doctrine and Conversation of John Baptist* (1642), 9 Dec. 1641.

D1014 —— *Anti-Christ Unmasked* (1645), 1 Apr.

D1022 —— *The Man of Sin Discovered* (1645), 1 Apr.

D1021 —— *The Levellers Designe discovered* (1649), 24 May.

D1024 —— *The Quaker no Papist* (1659), 16 Oct.

6626 DENT, ARTHUR, *The Plain Mans Path-way to Heaven* (1601).

D1259 DEWSBURY, WILLIAM, *The Discovery of Mans Returne To his First Estate* (1654), 14 Feb.

D1279 —— *A True Prophecy of the Mighty Day of the Lord* (1654), 18 Jan.

D1266 —— *A Discovery of the Ground* (1655), 12 Apr.

D1722 *Divine Light, manifesting the Love of God unto the whole World* (1646), 7 July.

D1737 *Divinity And Philosophy Dissected, and Set Forth, by a Mad Man* (Amsterdam, 1644).

E115 EATON, JOHN, *The Honey-Combe of Free Justification* (1643).

E222 EDWARDS, THOMAS, *Antapologia* (1644).

E228–30 —— *Gangraena*, 3 parts (1646), i, 26 Feb.; ii, 28 May; iii, 28 Dec.

E578 ELLIS, HUMPHREY, *Pseudochristus, or a True and faithful Relation . . . of William Frankelin and Mary Gadbury* (1650).

E612 ELLWOOD, THOMAS, *An Alarm to the Priests* (1660).

E714A EMMOT, GEORGE, *The Spiritual Quaker* (1655).

ERASMUS, DESIDERIUS, *Enchiridion Militis Christiani* (1515), English trans. (1533), ed. Anne M. O'Donnell (Oxford, 1981).

E3226   ERBERY, WILLIAM, *The Grand Oppressor, or The Terror of Tithes; First Felt and now Confest* (1652), 21 July.

E3223   —— *The General Epistle to the Hebrews* (1652), 8 Jan. 1653.

E3230   —— *The Mad Man's Plea* (1653), 28 Oct.

E3227   —— *The Great Earthquake, Revel, 16. 18, or Fall of all the Churches* (1654), 30 July.

E3239   —— *The Testimony of William Erbery* (1658).

E3384   ETHERINGTON, JOHN, *The Defence of John Etherington* (1641), Dec.

E3383   —— *The Deeds of Dr. Denison* (1642), May.

E3381   —— *The Anabaptists Groundwork For Reformation* (1644), 31 May.

E3382   —— *A Brief Discovery of the Blasphemous Doctrine of Familisme* (1645), 9 Apr.

E3468   EVANS, ARISE, *A Voice from Heaven to the Commonwealth of England* (1652), 25 Aug.

E3459   —— *The great and Bloody Visions* (1653), 15 Feb.

E3458   —— *The Euroclydon Winde Commanded to Cease* (1653), 25 July 1654.

E3473   —— *The Voice of the Iron Rod* (1654), 17 Mar. 1655.

E3462   —— *Mr. Evans and Mr. Pennington's Prophesie* (1655), 12 Jan.

10598   EVERARD, JOHN, *The Arriereban* (1618).

10599   —— *Somewhat: written by occasion of three sunnes seene at Tregnie in Cornwall* (1622).

E3533   —— *Some Gospel-Treasures Opened* (1653), 23 May.

E3531–32 —— *The Gospel-Treasury Opened*, 2 parts (1st edn., 1657; 2nd edn., 1659).

E3537   EVERARD, ROBERT, *The Creation and Fall of Adam Reviewed* (1649, 2nd edn., 1652).

E3536   —— *An Antidote for the Newcastle Priests* (1652).

E3540   —— *Nature's Vindication* (1652).

E3867   —— *An Exhortation to Catechizing* (1655), 30 Aug.

F39   F., I., *John the Divines Divinity* (1649).

F444   FARMER, RALPH, *Sathan Inthron'd in his Chair of Pestilence* (1657), 24 Oct. 1656.

F485   FARNWORTH, RICHARD, *The Heart Opened by Christ* (1654), May.

F494   —— *The Pure Language of the Spirit of Truth* (1655), 1 Mar.

F492   —— and Aldam, Thomas, *The Priests Ignorance* (1656), 28 Nov. 1655.

F567   FEAKE, CHRISTOPHER, *A Beam of Light, shining in the midst of much darkness and Confusion* (1659), 2 May.

F585   FEATLY, DANIEL, Καταβαπτισταὶ κατάπτυστοι. *The Dippers Dipt* (1645), 7 Feb.

F636   FELL, MARGARET, *A Testimonie of the Touch-stone* (1656).

F634   —— *A Loving Salutation to the seed of Abraham Among the Jewes* (1656), 31 Oct.

F628   —— *A Declaration And An Information From us the People of God called Quakers* (1660).

F629   —— *An evident Demonstration to God's Elect* (1660).

F626A   —— *The Citie of London Reproved* (1660).

F637   —— *This is to the Clergy* (1660).

F640   —— *A True Testimony from the People of God* (1660).

F642   —— *Women's Speaking Justified* (1666).

F954   *Fire from Heaven* (1649), 1 Sept.

F1049   FISHER, SAMUEL, *Christianismus Redivivus* (1655).

F1057   —— *The Scorned Quakers True and Honest Account* (1656), 17 Sept.

F1056   —— *Rusticus Ad Academicos* (1660).

F1046   —— *An Additionall Appendix* to *Rusticus Ad Academicos* (1660).

F1624   FOSTER, GEORGE, *The Sounding of the Last Trumpet* (1650), 24 Apr. and 15 Nov.

F1623   —— *The Pouring Forth of the Seventh and Last Viall* (1650), 15 Nov.

F1692–93 FOWLER, CHRISTOPHER, *Daemonium Meridianum*, 2 parts (i. 18 Sept. 1654; ii, 18 Feb., 1656).

F187   FOX, GEORGE, *Newes Coming up out of the North* (1654), 21 Dec. 1653.

F1991A   —— *A Word from the Lord* (1654), 25 Aug.

F1784   —— *A Declaration against all Profession and Professors* (1655), 28 Aug.

F1863   —— *A Message from the Lord, to the Parliament of England* (1654), 15 Sept.

F1980   —— *A Warning from the Lord* (1654), 16 Oct.

F1975–6   —— *The Vials of the Wrath of God* (1st edn., 1654; 2nd edn., 1655).

F1924   —— *The Teachers Of the World Unvailed* (1655), 8 June 1656.

F1838   —— *Here all may see, That Justice and Judgement is to Rule* (1656), 4 Aug.

F1785   —— *A Declaration concerning Fasting, and Prayer* (1656), 9 Aug.

F1779   —— *A Cry for Repentance* (1656), 1 Dec.

F1839   —— *Here are several Queries* (1656), 10 Jan. 1657.

F1929   —— *A Testimony of the True Light of the World* (1657), 24 Jan.

F1756   —— *A Catechisme for Children* (1657), 27 Feb.

F1882   —— *The Priests and Professors Catechisme* (1657), 25 Apr.

F1766   —— *Concerning Good-Morrow, and Good-Even* (1657), 25 May.

F1856   —— *The Law of God, The Rule for Law-makers* (1658), 3 Feb.

F1840   Fox, George, *Here is Declared The manner of the naming of Children* (1658).

F1958   —— *To the Parliament of the Comon-Wealth of England, Fifty nine particulars* (1659).

F1832   —— *The Great Mistery of the Great Whore Unfolded* (1659).

F1900   —— *The Serious Peoples Reasoning* (1659).

F1747   —— *An Answer to Thomas Tillams Book* (1659).

F1855   —— *The Lambs Officer* (1659).

F1841   —— *Here you may see what was the True Honour Amongst the Jewes* (1660).

F1786   —— *et al.*, *A Declaration from the Harmles & Innocent People of God, called Quakers* (1660).

F1802   —— *An Epistle General* (1660).

F1781   —— *Cunctis Christi, Apostolorum Sanctorumque Verba, Decentibus & Profitentibus* (1660).

F1993   —— *A Word In the behalf of the King* (1660).

F1916   —— *Something in Answer to the Old Common-Prayer-Book* (1660).

F1923   —— *The Summ of such Particulars as are charged against George Fox* (1660).

F1751   —— *A Battle-Door for Teachers and Professors* (1660).

         —— *The Journal of George Fox*, ed. J. L. Nickalls (1952, rev. rpr. 1975).

         Foxe, John, *The Acts and Monuments of*, ed. J. Pratt, 8 vols. (1877).

F2045   Foxon, William, *A Brief Discovery of the particular making out the infinite Reigning and Being of God in Mankind* (1649), 31 July.

11317   Francis of Sales, *An Introduction to the Holy and Devout Life*, trans. John Yakesley (Douai, 1613).

         Franck, Sebastian, *De Arbore Scientiae Boni et Mali* (Mulhouse, 1561).

F2066   —— *The Forbidden Fruit* (1642).

F2129   Freeman, Francis, *Light Vanquishing Darknesse* (1650), 29 Oct.

F2254   Fry, John, *The Accuser sham'd* (1648), Feb. 1651

         Fuller, Thomas, *The History of the Worthies of England* (1662), ed. P. A. Nuttall, 3 vols. (1840).

F2521   Fullwood, Francis, *Vindiciae mediorum & mediatoris* (1651), 27 May.

G261   Garment, Joshua, *The Hebrews Deliverance at Hand* (1651), 23 Aug.

G321   Gataker, Thomas, *God's Eye on his Israel* (1645), 31 Dec. 1644

G473   GELL, ROBERT, *Stella Nova, A New Starre, Leading wisemen unto Christ* (1649), 1 Aug.

G468   —— ΑΓΓΕΛΟΚΡΑΤΙΑ ΘΕΟΥ *Or, a Sermon Touching God's Government of the World by Angels* (1650), 8 Aug.

G471   —— *Noah's Flood Returning* (1655), 7 Aug.

G472   —— *Gell's Remaines*, ed. Robert Bacon (1676).

G606   GEREE, STEPHEN, *The Doctrine of Antinomianisme Confuted* (1644), 29 April.

G1146   GOODWIN, JOHN, *Anti-Cavalierisme* (1642), 21 Oct.

G1145   —— *Anapologesiastes Antapologias* (1646), 27 Aug.

G1163   —— *The Divine Authority of the Scriptures asserted* (1648), 18 Dec. 1647.

G1217   GOODWIN, PHILIP, *The Mystery of Dreames, Historically Discoursed* (1658), Feb.

G1225   GOODWIN, THOMAS; NYE, PHILIP; SIMPSON, SIDRACH; BURROUGHES, JEREMIAH; and BRIDGE, WILLIAM, *An Apologeticall Narration humbly submitted to Parliament* (1644), 3 Jan.

G1308   GORTON, SAMUEL, *Simplicities Defence* (1646), 7 Nov.

G1307   —— *Saltmarsh Returned from the Dead* (1655), 6 May.

G1320   GOSTELO, WALTER, *For the Lord Protector* (1654), signed 22 Jan. 1644/5.

G1319   —— *The Coming of God in Mercy, in Vengeance* (1658), 15 Apr.

G1597   GRAUNT, JOHN, *Truths Victory Against Heresie* (1645), 9 Apr.

G1862   GREENWAY, RICHARD, *An Alarm from the Holy Mountain of the Lord* (1662).

G1988   GRIFFITH, ALEXANDER, *Strena Vavasoriensis* (1654), 30 Jan.

H188   HAGGAR, HENRY, *The Order of Causes of Gods Fore-Knowledge, Election and Predestination* (1654), 24 May.

H441–2   HALL, THOMAS, *Vindiciae Literarum* (1st edn., 1654; 2nd edn., 1655).

B4682   HARFORD, RAPHA [publisher] *Reverend Mr. Brightman's Judgement, or Prophesies of what shall befall Germany, Scotland, Holland and the Churches adhering to them* (1st edn., 1641).

H768   —— *A Gospel-Engine, or Streams of Love and Pity* (1649), 2 Mar.

H1133   HASSAL, GEORGE, *The Designe of God in the Saints* (1648).

H1134   HASSELWOOD, HENRY, *Doctor Hills Funeral-Sermon*, 2 parts (1654), Dec.

H1139A   HATCH, JOHN, *A Word of Peace* (1646), Imprimatur dated 15 Apr.

H1217   HAYNE, THOMAS, *Christ's Kingdom on Earth, Opened according to Scriptures* (1645), 10 Apr.

13055   HELWYS, THOMAS, *A Short and Plaine Proofe* (?Amsterdam, 1611).

13056   HELWYS, THOMAS, *A Short Declaration of the mistery of iniquity* (?Amsterdam, 1612).

13054   —— *Objections: Answered by way of Dialogue* (?The Netherlands, 1615).

H1565–66   HERMES TRISMEGISTUS, *The Divine Pymander of Hermes Mercurius Trismegistus*, trans. John Everard (1st edn., 1650, 25 Sept. 1649; 2nd edn., 1657).

H1567   —— *Hermes Trismegistus, His Second Book, called Asclepius*, trans. John Everard (1657).

13369   HEYWOOD, THOMAS, *A True Discourse of the Two infamous upstart Prophets* (1636).

H1918   HICKOCK, RICHARD, *A Testimony Against the People call'd Ranters* (1659).

H1953   HIGGINSON, FRANCIS, *A Brief Relation of the Irreligion of the Northern Quakers* (1653).
        HOBBES, THOMAS, *Leviathan* (1651), ed. C. B. Macpherson (1968).

H2274   HOBSON, PAUL, *A Garden Inclosed* (1647), 29 May.

H2276   —— *A Treatise Containing Three Things* (1653), 24 May.

H2273   —— *Fourteen Queries . . . answered by Paul Hobson* (1655), 18 May.

H2654   HOOKER, THOMAS, *The Saints Dignitie and Dutie* (1651), 8 July.

H2902A   HOTHAM, DURANT (Durand), *The Life of one Jacob Boehman* (1644), 8 Nov.

H2951–2   HOW, SAMUEL, *The Sufficiencie of the Spirits Teaching* (1st edn., 1640; 2nd edn., 1644 [22 Jan. 1645]).

H2985   HOWARD, LUKE, *A Few Plain Words* (1658).

V500A   ISAIAH, PAUL, *A Vindication of the Christians Messiah* (1653).

J78A   JACKSON, JOHN, *A Sober Word to a Serious People* (1651), 19 Dec. 1650.

J78B   —— *Strength in Weakness* (1655).

J78   —— *Hosannah to the Son of David* (1657).

J687   JESSEY, HENRY, *The Exceeding Riches of Grace Advanced* (1647).

J698   —— *A Storehouse of Provision* (1650).

C753   —— (with Joseph Caryl) *An English–Greek Lexicon* (1661).

J694   —— *The Lords Loud Call to England* (1660).

P28   —— *A Looking-glass for Children* (1672).

14520   JESSOP, EDMOND, *A Discovery of the Errors of the English Anabaptists* (1623).

J1261   *A Jvstjfcajon of the Mad Crew* (1650), 21 Aug.

15040   KNEWSTUB, JOHN, *A Confutation of monstrous and horrible heresies, taught by H.N.* (1579).

K725   KNOLLYS, HANSERD, *The Shining of a Flaming-Fire in Zion* (1646), 11 Feb.

K724   —— *The Rudiments of the Hebrew Grammar* (1648).

L39   L., J., *A Small Mite In Memory of the late deceased . . . Mr. William Erbery* (1654), 20 Apr.

L669   LAWRENCE, HENRY, *Some Considerations Tending to the Asserting and Vindicating of the Use of the Holy Scriptures* (1649), 10 May.

L2020   *The Life and Light of a Man in Christ Jesus* (1646).

L2164   LILBURNE, JOHN, *The Prisoners Mournfull Cry* (1648), 9 May.

L2175   —— *The Resurrection of John Lilburne* (1656), 16 May.

L2240   LILLY, WILLIAM, *A Prophecy of the White King Raised* (1644).

L2228   —— *Monarchy or no Monarchy* (1651), 6 Aug.

L2720D   LLWYD, MORGAN, *Llyfr y tri Aderyn* (1653).

     —— *The Book of the Three Birds*, trans. from Welsh into English by L. J. Parry, *Transactions of the National Eisteddfod of Wales, Llandudno, 1896* (Liverpool, 1898), 192–275.

     —— *Gair o'r Gair* (1657).

     —— *A Discourse of God the Word*, trans. Griffith Rudd (1739).

     —— *Gweithiau Morgan Llwyd*, ed. T. E. Ellis and J. H. Davies, 2 vols. (Bangor and London, 1899, 1908).

     LUTHER, MARTIN, *The Works of Martin Luther*, ed. A. J. Holman, 6 vols. (Philadelphia, 1932).

F996   *The Marrow of Modern Divinity*, 2 parts (i. 2 June 1645; ii, 13 Oct. 1648).

M926   MASON, MARTIN, *A Check to the Loftie Linguist* (1655), 2 Nov.

     MATTHIAS, MAURICE, *Monuments of Mercy* (1729).

17766   MEDE, JOSEPH, *Clavis Apocalyptica* (1627).

M1600–01   —— *The Key of the Revelation*, trans. Richard More (1st edn., 1643 [27 Sept.]; 2nd edn., 1650).

M1735   MERCER, WILLIAM, *Angliae Speculum* (1646), 9 Mar.

     MILTON, JOHN, *Complete Poems*, ed. John Carey and Alastair Fowler (1968).

     —— *Selected Prose*, ed. C. A. Patrides (1974).

L1099   MODENA, LEON of, *The History of the Rites, Customes and Manner of Life of the Present Jewes throughout the World* (1650), 21 Apr.

M2650   MORE, HENRY, *Divine Dialogues* (1668, 2nd edn., 1713).

     —— *Philosophical Poems*, ed. G. B. Bullough (Manchester, 1931).

M2700   *The More Excellent Way* (1650), 22 Dec.

M2802   MORNAY, PHILIPPE DE, *The Soules Own Evidence for its own Immortality* (1646), 20 Feb.

     MUGGLETON, LODOWICK AND REEVE, JOHN, *A Volume of Spiritual Epistles* (1820).

N302   NAYLER, JAMES, *The Power and Glory of the Lord Shining out of the North* (1653), 17 Aug.

N272   —— *A Discovery of the First Wisdom from beneath, and the Second Wisdom from Above* (1653), 25 Apr.

N309   —— *A Salutation to the Seed of God* (1655), 3 Sept.

N280   —— *A Foole Answered According to his Folly* (1655), 25 May.

N294   —— *Love to the Lost* (1656), 9 Feb.

N263   —— *Antichrist in Man, Christ's Enemy* (1656), 5 March.

N331   —— *Wickedness Weighed: In An Answer to a Book, called The Quakers Quaking Principle, Examined & Refuted* (1656), 13 Mar.

N327   —— *Weaknes above Wickednes, and Truth above Subtilty* (1656), 18 July.

N305   —— *A Publike Discovery, of the Open Blindness of Babels Builders* (1656), 13 Mar.

T2789   —— *A True Narrative of the Examination, Tryall, and Suffering of James Nayler* (1657), 14 Jan.

        —— *A Collection of Sundry Books, Epistles and Papers Written by James Nayler.* (1716).

H3232   —— and HUBBERTHORNE, RICHARD, *A Short Answer to a Book called the Fanatick History* (1660).

N670   *A New Mercury* (1644), 9 Sept.

K395   NICHOLAS OF CUSA, Ὀφθαλμὸς Ἁπλοῦς *Or the Single Eye, Entituled the Vision of God*, published by Giles Randall (1646).

K394   —— *The Idiot*, trans. John Everard (1650), 22 May.

18562   NICLAES, HENDRIK, *A Publishing of the Peace upon Earth* (Cologne, 1574).

18559   —— *A New Balade* (Cologne, 1574).

18559   —— *Another of the Same Kynde* (Cologne, 1574).

18550   —— *Comoedia* (Cologne, ?1574).

N1126   —— *The First Epistle: A Crying Voice of the holy Spirit of Love* (Cologne, 1580; London, 1648).

N1129   —— *The Prophecy of the Spirit of Love* (Cologne, 1574; London, 1649).

N1131   —— *Terra Pacis* (Cologne, ?1575; London 1649), Imprimatur dated 6 Sept.

N1130   —— *Revelatio Dei* (Cologne, ?1575; London, 1649, 26 Sept.).

N1128   —— *An Introduction to the holy Understanding of the Glass of Righteousnesse* (Cologne, ?1575; London, 20 Oct. 1649)

N1123–4   —— *Evangelium Regni* (Cologne, ?1575; London, 1652).

N1125   —— *A Figure of the True & Spiritual Tabernacle* (1655), 23 Jan.

N1127 —— *The First Exhortation of H. N.* (Cologne, ?1575; London, 20 Feb. 1656).

See also Ainsworth, Henry.

NICOLSON, M. H. (ed.), *Conway Letters* (New York, 1930).

N1486 [NYE, PHILIP], *A declaration of the Faith and Order Owned and practised in the Congregational Churches in England* (1658).

0526 OSBORN, JOHN, *The World to Come* (1651), 7 July.

0784 OWEN, JOHN, *Of the Divine Originall, Authority, self-evidencing Light and Power of the Scriptures* (1659), Nov., 1658.

P174,181 PAGITT, EPHRAIM, *Heresiography* (1st edn., 1645 [8 May]; 6th edn., 1661).

B3540 PARACELSUS, BOMBAST VON HOHENHEIM, PHILIPP AURAL THEOPHRAST, *Paracelsus His Aurora* (1659).

P353 PAREUS, DAVID, *A Commentary upon the Divine Revelation of the Apostle and the Evangelist*, trans. Elias Arnold (Amsterdam, 1644).

P382 PARKER, ALEXANDER, *A Manifestation of Divine Love* (1660).

P486 PARKER, WILLIAM, *The Late Assembly of Divines Confession of Faith Examined* (1651), 20 June.

PATRIDES, C. A., (ed.), *The Cambridge Platonists* (1969).

P1136 PENDARVES, JOHN, *Arrowes against Babylon* (1656).

P1177 PENINGTON, ISAAC, *Light or Darknesse* (1650), 22 May.

P1217 —— *A Voyce Out of the thick Darkness* (1650), 1 Apr.

P1189 —— *Severall Fresh Inward Openings* (1650), 20 July.

P1163 —— *An Eccho From The Great Deep* (1650), 24 Nov.

P1169 —— *The Fundamental Right, Safety and Liberty of the People* (1651), 15 May.

P1175 —— *The Life of a Christian* (1653).

P1162 —— *Divine Essays or Considerations* (1654).

P1215 —— *To the Parliament, the Army . . . who have been faithful to the Good Old Cause* (1659), signed 18 March.

P1180 —— *The New Covenant* (1660).

P1158 —— *Concerning the Sum or Substance of our Religion* (1666).

—— *Works*, 4 vols. (3rd edn., 1784).

PENINGTON, MARY, *Some Account of Circumstances in the Life of Mary Penington* (1821).

P1305 PENN, WILLIAM, *The Invalidity of John Faldo's Vindication* (1673).

19699 PERKINS, WILLIAM, Επιείχεια: *Or, A Treatise of Christian Equitie and Moderation* (1604).

19652–53 —— *The Works of that Famous and Worthy Minister of Christ in the Vniversitie of Cambridge, M. William Perkins*, 3 vols. (i, 1626, ii and iii, 1631).

P1638 PERROT, JOHN, *A Visitation of Love* (1658).

P1619 PERROT, JOHN, *Immanuel The Salvation of Israel* (1658).

P1624 ——*John, To all Gods Imprisoned People For His Names-sake, Wheresoever upon the Face of the Earth, Salutation* (1660).

P1621 ——*J. P. The follower of the Lamb* (1660).

P1612 —— *Battering Rams against Rome* (1661).

P1629 —— *A Sea of the Seed's Sufferings* (1661).

P1903 PETTO, SAMUEL, *The Voice of the Spirit* (1654), 1 Sept.

P1900 —— *The Preacher Sent* (1658), 30 Jan.

M246   PINNELL, HENRY, and John Maddox, *Gangraenachrestum* (Oxford, 1646), 5 Sept.

P2280 —— *A Word of Prophesy, concerning the Parliament, Generall, and the Army* (1648), 5 Dec.

A2900 —— translator, *Five Treatises of the Philosophers Stone* (1652), 7 Nov. 1651.

P2279 —— *Nil Novi. This years F[r]uit, From the last Years Root* (1654) 31 Dec.

C7023 —— translator, *Philosophy Reformed & Improved in Four Profound Tractates* (1657), 1 May.

PISTORIUS, JOHANNES, *Artis Cabalisticae . . .* (Basel, 1587).

POCOCK, MARY, *The Mystery of the Deity in the Humanity* (1649).

T3151 PORDAGE, JOHN, *Truth Appearing through the Clouds of undeserved Scandal* (1654), 22 Dec.

P2967 —— *Innocencie Appearing Through the dark Mists of Pretended Guilt* (1655), 5 Mar.

P2974 PORDAGE, SAMUEL, *Mundorum Explicatio* (1661).

P3093 POWELL, VAVASOR, *The Scriptures Concord* (1646), 24 Oct.

P3087 —— *God the Father Glorified* (1649), 1 Dec.

P3092 —— *Saving Faith* (1651), Mar.

P3081 —— *Christ Exalted above all Creatures By God His Father* (1651).

P3078 —— תצפר בפח *or The Bird in the Cage* (1661).

See also Bagshaw, Edward.

P4234 PURNELL, ROBERT, *Good Tydings for Sinners* (1649), 1 June.

20548 QUARLES, FRANCIS, *Hieroglyphickes of the Life of Man* (1638).

Q148   QUATERMAYNE, ROGER, *Quatermayns Conquest over Canturburies Court* (1642).

R111   RABISHA, WILLIAM, *Adam Unvailed, and Seen with open Face* (1649).

R310   RAUE, CHRISTIAN, (Ravius Berlinas), *A discourse of the Orientall tongues* (1648).

R440   READ, ROBERT, *The Fiery Change* (1656), 3 Jan. 1657.

R450   READING, JOHN, *The Ranters Ranting* (1650), 2 Dec.

R681   REEVE, JOHN, *The Prophet Reeve's Epistle to his Friend* (1654).

R676 —— and Muggleton, Lodowick, *A Divine Looking-Glass* (1656, repr. 1661). See also Muggleton, Lodowick.

S365 RICH, ROBERT, *The Saints Testimony* (1657).

R1361 —— *Love without Dissimulation* (1666).

R1612 ROBERTSON, WILLIAM, שער או פתח אל לשון הקדש *A Gate or Door to the Holy Tongue; opened in English* (1653), 14 Nov.

R1675 ROBINSON, HENRY, *Liberty of Conscience* (1644), 24 Mar.

R1670 —— *Certain Proposalls In order to the Peoples Freedom and Accommodation in Some Particulars* (1652).

21109 ROBINSON, JOHN, *A justification of separation from the Church of England* (Amsterdam, 1610).

ROGERS, EDWARD, *Some Account of the Life and Opinions of a Fifth-Monarchy-Man* (1867).

21181 ROGERS, JOHN, *The Displaying of an horrible Secte of gross and wicked Heretiques* (1578).

21180 —— *An answere unto a wicked & Infamous libel made by Christopher Vitel* (1579).

R1808 ROGERS, JOHN, (1627–65), *A Godly and fruitful exposition* (1650).

R1814 —— סגריר *Sagrir. Or Doomes-day drawing nigh. With Thunder and Lightening to Lawyers* (1653), 7 Nov.

R1813 —— *Ohel or Beth-shemesh. A Tabernacle for the Sun* (1653), 7 Nov.

R1811 —— *Mene, Tekel, Perez, Or, A Little Appearance of the Hand-Writing (In a Glance of Light) Against the Powers and Apostates of the Times* (1654), 10 June.

R1809 —— *Jegar-Sahadvtha: An Oyled Pillar: Set up for Posterity* (1657) 28 July.

21205 ROGERS, RICHARD; PERKINS, WILLIAM; GREENHAM, RICHARD; WEBBE, GEORGE, AND MOSSE, MILES, *A Garden of Spiritual Flowers* (1609).

R2012 ROUS, FRANCIS, *The Balme of Love* (1648), 30 June.

R2160 ROYLE, THOMAS, *A Glimpse of Some Truths* (1648).

R2347 RUSSEL, RICHARD, *The Spirit of God in Man* (1654), 13 April.

R2394 RUTHERFORD, SAMUEL, *A Survey of the Spirituall Antichrist*, 2 parts (1648), Nov.

R2395 —— *A Survey of the Survey of that Summe of Church-Discipline* (1658).

S19 S., E., *The Saints Travell From Babylon Into their owne Countrey* (1643).

S413 SALMON, JOSEPH, *Anti-Christ in Man* (1647), 12 Dec.

S416 —— *A Rout, A Rout* (1649), 10 Feb., in *CRW*.

S5725 SALMON, JOSEPH, Letter to Thomas Webbe dated 13 Apr. 1650, printed in Edward Stokes, *The Wiltshire Rant* (1652), in
S494 *CRW*.
S415 —— *Heights in Depths* (1651), 13 Aug., in *CRW*.
21638 SALTMARSH, JOHN, *Poemata Sacra, Latinae & Anglicae scripta* (Cambridge, 1636).
21637 —— *Holy Discoveries and Flames* (1640).
S501 —— *A Solemn Discourse upon the Grand Covenant* (1643), 12 Oct.
S494 —— *A Peace, but No Pacification* (1643), 23 Oct.
S502 —— *A Solemn Discourse upon the Sacred League and Covenant of Both Kingdomes, Opening the Divinity and Policy of it* (1644), 21 Mar.
S506 —— *A Voice from Heaven* (1644), 19 Nov.
S476A —— *Dawnings of Light* (1645), 4 Jan.
S484 —— *Free Grace* (1645), 3 Dec.
S498 —— *The Smoke in the Temple* (1646), 16 Jan.
S489 —— *Groanes for Liberty* (1646), 10 Mar.
S495 —— *Perfume Against the Sulpherous Stinke* (1646), 19 Apr.
S496 —— 'Shadows Flying Away' in *Reasons for Unitie, Peace and Love* (1646), 17 June, repr. in D. M. Wolfe, *Milton in the Puritan Revolution* (1941).
S504 —— *Sparkles of Glory Or, Some Beams of the Morning Star* (1647) 27 May.
S507 —— *Wonderfull Predictions* (1648), 29 Dec. 1647.
S480 —— *England's Friend* (1649), 28 Oct. 1648.
I1047 SANDERS, JOHN, *An Iron Rod for the Naylers* (1655), 17 June.
S575 —— *An Iron Rod put into the Lord Protectors Hand* (1655).
S2359 SEDGWICK, JOHN, *Antinomianisme Anatomized* (1643), 2 Aug.
S2392 SEDGWICK, WILLIAM, *Zion's Deliverance* (1642), 29 June.
S2388 —— *Scripture a Perfect Rule for Church Government* (1643), 28 Dec.
S2390 —— *Some Flashes of Lightnings* (1648).
S2386 —— *The Leaves of the Tree of Life* (1648), 25 Aug.
S2385 —— *Justice upon the Armie Remonstrance* (2nd edn., 1649), 11 Dec.
S2391 —— *The Spirituall Madman* (1648), 20 Dec.
S2389 —— *A Second View of the Army Remonstrance* (1649), 23 Dec. 1648.
S2387 —— *Mr. William Sedgwicks Letter To his Excellency Thomas Lord Fairfax* (1649), 28 Dec. 1648.
S2383 —— *Animadversions upon a letter and paper, first sent to His Highness by certain gentlemen and others in Wales* (1656), 28 Jan.
S3166 SHEPPARD, SAMUEL, *The Joviall Crew, or the Devill turn'd Ranter* (1651), 6 Jan.

22479	SIBBES, RICHARD, *The Bruised Reede and Smoaking Flax* (1630).
22508	—— *The Soules conflict with it selfe* (1635).
22500	—— *The Successful Seeker* (1639).
22491	—— *Evangelical Sacrifices* (1640).
S3794	SIMMONDS, MARTHA, *When the Lord Jesus came to Jerusalem* (1655), 25 Apr.
S3791	—— *A Lamentation for the Lost Sheep* (1655), 20 Oct.
S3793	—— *O England; thy time is come*, n.p. (1656)
S3817	SIMPSON, JOHN, *The Perfection of Justification* (1648).
S3816	—— *The Herbal of Divinity* (1659).
S3818	SIMPSON, MARY, *Faith and Experience* (1649).
S4071	SMITH, HUMPHRY, *A Sad and Mournefull Lamentation* (1660), signed 16 Nov. 1658.
	SMITH, JOHN, *Select Discourses* (1660), ed. Henry G. Williams (4th edn., Cambridge, 1859).
	SMYTH, JOHN, *The Works of John Smyth*, ed. W. T. Whitley, 2 vols. (Cambridge, 1915).
S4905	SPEED, THOMAS, *The Guilty-Covered Clergy-man Unvail'd* (1657).
S5072	SPRIGGE, JOSHUA, *Christus Redivivus* (1649).
S5076	—— *A Testimony to an Approaching Glory* (1649).
S5476	STERRY, PETER, *The Comings Forth of Christ* (1650), 1 Nov. 1649.
S5725	STOKES, EDWARD, *The Wiltshire Rant* (1652), 2 July.
	STUBBS, JOHN, Letter to George Fox, 1661 (Liverpool, 1842).
S6084	STUBBS, THOMAS, *A Call into the Way to the Kingdome* (1655), 13 Sept.
S6086	—— *Certain Papers Given forth from the Spirit of truth* (1659).
S6212	SUTTON, KATHERINE, *A Christian Woman's Experience of the glorious working of Gods free grace* (Rotterdam, 1663).
T150	TANY, THOMAS, *The Nations Right in Magna Charta discussed with the thing Called Parliament* (1650), 2 Jan.
T158	—— *Theauraujohn his Theous Ori Apokolipikal* (1651), 13 Aug.
T152	—— *Theauraujohn High Priest to the Jewes* (1652), 15 March.
T155	—— *Theauraujohn Tani His Second Part of his Theous-Ori Apokolipikal* (1653).
T151	—— *Theauraujohn His Aurora in Tranlagorum in Salem Gloria* (1655), 24 Sept.
	TAULER, JOHANNES, *Opera* (Cologne, 1548).
T268	TAYLOR, CHRISTOPHER, *The Whirl-wind of the Lord gone forth As A Fiery flying Roule* (1655), 12 Sept.
T400	TAYLOR, JEREMY, ΘΕΟΛΟΓΙΑ ἘΚΛΕΚΤΙΚΗ, *A Discourse of the Liberty of Prophesying* (1647), 28 June.

TAYLOR, JEREMY, *Whole Works*, 10 vols. (1854).

T582   TAYLOR, THOMAS, *Some Prison Meditations* (1657), 18 Nov.

T590   —— *A Trumpet Sounded from under the Altar* (1658).

B3542   TENTZEL, ANDREAS, *Medicina diastatica, or sympatheticall mumie* (1653).

'*Der Frankforter*' ['*Theologia Deutsch*'] *Kritische Textausgabe*, ed. Wolfgang von Hinten (Munich, 1982).

Theologia Germanica, trans. L. Haetzer (Augsburg, 1531).

—— trans. Sebastian Castellio (Antwerp, 1558).

—— ed. and trans. Berthold von Chiemsee (Salzburg, 1561).

11786   —— Latin edn., (1632).

T858   —— trans. Giles Randall (1646, 2nd edn. 1648), 24 Oct.

T1153–4 TICKELL, JOHN, *The Bottomles Pit Smoaking in Familisme* (Oxford, 1st edn., 1651, [23 Sept.]; 2nd edn., 1652).

T1173   TILLINGHAST, JOHN, *Generation Work or A Briefe and Seasonable Word, offered to the view and consideration of the Saints and people of God* (1653).

24095   TOBIAS, *Mirabilia opera Dei* (?1650).

T1767   TOLDERVY, JOHN, *The Foot out of the Snare* (1656), 24 Dec.

T1770   —— *The Snare Broken* (1656), 31 Jan.

T1769   —— *The Naked Truth* (1656), 21 Feb., 1655.

T1978   TOWNE, ROBERT, *The Assertion of Grace* (1644), 20 Feb.

T1980   —— *A Re-assertion of Grace* (1654).

T2031   TRAPNEL, ANNA, *The Cry of a Stone* (1654), 7 Jan.

T2034   —— *Strange and Wonderful Newes from White-hall* (1654), 11 Mar.

T2032   —— *A Legacy for Saints* (1654), 24 July.

T2033   —— *Anna Trapnel's Report and Plea* (1654).

—— Untitled book of verse (1658), Bodl. Shelfmark S. 1. 42. Th.

T2035   —— *A Voice for the King of Saints and Nations* (1658).

Trismegistus: see Hermes Trismegistus.

T3197–8 TRYON, THOMAS, *A Treatise of Dreams and Visions* (1st edn., 1689; 2nd edn., 1695).

T3294   TURNER, JANE, *Choice Experiences* (1653).

UNDERHILL, E. B., ed., *The Records of a Church of Christ meeting in Broadmead, Bristol, 1640–1687* (1847).

—— (ed.), *Records of the Churches of Christ, Gathered at Fenstanton, Warboys, and Hexham, 1644–1720* (1854).

V75   VANE, SIR HENRY, *The Retired Mans Meditations* (1655), 2 July.

V67   —— *An Epistle General, to the Mystical Body of Christ* (1662).

H1401   VAN HELMONT, J. B., *A Ternary of Paradoxes* (1650), 20 Nov.

V659   *A Vision, which One Mr. Brayne . . . had in September, 1647* (1649) 18 Mar.

H979   VON FRANKENBURG, ABRAHAM, *Clavis Apocalyptica: or, A Prophetical Key*, trans. Samuel Hartlib, preface by John Dury (1651).

W376   WALKER, HENRY, *A Gad of Steele* (1641).

W384   —— *The Sermon of Henry Walker, Ironmonger* (1642), Mar.

W381   —— *The Protestants Grammar* (1648), 19 Apr.

W374   —— בראשית א , *The Creation of the World* (1649).

W385   —— *A Sermon Preached in the Kings Chappell at Whitehall* (1649), 15 July.

W386   —— *A Sermon Preached in the Chappell of Somerset House* (1650), 27 June.

W387   —— *Spirituall Experiences, Of sundry Beleevers* (1653) 6 Jan.

W390   —— , *TRAΓHMATA, Sweet-Meats* (1654), 20 June.

P3105   WALWYN, WILLIAM, *The Power of Love* (1643), 19 Sept.

W832   WARD, SETH, *Vindiciae Academiarum* (Oxford, 1654), 26 May.

W944   WARR, JOHN, *Administrations Civil and Spiritual* (1648).

W980   WARREN, THOMAS, *Vnbeleevers No Subjects of Iustification, Nor of mystical Vnion to Christ* (1654), 20 Apr.

W1032   WASTFIELD, ROBERT, *Christ coming in the Cloudes* (1647), 8 Sept.

W1206   WEBBE, THOMAS, *Mr. Edwards Pen no Slander* (1646), 21 May.

W1212–13   WEBSTER, JOHN, *The Saints Guide* (1st edn., 17 Aug. 1653; 2nd edn., 1654).

W1211   —— *The Picture of Mercurius Politicus* (1653), 12 Oct.

W1209   —— *Academiarum Examen* (1654), 19 Dec. 1653.

W1210   —— *The Judgement Set* (1654), 24 July.

    —— *The Secret Soothsayer* (1654), repr. 1713.

    —— *The Vail of the Covering* (2nd edn., 1713).

W1256   WEIGEL, VALENTIN, *Of the Life of Christ* (1648).

W1679   W[HISTON], E[DMUND], *The Life and Death of Mr. Henry Jessey* (1671).

    WHITE, B. R. (ed.), *Association Records of the Particular Baptists of England, Wales and Ireland to 1660*, 3 parts. (1971–4).

    WHITAKER, WILLIAM, *A Disputation on Holy Scripture* trans. and ed. William Fitzgerald (Cambridge, 1849).

W1975   WHITEHEAD, JOHN, *The Enmitie between the Two Seeds* (1655), 19 July.

W1986   WHITELOCKE, BULSTRODE, Sir, *Memorials of the English Affairs* (1682).

W2106   WIGHT, SARAH, *A Wonderful Pleasant and Profitable Letter* (1656), 20 Oct.

W2252   WILKINSON, ROBERT, *The Saints Travel to the Spiritual Land of Canaan* (1650).

25665   WILKINSON, WILLIAM, *A Confutation of Certaine Articles delivered unto the Family of Love* (1579).

W2762   WILLIAMS, ROGER, *Experiments of Spiritual Life and Health* (1652).

W3041   WINSTANLEY, GERRARD, *The Breaking of the Day of God* (1648), signed 20 May.

W3047   —— *The Mysterie of God, Concerning the whole Creation* (1648).

W3051   —— *The Saints Paradice* (?1648).

W3054   —— *Truth Lifting up its Head above Scandals* (1649), signed 16 Oct., 1648.

W3049   —— *The New Law of Righteousness* (1649), signed 26 Jan.

W3053   —— *The True Levellers Standard Advanced* (1649), signed 26 Apr.

W3050   —— *A new-Yeers Gift for the Parliament and Armie* (1650), 1 Jan.

W3056   —— *A Vindication . . . Or Some Reasons Given against . . . Ranting* (1650), signed 4 Mar.

W3043   —— *Fire in the Bush* (1650).

W3045   —— *The Law of Freedom in a Platform* (1652), signed 5 Nov. 1651.

          —— *The Works of Gerrard Winstanley*, ed. G. H. Sabine (Ithaca, N.Y., 1941).

          —— *England's Spirit Unfoulded or an Incouragement to Take the 'Engagement'*, ed. G. E. Aylmer in *P & P* 40 (1968), 3–15.

          —— *The Law of Freedom and Other Writings*, ed. Christopher Hill (1973, Cambridge 1983).

W3724–5 WRITER, CLEMENT, *The Jus Divinum of Presbyterie* (1646, 2nd edn. 1655).

W3723   —— *Fides Divina* (1657), 7 July.

C. SECONDARY WORKS

ADOLPH, ROBERT, *The Rise of Modern Prose Style* (Cambridge, Mass., 1968).

ALEXANDER, GILLIAN, 'Politics of the Pronoun in the Literature of the English Revolution', in R. Carter (ed.), *Language and Literature* (1983), 217–35).

ALLEN, D. C., 'Some Theories of the Growth and Origin of Language in Milton's Age', *PQ* 28 (1949), 5–16.

ATKINSON, DONALD, 'The Origin and Date of the "Sator" Word Square', *JEH* 2 (1951) 1–18.

BAILEY, M. L., *Milton and Jakob Boehme: A Study of German Mysticism in Seventeenth-Century England* (New York, 1914).

BALL, B. W., *A Great Expectation: Eschatological Thought in English Protestantism in 1660* (Leiden, 1975).

BARBOUR, HUGH, *The Quakers in Puritan England* (New Haven, 1964).

BARCLAY, R., *The Inner Life of the Religious Societies of the Commonwealth* (1876).

BAUMAN, RICHARD, *Let your words be few: Symbolism of Speaking and Silence among Seventeenth Century Quakers* (Cambridge, 1983).

BERG, CHRISTINE, and BERRY, PHILIPPA, 'Spiritual Whoredom: An Essay on Female Prophets in the Seventeenth Century', in Francis Barker (ed.) *1642: Literature and Power in the Seventeenth Century* (Essex, 1981), 39–54.

BEVAN, HUGH, *Morgan Llwyd y Llenor* (Cardiff, 1954).

BIRRELL, T. A., 'English Catholic Mystics in Non-Catholic Circles—I', *Downside Review*, 94 (1976), 60–81.

BLAU, J. L., *The Christian Interpretation of the Cabala in the Renaissance* (New York, 1944).

BRACHLOW, STEPHEN, 'The Elizabethan Roots of Henry Jacob's Churchmanship: Refocussing the Historiographical Lens', *JEH* 3 (1985), 228–54.

BRAILSFORD, H. N., *The Levellers and the English Revolution*, ed. and completed by Christopher Hill (1962).

BRAITHWAITE, W. C., *The Beginnings of Quakerism* (2nd edn. revised by Henry J. Cadbury, Cambridge, 1955).

BRAUER, J. C., 'Puritan Mysticism and the Development of Libertinism', *CH* 19 (1950), 153–79.

BROWNE, ALICE, 'Dreams and Picture Writing: Some Examples of this Comparison from the Sixteenth to the Eighteenth Centuries', *JCWI* 44 (1981), 90–100.

BROWNE, JOHN, *History of Congregationalism . . . in Norfolk and Suffolk* (1877).

BURKE, PETER, 'L'Histoire sociale des rêves', *Annales*, 28. 2 (1973), 329–47.

—— *Popular Culture in Early Modern Europe* (1978).

BURNS, N. T., *Christian Mortalism from Tyndale to Milton* (Cambridge, Mass., 1972).

BURRAGE, CHAMPLIN, 'Anna Trapnel's Prophecies', *EHR* 36 (1911), 526–35.

—— *The Early English Dissenters in the light of recent research (1550–1641)* (Cambridge, 1912).

CALDWELL, PATRICIA, 'The Antinomian Language Controversy', *Harvard Theological Review*, 69 (1976), 345–67.

—— *The Puritan Conversion Narrative* (Cambridge, 1983).

CAPP, B. S., *The Fifth Monarchy Men: A Study in Seventeenth-Century English Millenarianism* (1972).

—— *Astrology and the Popular Press: English Almanacs and Religion 1500–1800* (1979).

CHRISTIANSON, PAUL, *Reformers and Babylon: English Apocalyptic Visions from the Reformation to the Eve of the Civil War* (Toronto, 1978).

CLASEN, CLAUS PETER, *Anabaptism: A Social History, 1525–1618* (Ithaca, NY, 1972).

COHEN, CHARLES LLOYD, *God's Caress: The Psychology of Puritan Religious Experience* (New York and Oxford, 1986).

COHEN, MURRAY, *Sensible Words: Linguistic Practice in England, 1640–1785* (Baltimore, 1977).

COHN, NORMAN, *The Pursuit of the Millennium* (1957).

COLE, R. C. and MOODY, M. E. (edd.) *The Dissenting Tradition* (Athens, Ohio, 1975).

COLLINSON, PATRICK, *The Elizabethan Puritan Movement* (1967).

—— *The Religion of Protestants: The Church in English Society, 1559–1625* (Oxford, 1982).

COOLIDGE, J. S., *The Pauline Renaissance in England* (Oxford, 1970).

COPE, JACKSON, I., 'Seventeenth-Century Quaker Style', *PMLA* 71 (1956), 725–54.

DAILEY, BARBARA RITTER, 'The Visitation of Sarah Wight: Holy Carnival and the Revolution of the Saints in Civil War London', *CH* 55 (1986), 438–55.

—— 'The Husbands of Margaret Fell: An Essay on Religious Metaphor and Social Change', *The Seventeenth Century* 2 (1987), 55–71.

DAVIES, HORTON, *Worship and Theology in England. 2. From Andrewes to Baxter and Fox* (Princeton, 1975).

DAVIS, J. C., *Fear, Myth and History: The Ranters and the Historians* (Cambridge, 1986).

DAVIS, J. L., 'Mystical versus Enthusiastic Sensibility', *JHI* 4 (1943), 301–19.

DEBUS, ALLEN G., *The English Paracelsians* (1965).

—— *Science and Education in the Seventeenth Century* (New York, 1970).

DEJUNG, C., *Wahrheit und Häresie: Eine Untersuchung zur Geschichtsphilosophie bei Sebastian Franck* (Zürich, 1979).

DOUGLAS, MARY, *Purity and Danger: An Analysis of Concepts of Pollution and Taboo* (1966).

EBELL, J. G., 'The Family of Love: Its Sources in England', *HLQ* 30 (1966–7), 31–43.

EBNER, DEAN, *Autobiography in Seventeenth-Century England: Theology and the Self* (The Hague, 1970).

ELSKY, MARTIN, 'George Herbert's Pattern Poems and the Materiality of Language: A New Approach', *ELH* 50 (1983), 245–60.

EMORY, KENT, Jr., 'Mysticism and the Coincidence of Opposites in Sixteenth and Seventeenth-Century France', *JHI* 45 (1984), 3–23.

ENDY, M. B., Jr., *William Penn and Early Quakerism* (Princeton, 1973).

EVANS, B., *The Early English Baptists*, 2 vols. (1862).

EVANS, E. L., 'Morgan Llwyd and Jacob Boehme', *JBSQ* 1 (1953), 11–16.

FIRTH, K. R., *The Apocalyptic Tradition in Reformation Britain, 1530–1645* (Oxford, 1979).

FISCH, HAROLD, 'Puritanism and the Reform of Prose Style', *ELH* 19 (1952), 229–48.

FISH, STANLEY, *Self-Consuming Artifacts* (1972).

FONTAINE VERWEY, H. de la, 'The Family of Love', *Quaerendo*, 6 (1976), 219–71.

FOUCAULT, MICHEL, *Language, Counter-Memory, Practice*, ed. and trans. D. F. Bouchard (Ithaca, NY, 1977).

FRANK, JOSEPH, *The Levellers* (Cambridge, Mass., 1955).

FREUD, SIGMUND, *The Interpretation of Dreams* (1953 edn.), ed. and trans. J. Strachey (New York, 1971).

GEORGE, KATHERINE and CHARLES H., *The Protestant Mind of the English Reformation, 1570–1640* (Princeton, 1961).

GERSCH, STEPHEN, *From Iamblicus to Eriugena: An Investigation of the Pseudo-Dionysian Tradition* (Leiden, 1978).

GORDON, ALEXANDER, 'The Origins of the Muggletonians', *Proceedings of the Literary and Philosophical Society of Liverpool* (Liverpool, 1869).

GREAVES, R. L., *The Puritan Revolution and Educational Thought* (New Brunswick, NJ, 1969).

—— ed. *Triumph over Silence. Women in Protestant History* (Westport, Conn., 1985).

GREEN, IAN, ' "For Children in Yeeres and Children in Understanding": The Emergence of the English Catechism under Elizabeth and the Early Stuarts', *JEH* 37 (1986), 397–425.

HALLER, WILLIAM, (ed.), *Tracts on Liberty in the Puritan Revolution, 1638–47*, 3 vols. (New York, 1934).

—— *The Rise of Puritanism* (New York, 1938).

—— 'The Word of God in the New Model Army', *CH* 19 (1950), 15–33.

HALLEY, JANET E., 'Heresy, Orthodoxy, and the Politics of Discourse: The Case of the English Family of Love', *Representations*, 15 (1986), 98–120.

HAMILTON, ALASTAIR, *The Family of Love* (Cambridge, 1981).

HAYES, T. W., *Winstanley the Digger* (Cambridge, Mass., 1979).

—— 'John Everard and Nicholas of Cusa's *Idiota*', *N & Q*, NS, 28 (1981), 47–9.

—— 'A Seventeenth-Century Translation of Nicholas of Cusa's *De dato Patris luminum'*, *JMRS* 11 (1981), 113–36.

HAYES, T. W., 'John Everard and the Familist Tradition' in Margaret Jacob and James Jacob (edd.), *The Origins of Anglo-American Radicalism* (1984), 60–9.

HEAL, FELICITY, 'The Family of Love and the Diocese of Ely', *SCH* 9 (1972), 213–22.

HESSELS, J. H., 'Hendrick Niclaes: The Family of Love', *The Bookworm* (1869), 81–91, 106–11, 116–19.

HILL, CHRISTOPHER, *Puritanism and Revolution* (1958).

—— *Society and Puritanism in Pre-Revolutionary England* (1964).

—— *The Intellectual Origins of the English Revolution* (Oxford, 1965).

—— *The World Turned Upside Down* (1972).

—— *Milton and the English Revolution* (1977).

—— 'The Religion of Gerrard Winstanley', *Past and Present Supplement*, No. 5 (1978).

—— *The Intellectual Consequences of the English Revolution* (1980).

—— 'Radical Prose in 17th Century England: From Marprelate to the Levellers', *Essays in Criticism*, 32 (1982), 95–118.

—— *The Experience of Defeat: Milton and Some Contemporaries* (1984).

—— and Shepherd, Michael, 'The Case of Arise Evans', *Psychological Medicine*, 6 (1976), 351–8.

—— Reay, B. and Lamont, W. M., *The World of the Muggletonians* (1983).

HIRST, DÉSIRÉE, 'The Riddle of John Pordage', *JBSQ* 1 (1954), 5–15.

—— *Hidden Riches* (1964).

HORST, I. B., *The Radical Brethren: Anabaptism and the English Reformation to 1558* (Nieuwkoop, 1972).

HUDSON, ROY, F., 'Richard Sibbes's Theory and Practice of Persuasion', *Quarterly Journal of Speech*, 44 (1958), 137–48.

HUEHNS, GERTRUDE, *Antinomianism in English History* (1951).

HUTIN, SERGE, *Les Disciples anglais de Jacob Boehme* (Paris, 1960).

JACOB, MARGARET, and JACOB, JAMES (edd.), *The Origins of Anglo-American Radicalism* (1984).

JACOBS, LOUIS, 'Symbols for the divine in the Kabbalah', *Friends of Dr. Williams's Library, 38th Lecture* (1984).

JANSSEN, FRANS A., 'Böhme's *Wercken* (1682): Its Editor, Its Publisher, Its Printer', *Quaerendo*, 16 (1986), 137–41.

JOHNSON, G. A., 'From Seeker to Finder: A Study in Seventeenth Century English Spiritualism Before the Quakers', *CH* 17 (1948), 299–315.

JOHNSON, W. G., 'The Family of Love in Stuart England: A Chronology of Name-Crossed Lovers', *JMRS* 7 (1977), 95–112.

JONES, R. M., *Studies in Mystical Religion* (1909).

—— *Spiritual Reformers in the Sixteenth and Seventeenth Centuries* (New York, 1914).

—— *Mysticism and Democracy in the English Commonwealth* (New York, 1932).

JONES, R. TUDUR, 'The Healing Herb and the Rose of Love: The Piety of Two Welsh Puritans', in *Reformation, Continuity and Dissent: Essays in honour of Geoffrey Nuttall*, ed. R. Buick Knox (1977).

KATZ, D. S., *Philo-Semitism and the Readmission of the Jews to England 1603–55* (Oxford, 1982).

KEEBLE, N. H., *Richard Baxter: Puritan Man of Letters* (Oxford, 1982).

—— *The Literary Culture of Nonconformity in Later Seventeenth-Century England* (Leicester, 1987).

KENDALL, R. T., *Calvin and English Calvinism to 1649* (Oxford, 1979).

KERRIGAN, WILLIAM B., *The Prophetic Milton* (Charlottesville, Va., 1974).

KIBBEY, ANN, *The Interpretation of Material Shapes in Puritanism: A Study of Rhetoric, Prejudice and Violence* (Cambridge, 1986).

KNOTT, JOHN R. Jr., *The Sword of the Spirit: Puritan Responses to the Bible* (Chicago, 1980).

KNOX, RONALD A., *Enthusiasm: A Chapter in the History of Religion* (Oxford, 1950).

KOLAKOWSKI, LESZEK, *Chrétiens sans Église. La conscience religieuse et le lien confessionnel au XVIIe siècle* (Paris, 1969).

KONOPACKI, STEVEN A., *The Descent into Words. Jakob Böhme's Transcendental Linguistics* (Ann Arbor, 1979).

KOYRÉ, ALEXANDRE, *La Philosophie de Jacob Boehme* (Paris, 1929).

LAMONT, WILLIAM M., *Godly Rule: Politics and Religion, 1603–60* (1969).

—— *Richard Baxter and the Millennium* (1979).

LANGLEY, A. S., 'Seventeenth-century Baptist disputations', *TBHS* 6 (1918–19), 216–43.

LAPLANCHE, J. and PONTALIS, J. -B., *The Language of Psycho-Analysis* (1980).

LAURENCE, ANNE, 'Two Ranter Poems', *RES*, new series, 31 (1980), 56–9.

LEVERENZ, DAVID, *The Language of Puritan Feeling: An Explanation in Literary, Psychological and Social History* (New Brunswick, NJ, 1980).

LEWALSKI, B. K., *Protestant Poetics and the Seventeenth-Century Religious Lyric* (Princeton, 1979).

LLOYD-JONES, G., *The Discovery of Hebrew in Tudor England: A Third Language* (Manchester, 1983).

LODS, ADOLPHE, *The Prophets and the Rise of Judaism*, trans. S. H. Hooke (1937).

LUTAUD, OLIVIER, *Winstanley: Son œuvre et le radicalisme 'Digger'*, 2 vols. (Lille, 1973).

MACDONALD, MICHAEL, *Mystical Bedlam: Madness, Anxiety and Healing in Seventeenth-Century England* (Cambridge, 1982).

MACFARLANE, ALAN, *The Family Life of Ralph Josselin* (Cambridge, 1970).

McGEE, J. SEARS, 'Conversion and the Imitation of Christ in Anglican and Puritan Writing', *JBS* 15 (1976), 20–39.

—— *The Godly Man in Stuart England* (New Haven, 1976).

McGREGOR, J. F., 'Ranterism and the Development of Early Quakerism', *JRH* 9 (1977), 349–63.

—— and Reay, B. (edd.), *Radical Religion in the English Revolution* (Oxford, 1984).

MACK, PHYLLIS, 'Women as Prophets during the English Civil War', in Jacob, Margaret and Jacob, James (edd.), *The Origins of Anglo-American Radicalism* (1984).

MACLEAR, J. F., 'Quakerism and the End of the Interregnum: A Chapter in the Domestication of Radical Puritanism', *CH* 19 (1950), 240–70.

—— ' "The Heart of New England Rent": The Mystical Element in Early Puritan History', *Mississippi Valley Historical Review*, 42 (1955–6), 621–52.

MADSEN, WILLIAM G., *From Shadowy Types to Truth: Studies in Milton's Symbolism* (1968).

MANNING, BRIAN (ed.), *Politics, Religion and the English Civil War (1973)*.

—— *The English People and the English Revolution* (1975).

MARSH, CHRISTOPHER, ' "A Gracelesse and Audacious Companie?" The Family of Love in the Parish of Balsham, 1580–1630', *SCH* 23 (1986), 191–208.

MARTIN, J. W., 'English Protestant Separatism at Its Beginnings; Henry Hart and the Free-Will Men', *SCJ* 7.2 (1976) 55–74.

—— 'Elizabethan Familists and other Separatists in the Guildford Area', *BIHR* 51 (1978), 90–3.

—— 'Christopher Vitel: an Elizabethan Mechanick Preacher', *SCJ* 10. 2 (1979), 15–22.

—— 'Elizabethan Familists and English Separatism', *JBS* 20 (1980), 55–73.

—— 'The Elizabethan Familists: A Separatist Group as Perceived by their Contemporaries', *BQ* 29 (1982), 276–81.

MARTIN, L. F., 'The Family of Love in England: Conforming Millenarians', *SCJ* 3 (1972), 99–108.

MARTZ, LOUIS, *The Poetry of Meditation* (New Haven, 1954, rev. edn., 1962).

MATAR, N. I., 'Peter Sterry and the Ranters', *N & Q* NS, 29 (1982), 504–06.

—— 'Peter Sterry and Jacob Boehme', *N & Q* NS, 33 (1986), 33–6.

MILLER, PERRY, *The New England Mind: The Seventeenth Century* (Cambridge, Mass., 1954).

MITCHELL, W. F., *English Pulpit Oratory from Andrewes to Tillotson* (1932).

MORGAN, EDMUND S., *Visible Saints: The History of a Puritan Idea* (Ithaca, NY, 1963).

MORTON, A. L., *The World of the Ranters* (1970).

MOSS, J. D., 'The Family of Love and its English Critics', *SCJ* 6 (1975), 35–52.

—— 'Variations on a Theme: The Family of Love in Renaissance England', *RS* 31 (1978), 186–95.

—— ' "Godded with God": Hendrik Niclaes and His Family of Love', *Transactions of the American Philosophical Society*, 71. 8 (Philadelphia, 1981).

MULLETT, MICHAEL, *Radical Religious Movements in Early Modern Europe* (1980).

MULLIGAN, LOTTE, *et al.*, 'Winstanley: A Case for the Man as He Said He Was', *JEH* 28 (1975), 57–75.

NICKALLS, J. L., 'George Fox's Library', *JFHS* 28 (1931), 3–21.

NUTTALL, G. F., *The Holy Spirit in Puritan Faith and Experience* (Oxford, 1946).

—— *Studies in Christian Enthusiasm* (Wallingford, Pa., 1948).

—— *James Nayler: A Fresh Approach* (1954).

—— *Visible Saints: The Congregational Way, 1640–1660* (Oxford, 1957).

—— *The Welsh Saints, 1640–1660* (Cardiff, 1957).

—— *The Puritan Spirit, Essays and Addresses* (1967).

—— 'Puritan and Quaker Mysticism', *Theology*, 78 (1975), 518–31.

—— 'The Last of James Nayler, Robert Rich and the Church of the First-Born', *Friends' Quarterly*, 60 (1985), 527–34.

O'MALLEY, T. P., 'The Press and Quakerism, 1653–59', *JFHS* 54 (1979), 169–84.

ONG, W. J., S. J., *The Presence of the Word* (New York, 1967).

ORCIBAL, JEAN, *La Rencontre du Carmel Thérésien avec les Mystiques du Nord* (Paris, 1959).

ORMSBY-LENNON, HUGH, 'Metaphor and Madness', *ETC.: a review of general semantics*, 33 (1976), 307–18.

OZMENT, S. E., *Mysticism and Dissent: Religious Ideology and Social Protest in the Sixteenth Century* (New Haven, 1973).

PETTIT, NORMAN, *The Heart Prepared: Grace and Conversion in Puritan Spiritual Life* (New Haven, 1966).

PINTO, V. de SOLA, *Peter Sterry, Platonist and Puritan* (Cambridge, 1934).

POPKIN, RICHARD H., 'Spinoza's Relationships with the Quakers in Amsterdam', *Quaker History*, 73 (1982), 14–20.

REAY, BARRY, 'The Muggletonians: A Study in Seventeenth-Century English Sectarianism', *JHR* 9 (1976), 32–49.

—— *The Quakers and the English Revolution* (1985).

REEVES, MARJORIE, *Joachim of Fiore and the Prophetic Future* (1976).

—— and Hirsch-Reich, B., *The Figurae of Joachim of Fiore* (Oxford, 1972).

ROWLAND, CHRISTOPHER, *The Open Heaven* (1981).

RUSHE, HARRY, '*Merlini Anglici*: Astrology and Propaganda from 1644 to 1651', *EHR* 80 (1965), 322–33.

—— 'Prophecies and Propaganda, 1641 to 1651', *EHR*, 84 (1969), 752–70.

SALMON, VIVIAN, *The Works of Francis Lodwick* (1972).

SCHOLEM, GERSHOM, *Major Trends in Jewish Mysticism* (3rd edn., 1955).

SCHULER, R. M., 'Some Spiritual Alchemies of Seventeenth-Century England', *JHI* 41 (1980), 293–318.

SCRIBNER, R. W., *For the Sake of Simple Folk: Popular Propaganda for the German Reformation* (Cambridge, 1981).

SEAVER, PAUL, S., *The Puritan Lectureships: The Politics of Religious Dissent, 1560–1662* (Stanford, 1970).

—— *Wallington's World: A Puritan Artisan in Seventeenth-Century London* (1985).

SECRET, FRANÇOIS, *Les Kabbalistes chrétiens de la Renaissance* (Paris, 1964).

—— *Le Zôhar chez les kabbalistes chrétiens de la Renaissance* (Paris, 1964).

SIPPELL, THEODOR, *Zur Vorgeschichte des Quäkertums* (Giessen, 1920).

—— *Werdendes Quäkertum* (Stuttgart, 1937).

SLAUGHTER, M. M., *Universal Languages and Scientific Taxonomy in the Seventeenth Century* (Cambridge, 1982).

SMITH, N., 'George Herbert in Defence of Antinomianism', *N & Q* NS, 31 (1984), 34–5.

SOLT, L. F., 'John Saltmarsh: New Model Army Chaplain', *JEH* 2 (1951), 69–80.

—— 'Anti-Intellectualism in the Puritan Revolution', *CH* 25 (1956), 306–16.

—— *Saints in Arms* (1959).

SPUFFORD, MARGARET, *Small Books and Pleasant Histories: Popular Fiction and its Readership in Seventeenth-Century England* (Cambridge, 1981).

STEWART, STANLEY, *The Enclosed Garden: The Tradition and the Image in Seventeenth-Century Poetry* (Madison, 1966).

STRUCK, WILHELM, *Der Einfluss Jakob Boehmes auf die Englische Literatur des 17. Jahrhunderts* (Berlin, 1936).

TANNER, TONY, 'License and Licensing: To the Presse or to the Spunge', *JHI* 38 (1977), 3–18.

TAYLOR, J. H., 'Some Seventeenth-Century Testimonies', *Transactions of the Congregational Historical Society*, 16 (1949), 64–77.

TERRY, ALTHEA E., 'Giles Calvert's Publishing Career', *JFHS* 35 (1938), 45–9.

THOMAS, KEITH, 'Women and the Civil War Sects', *P & P* 13 (1958), 42–62.

—— *Religion and the Decline of Magic* (1971).

—— *Man and the Natural World: Changing Attitudes in England, 1500–1800* (1983).

THUNE, NILS, *The Behmenists and the Philadelphians: A Contribution to the Study of English Mysticism in the 17th and 18th Centuries* (Uppsala, 1948).

TOLMIE, MURRAY, *The Triumph of the Saints: The Separate Churches of London, 1616–1649* (Cambridge, 1977).

TOON, PETER (ed.), *Puritans, the Millennium and the Future of Israel: Puritan Eschatology 1600–1660* (1970).

TROELTSCH, ERNST, *The Social Teaching of the Christian Churches* (1931).

TURNBULL, G. H., *Hartlib, Dury and Comenius. Gleanings from Hartlib's Papers* (Liverpool, 1947).

TUVE, ROSAMUND, *Allegorical Imagery* (Princeton, 1966).

VAN BEEK, M., *An Enquiry into Puritan Vocabulary* (Groningen, 1969).

VANN, R. T., *The Social Development of English Quakerism* (Cambridge, Mass., 1969).

VICKERS, BRIAN (ed.), *Occult and Scientific Mentalities in the Renaissance* (Cambridge, 1984).

VON HARLESS, G. C. A., *Jakob Boehme and die Alchymisten* (Berlin, 1870).

WALES, KATHLEEN M., '*Thou* and *You* in Early Modern English: Brown and Gilman Re-Appraised', *Studia Linguistica*, 37 (1983), 107–25.

WALKER, D. P., *The Decline of Hell: Seventeenth-Century Discussions of Eternal Torment* (1964).

WALLACE, D. D., Jr., *Puritans and Predestination: Grace in English Protestant Theology, 1525–1695* (Chapel Hill, 1983).

WATKINS, OWEN C., *The Puritan Experience* (1972).

WATTS, M. R., *The Dissenters: From the Reformation to the French Revolution* (Oxford, 1978).

WEBBER, JOAN, *The Eloquent 'I': Style and Self in Seventeenth-Century Prose* (Madison, 1968).

WEBSTER, CHARLES, *The Great Instauration: Science, Medicine and Reform, 1626–1660* (1975).

WEIDHORN, MANFRED, *Dreams in Seventeenth-Century English Literature* (The Hague, 1970).

WESSENDORFT, K., 'Ist der Verfasser der "Theologische Deutsch" gefunden?', *Evangelische Theologie*, 16 (1956), 188–92.

WHITE, B. R., 'The Organization of the Particular Baptists, 1644–60', *JEH* 18 (1966), 209–26.

—— *The English Separatist Tradition* (Oxford, 1971).

WHITE, HELEN C., *English Devotional Literature [Prose] 1600–40* (Madison, 1931).

WILLIAMS, G. H., *The Radical Reformation* (1962).

WILSON, JOHN F., *Pulpit in Parliament: Puritanism during the English Civil War, 1640–48* (Princeton, 1969).

WITTREICH, J. A., Jr., *Visionary Poetics* (San Marino, 1979).

WOLFE, D. M., *Milton in the Puritan Revolution* (1941).

WOODHOUSE, A. S. P. (ed.), *Puritanism and Liberty* (1938, repr. 1951).

WOOLRYCH, AUSTIN, *From Commonwealth to Protectorate* (Oxford, 1982).

WORDEN, BLAIR, 'Toleration and the Cromwellian Protectorate', *SCH* 21 (1984), 199–233.

WRIGHT, LUELLA, M., *The Literary Life of the Early Friends, 1650–1725* (New York, 1932).

—— *Literature and Education in Early Quakerism* (Iowa, 1933).

ZAALBERG, C. A., *Das Buch Extasis van Jan van der Noot* Assen (1954).

INDEX